RIDGEWAY

ALSO IN THE
History *of* Canada Series

Death or Victory: The Battle of Quebec and the Birth of an Empire by Dan Snow

The Last Act: Pierre Trudeau, the Gang of Eight, and the Fight for Canada by Ron Graham

The Destiny of Canada: Macdonald, Laurier, and the Election of 1891 by Christopher Pennington

War in the St. Lawrence: The Forgotten U-Boat Battles on Canada's Shores by Roger Sarty

Canada's Warlords: Sir Robert Borden and William Lyon Mackenzie King by Tim Cook

The Best Place to Be: Expo 67 and Its Time by John Lownsbrough

Two Weeks in Quebec City: The Meeting That Made Canada by Christopher Moore

Ice and Water: The Future of the Arctic by John English

Trouble on Main Street: The 1907 Vancouver Race Riots by Julie Gilmour

Death on Two Fronts: Newfoundland by Sean Cadigan

RIDGEWAY

The American Fenian Invasion and the 1866 Battle That Made Canada

PETER VRONSKY

ALLEN LANE
CANADA

ALLEN LANE CANADA

Published by the Penguin Group

Penguin Group (Canada), 90 Eglinton Avenue East, Suite 700,
Toronto, Ontario, Canada M4P 2Y3 (a division of Pearson Canada Inc.)

Penguin Group (USA) Inc., 375 Hudson Street, New York, New York 10014, U.S.A.
Penguin Books Ltd, 80 Strand, London WC2R 0RL, England
Penguin Ireland, 25 St Stephen's Green, Dublin 2, Ireland (a division of Penguin Books Ltd)
Penguin Group (Australia), 250 Camberwell Road, Camberwell, Victoria 3124, Australia
(a division of Pearson Australia Group Pty Ltd)
Penguin Books India Pvt Ltd, 11 Community Centre, Panchsheel Park,
New Delhi – 110 017, India
Penguin Group (NZ), 67 Apollo Drive, Rosedale, Auckland 0632, New Zealand
(a division of Pearson New Zealand Ltd)
Penguin Books (South Africa) (Pty) Ltd, 24 Sturdee Avenue, Rosebank,
Johannesburg 2196, South Africa

Penguin Books Ltd, Registered Offices: 80 Strand, London WC2R 0RL, England

First published 2011

1 2 3 4 5 6 7 8 9 10 (RRD)

The credits on page 393 constitute an extension of this copyright page.

Manufactured in the U.S.A.

LIBRARY AND ARCHIVES CANADA CATALOGUING IN PUBLICATION

Vronsky, Peter
Ridgeway : the American Fenian invasion and the 1866 battle
that made Canada / Peter Vronsky.

(The history of Canada)
Includes bibliographical references and index.

ISBN 978-0-670-06803-6

1. Ridgeway (Fort Erie, Ont.), Battle of, 1866.
2. Canada—History—Fenian Invasions, 1866–1870.
I. Title. II. Series: History of Canada (Toronto, Ont.)

FC480.F4V76 2011 971.04'8 C2011-906112-0

Visit the Penguin Group (Canada) website at **www.penguin.ca**

Special and corporate bulk purchase rates available; please see
www.penguin.ca/corporatesales or call 1-800-810-3104, ext. 2477.

Dedicated to the memory and remembrance
of Canada's First Fallen

***

Ensign Malcolm McEachren
Sergeant Hugh Matheson
Corporal Francis Lackey
Lance Corporal Mark Defries
Private Christopher Alderson
Private Malcolm McKenzie
Private John Harriman Mewburn
Private William Smith
Private William Fairbanks Tempest

***

Second Battalion Volunteer Rifles of Toronto
"Queen's Own Rifles"

Killed in Action at Limestone Ridge
Battle of Ridgeway
Canada

June 2, 1866

It's been too long home boys to be forgotten.

CONTENTS

PART 3: THE HIDDEN HISTORY

INTRODUCTION TO THE HISTORY OF CANADA SERIES

Canada, the world agrees, is a success story. We should never make the mistake, though, of thinking that it was easy or foreordained. At crucial moments during Canada's history, challenges had to be faced and choices made. Certain roads were taken and others were not. Imagine a Canada, indeed imagine a North America, where the French and not the British had won the Battle of the Plains of Abraham. Or imagine a world in which Canadians had decided to throw in their lot with the revolutionaries in the thirteen colonies.

This series looks at the making of Canada as an independent, self-governing nation. It includes works on key stages in the laying of the foundations as well as the crucial turning points between 1867 and the present that made the Canada we know today. It is about those defining moments when the course of Canadian history and the nature of Canada itself were oscillating. And it is about the human beings—heroic, flawed, wise, foolish, complex—who had to make decisions without knowing what the consequences might be.

We begin the series with the European presence in the eighteenth century—a presence that continues to shape our society today—and conclude it with an exploration of the strategic importance of the Canadian Arctic. We look at how the mass movements of peoples, whether Loyalists in the eighteenth century or Asians at the start of the twentieth, have profoundly influenced the nature of Canada. We also look at battles and their aftermaths: the Plains of Abraham, the 1866 Fenian raids, the German submarines in the St. Lawrence River during World War II. Political crises—the 1891 election that saw Sir John A. Macdonald battling Wilfrid Laurier; Pierre Trudeau's triumphant patriation of the Canadian Constitution—provide rich moments of storytelling. So, too, do the Expo 67 celebrations, which marked a time of soaring optimism and gave Canadians new confidence in themselves.

We have chosen these critical turning points partly because they are good stories in themselves but also because they show what Canada was like at particularly important junctures in its history. And to tell them we have chosen Canada's best historians. Our authors are great storytellers who shine a spotlight on a different Canada, a Canada of the past, and illustrate links from then to now. We need to remember the roads that were taken—and the ones that were not. Our goal is to help our readers understand how we got from that past to this present.

Margaret MacMillan
Warden at St. Antony's College, Oxford

Robert Bothwell
May Gluskin Chair of Canadian History
University of Toronto

LIST OF MAPS

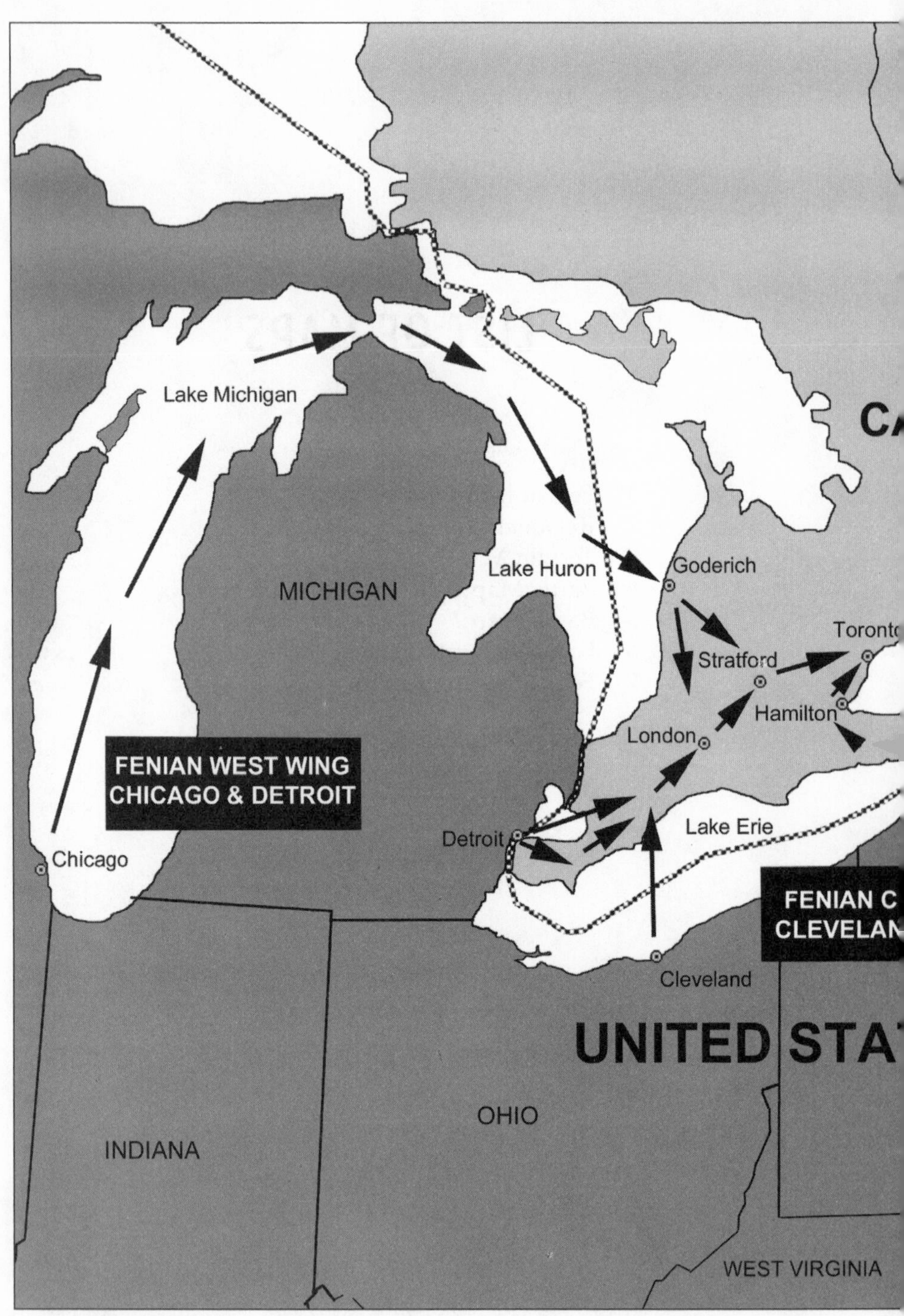
Lake Michigan
CA
Lake Huron
Goderich
MICHIGAN
Toronto
Stratford
Hamilton
London
FENIAN WEST WING
CHICAGO & DETROIT
Lake Erie
Detroit
Chicago
FENIAN C
CLEVELAN
Cleveland
UNITED STAT
OHIO
INDIANA
WEST VIRGINIA

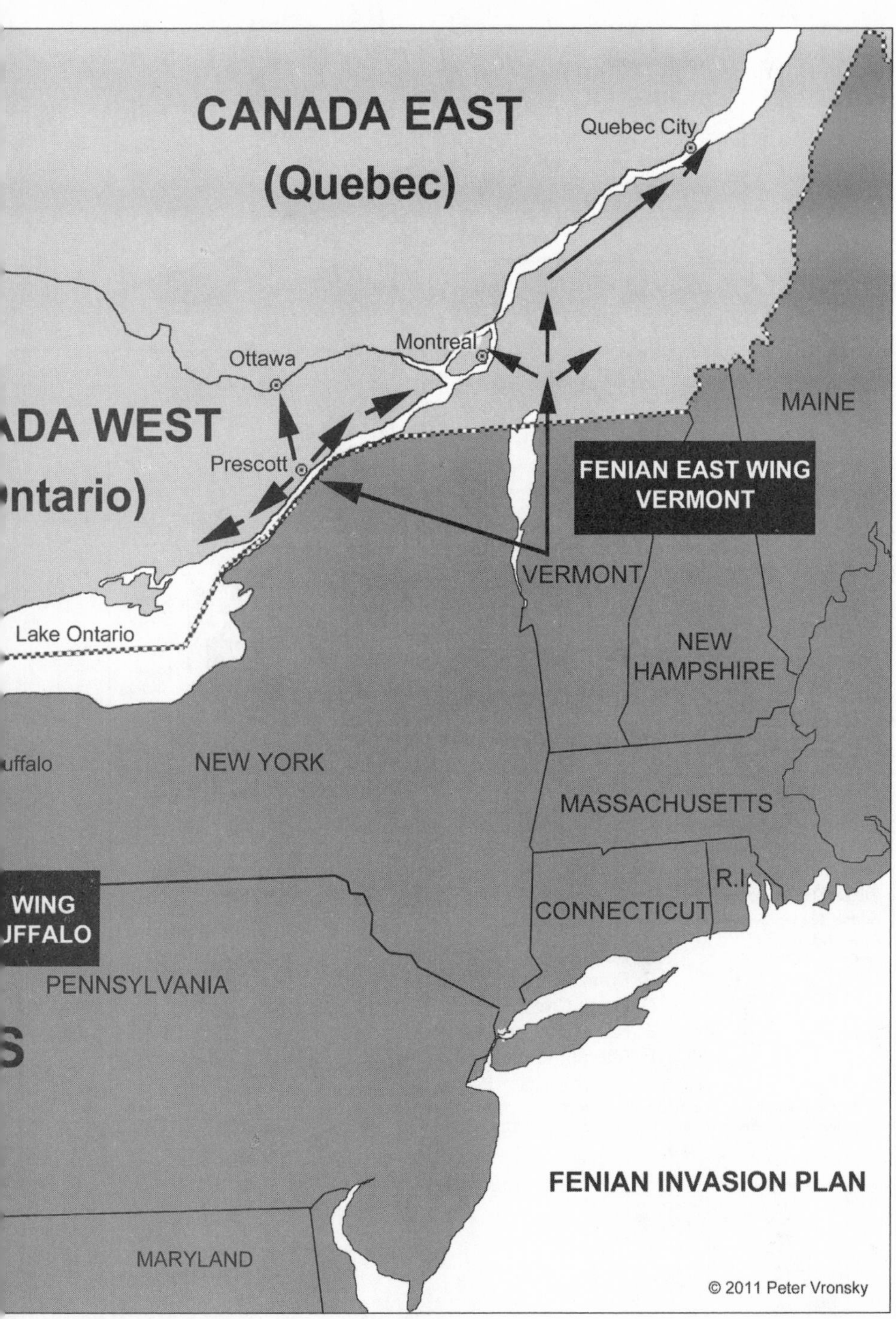
CANADA EAST
(Quebec)
Quebec City
Montreal
Ottawa
ADA WEST
ntario)
Prescott
Lake Ontario
FENIAN EAST WING
VERMONT
MAINE
VERMONT
NEW
HAMPSHIRE
uffalo
NEW YORK
MASSACHUSETTS
R.I.
CONNECTICUT
WING
JFFALO
PENNSYLVANIA
S
FENIAN INVASION PLAN
MARYLAND
© 2011 Peter Vronsky

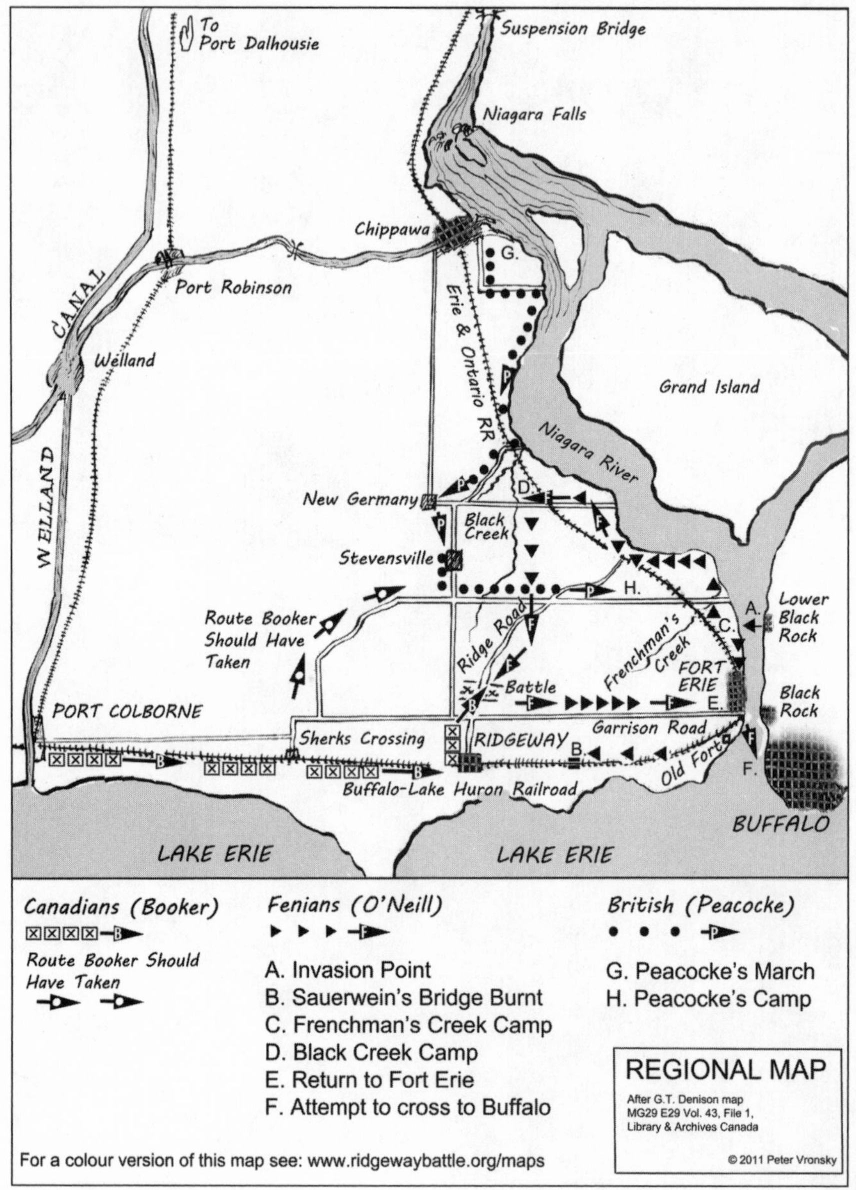

Canadians (Booker)

Route Booker Should Have Taken

Fenians (O'Neill)

A. Invasion Point
B. Sauerwein's Bridge Burnt
C. Frenchman's Creek Camp
D. Black Creek Camp
E. Return to Fort Erie
F. Attempt to cross to Buffalo

British (Peacocke)

G. Peacocke's March
H. Peacocke's Camp

REGIONAL MAP

After G.T. Denison map
MG29 E29 Vol. 43, File 1,
Library & Archives Canada

For a colour version of this map see: www.ridgewaybattle.org/maps

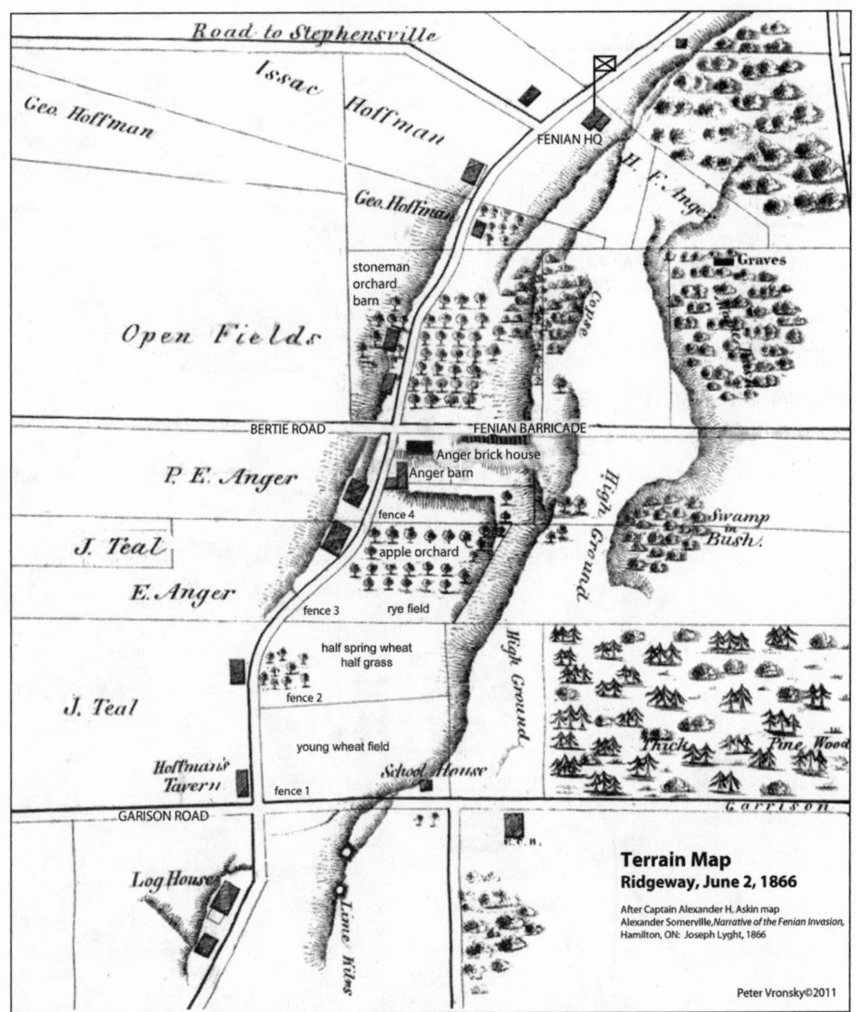
Road to Stephensville
Issac Hoffman
Geo. Hoffman
FENIAN HQ
H. F. Anger
Geo. Hoffman
Graves
stoneman orchard barn
Copse
Open Fields
BERTIE ROAD
FENIAN BARRICADE
Anger brick house
Anger barn
P. E. Anger
High Ground
fence 4
Swamp Bush
J. Teal
apple orchard
E. Anger
fence 3
rye field
half spring wheat half grass
High Ground
J. Teal
fence 2
Thick Pine Wood
young wheat field
Hoffman's Tavern
School House
fence 1
GARISON ROAD
Garrison
Log House
Lime Kilns
Terrain Map
Ridgeway, June 2, 1866
After Captain Alexander H. Askin map
Alexander Somerville, Narrative of the Fenian Invasion, Hamilton, ON: Joseph Lyght, 1866
Peter Vronsky©2011

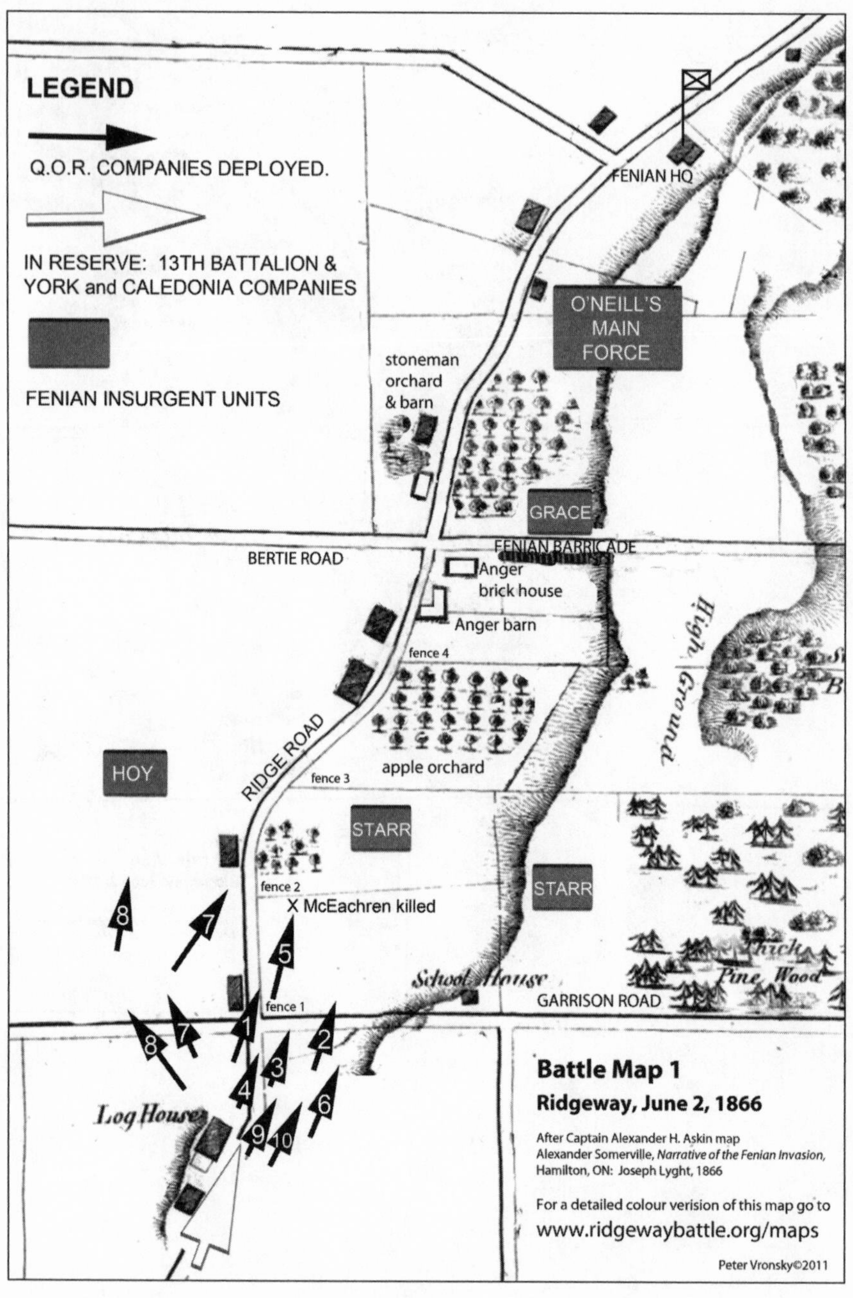
LEGEND
Q.O.R. COMPANIES DEPLOYED.
IN RESERVE: 13TH BATTALION & YORK and CALEDONIA COMPANIES
FENIAN INSURGENT UNITS
FENIAN HQ
O'NEILL'S MAIN FORCE
stoneman orchard & barn
GRACE
FENIAN BARRICADE
BERTIE ROAD
Anger brick house
Anger barn
fence 4
High Ground
RIDGE ROAD
apple orchard
HOY
fence 3
STARR
STARR
fence 2
X McEachren killed
8
7
5
School House
Thick Pine Wood
GARRISON ROAD
fence 1
1
2
8
7
3
4
6
9
10
Log House
Battle Map 1
Ridgeway, June 2, 1866
After Captain Alexander H. Askin map
Alexander Somerville, Narrative of the Fenian Invasion, Hamilton, ON: Joseph Lyght, 1866
For a detailed colour verision of this map go to
www.ridgewaybattle.org/maps
Peter Vronsky©2011

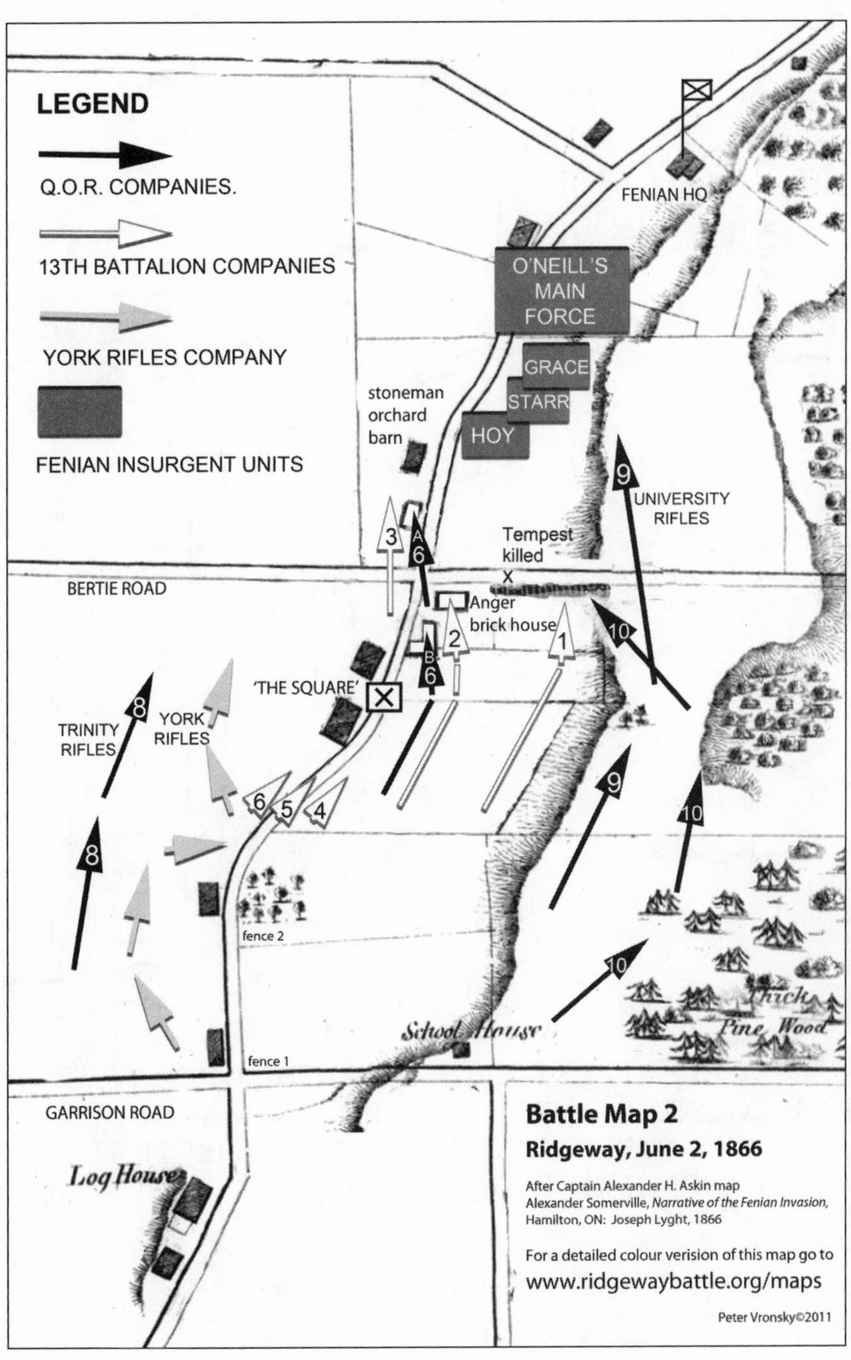

Battle Map 2

Ridgeway, June 2, 1866

After Captain Alexander H. Askin map
Alexander Somerville, *Narrative of the Fenian Invasion,* Hamilton, ON: Joseph Lyght, 1866

For a detailed colour verision of this map go to
www.ridgewaybattle.org/maps

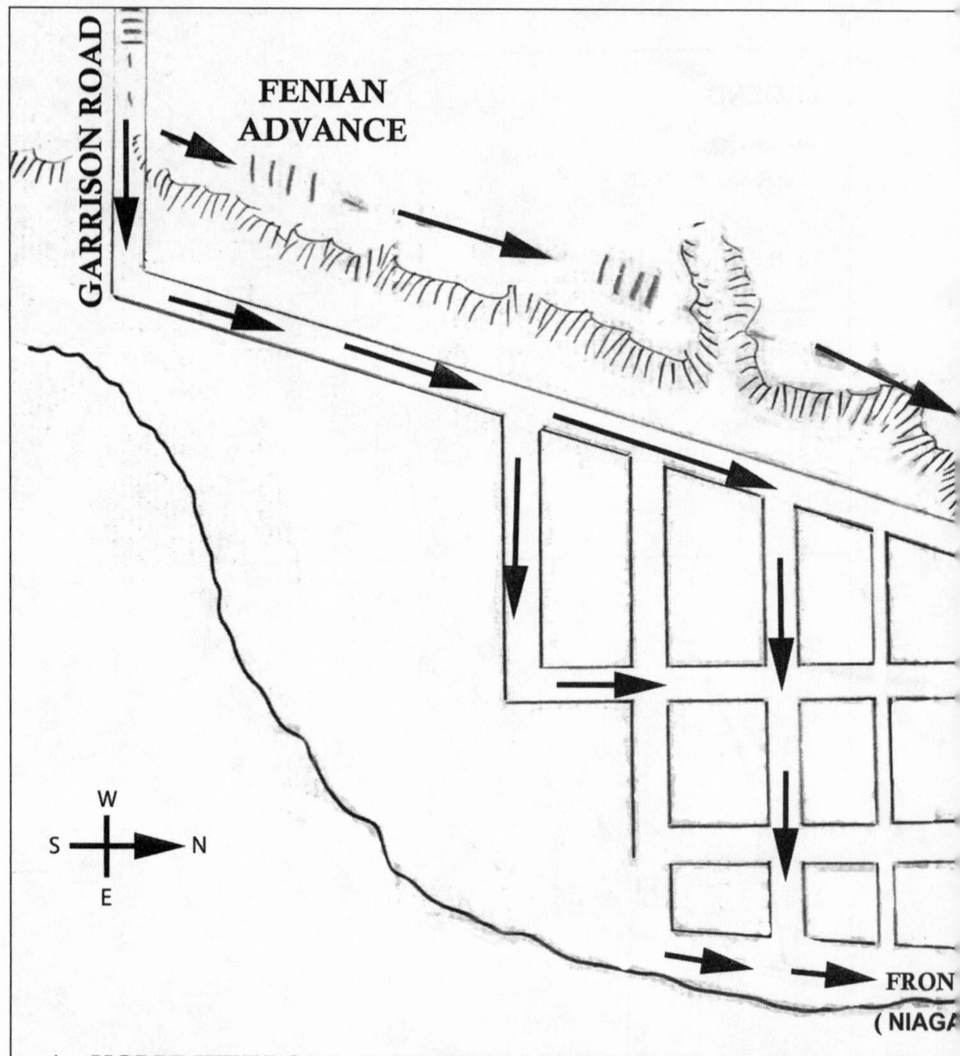

A. VOLUNTEERS MARCH FROM THE DOCK TO THIS POINT
B. COUNTER-MARCH TO HERE AND MAKE STAND
C. VOLUNTEERS RETREAT IN THIS DIRECTION
D. CAPTAIN KING AND HIS MEN

NIAG.

For a colour version of this map see: www.ridgewaybattle.org/maps

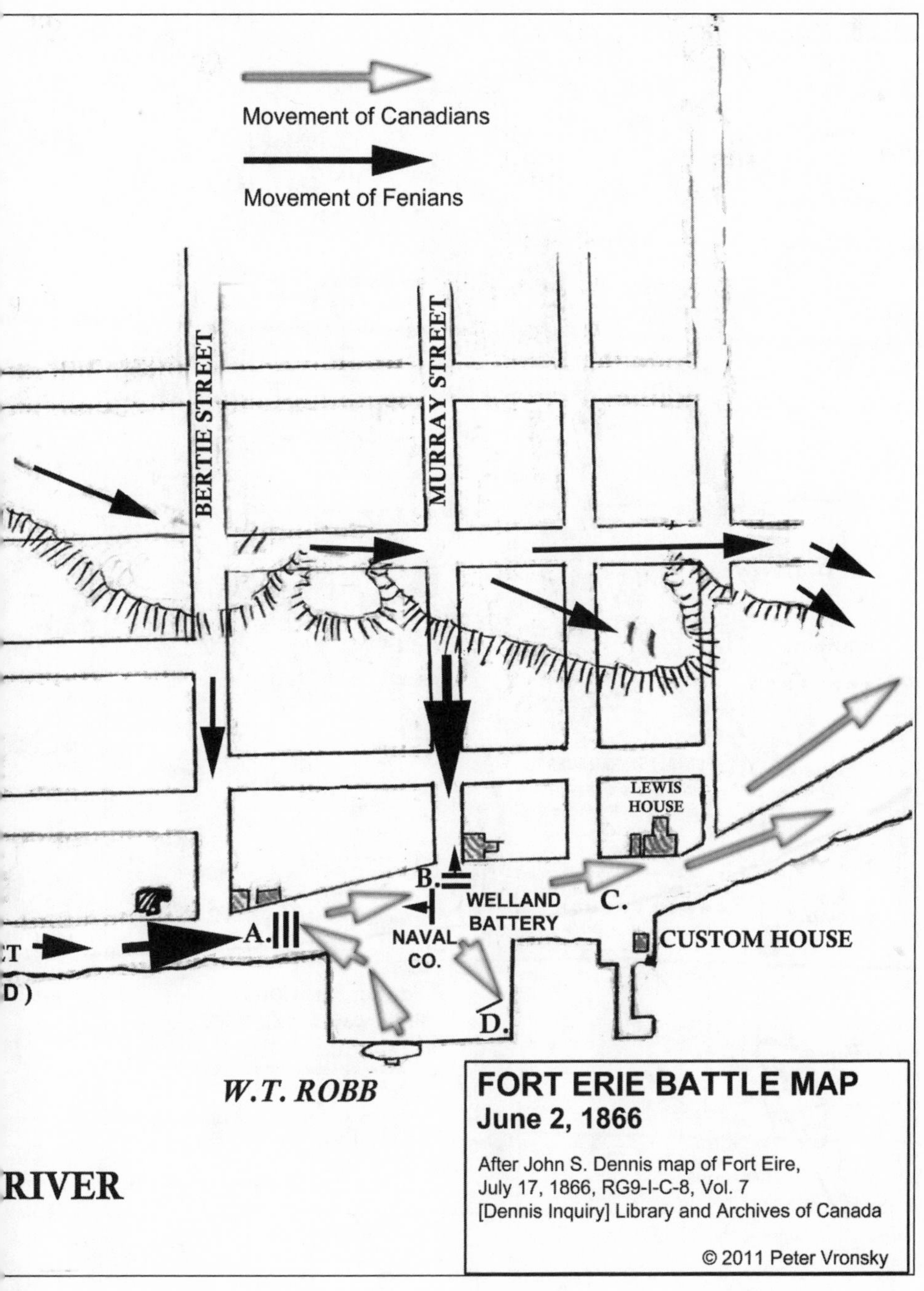

FORT ERIE BATTLE MAP
June 2, 1866

After John S. Dennis map of Fort Eire, July 17, 1866, RG9-I-C-8, Vol. 7 [Dennis Inquiry] Library and Archives of Canada

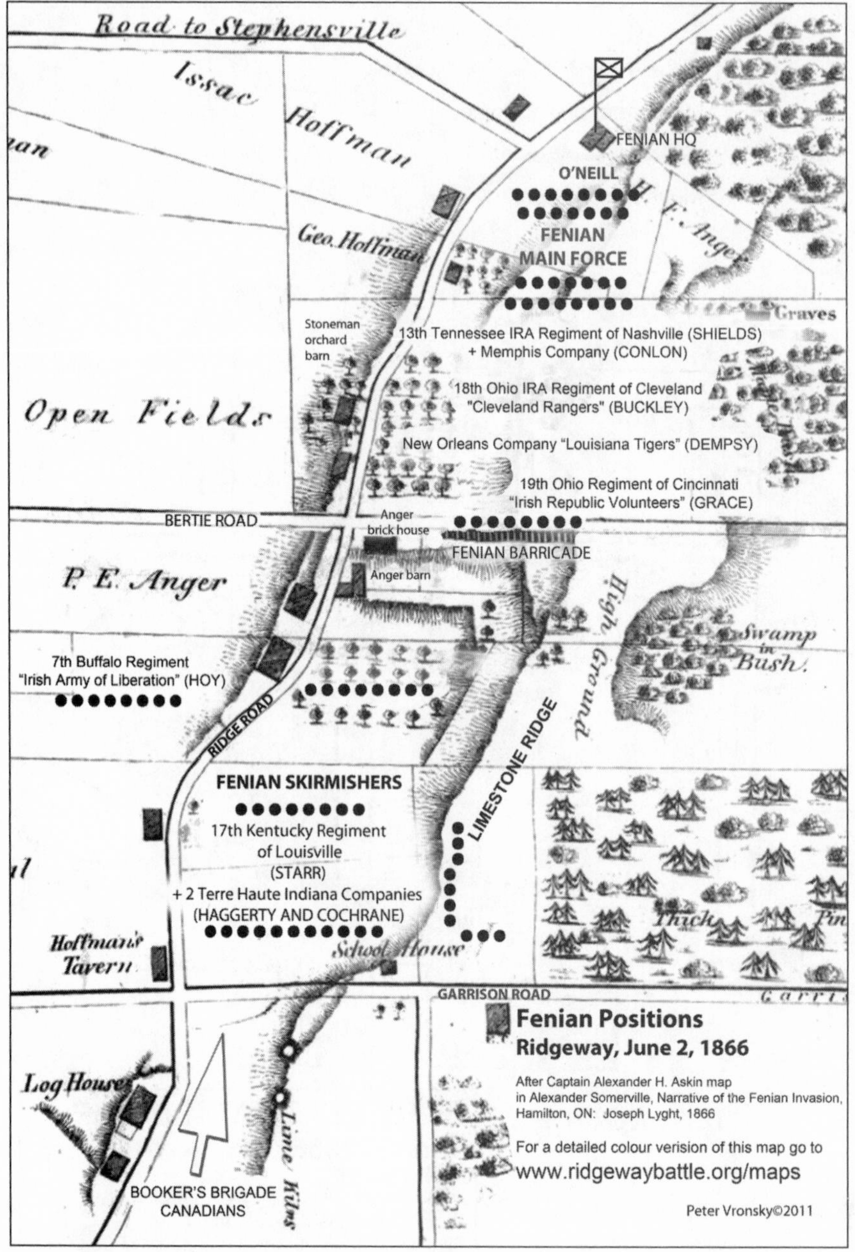

Road to Stephensville
Issac
Hoffman
Geo. Hoffman
FENIAN HQ
O'NEILL
FENIAN
MAIN FORCE
Graves
Stoneman
orchard
barn
13th Tennessee IRA Regiment of Nashville (SHIELDS)
+ Memphis Company (CONLON)
18th Ohio IRA Regiment of Cleveland
"Cleveland Rangers" (BUCKLEY)
Open Fields
New Orleans Company "Louisiana Tigers" (DEMPSY)
19th Ohio Regiment of Cincinnati
"Irish Republic Volunteers" (GRACE)
BERTIE ROAD
Anger
brick house
FENIAN BARRICADE
P. E. Anger
Anger barn
High Ground
Swamp in Bush
7th Buffalo Regiment
"Irish Army of Liberation" (HOY)
RIDGE ROAD
LIMESTONE RIDGE
FENIAN SKIRMISHERS
17th Kentucky Regiment
of Louisville
(STARR)
+ 2 Terre Haute Indiana Companies
(HAGGERTY AND COCHRANE)
Hoffman's
Tavern
School House
GARRISON ROAD
Log House
Lime Kilns
BOOKER'S BRIGADE
CANADIANS
Fenian Positions
Ridgeway, June 2, 1866
After Captain Alexander H. Askin map
in Alexander Somerville, Narrative of the Fenian Invasion,
Hamilton, ON: Joseph Lyght, 1866
For a detailed colour verision of this map go to
www.ridgewaybattle.org/maps
Peter Vronsky©2011

More than once during the Civil War newspapers reported a strange phenomenon. From only a few miles away a battle sometimes made no sound despite the flash and smoke of cannon and the fact that more distant observers could hear it clearly. These eerie silences were called acoustic shadows.

Ken Burns
"The Universe of Battle"
The Civil War[1]

A type of acoustical phenomenon that had been noted for two hundred years prior to Seven Pines and given the catchall name acoustic shadows ... an event in which a person who would ordinarily hear a sound does not ... These events also sometimes mean that those who should not hear the sound do hear it.

Charles D. Ross, *Acoustic Shadows in the Civil War*
Acoustical Society of America
136th Meeting, Lay Language Papers
Norfolk, Virginia, October 13, 1998[2]

Let them not be untrue to the dead.

George T. Denison III
Decoration Day Address, June 2, 1891
Canadian Volunteers Monument, Toronto[3]

No one is forgotten. Nothing is forgotten.

Olga Berggolts
Granite Inscription
Leningrad Blockade 1941–1944 Monument[4]

PREFACE

RIDGEWAY IN THE ACOUSTIC SHADOW OF HISTORY

On June 2, 1866, Robert Larmour saw something so horrible and painful that it would incessantly flash through his memory for the rest of his life. It was an unusually hot and gloriously sunny afternoon in Canada's Niagara region. Larmour was riding in the cab of a steam locomotive approaching the village of Ridgeway, the last stop before the town of Fort Erie on the Canadian border just across the river from Buffalo, New York. Suddenly he heard the train give a warning groan as the engineer bore down on the brakes. The cars shuddered, their steel wheels howling as they slowed. Leaning out from the cab, Larmour squinted through a shimmering curtain of heat waves rising from the sun-baked tracks ahead. He could not make sense of what he was seeing. It was enormous, so huge it spilled out from the tracks over the hillocks and surrounding fields as far as Larmour could see, a dragon-sized dark-green thing with scarlet red specks, hurtling straight at them at running speed.

Thirty-two years later, in 1898, Larmour would vividly describe it in his own words in *The Canadian Magazine*, as if it had happened to him only yesterday.[1]

Larmour was a twenty-five-year-old steampunk mid-Victorian office road-warrior. He lived and worked on the leading edge of the pre-electronic technology of his age. Larmour routinely travelled at the fastest land speed possible for humans at the time: twenty to thirty-five miles per hour, depending upon the condition of the railway tracks; a two-minute mile—50 percent of the average maximum highway speed limit today—exactly halfway between then and now, between the old and the modern. He could communicate with distant points on the continent of North America in seconds by sending "t-mails" over a Victorian internet of telegraph lines, and by the next year he could connect to England and Europe across the Atlantic by undersea cable.[2] As an assistant railway route superintendent, Larmour could do all this while riding comfortably in the plush, overstated nineteenth-century luxury of an empty first-class passenger coach or, as on this day, up front with the engineer on a jump seat in the locomotive's open cab, hot wind and coal ash streaming through his hair.

Larmour, a farm boy from Dundas, Ontario, was sixteen when he first joined the Grand Trunk Railway's telegraphic service, and he steadily rose in the company over the next nine years.[3] Recently he had been appointed to supervise railway operations on a route that connected Buffalo by way of Fort Erie to Port Colborne in Canada West, as Upper Canada, today Ontario, was then known. Ridgeway was halfway between Port Colborne and the border town of Fort Erie.

Two nights before, a thousand heavily armed Irish-American Fenian insurgents had made a surprise nighttime crossing of the Niagara River from their base in Buffalo and seized Fort Erie and its railway terminal. Their plan was to free Ireland by taking Canada hostage. It was feared that from Fort Erie the Fenians would strike next at the strategically vulnerable Welland Canal and the railway junctions. For the last thirty-six hours, Larmour had been supervising troop transports from a staging area at Port Colborne.

That morning he disembarked an 841-man Canadian militia brigade at Ridgeway, the last stop before Fort Erie and the Fenians. The Canadian volunteer brigade commander, Lieutenant Colonel Alfred Booker, was under orders to march and join with a column of British regular troops and together, under British command, interdict the Fenians.

When Larmour returned to Port Colborne he found an urgent telegram awaiting him: Before the brigade had been able to link with the British, it had been ambushed by the Fenians at Limestone Ridge a few miles north of Ridgeway. They were now engaging the enemy but running short of ammunition. Larmour quickly turned the train back, hauling two flatcars loaded with spare ammunition and a fresh company of infantry in support.

Shortly after his train left Port Colborne, Larmour began to see ominous signs. The closer the train chugged toward Ridgeway, the more the concession roads paralleling the tracks filled with frightened refugees, entire families on foot, on horseback, their children piled into wagons loaded with bedding and furniture, desperately driving their livestock ahead of them. This torrent of people and animals streamed away from the direction in which his train was headed. As the fleeing columns were left behind, Larmour's train rolled cautiously into eerily empty countryside. All the homes and farmsteads appeared to be shuttered and abandoned, no smoke rising from their kitchen chimneys. Occasionally Larmour would catch sight of small ghostly parties of armed horsemen flanking the train in the distance or popping up on the horizon. They would melt away into the countryside as fast as they had appeared.

When the train began to brake a few miles short of Ridgeway and the mammoth dark-green and red thing rushing at them got close enough to break into focus through the heat waves, Larmour recognized what it was: hundreds of soldiers running toward him. Their green and scarlet uniforms were torn and soiled, soaked with sweat, some in blood. Their faces were stained as black and indigo-blue as coal miners' by gunpowder residue from the hours of having fired their rifles in what must have been one futile shot after another. Their many eyes glowed a wild white from their grotesque blackface. Many of them in a panic had thrown away their weapons and ammo belts. Larmour would recall, "The railway track ahead of us was crowded from fence to fence, and in the fields on each side of the track they were scattered as far as could be seen. The train was brought to a stand, the whistle blown to attract attention."

It was the brigade he had detrained earlier that morning at Ridgeway. Something had gone terribly wrong. Having seen the train, the troops rushed toward it pell-mell in desperation. The relief company Larmour had been transporting deployed across the tracks in an attempt to stem the wave of men. It was to no avail.

Larmour remembered, "Like a stream of water they parted in front of the company, passed around its flanks, and again closed in the rear. As many as could get a foot-hold clung to the engine and two flat-cars. The scene that I witnessed from the foot-place of the engine was painful in the extreme. Some of the men were so utterly exhausted that they dropped in their tracks, and lay there as if dead. Many were without their arms and accoutrements. Some were weeping, while others tramped on in sullen silence, and yet others were cursing. Someone had blundered!"[4]

The scene Larmour describes is absent from Canadian history. Its ocean of grimy, disheartened soldiers clambering aboard the train through clouds of steam has the epic feel of widescreen movies about conflicts far from the Canadian experience: the disastrous railroad scenes of the Russian Civil War in *Doctor Zhivago* or the Great War in *Lawrence of Arabia*; the trains of the American Civil War in *The Good, the Bad and the Ugly*; something out of *Cold Mountain, Once Upon a Time in the West, Reds,* or *Europa*. But this scene actually happened to us, happened here in Canada, in Ontario's Niagara country, a mere year before Canadian Confederation. Why have we heard so little about it?

IN THE DARK of the early morning hours of June 1, 1866, more than a thousand Irish Americans invaded Canada. They were the spearhead in a planned assault calling for thousands of Fenians to cross the Canadian land and maritime borders with Michigan, Ohio, New York, and Vermont. The raid on the Niagara Frontier was led by the Fenian general John O'Neill, a former U.S. cavalry captain specializing in anti-guerrilla warfare during the recent Civil War. Crossing the Niagara River from Buffalo in barges, the Fenians occupied the town of Fort Erie, and after seizing horses and supplies and posting pickets, their main force headed inland.

The next morning on Limestone Ridge near the village of Ridgeway, they fought 841 militia volunteers under Booker's command from Toronto, Hamilton, and York and Caledonia counties. The Canadians lost nine men and dozens were wounded while resolutely advancing in a pitched two-hour battle. And then they suddenly appeared to break into a retreat never adequately explained to this day. Because the Fenians were aware that British and Canadian reinforcements were on their way, they did not pursue the withdrawing troops. Instead they wheeled back to the town of Fort Erie, just across the river from their invasion base in Buffalo.

The Fenians found Fort Erie now held by a seventy-one-man detachment of Canadian troops. The Canadians had landed that morning from a high-speed steamboat and had been patrolling the Niagara River shoreline, capturing straggling insurgents and pickets while the main Fenian force was fighting at Ridgeway. But now outnumbered ten-to-one by the returning Fenian army, the Canadians found themselves with their backs to the river and to the ship that had brought them there. To the soldiers' horror their commanding officer, rather than ordering them to board the tug and pull away from shore as their junior officers were urging, insisted instead that they make a stand. A vicious house-to-house battle ensued in Fort Erie's streets, in which several Canadians were severely wounded while thirty-seven were taken prisoner by the Fenians. Among the few who managed to escape was Lieutenant Colonel John Stoughton Dennis, the commanding officer of the detachment, who had insisted on making the hopeless stand.

While the Canadians were turned on the field, the raid itself was a failure for the Fenians. Early on June 3, finding their supplies and relief cut off by U.S. Navy gunboats, and with a numerically superior force of British and Canadian infantry, cavalry, and artillery assembling nearby, the Fenians began to withdraw across the river to Buffalo. They were taken prisoner in midstream by the U.S. Navy.

The battle at Limestone Ridge (or Lime Ridge) in the morning and the battle of Fort Erie in the afternoon of June 2, 1866, together referred to as "the Battle of Ridgeway," were the last battles fought in Ontario against a foreign invader. They were also Canada's first modern battles and the first to be fought exclusively by Canadians and led in the field by Canadian officers. Except for one British army private in Fort Erie who had been taken prisoner by the Fenians on the first day of the raid and released on his parole, no British military personnel were present in the battles.

The Battle of Ridgeway became the melancholy baptism of the Canadian army, in which it suffered its first nine battlefield deaths: its first officer, sergeant, corporal, lance corporal, and five privates killed in action or shortly afterward succumbing to their wounds.[5] Another six would die from disease within the next few weeks, while forty-one men sustained wounds, many of them serious enough to require amputation.[6]

The Canadian soldiers were really mostly teenage boys and young men, some as young as fifteen years old—farm boys, shopkeepers, apprentices, schoolteachers, store clerks, and two rifle companies of University of Toronto student volunteers who were hastily called out in the middle of their final exams. The Fenians who had assembled from all corners of the United States were almost all battle-hardened Civil War veterans, some from crack Irish brigades. They carried weapons with which they had intimate familiarity after having fought in dozens of apocalyptic battles in a war that killed 620,000 in four years—two percent of the entire American population—more dead than in all the wars combined that the United States has fought before and since. The Canadian boys on the other hand came from a generation that had not seen combat since the 1837–38 Rebellion—nearly thirty years earlier. While there had been freebooting raids across the border in 1838, no major invasion of Canadian territory had occurred since the War of 1812, a conflict their grandfathers had fought in. Strapped by the cost-saving policies of the colonial government, many of them had not even been given an opportunity to practise firing live rounds from the rifles issued to them the day before. Many were city kids from Toronto and Hamilton, unaccustomed to firearms, untrained, and only parade ground drilled.

They were led by gentlemen part-time officers: wealthy merchants, attorneys, engineers, professors, landlords, civil servants, politicians, and entrepreneurs who saw their military rank as a privilege, a status symbol, and a function of their social class to lead the "lower orders" forward in their duty to Queen and Empire. When on that Saturday morning of June 2 the Canadians collided with approximately eight hundred Fenian insurgents on Limestone Ridge, a single company of twenty-eight University of Toronto student soldiers took the brunt of the Fenian counterattack and suffered the most killed and wounded.

Two Canadian militia battalions, the dark green–uniformed Second Battalion "Queen's Own Rifles" (QOR) of Toronto and the traditionally redcoat-clad Thirteenth Battalion of Hamilton, reinforced by two rural companies from Caledonia in Haldimand County and the York Rifles from Essex County, were hit hard by expert insurgent rifle fire; and when the Fenians fixed bayonets and charged headlong howling the Celtic war cry, the inexperienced Canadian ranks, it was said, broke and ran, leaving their dead and wounded on the field. It was the first Irish victory over the forces of the British Empire since the Battle of Fontenoy in 1745, when in present-day Belgium the exile Irish Brigade in the service of the French King Louis XV—the "Wild Geese"—charged shrieking into the Duke of Cumberland's elite Coldstream Guards and scattered them like pigeons.[7]

The Battle of Ridgeway took place less than a year before Confederation finally brought together several British North American colonies in the Dominion of Canada on July 1, 1867. Because of

Ridgeway's proximity to Fort Erie and the Niagara region, the battle is sometimes confused with the War of 1812 that was fought in Canada between Britain and the United States. But by 1866 the fort at "Fort Erie" was an abandoned ruin, and the town was a booming border crossing and railway ferry terminal just across the river from Buffalo. The battle was fought in a world of telegraph communications, steam power, railways, newspapers, news wire services, photography, public opinion, and parliamentary democracy—all things that were undreamt of in the Canada of 1812 or even as recently as 1837–38, the last time there had been combat in Canada before Ridgeway. This first modern battle fought by Canadians was, significantly, fought *in* Canada. Ridgeway and the Fenian invasion were in many ways a midwife to Canadian institutional modernity and its aspirations to nationhood and union. They tested for the first time Canada's ability to defend itself, *by itself*, without British troops on the field of battle.

The Fenian incursion triggered a "national" security crisis, although Canada was still a year away from becoming a nation. It led to the mobilization of twenty-two thousand volunteer soldiers and put on alert every village, town, and city along the Canada–U.S. frontier. Civil rights were partly suspended under an emergency war measures decree for most of what remained of pre-Confederation Canada and were not reinstated until June 8, 1867, just three weeks before the July 1 Canada Day birthday.[8] The surging Fenian threat tested Canada's civil and military institutions, the viability of its infrastructure, its capacity for autonomy, its tenor of loyalty, its patriotism, and its commitment to its heritage traditions of personal liberty, justice, cultural and religious pluralism, and parliamentary integrity—everything that would define the nation it became. The Fenian Raid and the Battle of Ridgeway in which it culminated were the final events that persuaded some remaining reluctant colonial Canadians still unsure of the wisdom of Confederation to finally commit to nationhood; the crisis marked the beginning of an emerging national identity, a new sense of self.

Indeed, the soldiers' marching songs in 1866 celebrated a Canada not yet formally born as a nation:

> Tramp, tramp, tramp, the boys are marching,
> Cheer up, let the rabble come!
> For beneath the Union Jack, we'll drive the Fenians back
> And we'll fight for our beloved Canadian home.[9]
> Cheer up boys, come on, come on!
> It will not take us long
> To prove to their dismay, that their raid will not pay
> And wish that from Canadian ground
> They stayed away.[10]

Here is how, in 1931, the young C.P. Stacey, the future dean of twentieth-century Canadian military historians, described this new emerging sense of "national feeling" in Canada in the face of the Fenian invasion:

> Fenianism tended to engender among Canadians an attitude that gave practical significance to that platform phrase "the new nationality." No mere constitutional proposal could have aroused the feeling that was awakened by the threats ... The menace imposed itself strongly upon the popular imagination, and in such a fashion as to cultivate a patriotic feeling which was distinctively Canadian. The resistance to the Fenians was in defence of the British connection, but it was also an act of simple self-defence in which Canadian eyes turned as never before to local resources.[11]

Stacey was far from the first to make this claim. In 1866 the *St. Catharines Constitutional*, in a list of seven things "the Fenians have done," proclaimed the first four to be as follows:

1. They have drawn the parent country and her North American colonies into closer mutual sympathy and affection.

2. They have banded the British American provinces more closely together by a sense of common danger and a desire for mutual co-operation and defence.
3. They have consequently greatly promoted the Confederation scheme.
4. They have elicited a triumphant display of loyalty and courage of the inhabitants of the two Canadas, who have sprung to arms to defend their country with promptitude and energy never surpassed.[12]

A year after Ridgeway, a prominent veteran of the battle, Toronto schoolteacher Alexander Muir, composed what became anglophone Canada's unofficial national anthem, which proclaimed "Our watchword evermore shall be the Maple Leaf forever!"[13] It was at Ridgeway that Canadians first fought for the Maple Leaf before the Crown. It ushered in a new patriotism rooted in a rising sense of a "homeland" defined by an emerging national ideal, one that Canadians demonstrated they were prepared to fight and die for. Ridgeway was where British colonial *subjects* began their transformation into *citizens* of a unique, emerging, indigenous Canadian political community—a nation—that emphasized its "connection to Britain" as opposed to its former status as a loyal colonial province of it. Confederation in 1867 made Canada on paper; Ridgeway made it in its people's hearts. It was Canada's Bunker Hill, down to its subtext of national identity flowering in battlefield defeat, tempered by a common resilience to fight another day—to never surrender. When Canada was being made, Ridgeway was the battle that made Canada.

Ridgeway is also the battle that most Canadians today have never heard of.

That was not always the case. In 1897, thirty-one years after the battle, when two hundred veterans of Ridgeway marched through Toronto to the 1866 Canadian Volunteers Monument—Toronto's oldest standing public monument today—fifty thousand spectators lined the route, an extraordinary one-quarter of the city's population. Escorted by two thousand schoolchildren, the middle-aged "Veterans of '66" were showered in flower petals and bouquets. Another thirty-five thousand people assembled at the monument and decorated it in garlands and wreaths.[14]

The public commemoration of the Battle of Ridgeway had begun only in 1890 and evolved into Canada's memorial day. It was known originally as Decoration Day and until 1931 was commemorated in late May or early June on or near the anniversary of the battle. Decoration Day honoured not only the veterans and the fallen of Ridgeway, but also the Canadian soldiers killed in the Northwest Rebellion of 1885 and those killed subsequently in the South African War of 1899–1902 (Boer War) and the First World War (Great War) from 1914 to 1918.[15] This makes it all the more puzzling why today Ridgeway is a battle so obscure that even many Canadian historians themselves cannot meet the challenge of identifying, dating, or describing it without looking it up.

IN 1931, the anniversary of the Battle of Ridgeway ceased to be marked as Canada's memorial day when in an Act of Parliament R.B. Bennett's Conservative government moved it to November 11, the Great War Armistice Day, to "harmonize" it with Commonwealth practice, and officially renamed it Remembrance Day.[16] The Veterans Affairs Canada website bluntly states, "Remembrance Day commemorates Canadians who died in service to Canada from the South African War to current missions."[17] Neither Ridgeway's status as a pre-Confederation battle nor the official date of the founding of Canada's "permanent regular" army in 1883 explains why the casualties of 1866 are today excluded from the country's official military memorial heritage. Veterans Affairs Canada also excludes casualties in the Red River Rebellion (1869–70), the second Fenian Raids (1870–71), and the Northwest Rebellion (1885), even though many of the units that sustained those casualties are still as active today in the defence of Canada and its military as they were back then.

The assertion that only casualties sustained overseas qualify for national memorialization is, I suspect, rooted in Canada's political geography. That many Canadians are embarrassed by the armed conflicts in 1869–1870 and 1885 with the Metis and First Nations in the West goes without saying, but when it comes to defending home *at home* from external invaders, it could only mean one thing: fighting Americans, a taboo notion in Canada, where we have long celebrated the politics of the "undefended border." The boys who fell in 1866, 1870, and 1885, who left widows and orphans as broken-hearted as those of men lost overseas in South Africa, on Vimy Ridge, or at Dieppe, are just as dead yet completely forgotten. Their resting places, lacking Canada War Graves status, often are anonymous and uncared for; their names missing from Canada's national Books of Remembrance; their lives and sacrifice discounted.[18]

Remarkably, when Ridgeway was forgotten in the 1930s, it was not the first time the battle's memory had been erased from Canadian history. Ridgeway has been forgotten *twice.* We forgot that we had forgotten once before! The battle fell into a kind of historical acoustic shadow, audible to some but not to others, a self-cancelling echo from the past distorted by deep politics of myth, conspiracy, and nation building in the very midst of Canada's becoming not only itself, but modern too. Nationalism and modernity is an Orwellian two-punch knockout blow to truth and honesty typical of many national founding stories, not just Canada's. In the summer and autumn of 1866, what really happened at Limestone Ridge and at Fort Erie—already the subject of confused and often inaccurate newspaper reports—was hidden from Canadians; the colonial government led by John A. Macdonald and several rival factions of wealthy, socially prominent volunteer officers covered up and falsified the history through two military boards of inquiry, typically obscuring the truth rather than ascertaining it.

The Booker Inquiry, a one-day proceeding into the conduct of the commanding officer at Limestone Ridge, Lieutenant Colonel Alfred Booker, was a whitewash. Booker himself was the only one permitted to call witnesses and present evidence while the entire proceedings took place behind closed doors. A month later the Macdonald government published the transcripts of the carefully staged inquiry. These transcripts absolved Booker of any wrongdoing or fault other than inexperience on the field of battle, and generations of historians have since cited them as definitive.

The press objected at the time to how the Booker Inquiry was conducted. As a result, the subsequent inquiry into the conduct of Lieutenant Colonel John Stoughton Dennis at Fort Erie took several weeks and was more adversarial and objective. But the existence of the inquiry was not revealed to the press until the inquiry had finished sitting, while the testimony and evidence gathered by it was classified and suppressed, and although no longer classified today, still remains unpublished. Only a verdict and a statement absolving Dennis of any wrongdoing were released to the press when the inquiry had run its course. With a few recent exceptions, historians have not challenged the findings of these two inquiries or investigated the findings further to any extent.[19]

In the twenty-five years following the battle, Ridgeway was little mentioned and rarely commemorated. A leaden silence prevailed until the men who fought there, by then middle-aged, banded together and lobbied for recognition starting in 1890.[20] Their campaign triggered a period in which the Veterans of '66 were acknowledged and their sacrifice memorialized, culminating in 1900 when, thirty-four years after the battle, the federal and provincial governments finally, grudgingly, offered them token recognition in the form of medals and land grants.[21] Why the veterans *had to* lobby and what happened at Ridgeway are the two closely related subjects of this book.

In the subsequent decades, with no authentic history to sustain it and overshadowed by the enormous casualties of the South African War and then the First World War, along with the natural deaths of Ridgeway's veterans, the battle was gradually forgotten for a second time by the early 1930s. When Canada's Decoration Day was moved to November 11 and renamed Remembrance Day, Ridgeway was excluded from the memorialization, its history and significance virtually disappearing for good.

Ridgeway was the last battle fought in Ontario, the first modern battle fought by Canadians, and the first battle fought by what was about to become the Canadian army. The men who fell at Limestone Ridge were *de facto* Canada's first combat deaths—beginning with Ensign (Second Lieutenant) Malcolm McEachren—*the* first to fall. That alone is significant. That these battles took place in Canada only one year before Confederation and yet we not only know so little about them but barely know *of them* at all is a symptom of our great national cultural malaise: "What is wrong with Canadian history?" That question I will attempt to answer through a quest not only to explore the hidden history of the Battle of Ridgeway, but also to investigate how it came to be concealed and forgotten in the first place, and what that might mean to generations of Canadians who have been taught a different national past from the one revealed here in these pages.

PART 1
The Fenian Threat and the Canadian Army

We are a Fenian Brotherhood, skilled in the arts of war.
And we're going to fight for Ireland, the land that we adore.
Many battles we have won, along with the boys in blue.
And we'll go and capture Canada, for we've nothing else to do.

FENIAN DRINKING SONG, 1866[1]

The vile Kanucks, those savage hordes,
Shall fall beneath our Irish swords,
That soon shall cut the British cords
Which bind our liberty.

Advance upon the cowardly foe,
A thousand slay at every blow,
And let the whelps of England know,
Our valiant chivalry.

"GENERAL O'NEILL'S ADDRESS TO HIS ARMY"
FENIAN MARCHING SONG (EXCERPT)[2]

ONE
The Fenian Cause

Founded in 1858 simultaneously in Dublin and New York City, the Irish Republican Brotherhood (IRB) in Ireland and the Fenian Brotherhood (FB) in the United States were predecessors of the twentieth-century IRA. In fact the American Fenian insurgents who invaded Canada in 1866 called themselves the "Irish Republican Army"—the first known usage of that appellation.[1] Eventually the IRB became known as the "Fenians" even back home in Ireland, as well as in England, taking their name from ancient warrior clans, the *Fiana,* or *Fianna Eirionn*, who defended the coast of Ireland from invaders. The ancient *Fianna*, according to one source, "employed their time alternately in war, the chase, and the cultivation of poetry."[2] The modern Fenians' goal was the creation of an independent republican Ireland free of the British Crown. The contentious history of the relationship between the two peoples began with the conquest of Ireland by the Normans from Britain in 1170 and only became worse with the subsequent Protestant Reformation in England in the face of an Irish Catholic majority. This was followed by British-organized "plantations" of Protestant settlers, deportations of Catholic peasants to less fertile regions of the island, and so-called "Penal Laws" restricting the rights of Irish Catholics, the last vestiges of which would not be repealed until 1869.[3] Various attempts by England's rivals, Spain, France, and the Papacy, to exploit for their own interests the conflict in Ireland, along with the emerging threat of republicanism accompanying the French Revolution and the Napoleonic Wars, further intensified this ever-escalating history of conquest and division and drove both sides into increasingly brutal and radical responses, the effects of which are still felt to this day.[4]

When the Fenians were founded, the most recent in the long history of bloody Irish uprisings had been the 1798 United Irishmen Rebellion. It failed, leaving an estimated thirty to fifty thousand dead in its wake, and resulted in 1801 in the unification of Ireland with Great Britain through the Acts of Union, forming the United Kingdom.[5] For the next fifty years Irish nationalism and political dissent were channelled into peaceful legislative and constitutional reform by Daniel O'Connell, who spearheaded two great political movements one after the other: first the successful emancipation of Catholics from the discriminatory laws of Protestant Britain, and then his unsuccessful campaign to repeal the Acts of Union. But O'Connell's popular peaceful movement collapsed between 1845 and 1849 in an unprecedented calamity: the Irish Potato Famine. Its impact was the hardest on Catholic peasants, who depended upon the potato for their subsistence. It drove at least 1.5 million predominantly Catholic refugees to emigrate and killed another eight hundred thousand to one million by starvation and disease. This radicalized some of O'Connell's former disciples into a more militant Young Ireland nationalist movement. In 1848 they attempted an uprising that was quickly put down.

The Young Ireland rebel fugitives James Stephens and John O'Mahony fled to Paris and there came into contact with other European revolutionary secret societies. Stephens was tutored in Italian by the exile Guglielmo Pepe, a senior member of the quasi-Masonic secret society the *Carbonari* and a deputy of the 1848 Venetian revolutionary Daniel Manin.[6] The two exiles would become the founders of the Fenians ten years later—Stephens in Dublin on St. Patrick's Day in 1858, and O'Mahony in New York City at about the same time.

Whether the Fenians were nationalists, rebels, patriots, assassins, insurgents, bandits, irregulars, freedom fighters, pirates, murderers, martyrs, tribal militia, national revolutionaries, guerrillas, terrorists, or national founding fathers of the modern Irish Republic depends upon the observer's point of view. They were the first modern transcontinental insurgent group in the Western world, with cells in Ireland, England, Canada, the United States, South America, New Zealand, and Australia, and a banking centre in Paris. They organized themselves into cells called "circles." A Fenian circle was like a regiment: A colonel, the "centre" or "*A*," recruited nine "*B*s" or captains, who recruited nine "*C*s" or sergeants, each of whom chose nine "*D*s"—the rank-and-file privates. Whereas the Fenian Brotherhood could operate legally and openly in the United States, in the British Empire Fenian circles operated clandestinely. A chain of secrecy worked its way upward: The "*A*" was known only to his "*B*s," the "*B*s" only to their "*C*s," and so forth. Senior leaders in a city, territory, or state were called "head centres."[7] In Toronto and Montreal the Fenians infiltrated the leadership of an Irish Catholic self-defence organization, the Hibernian Benevolent Society (HBS), which was founded as a rival to the militant Protestant Orange Order and in Toronto had the blessing and sanction of the Catholic Archbishop, John Joseph Lynch.[8]

Steam power gave the Fenians transcontinental and transatlantic mobility; the telegraph linked them together with an internet's reach (albeit without its bandwidth); cheap newsprint and printing presses gave them a mass media voice; industrialism gave them an ocean of patriotic wage earners to fund their cause; the ascent of global capitalism offered a banking system to raise and distribute funds across oceans and continents; and the American Civil War would mobilize, arm, and train tens of thousands of Irish-American patriots.[9]

In their time the Fenians were perceived as an Irish Catholic version of al Qaeda, religious fanatics linked to the Papacy, with political ambitions and a mythical conspiratorial connection to the Vatican in Rome. Just as Muslim immigrant communities are sometimes suspected of harbouring Islamic terrorists today, Irish Catholics were suspected of Fenian allegiance in the 1860s.[10] The clandestine relationship between the Hibernian Benevolent Society in Canada and the Fenians, which the Toronto Police tracked closely, did not help Irish Catholic–Protestant relations.[11] The presence of Fenians in Canada contributed to the paranoid fear of a "fifth column" rising up among the Catholics—both Irish and French. The reality was that Fenianism went beyond religious sectarianism: One-third of the Fenians captured on the Niagara Frontier in 1866 were Protestants.[12] Fenianism was a republican movement and not exclusively a Catholic one.

The Fenians were classified as illegal combatants waging a "dirty war" even when fighting in conventional uniformed formations as they would at Ridgeway. They were frightening because they were something new in insurgency and as modern as the world around them. Entirely familiar to students of terrorism today was the Fenian operational use of encrypted communications; their quasi-autonomous cell-like structure; their use of public announcements, newspapers, rallies, and "fairs"; their use of disinformation, along with auxiliary cultural, educational, charitable, and recreational programs; their intelligence-gathering activities and deployment of "sleepers"; and their employment of sophisticated financial instruments in the international banking system. The Fenians were seen as *the* great subversive threat in the British Empire in the second half of the nineteenth century, until supplanted by anarchists, German spies, labour agitators, suffragettes, and Communists.

IN THE BRITISH EMPIRE, the first alarm about the global extent of the Fenian threat was not sounded until an incident occurred in Toronto, Canada, in November 1864. In the first five years after the organization's founding, British authorities had been aware of the Fenian ambitions but were not particularly concerned about the group's ability to carry them out. When Dublin Castle, the seat of the British administration in Ireland, issued an internal report on the Fenians in 1868, its authors would note, "To trace the history of the Fenian Brotherhood from 1859 to '63 would be tedious, as events are lacking to give it interest."[13]

Outside of Ireland, neither Britain nor Canada had a standing domestic intelligence agency to monitor the Fenian threat. Britain not only stopped spying at home after 1848, but also with a few exceptions (Ireland being the big one) was decidedly anti-spy.[14] Even in the colonies, where the British never hesitated to adopt a double standard, domestic spying was scrupulously avoided. As one historian of British domestic intelligence points out, "A strong aversion to the use of spies was one of the alien traditions of government which the British brought to India in the nineteenth century."[15]

British authorities did not appreciate the scope of the connection between Fenians in the United States and the IRB in Ireland until Stephens travelled to America in the summer of 1864.[16] It would be, however, an incident in Toronto on Guy Fawkes' Night in 1864 that would trigger the British Consul in New York City—the Truro, Nova Scotia–born Edward Mortimer Archibald[17]—to call for spies to be infiltrated into the Fenian organization in North America and to alert the British Foreign Office to the possibility of Fenian cells in Canada.[18]

On the night of November 5, reacting to rumours in Toronto's Catholic community that Orangemen planned to assemble and burn an effigy of Daniel O'Connell, along with one of Guy Fawkes, the Hibernian Benevolent Society and a Fenian cell secreted within it suddenly deployed some three hundred armed men into the streets of the city. Operating in small, highly disciplined squads, they rapidly seized strategic points, isolating the few on-duty Toronto Police constables in their stations and preventing those at home from being mobilized. Toward morning, the squads assembled into two large companies on opposite sides of the city and just before dawn fired their muskets into the air, rattling windowpanes everywhere.[19] Then they melted away as quickly as they had appeared, leaving in their wake a shocked and frightened Protestant populace fearing that they would be murdered in their beds in a sectarian massacre. The incident triggered a paranoid panic in Canada throughout November and December.[20]

The *Globe* reported, "It is quite evident that these men were completely organized and prepared for any emergency and had the Orangemen turned out, there would have been a scene of bloodshed such as Toronto has rarely seen."[21] In the following days, the Toronto Police raided a tavern on Queen Street where a Hibernian lodge was believed to meet and discovered a number of pike heads and staves, the traditional feared instrument of Irish massacre and rebellion. As it could not be proved that these pikes were carried in the Guy Fawkes' Night demonstration, the tavern proprietor, John McGuire, was released, whereas the pikes mysteriously "disappeared" while in police custody.[22]

The *Globe* went on to publish a letter without comment several weeks later, among the earliest references in its pages to the possibility of an active Fenian network in Canada. The letter writer warned:

> A second "massacre of Bartholomew" may be expected, unless we guard carefully against it. It is well known that the Fenian organization has a network throughout the whole of Canada, and at a given time the different corps will rise *en masse* and deal destruction to all Protestants ... In the Roman Catholic churches the "pikes" (of which we heard so much in this city), guns, pistols, and ammunition, are stored in great quantities, so as to be ready at the appointed time. These offensive weapons have been distributed through the connivance of Roman Catholic Custom-house officers ... Our hitherto peaceful country is to be devastated by similar horrors to those perpetrated by the midnight assassins in Ireland. Murder and arson will stalk through the land unless prompt action is taken to nip the rising spirit in the bud.[23]

In Canada itself, there was little appreciation of the nuances of the Fenians' republican program. Despite the emergence in Canada by the 1860s of a loyal and peaceable Irish Catholic middle class, the Fenians once identified by name were permanently associated in Protestant minds with the traditional radical Catholic rebel threat.[24]

The 1798 Rebellion in Ireland had unified urban republicans and predominantly Catholic peasants. Although the rebels consisted of both Catholics and Protestants (mostly Presbyterians), they targeted the so-called Protestant Ascendancy in Ireland and its British patrons. The uprising was characterized by sporadic massacres of loyal Protestant populations by rebels wielding pikes[25] and by brutally fierce reprisals from British troops and loyalist militia against the suspected Irish Catholic population, particularly in the rural regions.

Exaggerated reports of these horrific events, as they were depicted in the British press, would be carried to Canada with the early waves of mainly Protestant Irish immigrants who arrived after the Napoleonic Wars ended in 1815. When the Fenians invaded Canada in 1866, the atrocities in Ireland sixty-eight years earlier were still fresh in the collective memory of Protestants in Canada: The bloody pike massacres of 1798 defined in their imaginations what to expect from what they believed to be an Irish Catholic rebellion.

IN THE WAKE OF GUY FAWKES' NIGHT, the term "Fenian" began to appear in official Canadian correspondence.[26] John A. Macdonald, as Attorney General in Canada West, had formed an undercover police agency two months earlier, the Frontier Constabulary under Stipendiary Magistrate Gilbert McMicken. Often referred to as Canada's first secret service, its original purpose was to respond to clandestine U.S. Army recruiters ("crimpers") who were trying to replenish Union ranks thinned by Civil War combat by enlisting Canadian volunteers or deserting British soldiers stationed in Canada. To encourage British soldiers, recruiters often offered an enlistment bounty as lucrative as one thousand dollars.[27]

Now the Frontier Constabulary was assigned to deal with the Fenian threat.

The many stories of the Canada West Frontier Constabulary and Toronto Police agents who infiltrated Fenian circles in Canada and the United States in Buffalo, Chicago, Pittsburgh, New York, Detroit, Cincinnati, and Nashville are outside the scope of this book.[28] Independently of Britain, and with American co-operation, colonial Canada had an extensive intelligence network operating deep within U.S. territory. The history of this force between its founding in 1864 and the invasion at Fort Erie in June 1866 is preserved in the Canadian archives in some 3,422 pages of reports by McMicken and his nearly fifty agents.[29] Its full story still remains to be untangled and told.[30]

While the Civil War raged on, the Fenians could do little other than recruit Irish Americans into the brotherhood and direct them to enlist in the U.S. Army. The brotherhood encouraged its members to gain military experience for a future war of liberation in Ireland, and Fenian agitation within the U.S. Army units was tolerated by Washington as long as the Fenians fought for the Union first.[31] The war had a seminal role in the growth of the American Fenian Brotherhood. Combat of catastrophic proportions would radicalize, traumatize, and harden American militants who often fought in exclusively Irish volunteer regiments. The rise in Fenian membership was spectacular—from forty New Yorkers in 1858 to perhaps as many as fifty thousand members nationwide by 1861, and perhaps four or five times that number of sympathizers.[32] As tensions rose and fell and rose again between Britain and the United States from 1861 to 1864, some Fenians began to appraise Canada's potential as a battlefield stepping stone that could lead to the expulsion of Britain from Ireland.

The objective of the Fenian invasion of British North America, simply explained, was to trigger a political crisis in the British Empire and weaken its hold on Ireland by holding Canada hostage in the hope of provoking hostilities between the United States and Britain. While in the end the plan was poorly executed and miscalculated in some of its components, the concept was not as far-fetched as it may sound at first. It was intended to work on multiple levels. For centuries Britain had been obliged to commit enormous resources to control Ireland and suppress rebellion there. But in the wake of colonial expansion, the Crimean War, the Great Mutiny in India, and rising tensions in Europe, these resources were being strained by the 1860s. One of Britain's early responses was to pare down its military commitments in British North America and attempt to turn over the responsibility of defence to the colonies themselves.[33] Anything the Fenians could now do to keep the British busy in Canada would drain the resources and political will available for Ireland, or so the Fenians thought.

With the Fenian flag flying over Canada, Fenian ships could sail on the high seas without being deemed piratical. Meanwhile, the Fenian occupation could extract increased funding from a captive Canadian tax base for their planned war of liberation.[34] The Fenians were counting on two necessary conditions taking effect: that an expansionist United States hostile to Britain would recognize their seizure of Canadian territory, and that disgruntled Irish Catholics in Canada, as well as French Canadians, would rise up in aid of the invasion—or at least would stand by and do nothing. Neither of these conditions was fulfilled.

When the Civil War ended in April 1865, thousands of Irish-American U.S. Army and Confederate veterans could not immediately adjust to a peacetime life. As the Fenian ditty warned, "Many battles we have won, along with the boys in blue. / And we'll go and capture Canada, for we've nothing else to do."[35]

TWO

The Making of the Canadian Army, 1855–1866

The genesis of the Canadian army—and perhaps arguably of the Confederation of Canada itself—was Canada's fear of invasion by the United States and Britain's reluctance by the mid-1850s to maintain extensive troop deployments in Canada. The problem was not so much keeping troops in these territories as the enormous cost of relieving them and redeploying them in emergencies in other parts of the empire.[1] In 1846 Britain began a concerted effort to reduce its troop deployment in British North America, expecting that colonists in the future would undertake their own defence with a minimum of British help. The Crimean War in 1854 forced the issue as British troop strength in Canada was substantially reduced. In May 1857 the Indian mutiny broke out, and again there was a drain on the British army. This was followed by a crisis in Europe in 1859, when tensions between France and Austria escalated. Clearly this shuffling of British troops in and out of distant Canada could not go on—the Canadians had to defend themselves.

Under colonial Canada's early militia laws, all able-bodied men between the ages of eighteen and sixty were liable for military service with the exception of clergy and Quakers. Males were enrolled in militia companies and were required in times of peace to report for an annual muster. Other than that there was no drill or training. Officers were appointed for their social standing, wealth, and prominence rather than for their military knowledge or experience. Known by the quaint term "sedentary militia," these units could not take the field except in a local emergency or a military threat to Canada. As long as it operated with a robust deployment of regular British troops behind it, this system proved to be sufficient for the War of 1812, the 1837 Rebellions, and the Hunters Lodge patriot raids from the United States in 1838. While there was some tinkering with Canada's militia structure during the Oregon Crisis in 1845, Canada's defence system basically remained the same until the onset of the Crimean War.[2]

The Militia Act of 1855 introduced a string of reforms that would eventually lead to the development of the current Canadian military system. Today's permanent regular army was established in 1883 (replacing the British army). It is backed by a volunteer militia force, now called the Primary Reserve, whose origins go back to the 1855 Act.[3] Under the provisions of the 1855 Act, a five-thousand-man "active" paid militia was for the first time created in the Province of Canada. Its volunteer infantry and cavalry would undergo ten days of paid training and its artillery, twenty days. Backing this trained corps would be an unpaid reserve of "sedentary militia," consisting of all remaining males between the ages of sixteen and sixty who were required to muster in peacetime only once a year as before. The active militia was organized into independent companies of approximately thirty to fifty men each. Again, socially prominent citizens sponsored, organized, and led these volunteer companies.

In 1859 a more centralized command system began to be developed by grouping small independent companies into larger battalions. In Montreal, in Canada East, nine infantry companies were unified into the First Battalion of Volunteer Militia Rifles of Canada—today the Canadian Grenadier Guards. In Canada West in 1860, four rifle companies from Toronto and a company each from Barrie and Whitby were formed into the Second Battalion, which eventually took the name Queen's Own Rifles (QOR), celebrating at this writing 150 years of continuous service in the Canadian military going back to seven years *before* Confederation.[4]

The amalgamation of companies into battalions revealed an underlying problem whose significance would become apparent at Limestone Ridge. When an attempt was made to transfer men from one company to another to "equalize" the strength of companies in a battalion, there were protests and resignations. Each company was really a tight-knit social unit, a club reflecting the civilian class and professional origins of its members who were selectively admitted by fellow volunteers and who paid dues to join and serve in the company. The disruption of this social structure generated rival factions that jockeyed for seniority and command of the newly formed battalions.[5]

In the 1850s, relations and trade between the United States and Canada were friendly and lucrative enough that funding of the militia gradually began to decline until the outbreak of Civil War in April 1861. At first it seemed the conflict would have no repercussions for Canada other than an improvement in business supplying the U.S. war effort (and whenever possible the Confederate one as well). But on November 8, the U.S. Navy stopped in international waters and boarded a British postal steamer, *Trent*, taking prisoner two Confederate envoys on their way to England and France. The *Trent* Crisis threatened to lead to a war between Britain and the United States in which Canada would be caught in the middle. Canadian public opinion, which had been relatively hostile to the Confederacy, almost instantly turned against the Union. Canadians were once again reminded of the historical hostility between the monarchy and republicanism.[6] As tensions rose in November and December 1861, Britain was forced to make the largest single troop deployment to North America in its history—some fourteen thousand British army regulars were hastily shipped over, raising the British troop strength to a total of eighteen thousand.[7] This was not what Britain wanted.

The threat to Canada unleashed at home a surge of volunteers into the militia. Men absent from drill for years suddenly returned enthusiastically. With a new Militia Act of 1862 the colonial provincial government established a Department of Militia, headed by John A. Macdonald, the Attorney General in Canada West and a premier in the Macdonald-Cartier coalition, whose Liberal-Conservative Party had governed Canada since 1854 (except for a brief interruption in 1858). The act increased funding for the militia, and now anybody who wanted to be somebody rushed in to sponsor and organize a company of militia.

HENRY HOLMES CROFT, a forty-one-year-old chemistry professor at University College, one of the schools that would eventually be amalgamated into the University of Toronto, dreamt of a glorious military career. The son of William Croft, the Deputy-General Paymaster of Ordinance under the Duke of Wellington, Croft had studied in Germany and upon graduation, with Michael Faraday's recommendation, came to Toronto to be the university's first professor of chemistry in 1843. In December 1861 as the *Trent* Crisis was unfolding, Croft assembled the students in the convocation hall and delivered a passionately patriotic lecture, exhorting them to form a volunteer rifle company against the threatened Yankee invasion. The students, as was customary at the time, elected their company officers: Professor Croft as captain and company commander; John Cherriman, a professor of mathematics, as lieutenant.[8]

By Christmas Day, the University College Rifles were at full strength and would eventually be assigned to the Queen's Own Rifles Second Battalion as Company 9, "University Rifles." Captain Goodwin, a gym teacher at Upper Canada College and a veteran of the Battle of Waterloo, was chosen by Croft to drill the University Rifles. Croft now had a company of infantry to play with, drill, compete, parade, and host balls and picnics with.[9] A laudatory biography of Croft reports that his rifle company, "with the exception of the College Literary and Scientific Society, was the most potent element in the University for promoting sociability and *esprit de corps* amongst all classes of University men. Academic distinctions found no place in its ranks; in its earlier years the messenger elbowed the graduate, the freshman, the sophomore, and the professor freely reproved both for treading too heavily on his heels; its pleasant comradeship was a bond between the faculties and the student body."[10]

The Anglican Trinity College likewise formed a student company, which was eventually designated QOR Company 8. Normal School and Education Department employees and teachers formed Company 7, the Civil Service or Educational Department Company, while companies 4 and 5, consisting of store and warehouse proprietors and their clerks, were known respectively as the First and Second Merchants Companies.[11] Scots assembled in Company 10, "Highlanders." The newest unit, Company 6 from Upper Canada College consisting of upper-class high schoolboys, was nicknamed "The Babies."[12]

THE AVAILABILITY OF NEW FUNDING for the militia unleashed a feeding frenzy among Canada's gentlemen elite. It also triggered bitter rivalries as companies were amalgamated again into newly funded battalions and the issue of officer seniority became contentious. Civilian-life rivalries were often carried over into the military sphere. In Hamilton, several prominent citizens who had sponsored militia companies would clash as they came to be amalgamated. James Atchison Skinner, a wealthy china merchant, organized and uniformed a company of Highlanders at his own expense. Alfred Booker, a prominent local auctioneer and consigned-goods dealer, financed his own artillery battery.[13] Isaac

Buchanan, a Scottish merchant, railway investor, and member of the legislature, formed a company of infantry. All held captain's rank and had near-absolute authority over their own men in the absence of any superior officer, but once drawn together into battalions they found themselves chafing under one another's command. As new militia districts and commands were created in 1862, some of the officers moved up into those positions: Booker was promoted to lieutenant colonel and became the commandant of the Hamilton Militia while retaining personal command of his artillery battery.[14] Other prominent captains like Skinner were promoted to the rank of major and given battalion-level responsibilities.

The independent rifle companies in Hamilton were amalgamated in December 1862 into the Thirteenth Battalion Volunteer Militia of Canada (today the Hamilton Light Infantry Regiment) and put under the command of Isaac Buchanan. The ambitious James Skinner allied with several other disgruntled company captains and immediately began to feud with Buchanan over myriad issues ranging from drill instruction to the "equalization" of companies. Some of the captains resigned. By 1864 Buchanan was fed up and announced that he was resigning from the command of the Thirteenth. Skinner as the next senior officer was now the obvious choice to lead the battalion, but Buchanan had one last surprise for him. Before he left, the well-connected Buchanan invited the more senior-ranking Hamilton District commander, Alfred Booker, to take personal command of the Thirteenth Battalion. Despite protests and threats of resignation from Skinner and several other company commanders, the unpopular Alfred Booker, who had no experience in leading infantry in the field, took command on January 27, 1865.[15]

In smaller rural communities with fewer social climbers, the going was easier. At a junction seven miles from Port Colborne on the Welland Canal, a twenty-one-mile navigable feeder canal led to Dunnville on the Grand River near Lake Erie.[16] There, forty-year-old Scottish-born Lachlan McCallum owned stores, mills, shipyards, and a fleet of tugs for towing rafts of lumber, grain, and other freight. In 1863 he formed the Dunnville Naval Brigade—a marine rifle company. McCallum paid out of his own pocket for the company's navy blue uniforms with their silver buttons. The men of the company consisted of local merchants, small businessmen, and McCallum's employees and family members.[17] McCallum, a short-tempered, foul-mouthed mariner, was of course "elected" as captain, a naval rank equivalent to colonel. Angus McDonald, McCallum's first cousin and employee, was elected as the company's lieutenant.[18]

In 1864 McCallum built a steam-powered tugboat that he christened the *W.T. Robb,* after his close friend Walter Tyrie Robb, whom he made captain. The powerful vessel was reputed to be one of the fastest on the Great Lakes.[19] McCallum dreamt of converting the *Robb* into a high-speed gunboat crewed by his company of marines and able to deploy rapidly anywhere along the frontier on lakes Erie and Ontario, and in the Niagara River and the Welland Canal system. In 1865 he wrote to Macdonald proposing that the *Robb* be fitted with two guns and leased to the government, arguing that his vessel of marines would be as cost-effective as five or six companies of land-borne infantry.[20] Macdonald declined the offer, but McCallum continued to finance the unit and the war tug, drilling its crew and marines incessantly in shoreline landings.

On the Welland Canal itself, Captain Dr. Richard Saunders King, M.D., a highly respected physician in Port Robinson, took command of the Welland Canal Field Artillery Battery. The battery would be headquartered in Port Robinson and equipped with four 9-pounder Armstrong brass field guns supplied by the British army at Hamilton. Its gunners would be trained by a veteran Royal Artillery bombardier detached to them, Sergeant James McCracken.[21]

It was from Toronto's upper-crust milieu, however, that one of the most eccentric of Canada's Victorian militia commanders rose to prominence—George Taylor Denison III. The "Fighting Denisons" may still today be Toronto's premier military family. Their monumental cenotaphs and tombstones in their private cemetery in the west end of Toronto are lined up by rank like soldiers on parade. The Ontario Archives preserves locks of their hair like saintly reliquaries,[22] while a Canadian Armed Forces armoury in north Toronto bears the George Denison name and houses a regiment the family founded nearly two hundred years ago—the Governor General's Horse Guard, today an armoured reconnaissance unit with a squadron of ceremonial cavalry.[23]

The family patriarch, great-grandfather John Denison, a brewer and farmer from Yorkshire, immigrated to Upper Canada in 1792 and acquired a one-thousand-acre grant in what is today the College-Dovercourt area of Toronto. The Denison progeny grew into a robust line of successful Toronto land speculators, politicians, and lawyers, which, along with their marriages into United Empire Loyalist families, by 1853 made the Denisons reputedly the wealthiest private landowners in Canada West.

Back in 1822 the grandfather, George Taylor Denison I, formed one of Upper Canada's earliest cavalry regiments, the York Dragoons. The regiment was renamed "Denison's Horse" in 1839 after the government stopped subsidizing the Denisons, but the family continued financing the unit like a feudal cavalry for the next twenty-three years, until the *Trent* Crisis brought it back onto the active lists in 1862 as a troop in the First York Cavalry. Over the years, command of the troop was transferred from its founder, George T. Denison I, to his son George T. Denison II, an attorney and alderman for St. Patrick's Ward in Toronto from 1843 to 1853 and one of the founders of Ontario's Queen's Plate thoroughbred racing classic. Then the command passed to *his* eldest son, George T. Denison III—the great-grandson in this ever-expanding family of enterprising cavalrymen.[24]

George T. Denison III was born in Toronto in 1839. Educated at the elite Upper Canada College, Denison enrolled in the equally prestigious Trinity College and was then promptly expelled for insubordination by Bishop Strachan himself. Denison transferred to University College, where he completed a law degree and was called to the bar in 1861 at the age of twenty-two. Denison's real passion, however, was service in his father's cavalry. He was fifteen years old when he was made a cornet (cavalry second lieutenant) and only eighteen when he was promoted to the rank of captain and appointed the troop's commanding officer in 1857.[25]

After a new Militia Act in 1862 authorized increased funding, George Denison relentlessly lobbied the government for arms, equipment, uniforms, and saddles for his force of fifty-five horsemen. Always status-conscious, he petitioned Governor General Viscount Monck to grant his troop the title "Governor General's Body Guard for Upper Canada"—an acknowledgment that it was the oldest cavalry unit in Upper Canada and was to be given eternal precedence over other units in parades and ceremonies. In April 1866, by which time George Denison held the rank of major, the troop was granted the title he asked for, which eventually was amended to the Governor General's Horse Guard. The unit operates under this name today as Canada's senior reserve armoured regiment, and its ceremonial horsemen still escort members of the Royal family when they are on formal visits in Ontario.[26]

In 1861, when the Civil War broke out but before the *Trent* Crisis, Denison published under the pseudonym "a native Canadian" a pamphlet titled *Canada, is she prepared for war? Or, a few remarks on the state of her defences.* In it Denison condemned the poor state of the militia and the lack of martial spirit among Canadians. The pamphlet drew vigorous condemnation from the Toronto *Globe* for its "military fever" and "martial ardour" that threatened to be costly to the province.[27]

As the *Trent* Crisis began in November, Denison published a second pamphlet, *The National Defences,* this time in his own name. In it he insisted that any country bordering with a country at war needed a strong army to defend its neutrality. Prophetically, he also warned, "When peace is proclaimed between the Southern and Northern States, a large body of armed men will be thrown out of employment, and may in some instances be induced to make filibustering expeditions into our territory for the sake of plunder."[28]

Denison inherited his family's historical hatred of the American republic. During the Civil War, he became a secret agent in Confederate Secret Service operations in Canada against the northern United States. Denison's connection to the Confederacy came through his uncle George Dewson, who had immigrated to Florida in the 1850s and was a colonel in the Confederate Secret Service.[29] In his autobiography, Denison described how he had helped a Confederate operative infiltrate the United States across the Canadian border. As U.S. authorities became aware of photo microdot dispatches being smuggled from Canada to the United States inside of metal buttons on couriers' clothing,[30] Denison's wife sewed encrypted secret service dispatches written in pencil on silk into the lining of agents' coat sleeves; these were unrecognizable to the touch if the men were searched.[31] Denison fronted his name and money for the purchase of a ship in Canada, the *Georgian,* which the Confederate Navy planned to secretly outfit with guns and torpedoes in Collingwood and unleash on the Great Lakes against U.S. shipping and POW camps.[32] Before the mission could be carried out, at the urging of the United States, Macdonald ordered the vessel to be seized, and Denison spent enormous energy unsuccessfully suing the government for its return. Eventually the Crown surrendered it to the United States as part of a compensation payment for damages inflicted by Confederates operating from British North American territory.[33]

Like his father, Denison was an alderman in Toronto. In April 1865 after Abraham Lincoln's assassination, when Toronto City Council voted on a resolution offering condolences to the American people, Denison was the only member to vote against it.[34] After the Civil War, Denison became friends with the Confederate General Robert E. Lee and the former Confederate President Jefferson Davis, who would stop at Denison's residence, Haydon Villa in Toronto near Dovercourt and College streets, during his several postwar visits to Canada. As Denison's biographer, Carl Berger, explained, "Denison's sympathy for the Southern cause in the Civil War was instinctual and rooted in the loyalist tradition of his family. He adhered to the same values that legend and propaganda had attached to the plantation life and the Confederacy—the martial values and chivalric code of honour; the adulation of conservative, landed society; and the detestation of capitalistic business. Bathed in pastoral imagery of romance, the South seemed to represent the hierarchical order for which the Family Compact had also stood."[35]

Berger might be describing the sentiments not only of Denison, but also of many Canadians during the Civil War. When Jefferson Davis was released from prison in 1867 and travelled to Canada to recover his presidential papers from a bank safety deposit box where they were deposited after the fall of the Confederacy, thousands of people gathered at the docks in Toronto to cheer him. Standing on a pile of coal leading the cheers was Denison.[36] George T. Denison III played a minor role in the fighting at Ridgeway, but his place in the subsequent writing and rewriting of the battle's history, both with pen and gavel, would be titanic. Not only would he preside over the two military boards of inquiry, but he also would publish an influential "instant history" of the invasion ten weeks after it had occurred.[37]

From 1861 to 1865, the volunteers and their officers paraded, drilled, and feuded, but as the Civil War drew to an end it appeared that the threat from the United States was diminishing. Canada's militia once again began to show signs of decay as enthusiasm for drilling waned and government resolve to pay for it flagged. Fewer volunteers showed up for drill, and company enrolments dropped dramatically while funding was once again cut.

THREE

The Threat of Invasion, 1865–1866

In April 1865, the American Civil War ended and freed up thousands of Fenians serving in the U.S. and Confederate armies. The Fenian chief in Ireland, James Stephens, had been calling on American Fenians to prepare for the "Year of Action" in 1865—his plan for an incursion into Ireland once the war was over—but his plans came to nothing. In the meantime, the American Fenians split into two factions—the traditionalist "Ireland First" Wing led by the original founders, Stephens and O'Mahony, and a dissident so-called "Senate Wing," or "Roberts Wing" (sometimes also called the "Canadian Wing"), led by William R. Roberts. The dissidents challenged the Stephens–O'Mahony executive by calling for the deployment of a Fenian army "by the shortest route to meet the common enemy of Ireland and the United States," meaning an attack on Canada.[1]

In September 1865, after years of passive near-indifference, British authorities in Ireland finally reacted to the Fenians by seizing their *Irish People* newspaper and arresting senior Irish Republican Brotherhood

(IRB) leaders. Stephens became a fugitive and eventually escaped to the United States. The arrests in Ireland triggered new alarm in Canada, and Macdonald ordered secret service chief Gilbert McMicken to hire and infiltrate undercover agents deep into Fenian centres throughout the United States to keep careful track of any Fenian plans to strike against Canada in lieu of their failure in Ireland. Macdonald wrote to McMicken, "The Fenian action in Ireland is serious, and the Imperial Government seems fully alive to it. *We* must not be caught napping. Keep me fully informed."[2]

In October 1865, the Fenian Brotherhood met in Philadelphia for its Third Congress. News of the arrests in Ireland triggered a revived call for an invasion of Canada instead. A Canadian intelligence report in September 1865 enclosed an editorial from the *Cincinnati Daily Gazette*, which claimed:

> The Fenian [*sic*] is essentially an American organization. It commenced about seven years ago for a very different object than freeing Ireland from the English yoke. It is not entirely composed of Irishmen. At the present moment it numbers many thousands native Americans and Americanized Germans, and has a large treasure at its back. The exact number of enrolled members at the beginning of last August was 273,581. Notwithstanding the statements of the Fenian orators at picnics and other gatherings in the United States that its object is to free Ireland, I know that such is not the case. Those statements are put forward to mislead the public and keep the British authorities off the scent. The real object is to attack and conquer Canada and divide the immense territory of Britain on the American continent among the exiles of Erin. The United State authorities not only wink at the Fenian movement, but the movement is sanctioned by the Government, and ruled by Mr. Seward, the Secretary of State.[3]

While of little veracity, the editorial dramatically highlights the fears arising in Canada at the time. It also underscores the Fenians' own belief that the U.S. government was going to back their invasion. Both the

Canadians and the Fenians had good reasons to worry. After Abraham Lincoln's assassination, Andrew Johnson's Republican-led administration held only a tenuous control over Congress that would be threatened in upcoming elections by a massive Irish vote that traditionally supported the Democratic Party. As the Fenians met and paraded in the United States and proclaimed their plans to invade Canada, the U.S. government appeared to do nothing that could alienate the Irish vote. Before long the Fenians were claiming they had the backing of the U.S. government, and many historians today still share their conviction, including the Canadian Armed Forces historical branch, which in 1965 concluded, "There seems little doubt that the Fenian raids of 1866 were undertaken with, at the very least, the tacit encouragement of the President and Secretary of State."[4] Most histories of the Fenian invasion of Canada characterize Johnson's and his Secretary of State, William Seward's, policy toward the Fenians as "ambiguous," "ambivalent," or "complacent," always hinting at the possibility of a clandestine U.S. government hand in the invasion.[5] What was not known, or at least left unsaid until now, was that Johnson and Seward privately resented the power of the Irish lobby and held Irish Americans and their cause in disdain, and they were going to make their feelings perfectly clear to the British.

WHILE THE UNITED STATES and Britain nearly went to war against each other during the Civil War, they discreetly kept a cordial relationship in one corner of the world: China. Britain and the United States, along with their European partners, all supported a Chinese Emperor compliant with their colonial interests in the region. When the Taiping rebels threatened the Emperor's rule, the British envoy William Frederick Adolphus Bruce came up with a plan, sanctioned by the United States, to supply the Chinese navy with a fleet of gunboats crewed by Europeans but under the command of the Chinese admiralty—the so-called "Vampire Fleet," or the "Osborne Flotilla."[6] But the plan went off the rails over who really commanded the fleet. The Emperor who had paid for the gunboats ordered them to be returned and sold off when their British officer refused to take direct orders from superior Chinese naval officers. The flotilla was in danger of falling into the hands of purchasing agents from the Confederate Navy, but Bruce, who had developed a close friendship in Peking with the U.S. envoy Anson Burlingame, foiled the Confederates by ordering the fleet's evacuation at British expense from China to Bombay.[7] The Americans were grateful to Bruce, although in view of hostilities between the United States and Britain everywhere else, they kept their gratitude confidential.[8]

As the Civil War was coming to an end in 1865, the British Foreign Office, anxious to improve relations with the United States, sent Bruce to Washington as the new British envoy. In the autumn and winter of 1865–66, he met numerous times with Seward to defuse the growing threat posed by the Fenians to the British provinces in North America. In those meetings, according to Bruce, Seward stated that:

> The conduct of the Irish during the War in spite of their military service, has not rendered them popular. In point of sentiment they did not show themselves friendly to Northern ideas, and they went with the Democratic, and not with the Republican party. If they were strong enough to make the independence of Ireland a probable result of their enterprise, the irritation against England would acquire for them considerable moral support, but there is no faith in their success, and no real sympathy with Celtic aspirations, and the humiliation of England is not of sufficient interest to the United States, to induce them to ally themselves with a desperate cause, in the struggle which such an enterprise would produce.[9]

In February 1866, Bruce was snuck in through the back door to meet the President on a pretext of "visiting the ladies of the White House." Johnson appeared in the parlour as if by accident and was introduced to the British envoy. The President assured him that the Fenian movement "met with no sympathy on the part of the Government, which on the contrary was anxious to discourage it, that he was much dissatisfied with the *imperium in imperio* the Irish wished to create in this country, that the attempt to combine particular nationalities on this continent was contrary to American interests and inconsistent with their duties as American citizens ..." Bruce reported to London that Johnson "dwelt on the inconsistency of the Irish who, while invoking aid on their own behalf as an oppressed race, were themselves the most bitter opponents of all attempts to improve and elevate the condition of the Negro in the United States."[10]

In February 1866, the British agreed to a proposal from Seward not to make American Fenian activity a subject of formal diplomatic correspondence, thus soothing the Republican administration's concern over being forced to publicly adopt measures that could alienate Irish-American voters. The British intended to exploit the growing divide between the O'Mahony and Roberts factions by explicitly requesting that the United States *not* interfere with any Fenian meetings or activities inside U.S. territory except to intervene in any direct attempt to violate the border.[11] For their part Seward and Johnson would make bona fide efforts to keep the Fenians away from the British North American provinces, while the British would share with U.S. authorities their own and the Canadians' intelligence on Fenian movements and arms purchases in the United States. While U.S. government arsenals sold thousands of war surplus rifles and tons of ammunition to the Fenians, the U.S. Army and Department of Justice made numerous unpublicized attempts from March to June 1866 to seize these same arms before they could be used in an invasion.[12]

The Canadians were apparently not privy to this secret agreement and were unaware that the British Foreign Office was sharing their intelligence (even including the identity of John A. Macdonald's spy deep within the Fenian circle in Buffalo) with the U.S. State Department.[13] At one point the Canadians almost wrecked the agreement by vigorously and publicly demanding that Britain formally protest the apparent American inaction in the face of the rising Fenian threat.[14]

Within weeks of its conclusion, from February to March 1866, this agreement was tested when British authorities in Ireland began making mass arrests of Fenians under an emergency Suspension of Habeas Corpus Act. Home Office officials refused to recognize the naturalized U.S. citizenship of British-born Fenians arrested in Ireland. As a sign of its goodwill, the Foreign Office pressured authorities in Ireland to release most of the arrested Irish-American citizens if they agreed to leave Ireland immediately. This sealed the agreement between the United States and Britain. In mid-March instructions went out through the U.S. War and Justice departments to military and judicial officials in the border states to proactively intervene in Fenian attempts to mobilize and arm on the frontier of the British provinces.[15] There was no tacit or any other kind of encouragement from Johnson or Seward of the planned Fenian invasion.

U.S. authorities were sincere in their commitment to contain the Fenians, but they would fail in their efforts. The border was too long to patrol effectively, post–Civil War America too full of guns and ammo for authorities to intercept every shipment. And the U.S. Army in the north was too heavily demobilized, with most of its commitment in the southern states and on the western frontiers, to guard every point of entry. In early April 1866, there were only 357 U.S. Army officers and men on the entire Canada–New York border, and none on the frontiers of New Hampshire, Vermont, and Maine.[16] On June 4, *after* the Fenian invasion, U.S. Army strength on the border from Maine to New York had been increased to only one thousand two hundred troops in total—about the number of Fenians who took part in the raid.[17] Nor did Fenian arms seizures proceed effortlessly, as the Fenian Brotherhood retained lawyers who fought the seizures in court while at least some U.S. Army personnel sympathetic to the Fenian cause dragged their feet.[18] But the rumours of an invisible U.S. government hand in the Fenian invasion of Canada were just that: rumours.

THE ROBERTS FACTION had been preparing an invasion force since autumn 1865. On October 28, they appointed the one-armed forty-six-year-old Thomas W. Sweeny, a distinguished U.S. Army general, as the Fenian Secretary of War to mount the invasion of Canada.[19] One of the first things Sweeny did was to establish a Fenian intelligence network in Canada, seeded with one thousand five hundred dollars.[20]

Major John C. Canty (also Cautie or Cauntie or Kantie), a spy from the Buffalo Fenian circle,[21] crossed into Canada in December 1865, purchased a house in Fort Erie, and settled there as a Fenian "sleeper."[22] Finding employment as a section foreman on the Grand Trunk Railway line, Canty for the next six months meticulously collected maps and intelligence and sketched and surveyed the local topography, the Welland Canal, ferries, bridges, railway junctions, roads, and telegraph systems.[23] The town of Ridgeway and Limestone Ridge were likely part of the terrain Canty surveyed during his mission.

Sweeny acquired detailed intelligence on the defence of the Welland Canal from Fenians serving on the crew of a U.S. Navy gunboat on Lake Erie, the U.S.S. *Michigan*.[24] (More on this later.) Fenians in Montreal transmitted to Sweeny warnings about a Canadian spy on the way to infiltrate the Fenians in New York. [25] A Fenian organizer in Quebec City sent information of troop deployments there.[26] Some Fenian circles in Montreal, when they became aware of the factional split in the organization, came over to Roberts Wing "ready to go in" if there was an invasion.[27] The Fenians in Toronto, however, led by Michael Murphy, a tavern-keeper and the president of the Hibernian Benevolent Society, according to Toronto Police reports, remained loyal to the Stephens–O'Mahony Ireland First Wing and vehemently condemned any planned invasion of Canada.[28]

In January 1866, the split between the O'Mahony and Roberts wings became irreconcilable and the two factions went their separate ways. At the end of February, Sweeny presented his strategy for the invasion of Canada to the Fourth National Fenian Congress in Pittsburgh, now dominated by the Roberts Wing. Two Frontier Police secret service operatives infiltrated the meeting and reported that the Fenians on February 25 had approved the plan to invade Canada. The agents mistakenly believed the invasion was scheduled for March 17—St. Patrick's Day.[29] These reports triggered a massive call-out of Canada's militia in March, but the Fenians never came.

Sweeny's plan actually projected an invasion for the following winter, when frozen waterways would facilitate crossing and make the movement of reinforcements from Britain and Halifax more difficult. He called for a three-pronged attack to be launched from Chicago and Detroit in the west, from Cleveland across Lake Erie in the centre, and from New York and Vermont in the east, involving a total of twenty-five thousand Fenian insurgents, including five cavalry regiments and three artillery batteries. A smaller diversionary attack was planned from Buffalo into the Niagara region and the network of railways there to draw troops away and, if possible, seize the Welland Canal, while the main Cleveland prong would drive into the centre toward London and eventually join with the smaller Buffalo force. The strategy called for cutting across the railway and canal links between Windsor, Sarnia, Toronto, and Montreal, segmenting and isolating large pockets of Canadian territory bordering on the United States.[30] (See Fenian Invasion Plan Map.)

The operation was budgeted at four hundred and fifty thousand dollars. To support the initiative, the Fenians had even tested a submarine at the depth of seventeen feet in New York's East River. It survived a test detonation of a twenty-five-pound depth charge fifteen feet away from it.[31] (Early Fenian submarine development remains a subject of naval lore to this day.)[32]

Sweeny's plan was neither a comic opera nor a burlesque proposal, as many have characterized it. As historian Kerby Miller notes, at the end of the Civil War, "Fenianism had about 50,000 actual members, many of them trained soldiers, and hundreds of thousands of ardent sympathizers; in just seven years, and despite clerical condemnation,

Fenianism had become the most popular and powerful ethnic organization in Irish-American history."[33]

Concerned about the momentum the Roberts Wing was gathering with its planned invasion of Canada, O'Mahony in early April launched his own invasion of New Brunswick from Maine at some remote islands near Campobello in an attempt to steal his rivals' thunder.[34] The British and U.S. navies quickly dispersed the feeble attempt.[35] Michael Murphy's Toronto Fenians, loyal to O'Mahony, or perhaps less loyal to New Brunswick than to their own developing attachment to Upper Canada, attempted to join the invasion but were arrested at Cornwall aboard an eastbound train. That effectively ended any further Toronto Fenian activity or any role in the invasion of Canada when it came in June. Murphy and several of his companions sat out the battle in jail. In September they broke out and fled to the United States.

The Campobello raid, as much as it was a failure and an embarrassment to the O'Mahony wing, spurred the Roberts faction to act sooner than they had originally planned. While the invasion preparations were far from complete, Sweeny was now ordered to proceed with an invasion he believed he had until next winter to prepare fully.

IN MAY SWEENY BEGAN issuing orders for the Fenians to assemble. Despite having received numerous reports throughout the month of large groups of Fenians moving by train toward the border, Canadian authorities failed to act. They had spent too much money and exhausted too much of the volunteers' goodwill on false alerts; they had cried wolf too often. Macdonald had called out the militia for frontier duty twice—in November 1865 and March 1866. These alerts were expensive and caused enormous disruptions in the labour supply, commerce, and business, and in the personal lives and careers of the young volunteers and their officers.[36] Had the Fenians come, these disruptions would have been forgiven, but the invasion had not materialized. It appeared to many that the Fenian plans were all talk and bluster.

Did Gilbert McMicken and the Frontier Constabulary fail in assessing the urgency of the Fenian threat that May? In the final month before the invasion, Macdonald, McMicken, D'Arcy McGee, and many others were convinced that the Fenians were on the brink of extinction.[37] The phenomenon that the Canadians were experiencing is known in military intelligence as "conditioning," when after numerous feints by an enemy, deliberate or not, the defender is no longer able or willing to recognize a real attack when it comes.[38] The Fenians had announced their invasion plans so many times that Mark Twain would later comment, "A regiment of Fenians will fill the whole world with the noise of it when they are getting ready to invade Canada."[39]

It should be noted, however, that Canada's Adjutant General of Militia, Patrick L. MacDougall, had been arguing since the first alert in November 1865 for a defence policy that involved assembling the volunteers at strategic centres away from the frontier *after* a Fenian landing and then launching focused counterattacks, rather than rushing the militia blindly to the immense frontier at every rumour of their approach.[40] McMicken strongly opposed this strategy, arguing that if the Fenians were allowed to penetrate Canadian territory "it would raise an excitement in the United States very difficult to control."[41] MacDougall did not get his way during the second Fenian scare in March 1866, when volunteers were again called out and deployed to the frontier needlessly. But in the wake of the March alarm and its renewed financial and political costs, it appeared that MacDougall's argument would prevail. No troops would be called out and deployed until the day the Fenians actually began moving on to the border.

McMicken would later vehemently hold the military chain of command responsible for allowing the Fenians to penetrate Canadian territory, writing to Macdonald, "Are you aware that I telegraphed Gen Napier [British Military Commander for Canada West] on 30th May suggesting the propriety of sending a force to Port Colborne? Had he done this perhaps all would have been well, but I believe he was at some

Lady fair's [*sic*] when he got my telegram and putting it in his pocket probably never saw it or even thought of it again."[42]

IN THE LAST WEEK OF MAY, spies and newspapers were reporting the arrival by train of hundreds of Fenians at Buffalo from Tennessee, Kentucky, Ohio, Indiana, and even from as far away as Louisiana. The men arrived in regimental groups but in civilian clothing and unarmed. Upon arrival they were barracked and armed by the Buffalo Fenians. Other Fenian units were slowly arriving in Malone and Ogdensburg, New York; at St. Albans, Vermont; at Cape Vincent; Oswego; Rochester; and other points along the Upper St. Lawrence and Lake Ontario. But only at Buffalo were their numbers significant; everywhere else the flow of volunteers was a sluggish trickle.[43] At some critical launching points, such as Chicago, Detroit, and Cleveland, there was hardly any Fenian mobilization at all. In the end, when the time came to act, many of the Fenian volunteers that Sweeny was counting on failed to appear.

The problem for the Fenians was not their plan but its hasty and disorganized execution by a faction-torn movement that had over the years made so many futile calls for action that when the genuine call came, many refused to believe it. Ironically, they were hindered by the same "cry wolf" that conditioned Canada's leaders to stand down the militia at this critical moment. The Civil War had been over for fourteen months, and many Fenian veterans had settled down. After so many false starts, they were not as ready to drop everything as they might have been earlier. There was also a distinctly cavalier and undisciplined culture among American Fenians compared with that of the Irish revolutionaries back home.[44] The Roberts Wing leadership was not the same hardened generation of rebel exiles that O'Mahony and Stephens represented. O'Mahony would say of his own American Fenians, "I am sick of Yankee-doodle twaddle, Yankee-doodle selfishness and all Yankee doodledum! It is refreshing to turn to the stern front and untiring constancy of the continental apostles of liberty."[45]

When in the last week of May Fenian forces in Cleveland failed to secure the necessary boats to cross Lake Erie, Sweeny ordered those units to deploy to Buffalo instead.[46] Claiming to be migrant railway workers, the Fenians avoided surveillance at the Buffalo central station by having their trains slow down on the outskirts, jumping off, and making the rest of the journey into the city on foot.[47]

At 11:55 P.M. on May 30, the general-in-chief of the U.S. Army, Lieutenant General Ulysses S. Grant, warned Major General George G. Meade, commander of the Military Division of the Atlantic, that the Mayor of Buffalo had telegraphed that six hundred Fenians were on their way from Cleveland to join those already assembling in Buffalo and that Seward had intercepted orders for Fenians headed to St. Albans to prepare to move on Canada. Meade was ordered to "take the best steps you can to prevent these expeditions from leaving the United States."[48]

So many Fenians had now assembled in Buffalo that on May 31 the U.S. Attorney there, William A. Dart, alerted the navy gunboat U.S.S. *Michigan* at Buffalo, ordering the closing of the port to outbound traffic between 4 P.M. and 9 A.M. and prohibiting in other hours any outbound traffic without the vessels' first being inspected by U.S. Customs.[49] The *Michigan* was a formidable vessel, armed with a 64-pounder eight-inch pivot gun, a 30-pounder Parrott rifled gun, six 24-pounder Dahlgren smoothbore howitzers, five 20-pounder Parrott rifles, and two 12-pounder Dahlgren boat howitzers.[50]

Sweeny now had to act before U.S. authorities shut down his operation completely. Despite the fact that the Fenian forces had not assembled as planned on the other points of the frontier, or perhaps to inspire them to mobilize faster, Sweeny transferred the Fenians assembled in Cleveland over to Buffalo (as Grant had warned Meade) and telegraphed the attack code: "You may commence work."[51] What was originally intended as a diversionary prong suddenly became the main invasion force.

WHEN FENIAN GENERAL William F. Lynch failed to appear at Cleveland to lead the centre wing, Sweeny turned at the last minute to the most senior available Fenian officer, a former U.S. cavalry captain, the thirty-two-year-old Fenian Colonel John O'Neill commanding the Thirteenth Fenian Regiment of Nashville, Tennessee. O'Neill had arrived by train with his men the day before.[52] Sweeny promoted O'Neill to brigadier general and put him in command of the invasion on the Niagara Frontier. Much of what happened to the Canadians at Ridgeway had to do with the skills and character of O'Neill. Sweeny could not have made a better choice.

John O'Neill was born on March 9, 1834, in Drumgallon, County Monaghan, Ireland. His widowed mother immigrated to the United States, leaving John in the care of his paternal grandfather, who engaged a private tutor to educate him in the fear that a national school would endanger his Catholic faith. John joined his mother in the United States when he was fourteen as part of the famine migrations in 1848.[53] He completed one more year of schooling in Elizabeth, New Jersey, and then travelled as a sales agent for Catholic publishing houses. In 1855 he opened a Catholic bookstore in Richmond, Virginia, and became a member of the Emmet Guard, then the leading Irish nationalist organization in Virginia. In 1857 he gave up his business and joined the U.S. Cavalry, fighting in the Second Mormon War in Utah from 1858 to 1859. Afterward he went off to California to seek his fortune.

When the Civil War broke out, O'Neill joined the Seventh Michigan Cavalry as a sergeant and served in the Army of Potomac's Peninsula Campaign in Virginia in 1862. After the withdrawal of the army from the peninsula, he was commissioned as a lieutenant and dispatched to Indiana, where he was retained for some time as instructor of cavalry, drilling the officers of a force then being raised for defence against incursions by Confederate guerrillas. He subsequently entered the Fifth Indiana Cavalry and served with that regiment from 1863 to 1864 in Indiana, Ohio, Kentucky, and Tennessee.

O'Neill developed a reputation as an anti-insurgency specialist and was assigned to hunt down the legendary Confederate cavalry commander Brigadier General John Morgan, whose Morgan's Raiders terrorized Ohio, riding in as deep as the suburbs of Cincinnati in July 1863. On July 19 Morgan was crossing from Ohio into West Virginia over Buffington Bar in the Ohio River with 2,460 men, artillery, and plunder when they were charged by O'Neill leading a troop of just fifty horsemen. O'Neill's attack was so sudden and savage that Morgan was forced to abandon his guns and supplies while six hundred of his men were driven toward U.S. Navy gunboats and captured. Without supplies or artillery, Morgan surrendered several days later. O'Neill distinguished himself as an aggressive cavalry officer, cutting down his enemies with his sabre in an era in which cavalry charges were few and rare. His feats would be mentioned in dispatches several times.[54] His men were quoted as saying, "We know of seven rebels he has killed with his own hands. We know he charged and put to rout 200 rebels with 33 men. We know he charged two regiments of Morgan's command with fifty men, and took three of their guns. Let every officer in the service do that well, and the privates will soon finish the balance."[55]

In December 1863, O'Neill was severely wounded at the battle of Walker's Ford on the Clinch River in east Tennessee.[56] Frustrated by his lack of advancement, O'Neill at his own request was appointed captain in the Eleventh U.S. Colored Infantry and was detailed to the Military Examining Board, sitting at Nashville, Tennessee.[57] He was promised the colonelcy of a black regiment of cavalry, but the organization of these troops was dispensed with toward the close of the war.[58] As O'Neill's wound was becoming troublesome, he resigned his commission in November 1864 and married May Crowe of San Francisco that month.[59] Settling at first in Pulaski, Tennessee, O'Neill opened a military service claims office, assisting demobilized veterans with their claims. While his previous Fenian activities are unknown, O'Neill in May 1865 moved to Nashville where he founded a Fenian circle. As his biographer commented, "O'Neill did not originate these notions, but he became their high priest ..."[60]

On May 27, 1866, in answer to Sweeny's call, O'Neill and his 115-strong Nashville Fenian "regiment" (really of slightly more than company strength) left by train first for Louisville, Kentucky, where they joined up with another Fenian unit, and then on to Cleveland before finally arriving at the outskirts of Buffalo in the early morning of May 30.[61]

Almost everyone in authority on both the Canadian and U.S. sides was still stubbornly refusing to believe the warnings of a Fenian buildup until the anti-Fenian Mayor of Buffalo, Chandler J. Wells, and U.S. Attorney William Dart began telegraphing urgent alerts to the mayors of Hamilton and Toronto on May 31.[62] As thousands of Fenians converged on Buffalo behind him, O'Neill suddenly took a force of about a thousand men across the Niagara River into Canada in the early morning hours of June 1. Over the next eight hours several hundred more Fenians would follow, raising the final number of insurgents crossing into Canada to about 1,250, and maybe even 1,500, while the U.S.S. *Michigan*, despite having been put on alert, sat helplessly first in Buffalo and then a little farther downriver at Black Rock, the Fenians having sabotaged the vessel.

THE 120-MAN CREW of the *Michigan* had been thoroughly infiltrated: There was a seventeen-man circle of Fenians aboard led by one of the mates, William E. Leonard, who was in direct communication with Sweeny in New York and with Patrick O'Day, the Fenian "centre" in Buffalo.[63] The *Michigan* Fenians had raised one hundred dollars for the cause and sent a map of Lake Erie, together with detailed intelligence about the Welland Canal and its locks and defences.[64] The Fenians were acutely aware of the danger presented to their plan by the *Michigan* and of the need to somehow take the vessel out of action.[65] The assignment was given to Second Assistant Engineer James P. Kelley.[66] On the night of May 31, when the crew were ordered to report to the vessel, Kelley diverted the ship's pilot, Patrick Murphy, by a generous flow of whiskey and cigars, along with the tender attentions of "a lady friend."[67] Kelley and Murphy staggered aboard the *Michigan* only at 5 A.M. after the main body of Fenians had successfully finished crossing the Niagara River. Both were immediately arrested, but Murphy was ordered nonetheless to pilot the ship toward the Fenian base. Murphy guided the vessel as far as the ferry docks at Black Rock but then begged off from continuing, claiming he was not familiar with the river beyond. The *Michigan* came to a halt again.

As the *Michigan* lay helpless, a little farther down the river Fenian tugs and barges continued to cross back and forth unhindered, bringing supplies and reinforcements to the Canadian shore. The last successful crossing was made in daylight at 11 A.M. on June 1. It was only after another river pilot was brought on board that the *Michigan* finally steamed out at 11:20 A.M. and took its position to block any further Fenian reinforcements.[68] The Fenians had been crossing unhindered for nearly twelve hours. The next and last attempt to re-supply the Fenians was made by a tug towing a barge at 2:50 P.M., but it was promptly intercepted and seized by the *Michigan*.[69]

THE FENIAN ARMY that crossed into Canada is frequently portrayed as a drunken Irish mob, its plan dismissed as folly, born out of a misguided romantic dream. But as military historian James Wood recently commented:

> The works of Canadian historians have echoed trends in the wider historiography of military professionalism. Notwithstanding defeats suffered by the French in Algeria, the Americans in Vietnam, the Soviets in Afghanistan, and today's ongoing difficulties in that region and in the Persian Gulf, many military historians still find it difficult to view the history of armed conflict outside a professional mould in which civilians are clearly and easily distinguished from soldiers. If anything,

> events of recent years have taught us that whatever designation is used—soldiers, insurgents, terrorists, tribal militias, bandits, or worse—failure or refusal to conform to the standards of regular soldiers does not necessarily render an adversary any less dangerous.[70]

Ironically for my purposes, Wood was thinking of the Canadian citizen militia when he wrote those words, not of the Fenians, but as we shall see when it comes to the Battle of Ridgeway, his observations apply equally to both sides.

PART 2
The Battle of Ridgeway

Tramp! Tramp! Tramp! The Boys Are Marching

In the morning by my side sat the darling of my
pride,
While our happy children round us were at play
When the news spread through the land that the
Fenians were at hand,
At our country's call we'll cheerfully obey.

Tramp! Tramp! Tramp! The boys are marching!
Cheer up, let the rabble come!
For beneath the Union Jack we will drive the
Fenians back,
And we'll fight for our beloved Canadian home.

Old Mahoney needs some cash and he
contemplates a dash
With his troops upon our soil to raid,
But he'll find to his dismay that the thing will
never pay
And wish that from Canadian ground he stayed
away.

Tramp! Tramp! Tramp! The boys are marching!
Cheer up, let the rabble come!
For beneath the Union Jack we will drive the
Fenians back,
And we'll fight for our beloved Canadian home.

CANADIAN VOLUNTEER MARCHING SONG, 1866
(ONE OF MANY VARIATIONS)[1]

FOUR

The Fenian Invasion of Fort Erie, Morning, June 1, 1866

In the early morning hours of Friday, June 1, the Fenian forces in Buffalo crossed the Niagara River on their wing of the planned invasion of Canada. Their embarkation site was at Lower Black Rock, a river-front industrial suburb on the mouth of the Erie Canal, approximately three miles north of Buffalo. This was one of the narrower segments of the Niagara River in the Buffalo–Fort Erie sector of the U.S.–Canada border: approximately eight hundred to a thousand yards wide.[1]

Two days earlier, Fenians working at the Pratt's Iron Furnace at Lower Black Rock (at the foot of Hertel Avenue in Buffalo today) chartered two steam tugs and four canal barges ostensibly to transport employees on a picnic to Falconwood, a resort and nature preserve on Grand Island.[2] The main landing zone for the Fenians was directly across the river from

Pratt's dock on the Canadian side, at the Lower Ferry Docks at Bowen Road, about a mile and a half north of the village of Fort Erie.[3]

The Fenian invasion force referred to themselves as the "Irish Republican Army"—IRA—a very early use, if not *the* first use of this nomenclature.[4] Depending upon their unit, they wore an assortment of U.S. uniforms with green facing, Irish-green tunics with brass buttons sometimes emblazoned with "IRA," or green shirts and U.S. Army trousers, while some were reported to be wearing grey Confederate Army tunics.[5] Many were simply dressed in civilian clothes and black felt hats with green scarves. John O'Neill himself was reportedly wearing "drab" civilian dress and was later described by a witness as "a gentleman-like man, pale and freckled; more like a dry-goods clerk than the leader of a marauding party."[6]

This is as complete a description of the Fenian force as possible from available sources:

Fenian IRA Brigade
Order of Battle and Strength on the Niagara Frontier

General John O'Neill, commanding officer; Colonel George Owen Starr, second-in-command; Major John C. Canty (Fort Erie, C.W.), chief of staff/intelligence; Lieutenant Rudolph Fitzpatrick, aide-de-camp.

- O'Neill's **Thirteenth Regiment** of Nashville, Tennessee (115 men), now commanded by Captain Lawrence Shields (Nashville) with Captain Philip Mundy (Chattanooga), Captain McDonald (Pulaski), Lieutenant James J. Roach (Nashville), and Lieutenant John Maguire (Nashville) and reinforced by Memphis companies (200 men)[7] under Captain Michael Conlon (Memphis). Total 115 + 200 = 315 men.
- **Seventh Regiment** of Buffalo "Irish Army of Liberation" commanded by thirty-four-year-old Colonel John Hoy [Hoye], a former first

lieutenant in the 179th New York Volunteers, with Lieutenant Colonel Michael Bailey, former captain in the 100th New York Volunteers, Captain John M. Fogarty, Captain William V. Smith, Lieutenant Edward Lonergan, and Color Sergeant John Smith of Company "G." A very conservative estimate, considering Buffalo's proximity to the scene of action, is 150 men.

- **Seventeenth Regiment** of Louisville, Kentucky, uniformed in blue army jackets with green facings and led by O'Neill's second-in-command, Colonel George Owen Starr, with Lieutenant Colonel John Spaulding (Louisville), Captain Timothy O'Leary (Louisville), Captain John Geary (Lexington, Kentucky), Lieutenant Patrick J. Tyrrell (Louisville), and Lieutenant Michael Boland (Louisville), (144 men); and attached to the Seventeenth were also two infantry companies from Terre Haute and Indianapolis, Indiana, under Captain Hugh [James] Haggerty (Indianapolis) and Color Sergeant Michael Cochrane (130 men).[8] Total 144 + 130 = 274 men.
- **Eighteenth Regiment** "Cleveland Rangers" under Captain Buckley (Cleveland) and Lieutenant Timothy Lavan (Cleveland). Exact strength unknown; estimate 50 men.
- **Nineteenth Regiment** Cincinnati "Irish Republic Volunteers" (120 men),[9] both units from Ohio dressed in green caps and green shirts and led by Lieutenant Colonel John Grace (Cincinnati), with Captain Sam Sullivan (Cincinnati) and Lieutenant John J. Geoghan (Cincinnati) and Captain Donohue commanding a company of mounted scouts of unknown strength. Approximate total strength: 220 men.
- **New Orleans Company** "Louisiana Tigers" under Captain J.W. Dempsey, wearing grey Confederate uniforms. Unknown strength; estimate 25 men.[10]
- A small unidentified troop of mounted scouts believed to be from Buffalo, of unknown strength and riding horses, seized on the Canadian side. Estimate 25 men.[11]
- A total Fenian strength of approximately 1,000 to 1,200 men.[12]

(Note: I do not furnish an order of battle for the Canadians and British the next day, as many other sources have adequately done so. Links to these can be found on www.ridgewaybattle.org.)

The actual number of Fenians who crossed into Canada has never been conclusively determined and has been estimated at as low as six hundred to as high as two thousand. The problem is that the Fenians crossed at different points and at different times between midnight and noon the next day; observers thus made their estimates at different locations and times.

The frequently cited figure of one thousand is most likely the correct *minimum* number of Fenians crossing into Canada in the first twelve hours of June 1. Perhaps as many as 1,350 to 1,500 made the crossing, of whom some 800 fought the Canadian forces at Ridgeway on the morning of June 2 and in Fort Erie in the afternoon. That figure of eight hundred, incidentally, was the typical wartime *actual* strength of two seasoned American Civil War infantry regiments—two formidable killing machines.[13] The British Consul in Buffalo reported 850 as being *the last* of the Fenians to withdraw from Canada on June 3 in the early morning after the battle, of which 700 were reported as captured and held by the U.S.S. *Michigan*, again suggesting that a minimum of 1,000 crossing is a likely figure.*

Of the remaining Fenians unaccounted for, three to six hundred who landed on June 1 but did not fight at Ridgeway, some held scattered positions along the Niagara River and its outlying roads from Black Creek in the north to Fort Erie in the south. Many had deserted by the end of the first day and returned to Buffalo, while others surrendered or were captured the following day by advancing British and Canadian troops.[14] After the battle the remainder trickled over to Buffalo undetected or hid in the surrounding countryside—some possibly with sympathetic locals.

---

* Full details and the evidence for the figure of one thousand can be found in my University of Toronto 2011 doctoral dissertation, *Combat, Memory, and Remembrance in Confederation Era Canada: The Hidden History of the Battle of Ridgeway, June 2, 1866*, or on my websites, www.fenians.org and www.ridgewaybattle.org.

At least one wounded Fenian, twenty-four-year-old Patrick J. O'Reilly of Buffalo, was reported to have later eloped in Niagara Falls with a farmer's daughter who, without her family's knowledge, had hidden him in a barn for a week and nursed his wound before helping him escape across the river. Another was rumoured to have been held captive secretly by a farmer as an unpaid hand.[15]

The Fenians were armed with standard U.S. military-issue single shot muzzle-loading Springfield .58-calibre percussion rifle-muskets, comparable to the weapons carried by the British and most of the Canadians. The Fenians, however, were better supplied with ammunition than their Canadian opponents. A Canadian secret service agent in Buffalo reported that the Fenians had five large double wagons and four furniture wagons with an almost unlimited supply of ammunition and a 1,500 stand of arms, a "stand" being a rifle plus bayonet, scabbard, ammunition, and cap pouches and belts.[16] Other sources estimated that 2,500 arms were taken into Canada, as the Fenians had anticipated support from local sympathizers to whom some of the arms would be distributed.[17] The extra weapons were also intended for delivery in Canada to smaller parties of Fenians that slipped by U.S. customs inspectors on other points along the frontier. So huge was the Fenian surplus of arms that in the morning before the Battle of Ridgeway, they destroyed a large portion of it. At least 250 or 300 rifles were thrown into fires and smashed against apple trees because, according to one witness, "they had more rifles than men."[18] Another witness testified to discovering forty rifles and nineteen thousand rounds of ammunition thrown into Frenchman's Creek in bayonet-punctured crates.[19] So many rifles were abandoned that a company of Canadian volunteers pursuing the Fenians the next day suddenly came to a halt while some of its men dove into the water to retrieve souvenir rifles.[20]

THE FENIAN INVASION unfolded in three waves. The first wave was the smaller advance party led by O'Neill's second-in-command, Colonel

George Owen Starr from Louisville, a former Union Army officer from the Second U.S. Kentucky Cavalry. As the rest of the Fenian army was loading its chartered barges, Starr's men seized at gunpoint a Buffalo steam tug, the *J.H. Doyle*, and a large Canadian timber scow belonging to Thorold timber dealers John and Thomas Conlon. The scow had just finished unloading at Lower Black Rock and was still docked on the American side.[21] Starr's advance party was the first to cross the river, springing onto the Canadian shore and unfurling a large Fenian green flag with a gold Irish harp at about 1:30 A.M. under a bright moon three days past full. It was the only Fenian flag with a harp—all other Fenian battle standards bore the gold sunburst.[22]

At Lower Ferry, Starr's advance party would have found a small but busy hamlet consisting of a shingle factory, a boathouse, a tavern, a house with a customs revenue officer, and several small frame dwellings.[23] They quickly seized control of the landing site, and after leaving a small unit holding the docks for the arrival of O'Neill's main force, Starr's men proceeded south along Niagara Road toward the town of Fort Erie a little over a mile away.

A group of young men were spearfishing by torchlight when they spotted Starr's unit crossing the river. They immediately rode off into the village, hammering on their wagon boxes and raising the alarm at every house they passed. The reports of Fenian forces gathering in Buffalo had been drifting back to Fort Erie for days, and few locals were caught unprepared that night.[24] While the U.S. Attorney's May 31 order restricted all river traffic from Buffalo to Canada, inbound traffic from Canada was not embargoed.[25] Many of the villagers crossed over to the safety of the American side in Buffalo by ferry and smaller boats.[26] Others drove their horses, wagons, and cattle west out of town. As the Fenians began occupying the town, the U.S. Consul in Fort Erie, Freeman N. Blake, raised the American flag in front of his home, which had been crowded with frightened villagers seeking protection. Blake reported that he had raised the flag "to indicate the prerogative of the United States over the premises occupied by me" but the passing rank and file of the Fenians misinterpreted the gesture as official U.S. support for the invasion and broke into loud applause. Colonel Michael Bailey, a forty-four-year-old ship's carpenter, a member of the Buffalo Seventh Fenian Regiment, and a former captain in the 100th New York Volunteers, accompanied by Major Canty, the spy, and a third unidentified officer (probably Owen Starr), briefly called on Blake and assured him of their "respect to the United States authority accredited here."[27]

Starr's scouting party appeared to have a fairly specific list of local targets provided by Canty,[28] who had been living in Fort Erie for over six months[29] meticulously collecting intelligence.[30] It was probably Canty who acquired and supplied the Fenians with detailed road maps of Welland County, which were readily available even in schools.[31] During the invasion Canty would serve as O'Neill's chief of staff and intelligence officer, while his house in Fort Erie was used to stockpile weapons and later to shelter Fenians.[32]

Starr's advance party was approaching the outskirts of Fort Erie when the Fenian main force under O'Neill began its crossing behind them. Although formally named Waterloo, the town was popularly called "Fort Erie" for the War of 1812 ruins that stood at the far southeast end of town. The town itself, with about a thousand inhabitants and transients, stood slightly north of Buffalo, directly across from Black Rock. (Ferry Street in Buffalo today pinpoints where the Fort Erie ferry used to land on the American side.)

Fort Erie was over twenty-five city blocks in size. With the exception of four brick buildings, it consisted entirely of two-storey frame houses, storefronts, hotels, taverns, boarding houses, workshops, feed stores, foundries, a bakery, a market, a schoolhouse, three churches and graveyards, a post office, a customs house, a railway station, and a one-hundred-ton steam ferry to Buffalo.[33] (The only working bridge connecting the United States and Canada across the river was at Clifton at Niagara Falls. A gale had destroyed the bridge at Lewiston in 1854.)

There was also housing for retired army personnel, a "Negro" quarter consisting of small wooden cottages, and fishermen's huts near the ruins of the fort.[34] From Front Street running along the river, the backstreets of Fort Erie rose up a steep slope toward a crest called Garrison Hill about 250 yards away. Beyond that to the west, the town levelled out into fields and orchards until the next big village about ten miles away: Ridgeway.

Fort Erie was a rough border town: Its taverns were far more numerous than convenience stores today. George Denison, who served on frontier duty in the region, described the town as "a most extraordinary place, the population consists entirely of tavern keepers, and they make a living by going around drinking in each other's bars."[35]

SAM JOHNSTON, a local-born twenty-two-year-old whiskey and coal oil smuggler, was staying at a Fort Erie hotel that night. Two years earlier, like an estimated twenty thousand other Canadians, Johnston had crossed into the United States during the Civil War in search of adventure and an enlistment bounty from the U.S. Army.[36] Serving in General Grant's Army of the Potomac, Johnston fought from the Rappahannock to the James River in the final campaign against Robert E. Lee's Confederate Army of Northern Virginia.[37]

It was after midnight, but Johnston was still up when two local villagers came into the hotel with news that Fenians were gathering for a crossing from a dock at Lower Black Rock. About an hour later people began to pour into the village, shouting that a large body of armed men was coming up the road. In the street Johnston encountered Corporal Nolan, who was in charge of the only military presence in the vicinity: five unarmed soldiers in civilian dress from a British unit, the Royal Canadian Rifles, stationed in Fort Erie to detect and arrest British troops attempting to desert over the U.S. border. Nolan was on horseback, nudging the animal through the current of townspeople, trying to break through and ride out to the Grand Truck Railway yards at the far end of the town to telegraph Toronto that Fenian forces had invaded Canada.[38]

Johnston alerted several families he was acquainted with in the village and then took a double-barrelled shotgun into one of the stores and asked for it to be loaded. By now the Fenians were pouring into the town. When they saw that Johnston was armed, several Fenians opened fire, but he managed to escape over a picket fence without being hit. Once out of range, he began to circle back across the top of the village to scout out the strength of the Fenians approaching from Lower Ferry.[39]

Starr's advance unit had entered Fort Erie at daybreak—sunrise had been at 4:40 that morning.[40] They immediately sought out and took prisoner the five unarmed British soldiers and Corporal Nolan.[41] They also occupied the smaller ferry docks but did not seize the ferry itself, which continued to run hourly, taking Canadian refugees to Buffalo and bringing back unarmed Fenian reinforcements smuggled past U.S. inspectors.[42] The ferry continued to operate throughout the next day as the battle unfolded at Ridgeway.[43]

On the southeastern outskirts between the town and the ruins of the fort was a railway yard. It connected to a massive ferry, the *International,* which could transport twenty railway cars at a time. A spur led to a locomotive roundhouse and repair shops.[44] Many of the inhabitants of the town were locomotive and rail yard workers from the Buffalo & Lake Huron Railway (B&LH), which ran from Fort Erie to the Welland Canal at Port Colborne about fifteen miles away. From there the route continued to Goderich on Lake Huron. It had been recently purchased by Grand Trunk Railway and was being refurbished, its iron rails being replaced by steel. The Fenians turned toward this train yard.

Robert Larmour, the assistant route superintendent of B&LH, had been aware for months of the rising Fenian threat and the vulnerability of the terminal and ferry. The Grand Trunk telegraph system and its employees made for an effective intelligence network. A Canadian ticket agent for Grand Trunk in Buffalo—R. Calvert—kept Larmour up to date by telegraph on Fenian movements there. Larmour was in Brantford on

Thursday night when Calvert telegraphed him that the Fenians were apparently assembling for some "important move."[45] Larmour boarded the first Buffalo-bound train through Brantford and rode it to Fort Erie, arriving there at 4 A.M. As the train and its passengers were rolled onto the ferry for the final leg of the journey to Buffalo, one of the Canadian customs officers, Mr. Treble, came running from town in a panic, crying, "The Fenians have landed in the village and are killing everybody."[46]

Larmour ordered the *International* to embark immediately with the train and passengers but to remain in midstream without landing in Buffalo, where he feared the vessel could be seized by Fenians. Larmour then ordered all the railroad cars to be coupled in a single line to three locomotives and telegraphed Toronto to alert Major General George Napier, the British Military commander for Canada West.[47]

Larmour recalled that the process took about an hour. Because the Fenians were delayed by their foraging for food and tools in the village, he had just enough time to load telegraph equipment and valuables from the station and freight sheds. The long train and two dead locomotives were pulled by a single third locomotive, and the train had difficulty making its way up the steep grade along the spur from the docks. It was early daylight and Larmour saw ranks of Fenian troops with rifles and bayonets advancing toward the train at a right angle from the village. The engineer opened the throttle in a panic, but it appeared to Larmour that the Fenians would overtake them before the train made it up the grade.[48] Larmour recalled, "I fully expected before we passed that point we should be fired upon, as we were within easy range, but for some reason I have never fully understood they allowed the train to proceed, and it reached the junction switch no more than 200 yards ahead of the advancing column. As the train turned the curve at this point it presented only the rear end, and as the speed had been increased by this time we felt safe. The engineer signified this by a farewell 'toot toot' with his whistle, and we soon lost sight of the enemy as we steamed away for Port Colborne."[49]

Fenian Captain John Geary of the Seventeenth Kentucky Regiment and several men gave chase to the train in a handcart but could not overtake it. Nonetheless, Geary continued west along the railway behind the train to Six Mile Creek, about a mile and a half before the town of Ridgeway. There Geary set fire to Sauerwein's Bridge across the creek and pulled up a portion of the railway track, cutting off the western rail approach from Port Colborne and Ridgeway, before returning to Fort Erie.[50]

Larmour's escape did not end well. The train was now proceeding too fast for the condition of the old iron tracks, and shortly after rumbling through Ridgeway, about three miles short of Port Colborne, it hit a swampy patch. There the train derailed and "plunged into the ditch. The whole aggregation of engines, passenger cars, box cars and flat cars in the rear were piled up in a confused mass. A worse wreck could scarcely be imagined."[51] Nobody was hurt and Larmour telegraphed for all work crews to be immediately sent down to begin clearing away the wreckage. He was very much aware of how critical it was to the upcoming military operations to reopen the line between Port Colborne and Fort Erie.[52]

THE SECOND WAVE, consisting of O'Neill's force of about six to eight hundred Fenians and nine wagons of arms, had boarded the four chartered barges back in Buffalo at Pratt's Dock. They set out at approximately 3:15 A.M.—about ninety minutes before dawn.[53] Upon disembarking in Canada, O'Neill dispatched some of Lieutenant Colonel Hoy's one hundred Buffalo Fenians north down Niagara Road, away from Fort Erie, to seize control of the road and railway approaches in that direction from the landing zone.[54] Hoy's men sealed off the approach from Chippawa in the north. The main force of the Fenians under O'Neill now poured into Fort Erie. The third wave would trickle in over the next six hours until the U.S.S. *Michigan* cut off further crossings in the afternoon.

In Fort Erie the Fenians searched out the home of fifty-two-year-old Dr. Peter Tertius Kempson, who lived in a large house overlooking the Niagara River. Kempson had graduated from the Royal College of Surgeons in England. He settled in Fort Erie in 1854 as a gentleman farmer while pursuing a career as a surgeon in Canada and Buffalo, and was eventually elected as the village reeve (mayor).[55] In the winter of 1861, as President-elect Abraham Lincoln travelled a circuitous route to Washington, Kempson was presented to him at his stop in Buffalo.[56]

When the Fenians began hammering on Kempson's door, it was opened by his twenty-five-year-old wife, Clara, who at first refused to call her husband. Owen Starr presented himself and demanded axes and spades, and Clara directed him to the barn. Starr ordered his men to cut down telegraph wires connecting with the interior of Canada.[57] Throughout the village, wires were strewn across the roads and several telegraph poles were chopped down.[58]

Once again Clara was asked to have her husband appear, or the Fenians would enter the house and seize him by force. Nobody knew how the Fenians were going to conduct themselves with the civilian population, and Starr had to assure Clara several times that while they intended to place her husband under arrest, they otherwise meant no harm to him. She finally relented and called her husband to the door.[59]

Kempson was escorted into town and told to instruct the villagers to surrender their horses and tools. Two of his horses were seized, as were several horses from the Niagara Street Railway Company pasturing on his property.[60] O'Neill chose a cream-coloured charger, which he would ride the next day. The horse would be returned to its owner on June 3 "considerably jaded," according to a contemporary report. Another horse, upon its recovery, was subsequently renamed "Fenian."[61] By the end of the day the Fenians had seized some forty to fifty horses, giving them a sizable force of scouts, but they would have no saddles or stirrups and rode bareback.[62]

The Fenians occupied the town and took its officials prisoner, ordering them to have the townspeople prepare one thousand rations of breakfast[63] for which they offered to pay in Fenian bonds, but the offer was refused.[64] Adult males in the village were rounded up and read a proclamation assuring them that the Fenians' fight was with the British Crown and not with Canadians. Afterward they were sent home under house arrest. A villager later testified at the Fenian trials, "The Fenians took me prisoner and some others. They made us go into the ranks ... I was there fifteen minutes. I was marched three-quarters of a mile along the road and dismissed. The men said they were going to Toronto and Quebec. They asked if Canada was seven miles across. I said it was ten miles."[65]

THE BREAKFAST SERVED to the Fenians that morning was a raucous, drunken affair, later described by a Hamilton journalist:

> The operations in the principal hotel were of this kind: The three lower sitting rooms were filled by men, who awaited their turn to pass into the bar-room. Sentries with loaded revolvers stood in front of the bar: the landlord stood behind it filling his liquors as long as bottles and jars held out. When these were drained he was escorted to his cellar by other guards with revolvers loaded and capped and assisted by willing "helps" to carry his liquid stock to the floor above. When all was drained, his cellar and bar empty, he was thoroughly cursed for not having more liquor on hand; and, at point of bayonet, driven to make haste and "help get breakfast ready." All the butcher's meat and cured hams in the hotel were cut up and cooked; coffee was made in pails and tubs and carried to a rising ground west of the village, on which O'Neil and his officers had posted the main body of their force.[66]

This was not exclusively a Fenian bash. Some Fort Erie citizens joined the Fenians in drinking, having recognized acquaintances from Buffalo among them. Alexander Milligan, a Fort Erie tailor and a former tavern keeper, was awakened by the arrival of the Fenians in the village between 5 and 6 A.M. He joined them in Barney McManey's tavern and was "as sociable as possible" by offering to buy them rounds. According to Milligan's later courtroom testimony, "They said I should not pay—they could pay better than I could. I had four or five horns, and remained there till 9 ... I was not drunk the morning of the 1st June. I asked, when I went to drink, whether I should go; they said I need not, for they were not going to hurt us: outside they said the same thing."[67] His drinking session was interrupted around 9 A.M. when Fenian officers began to round up the carousing troops and ordered them back into ranks. This is the closest the Fenian insurgents came to being the drunken mob they are often portrayed as.

Except for the seizure of livestock, tools, liquor, and horses, the Fenians had not committed any outrages against the inhabitants, but rumours of killing and massacres continued to drift out of Fort Erie. Newspapers on June 1 reported that Reeve Kempson had been shot dead while attempting to read the Riot Act.[68] All along the roads leading from Fort Erie, people were being awakened by the sound of wagons rolling by loaded with refugees and belongings. In Stevensville, a five-year-old boy was horrified when he heard a woman on a wagon loaded with frightened people warn his mother as they passed the house, "The Fenians are coming. They are only a few miles behind. They are killing men, women and children as they go."[69] It was the deeply ingrained Protestant fear of a repetition of the 1798 Irish rebellion massacres that was fuelling the rumours. As the alarm spread, an eleven-year-old farm boy, Ernest Cruikshank, was awakened by his father at 6 A.M. and told to help their ploughman take their dozen horses beyond the reach of the Fenians. His father had read in newspapers that during the Confederate invasion of Pennsylvania in 1863, which culminated in the Battle of Gettysburg, the first thing the Confederates did was to "requisition" farmers' horses into their army. He assumed the Fenians would do the same. Ernest rode out with the farmhand in a buggy trailing a string of horses and looked nervously over his shoulder until they joined up with his brother-in-law driving his own animals to safety.[70]

Sam Johnston, in the meantime, after having counted the Fenians marching by in column (he counted 1,088)[71] and evading them on the road through Fort Erie, made his way across the back lots of the town to Henry Benner's house on the outskirts. Henry had already hitched up a team of horses and was moving his family out in a wagon. Johnston asked for a horse and Benner offered him one from his Kentucky stock. According to Johnston, he now "had the best bred horse in Welland County."[72] Sam Johnston began his wild ride, which, until its telling disappeared from popular memory in the 1920s, would earn him the appellation "Canada's Paul Revere."[73]

THE FENIAN ARMY, with their arms and ammunition and some fifty to sixty plundered horses, plus chickens, tools, and other provisions, moved out of Fort Erie at around 10 A.M., heading back north on the Niagara Road and a few hundred yards past their initial landing site at Lower Ferry.[74] They stopped at Joseph Newbigging's farm on the southern bank of Frenchman's Creek, a deep, sluggishly flowing stream approximately seventy feet across that emptied into the Niagara River.[75] O'Neill estimated that if any British and Canadian forces were nearby, they would logically approach from Chippawa in the north to attack him.

After seizing the eighty-foot bridge across the creek, O'Neill positioned his forces in Newbigging's apple orchard and wheat field on a U-shaped bend in the creek.[76] With his back to the Niagara River, O'Neill had an unobstructed view across approximately eight hundred yards of cleared farmland in the direction of Chippawa. The creek, which bent around the northern, southern, and western flanks of this ground, afforded O'Neill an additional water barrier between himself and any attackers coming across the open fields. Before allowing his men to rest, O'Neill had them dismantle the wooden-rail "snake" fences in the vicinity. A quarter mile of fencing in each direction from their position was torn up.[77] The rails, made mostly of oak about six inches thick, were then used for the construction of defensive breastworks along the perimeter of their position.

The defences were laid out in a broken checkerboard pattern alternating at a distance of twelve to twenty yards in advance or to the rear of each other and scattered irregularly, which would have limited the damage done to them by artillery fire. More fence rails were piled up on the bridge in prepared pyres in case it needed to be destroyed in the face of an oncoming attack.[78]

John O'Neill, with his years of combat experience, could not have chosen better ground to repel an attack nor prepare it any more efficiently. It is likely that this position was chosen days, if not weeks or months, earlier—perhaps by Canty the Fenian spy. For all the drinking that might have gone on in Fort Erie, when it was time to prepare for fighting, O'Neill's experienced Fenian infantry was digging in like a well-oiled machine.

Inquisitive Canadian townspeople and American journalists from Buffalo began arriving at Frenchman's Creek to look over the Fenian camp. John Cooper, the postmaster from Chippawa, rode in on his horse without being challenged by Fenian pickets. He inspected the camp and estimated that some five hundred men were there. He noticed several wearing Confederate uniforms and was told they were veterans of the Louisiana Tigers from New Orleans. Cooper had a harder time getting out of the area, as some Fenians attempted to seize his horse, but he managed to break away and return to Chippawa to report everything he saw.[79]

Late in the afternoon, Canada West Frontier Constabulary agent Charles Clarke infiltrated the camp as well. He was introduced to O'Neill and remained in the camp until 10 P.M. He had been sent by a Canadian officer who had already arrived with his force at Port Colborne.[80] Clarke would report the next day (too late to be of any use) his estimate of Fenian strength in the camp at 450, warning that an additional 200 would reinforce them during the night.[81]

The Fort Erie customs officer, Mr. Treble, was also inside the Fenian camp. At around 6 P.M. he introduced his superior, customs inspector Richard Graham, into the camp.[82] This introduction would have significant consequences in the next twenty-four hours.

FIVE

The Military Response, Afternoon, June 1, 1866

As John O'Neill was digging in at Frenchman's Creek, Canadian and British troops were already deploying in the Welland-Niagara region. The reports from Buffalo had finally spurred the Canadian government to mobilize the militia on the afternoon of May 31, about twelve hours before the Fenians crossed the river. British army Colonel Patrick L. MacDougall, the Adjutant General of Militia and overall commander of the Canadian Militia, ordered a battalion of four hundred men to be assembled in Toronto and dispatched to the Fort Erie region.

At 6 P.M. on May 31, Major Charles T. Gillmor, commanding officer of the Queen's Own Rifles (QOR) in Toronto, received orders to assemble four hundred men by 5 A.M. at the Simcoe Street drill shed and to proceed to the docks where, at 6:30 A.M., they were to board the steamer ferry *City of Toronto* for a three-hour trip across Lake Ontario to Port Dalhousie near the mouth of the Welland Canal.

From there they were to continue to Port Colborne on Lake Erie by the railway paralleling the canal.[1] Church and fire bells in Toronto began ringing that evening, alerting volunteers to report. The battalion adjutant, Captain William Otter, found a large number of QOR men at a banquet, which made the task of assembling them easier. The soldiers were presented with lists of names and sent out to find the other members of their unit.[2]

Fred McCallum, a fifteen-year-old volunteer in QOR Company 5, was at a soldiers' bazaar that evening in the former Governor's residence at King and Simcoe streets. He was admiring a hanging quilt in a military pattern made from patches of different-coloured uniforms when, at about 9 P.M., a sergeant tapped him on the shoulder and informed him that the battalion had been called out. He was handed a list of names and ordered to find them. Afterward McCallum went home to get a few hours' sleep. Fearing that his parents would not allow him to go, he snuck into the house without waking them. Early in the morning he dressed in his uniform and slipped out quietly without having breakfast lest he awaken them. He would later regret not having brought anything to eat from home.[3]

Ensign Malcolm McEachren, also from Company 5, anxiously reported to duty at the drill shed early in the evening. McEachren, at thirty-five, was older than the average militia volunteer. Born in Islay, Scotland, and raised in Lower Canada, he came from a humble background and had originally wanted to be a minister. Born a Presbyterian, he had only recently joined the Wesleyan Methodists and was a Sunday school teacher. McEachren was married to Margaret Caroline, aged thirty-one, and the couple had five children: two boys, eight and twelve, and three daughters, two, four, and six years old. He was a store manager in Toronto with an annual salary of nine hundred dollars, plus free rent for the family in an apartment above the premises. McEachren was sufficiently organized to have purchased life insurance but not sufficiently wealthy to acquire more than a $250 policy—in today's dollars about

$6,675.[4] (One Canadian dollar in 1866 had the approximate purchasing power of $26.70 in 2005.)[5]

Malcolm McEachren was the Protestant ideal of a lower-middle-class white-collar clerk Upper Canadian. He was described as "studious, circumspect, and industrious in his habits, and moreover possessing an unobtrusive and amiable disposition ... He sought as a Christian to be useful ... In his commercial relations he was regarded as a man of strictest integrity; he was industrious and painstaking and hence he had the confidence of all who knew him in this department of life ... one capable of varied and prolonged activities, and as eminently qualified, in this particular, for the part he essayed in the defence of his country. He had disciplined himself to integrity and a high sense of honour, and was one to whom the honour of his country had long been a sort of passion. Not thirsting for strife, he was prepared to meet it; not seeking occasion, he must do or die if it [*sic*] offer."[6]

LANCE CORPORAL WILLIAM HODGSON ELLIS, a twenty-one-year-old chemistry student born in Bakewell, Derbyshire, England, belonged to QOR Company 9, which consisted almost exclusively of Toronto's University College students. The "University Rifles" had been formed in a frenzy of patriotism in 1861 by the college's professor of chemistry, Henry Croft.[7] Ellis was studying for an exam scheduled for the following day when, at 11 P.M., a non-commissioned officer from his company knocked at his dormitory door with orders to report for duty at the drill shed.[8]

Ellis was joined by fellow student Malcolm McKenzie, a farmer's boy from Zorra, Oxford County, between London and Woodstock, Ontario.[9] McKenzie was the elder of two sons whose father had died and left each of them fifty acres of farmland. But Malcolm wanted to pursue a college education, and so he leased his land to his brother for seventy dollars a year, borrowed an additional ninety dollars from his brother-in-law, and enrolled at University College in Toronto.[10]

Another student volunteer called out that night was John Harriman Mewburn, twenty-one, who had just completed his third year of studies. He was the only son of Harrison Chilton Mewburn from Stamford, near Niagara Falls. His father had scraped together nearly $400 ($10,680 in 2005 dollars) to put him through a year of school, but his grades were so good that he was expected to win the annual University College Scholarship.[11]

William Fairbanks Tempest, a twenty-year-old volunteer with the University Rifles, was likewise ordered to report that night. Tempest was a Presbyterian from Oshawa and now a promising medical student in his final year of studies.[12] He was the elder son in a family of three sisters and two brothers. His father, Dr. William Tempest Sr., a physician in Oshawa, had made plans with his son to form a medical partnership and had recently moved his practice to Toronto so the two would be closer. Dr. Tempest had happily paid William's prep school, university, and medical school tuitions.[13] William did not disappoint his father. A graduate of Upper Canada College, he matriculated in medicine at University College when he was seventeen and was now attending the Toronto School of Medicine while boarding at UC. In his examinations, Tempest never achieved a mark below 96 percent. He was interning at a hospital in Toronto and attending dissection with only a year left before completing his medical degree.[14]

Several years earlier, when Tempest was seventeen, he had volunteered with the Oshawa Infantry Company commanded by his uncle, Captain L.B. Fairbanks. He immediately took to soldiering. During his summer breaks, William attended one of the militia schools organized to give additional training to the volunteers and graduated with a Military Certificate Second Grade. This qualified him for an officer's commission as an ensign (second lieutenant), but Tempest preferred to drill and serve as a private in the ranks.

After Tempest moved to Toronto in 1865 to complete his medical studies, he transferred to the University Rifles, commanded by

Captain Croft, his chemistry professor from University College. William was close to Professor Croft and had worked for him the previous year as a teaching assistant. In the rifle company, Tempest was permanently assigned the right-hand front rank position ("right marker"), entrusted to act as an anchor around which the company formation moved during drill and field manoeuvres.

During the Fenian alarm in March, Tempest had been called out to frontier duty but managed to keep his high 90-percent grades with only one night's studying prior to writing the exams. His mother had become worried about how much time he was dedicating to militia service, while William himself was growing concerned about the threat he might face and his unit's military preparedness. He felt uneasy that no surgeon had been assigned to the QOR, despite the fact that the unit would likely be deployed on the front line in any confrontation with the Fenians. A surgeon was finally appointed only a week before the battle.[15] His father later recalled that in the weeks before Ridgeway, "he had a presentiment that the Fenian movement was more serious than people thought at that time and had expressed his belief to a sister that he had not long to live."[16]

Anxious to see action and unable to sleep, many of the volunteers arrived at the drill shed early. Colonel Durie told them to return to their dormitory: So many students had completed their examinations and gone home, away from Toronto, that the university company was too scattered and under-strength to be mustered that night.

The boys returned to their residence, bitterly disappointed. But then at 5:50 A.M., Tempest was awakened by a friend hammering on his door. Church bells were still ringing throughout the city. The battalion was short of the required four hundred volunteers and would now be taking on men from any company. Tempest quickly donned his uniform and dashed down to the docks at the foot of Yonge Street, pushing his way through the chaos of families, friends, and spectators seeing off the soldiers to the ferry as a brass band played "Tramp! Tramp! Tramp! The Boys Are Marching."[17]

The song was a popular adaptation of an 1863 Civil War song by George F. Roots, "Tramp! Tramp! Tramp! The Prisoner's Hope," about Union prisoners of war held in Confederate camps.[18] The song came to have different adaptations, including a more imperial colonial version sung frequently in Lower Canada with a chorus that went as follows:

> Shout! Shout! Shout! Ye loyal Britons.
> Cheer up, let the Fenians come ...
>
> Should this poor deluded band set foot upon our land
> Or molest the rights of England's noble Queen,
> They will meet with British pluck—English, Irish, Scot, Canuck—
> And they'll wish themselves at home again, I ween.[19]

"Tramp! Tramp! Tramp!" became Canada's longest-lasting military marching song, with a version for every conflict: the Pacific Border tensions in 1869, "Tramp, tramp, tramp, the New Dominion now is knocking at the door"; the Northwest Rebellion in 1885, "And beneath the Union Jack we shall breathe the air again, and be happy in our own Canadian home"; the South African War in 1900, "And beneath the Union Jack we will drive old Krueger back"; and the First World War in 1914, "... we will drive the Germans back."[20]

Attaching himself to Company 8, Trinity College Rifles, Tempest managed to clamber aboard the *City of Toronto* just before it sailed at 6:40 A.M.[21] A total of 356 men were on board.[22]

William Ellis, in the meantime, had been ordered earlier to stay in Toronto and help search out more members of his company.[23] The university now offered to waive further examination requirements for any student reporting for duty, while those who were up for honours would have their standing decided by their average on the examinations already held, together with their records in previous years.[24] Eventually enough of the students were located to assemble Company 9. They would cross the lake in a second transport of 125 additional men and arrive at Ridgeway at dawn on June 2, just in time for battle but without their professor officers, who were, it was later reported, detained by "academic duties."[25]

THE FIRST OF THE Queen's Own Rifles disembarked from the *City of Toronto* at Port Dalhousie at around 10:30 A.M. They arrived woefully ill-equipped for battle, notwithstanding General Napier's speech to them at the drill shed prior to their departure, in which he said they might be engaged with the enemy within twelve hours.[26]

Forty-nine men of Company 5 were going to be equipped with state-of-the-art seven-shot repeating Spencer Rifles requiring unique brass cartridge ammunition, of which they were given exactly four packages of seven rounds each—a total of twenty-eight rounds per man.[27] The rest of the battalion carried standard muzzle-loading single-shot Enfield rifles and were sent on their way with only five rounds of ammunition each![28] The normal load for an infantryman going into combat in the mid-nineteenth century was forty to sixty rounds.

They had no tents, no blankets, no cooking or eating utensils, no food nor any knapsacks to carry it in had rations been available. They had no stretchers, no medical supplies, and no trained medical orderlies. They carried no spades, axes, or entrenching tools, the very items that the Fenians diligently expropriated immediately upon landing at Fort Erie.[29] Most did not even have canteens for water. They brought their heavy wool greatcoats, but by 10 A.M. in the heat of that June morning when they took them off, the men discovered they had no straps to fasten the coats with. They ended up having to carry them over their arms.[30]

Nor were the Queen's Own Rifles the only battalion so poorly equipped. Alexander Somerville, a freelance journalist with the Hamilton *Evening Times* and the Hamilton *Spectator*, and a former combat veteran who had served in the British Legion in Spain from 1836 to 1837, described how poorly equipped the Thirteenth Battalion from Hamilton was:

> They were sent out without canteens to carry water when on the line of march or on the battlefield. On the field of action and on the retreat they drank from swampy ditches, lifting the water in their shakos and caps and shoes; many were in consequence sick ... They had no knapsacks in which to carry changes of underclothing or the usual military necessaries. They had no mess tins in which to divide food and carry it when not all at once consumed. They had no haversack to carry bread and small articles indispensable to personal cleanliness and health, and not second to these, indispensable in keeping the rifle in working order. They had not a wrench in the battalion to unscrew locks, not a worm screw, of which every man should have one wherewith to draw charges from rifles. The [rifle] nipples of some were, after the action, plugged with dirt and could not be fired off. There was no battalion armourer. They had no oil for springs, or to protect burnished steel from rust. They had no portable camp kettles, to cook food which should have been supplied by a Government commissary. There were commissary agents who had no stores. The Government were said to be ready for any emergency. The 1st and 2nd of June proved that they had made no adequate preparation.[31]

The officers had no maps or, at best, general maps. The British commander of the operation, Lieutenant Colonel George Peacocke, had only a postal map torn from an almanac, on a scale of ten miles to the inch and showing mail delivery routes but no roads or topographical features.[32] The Fenians on the other hand arrived with detailed county-level road maps previously acquired by their intelligence service.[33]

The QOR were met at Port Dalhousie wharf by Mr. McGrath, the general manager of the Welland Railway and a captain in the militia, who had prepared a special train for them. McGrath was puzzled to see the soldiers unloading personal luggage as if they were on holiday, "trunks, hatboxes and the usual accompaniments of railway travellers when on long journeys."[34] McGrath wanted to know where they thought they were going with all that luggage. The QOR officers explained that they expected to be in garrison at Port Colborne for quite some time. McGrath responded that most likely they were going to be in combat before they got to Port Colborne and that there was no space for the luggage on the train. Several minutes later, McGrath realized that the QOR had arrived with no equipment, provisions, or ammunition, save the few rounds issued to each man. Space for the hat boxes and valises was easily found.[35]

AS IF ALL THE SHORTAGES were not enough to hobble the soldiers, they also faced a scramble between their amateur officers to seize command of the operation and presumably the glory as well. Shortly before leaving Toronto, Major Gillmor was informed that the QOR had been put under the direct field command of the local district brigade major, forty-six-year-old militia Lieutenant Colonel John Stoughton Dennis. The battalion had never been under the direct field command of Dennis, nor had it drilled or exercised with him.

Dennis was a wealthy Ontario land surveyor whose family's military history had put a lot of pressure on him to live up to its reputation. His grandfather was a Loyalist from Philadelphia, while his father had served as a lake captain in the War of 1812. A graduate of Victoria College, Dennis was the lead surveyor of a number of railway routes in Canada. In 1851 he had been appointed to the board of examiners for provincial land surveyors. He served on a number of institutional boards, including those of an institution for the deaf and blind in Hamilton and the Canadian Institute. A prominent socialite believing himself to be "descended of martial ancestors," Dennis actively sought out commissions and appointments in the Volunteer Militia.[36]

After having served in Denison's cavalry, John Dennis was made lieutenant of his own cavalry troop in 1855 but failed to raise and maintain the troop, according to George T. Denison's memoirs.[37] The next year John Dennis took command of the volunteer Toronto Field Battery, which he led for two years before managing to leverage the position into an appointment as lieutenant colonel and brigade major commanding the Fifth Militia Military District—a command that included the City of Toronto, Peel and Ontario Counties along Lake Ontario, and areas to the north as far as the shores of Georgian Bay, Penetanguishene, and Lake Simcoe regions.[38] He had no experience leading infantry.

Dennis was distinguished by his elaborate Dundreary-style whiskers that, even by Victorian standards, were spectacular. They grew out from huge "mutton chops" that descended to his upper chest just below his shoulders like two small, poodle-sized beards. George Denison described him as "a very good office man in time of peace, the exact type of man to be dear to the official heart, a good red tape courtier, but useless as a soldier. He was an ambitious man, carefully anxious not to let any opportunities pass him."[39]

As soon as the alarm was raised, Dennis immediately telegraphed MacDougall in Montreal asking to be put in command of the militia forces dispatched from Toronto.[40] Despite the fact that the Queen's Own Rifles had been for months training and drilling under Major Gillmor, they were now much to their resentment put under Dennis's command.[41] George T. Denison later commented, "His appointment created an unpleasant feeling, which had an indirect but evil influence on the campaign."[42]

Dennis's orders from General Napier were to proceed with the QOR by railway to Port Colborne and, if necessary, entrench there against any advancing Fenians. Dennis was told that Fenian strength was estimated at 1,500, and he was warned not to engage them before reinforcements and further orders had arrived.[43]

PORT COLBORNE WAS DEFENDED by the Welland Canal Field Battery, under the command of Captain Dr. Richard Saunders King, a local physician.[44] Three officers and fifty-nine men from the unit would report for duty by the end of the day.[45] Headquartered in Port Robinson, the battery was originally equipped with four 9-pounder Armstrong brass field guns and had been well trained in their use by a British artillery bombardier, James McCracken.[46] The guns had been divided equally between Port Colborne and Port Robinson, which were twelve miles apart on the canal. But earlier in the year, after failing to post guards at the wooden sheds where the artillery pieces were stored, British army Lieutenant Colonel Charles C. Villiers ordered that the guns and their accoutrements be taken away from the battery. They were moved to Hamilton where they would be put under the guard of regular British troops. And there the guns remained.[47]

With the artillery gone, Bombardier McCracken drilled the men in infantry tactics throughout the winter of 1866.[48] Half the men in the Welland Canal Field Battery were armed with standard-issue Long-Enfield rifles, but the other half were issued Victoria carbines[49]—an obsolete British firearm with limited range, which had been designed in 1839 and withdrawn from service in the British army back in 1853.[50] The surplus carbines had been supplied to the Canadian Volunteer Militia during the *Trent* Crisis in 1861.

It was not going to be easy to muster the Welland Battery. Most of the men were scattered throughout small villages and farms over a twenty-mile radius of the countryside, while others were at work on ships in the Great Lakes. On the morning of June 1, in the village of Byng just across the Grand River from Dunnville, Stephen Beatty, a corporal in the battery, was opening the doors on the first day of his new business, a gristmill that he had begun renting that month. Beatty had already lost a flour and feed store in Port Robinson when, during the March Fenian scare, he had been called to duty and had had to leave behind instructions for his entire stock to be liquidated at any price.[51] The March scare and then the alert in April, when the Fenians raided Campobello, strained the lives of all the volunteers. Beatty complained:

> All previous programme [*sic*] was paralysed. Some had lost their business like myself, others had their positions occupied by new comers and must look for other situations. The farmers of the Battery found a good deal of the work they had planned to do was not done ... Some employers of labour were loathe to engage a volunteer into their service

> for the opinion was general that a raid would occur and they did not feel like engaging a man to be employed by him [*sic*] for only a few days.[52]

No sooner had Beatty unlocked his door and set about organizing the mill with an employee he had just hired than a soldier appeared on the scene with news that the Fenians had invaded at Fort Erie. Beatty hoped the rumour was untrue and continued to work through the morning, but then, unable to resist any longer, he crossed the river into Dunnville to see if there was any news. He found an excited crowd gathered around the railway telegraph office and a mass of rumours: Two thousand Fenians had crossed the Niagara River; the reeve of Fort Erie had been shot; the Fenians were headed toward Port Colborne.

At the telegraph office Beatty found no orders awaiting him. He then telegraphed Captain King for instructions and returned to the mill. In the early afternoon he came back to the telegraph office to find the crowd still there, desperate for any scrap of news. The culture of keeping firearms in Canada in the 1860s, even in relatively rural Dunnville, appears to be different from that in the United States; firearms were scarcer, and a townsperson telegraphed Ottawa asking that a hundred stand of rifles be sent for a Home Guard. Pushing through the crowd, Beatty found a message waiting for him: Captain King ordered him to report to Port Colborne twenty-two miles away. But as the trains were not running, Beatty had no way of getting there.[53]

As Beatty made his way back through the crowd, he recalled being accosted by "one very stout old lady whose husband had been a British Army officer but was now dead. I was joking the people [*sic*] about being so excited, she said to me, 'if you are a good British subject you will put on your uniform and go and fight the enemy.' I replied that I would be there in due time."[54]

Beatty had had his uniform with him at the mill, as he was planning to attend a military ball later that evening. Now he returned to the mill, donned his uniform, and paid a month's wages to his worker, even though the employee had only worked a day. He then closed and locked the mill, the Fenians having ruined his second business. Beatty still did not know how he was going to get to Port Colborne—twenty-two miles was too far to walk.

In Port Colborne, meanwhile, the B&LH railway superintendent, Larmour, had sent out an employee on horseback to scout the tracks running to Fort Erie. A citizen had provided the horse, but only after Larmour guaranteed its price should it be captured by the Fenians. When the rider returned, he reported that Sauerwein's Bridge had been set on fire and that the Fenians were foraging in the countryside for horses but did not appear to be moving toward Port Colborne.[55] Lieutenant Colonel Dennis arrived with the QOR shortly afterward, at about 1 P.M. After meeting with Larmour he decided that there was no need to entrench, as the Fenians did not appear to be advancing toward the town. Dennis dispatched local scouts in an attempt to reconnoitre the Fenian positions. Some men from the Welland Canal Field Battery who had reported for duty were now assigned to escort the railway workers sent to repair Sauerwein's Bridge and to clear the wreckage of the train that had derailed earlier that morning.[56] They remained on the site until it was cleared at midnight.[57] Dennis also had at his disposition Frontier Constabulary undercover agent (and Toronto Police Sergeant) Charles Clarke, a British army veteran who had seen action at Kandahar during the First Afghan War. Dennis ordered him to infiltrate the Fenian positions in Fort Erie and to remain with them collecting information until 10 P.M.[58]

TOWARD LATE EVENING on May 31, when the intentions of the Fenians at Buffalo became obvious, the Hamilton Volunteer Thirteenth Infantry Battalion had been put on alert. A sergeant from the unit began calling on the homes of its men, ordering them to report to the drill shed on James Street at 6 A.M. the next morning.[59] Private George Alan Mackenzie, seventeen years old, who was home for the summer from Trinity College in Toronto, was typical of the Hamilton Thirteenth Battalion troops.[60] Of the 250 militia volunteers who reported for duty that day, 150 were under the age of twenty, and only 180 had previously fired any live ammunition.[61] Mackenzie's father, the rector of Christ Church, had a year earlier given his underaged son consent to enlist when the boy was only sixteen. Mackenzie later recalled that when he joined with some other boys of his own age:

> We were thrilled at the prospect of getting a taste of military life, of wearing a scarlet tunic and marching to the music of a military band. Young and immature as we were, I do not imagine that any of us were inspired by any definite feeling of patriotism, although, in the event, we were all highly lauded as patriots. We thought it would be good fun to play at soldiering. We were looking for a "lark," that might prove adventurous and exciting. And we found it![62]

The mustering of the Thirteenth Battalion that morning was announced by the booming of cannon fired at the drill shed. Mackenzie heard the first report of the cannon but drifted back to sleep. It was only after the second blast that he awoke and made his way down to the drill shed. Like most of the men that morning, he had not had breakfast. The commanding officer of the Thirteenth Battalion, Lieutenant Colonel Alfred Booker, in his statement to the Military Board of Inquiry, claimed, "As many came without overcoats or breakfasts, I caused them to return home for breakfast and report again within the hour, instructing them to bring their overcoats, and those who had them, their haversacks with food. I cautioned them that I could not tell when nor where they would have the next opportunity for a meal."[63]

Mackenzie remembered it slightly differently: "Having met him on familiar occasions, and not realizing the great and terrible distance that separates a private soldier from his commanding officer, I approached him this morning in all innocence and asked him if there would be time for me to go home and get some breakfast and a few sandwiches for future emergencies. He turned away with considerable hauteur and said brusquely, 'Go and ask your corporal!' I had learned a much-needed lesson in military etiquette and the distinctions of rank in the army."[64]

Only about 20 percent of the men in the Thirteenth had knapsacks. Booker's address to the men prior to their beginning the march acknowledged this. He said, "Men of the Thirteenth, you are once more called out for duty. You will now, as you did before, *follow me*. You have no knapsacks, but I can promise that if you do not behave yourselves before the enemy as soldiers do, you will get plenty of 'knapsack drill.'"[65] This threat of punishment by being drilled while wearing weighted knapsacks struck an ironic chord with many of the men. Booker's awareness that they lacked proper equipment and his failure to do anything about it were, after all, defects of command. More tellingly, the unit had recently been on frontier duty for five months at Windsor, and the officer who led them had not found it necessary to punish them even once. Booker's "follow me" would stick in their craws.

The forty-two-year-old Alfred Booker Jr., Esq., had been born in Nottingham, England, in 1824, one of eight children of a Baptist clergyman. As Baptists, the family were virtually outcasts in Anglican society, and they immigrated to Canada. After a year in Montreal the Booker family moved in 1843 to Hamilton, where the father established a church on Park Street and became one of the founding members of the Baptist Church in Canada. Alfred Booker Sr. was killed in a railway accident on the Desjardins Canal Bridge in 1857.[66]

Alfred Jr. had by 1850 established a thriving auction house on James Street where he sold real estate, horses, dry goods, and inventories of bankrupt merchants. By the 1850s, being a Baptist in Canada had acquired less of a stigma, and Booker became a wealthy member of Hamilton's elite. He was a member of the St. George Society and of his father's church, and a founder of the St. John's Masonic Lodge. Another way of forging social connections was through voluntary military service, and Booker sought a commission as an ensign in the

Wentworth Militia in 1851. He went on to finance his own artillery battery, personally paying for the casting of its guns (of dubious quality beyond firing ceremonial blanks) in the Hamilton locomotive works of the Great Western Railway.[67] In 1855 Booker was promoted to captain and then, in 1857, to major. In 1858 he was given command of all Volunteer Militia forces in Hamilton and was promoted to the rank of lieutenant colonel. During the American Civil War period, Booker served as a liaison officer with British forces deployed in the region.[68]

In 1862 the Thirteenth Battalion was assembled from local independent companies and placed under the command of Isaac Buchanan, but in 1865 he resigned after clashing with a group of insubordinate officers led by the battalion's popular second-in-command, Major James Atchison Skinner. In a parting shot at his persecutors, Buchanan ensured that Booker, while remaining in overall command of the Hamilton militia district, also took personal command of the Thirteenth Battalion rather than Major Skinner.[69]

Buchanan acted out of spite. Earlier he had written, "Booker ... deserves credit, and no one has borne more testimony to this than me, but as to there ever being a great military organization under him, the thing is absurd."[70] The bad blood left behind by the conflict between Buchanan and Skinner would end tragically. It would also have an enormous impact on how the history of Ridgeway would be written.

In principle, Booker was neither no more nor no less competent than any other Canadian militia officer; few had had the opportunity to see combat since the Hunters Lodge patriot border raids of 1838. Booker was certainly *qualified* to command a battalion, having completed a series of training exercises and earned a Militia Certificate First Grade.

In his personal life, Alfred Booker was no doubt a typically pompous Victorian gentleman making his way up the social ladder through community, church, and militia service. He was remembered by one Hamiltonian, his son's boyhood friend, as "a clever and versatile Englishman, an auctioneer by calling, fluent of speech and somewhat florid in manner. In private life he was good-natured and kind, and sometimes amused us boys in his own house by ingenious marionette shows of his own constructions and tricks of ventriloquism."[71]

How much blame for the ill-equipped state of the Thirteenth Battalion can be laid on Booker is debatable. The QOR, most of its men armed with only five rounds of ammunition, were in even worse condition than the Thirteenth and would eventually have to draw extra ammunition from Booker's supply. But Booker himself was ill-prepared: He departed without a map or even a pencil and paper with which to issue orders, and without his horse. Only one of the sixteen officers was mounted—Major Skinner. Later an apocryphal story was circulated that when an officer at Hamilton asked Booker if he was going to remain dismounted, Booker poked the officer in the side with his finger and said, "Skinner! There is Skinner with his horse; I'll dismount him."[72]

The Thirteenth Battalion departed the drill shed at 9 A.M. and marched through the streets to the Great Western Railway station past a multitude of cheering Hamiltonians as a brass band from the British Sixteenth Regiment played "The Girl I Left Behind."[73] The Thirteenth had been ordered to Dunnville on the Grand River. After a slow and tedious circular journey via Paris, Ontario, then a stop in Caledonia to pick up four officers and forty-four men of the Caledonia Rifle Company, the Thirteenth Battalion arrived in Dunnville shortly before 4 P.M.[74] They marched into the centre of town and were billeted among the homes there. Some of the soldiers were given dinner by the townspeople, but others went hungry.[75] Thomas Kilvington, one of the two remaining Thirteenth Battalion veterans of Ridgeway still living in 1936, recalled, "An old lady ten of us were billeted with couldn't do much for us. She hadn't enough food for her own family."[76] Booker himself had no problems finding a meal.[77]

In the meantime, Corporal Beatty of the Welland Battery had hoped to take the train farther east to Port Colborne but discovered that it was now halted there with the Thirteenth Battalion, pending further orders.

He finally decided to hire a driver, horse, and buggy to take him to Port Colborne for twenty dollars.[78] Beatty wrote, "The price asked was extortion but what did that matter if one is going to his death."[79]

Along the way Beatty and his driver encountered refugees, their wagons overloaded with household belongings, headed the other way. Nobody knew where the Fenians were, only that they were advancing, it was said, on Port Colborne to destroy the Welland Canal. As they began approaching Port Colborne, Beatty and his driver heard the sound of a brass band playing and the driver became frightened. Although Beatty "did not know if it was the British or something else, as I was not brought up with a musical ear," he persuaded the driver to push on.[80] They entered the town safely, and after reporting for duty, Beatty was issued an Enfield rifle, but no bayonet, haversack for provisions, or ammunition pouches for his caps and cartridges—those he had to stuff into the pockets of his uniform. He considered himself lucky, however, to have a Long Enfield rather than the obsolete Victoria carbine that half the men in his battery were issued.[81]

BACK IN HAMILTON, a twenty-six-year-old Victoria College graduate and recently ordained Wesleyan Methodist minister, Nathanael Burwash, was returning from the train station with several other churchmen after having seen off the Thirteenth Battalion. Privately, Burwash was experiencing a crisis of faith. With the publication of Darwin's *Origin of the Species* in 1859 and of a series of biblical criticisms known as *Essays and Reviews,* debate among young "Common Sense Realist" Methodist theologians had reached new heights. At issue was the challenge that rationalization, or reduction to an intellectual process, posed to the innate "work of the Spirit," which was at the heart of Methodism. For Methodists the essence of true religious experience was in the regenerative power of the "witness of the Spirit"—the inner assurance of faith, the redemptive power of divine grace. The scientific rationalism of the Victorian era challenged the basic premise in almost all Christian faiths that nature contained the clear signs of a benevolent Creator and that this God had provided additional, completely reliable information about Himself in the Scriptures.[82] With the nature of his faith under siege, Burwash found himself troubled by doubts. He would later recall, "I read the books and sometimes seemed to feel all certain ground sinking from under my feet."[83]

As they walked home the churchmen decided that it would be a good idea to send a pastor to minister to the men sent to the front. They convened a meeting of the Hamilton Ministerial Association to choose who among them might go. Burwash argued passionately for the appointment. One of the ministers later said, "I recall especially the impression made upon him by the thought of the ruffians who had invaded our borders. I question if he had ever entertained as strong and bitter a feeling at any time; it reminded me of some other man rather than the quiet, unassuming Methodist preacher I had known. I could fancy the highland strain was dominant ..."[84]

Appointed chaplain along with Burwash was Reverend Dr. David Inglis of the McNab Street Presbyterian Church. The forty-two-year-old Scottish-born Inglis had graduated from the University of Edinburgh, and after studying divinity, came to America in 1845, serving congregations in Detroit, New York City, Bedford, N.Y., and Montreal before arriving in Hamilton in 1855.[85] He was a fiery preacher and a militant Protestant, believing all other Christian communions to be "superstitious" and "anti-Christian."[86]

The two men would become the first chaplains to accompany Canadian troops into combat.[87] Their only problem was how to get to the front. With the telegraph lines cut at Fort Erie and the whereabouts of the Fenians unknown, the two churchmen got only as far as Brantford, where they found all scheduled trains had been cancelled. They began earnestly to search for a way to catch up with the Thirteenth Battalion.[88]

HAMILTON, THE LARGEST CITY in the vicinity of Fort Erie, was the nearest place with regular British troops: the Bedfordshire Regiment (Sixteenth Foot, Right Wing), consisting of four companies of two hundred officers and men under the command of Lieutenant Colonel George J. Peacocke.[89] He was a professional and able British officer thought highly of by his fellow officers and liked by his men. He was not overly insistent on military ceremonial protocols and would surprise a Canadian officer by shaking hands with a volunteer private he encountered on the road during the upcoming campaign. When the officer asked him about this breach of etiquette, Peacocke replied, "When I am in Hamilton I am often at that young man's home. I dine often with his father and family, and meet him there. He is a young man of good social position, and because he puts on a uniform and shoulders his musket to defend his Queen and country, should that degrade him? I think I should shake hands with him all the more on that account."[90]

Early in the morning, Major General George Napier, the British commander in Canada West, headquartered in Toronto, appointed Peacocke as commander-in-chief of the entire Niagara region operation but failed to give him any specific orders. Napier has been described by Viscount Wolseley as "not a shining light … In private life a charming man, he was quite useless at all times as a commander."[91] As volunteer troops from Toronto and Hamilton steamed out toward the Lake Erie region of the Welland Canal, British troops in the Hamilton area remained in their barracks with no orders to move.

In Toronto, George T. Denison had been following the reports from Buffalo for days, expecting to be called out with his troop of cavalry. He calculated the possible Fenian movements and their likely travelling times. When he was awakened by his brother on the morning of June 1 and informed that the QOR had been sent out overnight, he was surprised that there were no orders to assemble his horsemen.

Frustrated, Denison went to his law office in downtown Toronto. At about noon he received a message asking him to report to Napier at his headquarters. When Denison arrived, he was shocked to find Napier completely ignorant of the geography of the Niagara region and in possession of only a single large-scale map of Upper Canada, which hung on his office wall. Napier began to pepper him with questions, and from their nature Denison realized that Napier had still not issued comprehensive deployment orders for troops. Worse, it became apparent that Peacocke's British forces were holding uselessly at Hamilton while the critical bridges at nearby Clifton and Chippawa were undefended and the Welland Canal was exposed to the Fenian threat.[92] To complete his frustration, Denison saw that Napier intended to send Peacocke's forces in the exact same direction he had sent the Canadian volunteers—toward Port Colborne, leaving the bridges undefended. Denison heatedly pointed out the vulnerability of the bridges,[93] persuading Napier to order Peacocke to proceed to St. Catharines instead, to make his headquarters there, and to deploy troops throughout the region as he saw fit.[94] To Denison's disappointment, however, when he asked to be deployed with his troop of cavalry, Napier replied that he had "no permission" to order out cavalry. Denison returned to his office seething with frustration.[95]

PEACOCKE DID NOT GET MOVING until 2 P.M.[96] His late start would set in motion a series of consequences for the battle the next morning. Loading his troops aboard a train, he cautiously advanced toward the Niagara Frontier, stopping frequently to pick up additional units or responding to false rumours of approaching Fenians. After securing the suspension bridge at Clifton at Niagara Falls late in the afternoon, Peacocke advanced to Chippawa, arriving there at 8 P.M. or perhaps even as late as 9 P.M.[97] Once there, he disembarked his infantry and attempted to determine the precise location of the Fenians while waiting for additional reinforcements and artillery to arrive in the early morning from Toronto. He also ordered Booker and the Thirteenth Battalion to abandon Dunnville, advance by train to Port Colborne an hour away, and join with Dennis's force.[98]

When the Fenians had dug in at Frenchman's Creek at noon, O'Neill had sent mounted scouts northward in the direction of Chippawa. Early in the afternoon, Captain Donohue of the Eighteenth Fenian Regiment, "Cleveland Rangers," rode out with a small scouting party as far as Black Creek, five miles northwest of their position and about halfway to Chippawa. There Donohue encountered civilian mounted scouts approaching across the fields from Chippawa. After turning them away with several volleys of fire, Donohue sent word of his encounter back to O'Neill.

O'Neill now ordered one hundred men under Colonel Hoy from the Seventh Buffalo Regiment to proceed north to take control of the bridge over Black Creek.[99] Once there, the Fenians dug in to an elevated bank behind the creek over which they had clear sight of open fields in the direction of Chippawa—today, roughly in the vicinity of Shagbark Lane at the intersection of Townline and Switch roads near the bridge over the present-day QEW highway. The position was topographically similar to the one the Fenians held at Frenchman's Creek, except it was about two miles inland from the Niagara River. This was the farthest north the Fenians would penetrate in force during the raid.

At around 6 P.M. Hoy spotted mounted scouts again approaching from the north, most likely civilian riders sent out by the reeve of Chippawa.[100] Again, they were turned away by several rounds of fire. The assumption was made that these were scouts from Crown forces, and the encounter was again reported to O'Neill.

Peacocke was now receiving mixed reports on the Fenian positions, with some indicating the Fenians were at Frenchman's Creek while others insisted they were at Black Creek. With only a clipping of a postal map showing neither road nor topographical details, Peacocke now made a critical error.[101] According to historian Brian Reid, Peacocke confused Black Creek with Frenchman's Creek.[102] Assuming that the Fenian main force was at Black Creek, closest to Chippawa, Peacocke now planned to join with the forces from Port Colborne at Stevensville, eight miles south of Chippawa and about three miles by road southwest of the Fenian positions at Black Creek. (See Regional Map.)

Peacocke scheduled the rendezvous for between 10 and 11 A.M. the next morning. He later stated that he chose such a late hour because he was awaiting reinforcements from Toronto and St. Catharines. He estimated that they would arrive in Chippawa at 4:30 A.M. and that he would not be ready to leave for Stevensville until 6 A.M. Peacocke claimed that he expected the brigade at Port Colborne to leave at approximately the same time, 6 A.M., for the rendezvous at Stevensville later that morning, but did not specify the route they were to take.[103] This late (4:30 A.M.) arrival of Peacocke's reinforcements was subsequently questioned by the press but never adequately explained, as the reinforcements spent the night "cooling their heels" on a train inexplicably halted overnight at Clifton.[104]

This union of two columns was meant to be coordinated with a third column to be landed on the Niagara River from a steamboat, with orders to cut off any Fenian retreat to Buffalo. Peacocke had already telegraphed Dennis at 5 P.M. to tell him he was requesting the British Consul in Buffalo to dispatch the ferry, *International,* to Port Colborne and that Dennis was to place troops aboard it to flank the Fenians from the shore of the Niagara River between Fort Erie and Chippawa.[105]

To ensure that Booker and Dennis understood his plan, Peacocke dispatched Captain Charles Akers of the Royal Engineers (RE) to explain his orders in detail and assist the two Canadian officers. Akers left by train at midnight and Peacocke telegraphed Port Colborne, advising Booker and Dennis to expect Akers's arrival at around 1:30 A.M. But the telegram would not be delivered to the commander at Port Colborne until 12:45 A.M., another seemingly inconsequential but actually significant link in the chain of events leading to the debacle.

BACK IN PORT COLBORNE, Robert Larmour and Major Thomas Patterson cautiously reconnoitred the railway line in a handcar. As they approached

Fort Erie they saw columns of refugees escaping southward from the countryside toward the shore of Lake Erie, but they saw no sign of Fenians.[106] At around 10 P.M. they pulled in to the railway yards to find them almost completely deserted, except for the solitary figure of Her Majesty's Collector of Customs, Richard Graham, who was making his way up the tracks on foot with a message for the commandant in Port Colborne. Graham told Larmour and Patterson that the Fenians had abandoned Fort Erie and that, at around 6 P.M., he had visited their camp at Newbigging Farm on Frenchman's Creek, where he claimed he had found them reduced to not more than four hundred men and in a disorganized and drunken state. Graham had prepared a written dispatch reporting that he believed the Fenians were vulnerable.[107] Larmour and Patterson convinced Graham to return with them. They took him up onto the handcar and returned to Port Colborne at about midnight.[108]

Meanwhile Booker and the Thirteenth Battalion, which Peacocke had ordered to advance by train from Dunnville to Port Colborne, arrived sometime between 11 P.M. and midnight.[109] The ambitious Booker, having marginal seniority over Dennis, immediately relieved him of his command. Combining the various units that had arrived and were still arriving at Port Colborne (Thirteenth Battalion Hamilton, Second Battalion QOR Toronto, Caledonia and York Rifle companies, and the Welland Canal Field Battery), Booker found himself in command of a brigade, a formation normally commanded by a general. On the train from Hamilton, Booker was reputed to have bragged to his fellow officers that he technically outranked every lieutenant colonel in the region and that within days he would be in command of a force of three thousand men. One of the officers later remarked, "He talked as if he were competent to command fifty thousand men."[110]

These developments delighted the Queen's Own Rifles, who, with Dennis gone, returned to the direct command of their own Major Gillmor, but the developments also sent Dennis searching for a command of his own, away from Booker, a search that would also end in disaster.

At about the same time, Larmour arrived from Fort Erie with the customs collector, Graham, and the claim that he had seen the Fenians at Frenchman's Creek, drunk, disorganized, and so few in number that "400 good men will gobble them up before day."[111] According to another witness of the meeting, the customs official assured Dennis that the way ahead was easy. "Graham stated that the Fenian force here at one time at from [*sic*] two hundred and fifty to three hundred, the highest number he mentioned was four hundred. He said he had been in their camp and was introduced there by Mr. Treble, that the Fenian force was drunk and disorganized and if Col Dennis was to move down with two hundred men he could bag them all, and if he did not they would recross the river before sunrise."[112]

Peacocke believed that the Fenian main force was inland at Black Creek, eight miles northwest of Fort Erie, while Dennis and Booker now came to believe they were a mere two and a half miles outside of Fort Erie at Frenchman's Creek.

They were all wrong.

IN ALL THE HISTORIES written about the Battle of Ridgeway, nobody has determined how the Fenians ended up at Limestone Ridge. Generally their presence has been portrayed as an accident. It was not.

Perhaps weeks before the invasion, Ridge Road and Limestone Ridge had been carefully reconnoitred by the Fenians, likely by John C. Canty. According to John O'Neill in his *Official Report,* he knew by 8 P.M. that the Crown forces would be advancing in two columns from Chippawa and Port Colborne—several hours *before* Peacocke formulated his plan to do so. As an experienced officer with a good map, O'Neill could have easily deduced this. Remarkably, O'Neill also mentions that he knew a third column would be landed on shore to outflank him.[113] The Fenians very likely had spies in or near Peacocke's headquarters who were perhaps even tapping into the telegraph line and using it themselves to transmit intelligence.[114] When around 10 P.M. Peacocke telegraphed his orders to Booker to proceed to Port Colborne, O'Neill ordered his Fenians at Frenchman's Creek to pack up and start moving toward Black Creek. Then at midnight, exactly when Peacocke had completed his plan and telegraphed Port Colborne that he was dispatching Captain Akers, O'Neill reports that he suddenly "changed direction and moved on the Limestone Ridge road leading towards Ridgeway—halting a few hours on the way to rest the men: this for the purpose of meeting the column advancing from Port Colborne. My object was to get between the two columns, and, if possible defeat one of them before the other could come to its assistance."[115] O'Neill was following a classic military doctrine of "destruction in detail," in which a smaller force defeats a larger one by concentrating on a smaller part of its enemy, destroying it piece by small piece.

George Whale, who lived just south of Townline Road on the Niagara River about three miles north of Frenchman's Creek, later testified that between 10 and 11 P.M. a force of what he estimated to be between five and six hundred Fenians appeared at his door. According to Whale, they compelled him to show them the road to Ridgeway. He testified that they stopped to rest at Black Creek and then, at around 3 A.M., he led them south through a cedar swamp toward Ridge Road. The Fenians were in such a hurry to get there that they abandoned their ammunition wagons when they got mired and threw any munitions they could not carry into the creek.[116]

Whale's testimony suggests that the move onto Ridgeway had been in the Fenian plan at least two hours before Peacocke sent Captain Akers from Chippawa, and perhaps days or even weeks before then. It was certainly not an accident. George Denison was impressed by the Fenians' choice of position. Of their ground at Black Creek, he says, "Their position here was admirable—how they happened to discover it so soon is extraordinary and tends to show that they must have had the ground reconnoitred and the position of their camp chosen before they came over."[117]

The Fenians now established their full force at Black Creek, uniting the units from Frenchman's Creek with Hoy's Buffalo unit of one hundred men and Donohue's small mounted detachment. They held the position just in case Peacocke attempted an early-morning assault there, or perhaps to deliberately mislead and lure him into assembling his forces to target that position, as Peacocke apparently did. Peacocke's scouts would have reported the Fenian presence at Black Creek all through that night as he prepared to unify his forces at Stevensville for the late-morning operation.

Just before dawn, when it became evident that Peacocke would not launch an early-morning attack from Chippawa without first joining with the units from Port Colborne, the Fenians united and moved south toward Ridgeway with a full force of about eight hundred men. There they expected to intercept what they believed to be the weaker of the two columns—the one without artillery—which was moving up from Port Colborne under Booker's command.

It does not appear that O'Neill left many men behind at Black Creek. Somehow the Fenians either knew that the troops from Port Colborne would disembark at Ridgeway or expected the move to come from Stevensville, northwest of Ridge Road, as planned. Either way, the diagonal Ridge Road flanking the top of Limestone Ridge was the perfect ground to defend against an attack either from Ridgeway in the south or Stevensville in the north.

Denison would comment, "This march at early day break was so skilfully and secretly effected that for many days after they left, their movements were a perfect mystery ... The Fenians ... moved by a side line on to the Ridge Road which runs along on the top of the Limestone Ridge which extends in a circular direction from Lake Erie around the Niagara River. To the west of this ridge where they came upon it for a mile and a half or two miles wide extends an unbroken plain of open cultivated fields. Troops could be seen distinctly for two or three miles if coming from that direction. If therefore the Fenians had been attacked at any point on this march on their right flank by merely facing to the right they occupied a beautiful position on the top of a hill 30 or 40 feet high thickly covered with shade trees and woods which would hide their position and give them cover, while the broad expanse of level unbroken country formed a glacis that would not afford the slightest cover to an attacking force against the heavy fire that might be brought to bear against them."[118]

At about 5 A.M. O'Neill arrived at the farmhouse of Henry F. Angur (also Anger or Ankur) on Ridge Road about a half mile north of Bertie Road, near Farm Road today.[119] Angur was a seventy-three-year-old farmer of German origin who suffered from gout and could move about only on crutches. Members of his family who had nearby farms had evacuated their livestock and left the day before, but Angur, a veteran of the War of 1812 and of the 1837–38 Rebellion, told his family to leave without him as "he had been in two wars and would risk a third." When O'Neill entered his house, Angur was surprised that O'Neill already knew his name, the names of his neighbours, where they resided, and even how many horses they all had. The Angur house became the Fenian headquarters.[120]

Whereas the Fenians had reconnoitred the ground and acquired accurate maps and detailed information about the local population, Peacocke, Booker, and Dennis were bumbling about with dime-store postal maps and knew nothing of their own home ground, let alone that of the Fenian positions.

The Fenians, however, had not been moving entirely unobserved. The Fort Erie smuggler, Sam Johnston, had been steadily tracking their movements along their western flank all day long. When darkness fell, Johnston began stalking the Fenians, sometimes getting close enough to hear their voices. He continued to track the Fenians into the morning hours, only stopping off at Buck's Corners to get a rusty revolver oiled. At one point several Fenian horsemen spotted him and gave chase, but Johnston's horse managed to outrun them.

By 6 A.M., Johnston knew that the Fenians were following a line south along Ridge Road toward Ridgeway. Taking a parallel road that led directly into the town, Johnston galloped into Ridgeway just as the train with the brigade from Port Colborne was pulling into the station. Johnston had no idea that their commander believed the Fenians were as far as eight miles away at Frenchman's Creek. But just the same, he was determined to warn them of the proximity of the approaching Fenians. As the troops poured off the train onto the platform, he began impatiently riding up and down their ranks attempting to find Booker.[121]

SIX

Marching Orders, Night, June 1–2, 1866

To understand what might have gone wrong at Ridgeway, we need to backtrack some six hours before the arrival of the brigade at the railway station, as Sam Johnston was galloping into the town. While Johnston was shadowing the Fenians throughout the year on the road to Ridgeway, Lieutenant Colonel John Stoughton Dennis and Lieutenant Colonel Alfred Booker were trying to make sense of Richard Graham's report that the Fenians were still camped at Frenchman's Creek, understrength, and vulnerable. Dennis was arguing for an immediate advance into Fort Erie. Booker might have reminded him that the original order Dennis had received was to proceed to Port Colborne and hold there until further orders, and that this order was now binding on Booker himself as the new commander. Although at midnight Peacocke had telegraphed the brigade at Port Colborne that he was sending Akers to advise them, that message would not be delivered to Booker until 12:45 A.M.[1] In the meantime Graham was persuading Dennis and Booker that Peacocke "was endeavouring to keep the volunteers back in order that the regulars should have all the credit of capturing the Fenians."[2] Booker must have relented under the pressure from Dennis and Graham. He sent a message to Peacocke at 12:30 A.M.: "Erie is open. I have given orders to attack."[3]

Booker then ordered the sleeping troops to be awakened and the train prepared for an advance toward Fort Erie.[4] Fifteen minutes later he received Peacocke's telegram announcing Akers's imminent arrival, but it would not have changed Booker's order to prepare the train, only its eventual destination.

Five minutes later, at around 12:50 A.M., Frontier Constabulary agent Charles Clarke arrived on the scene. He too had been in the Fenian camp, having been sent there in the afternoon by Dennis. He confirmed both its position on Frenchman's Creek and Graham's estimate of approximately 450 Fenians at most, but warned that they were to be reinforced by 200 more at 3 A.M.[5] Clarke would have left the Fenian camp at around 10 P.M. If he already knew that an additional two hundred Fenians were on their way to join O'Neill, then it follows that O'Neill had already set his marching orders and planned the night-time junction between his main force and advance guard. O'Neill would hold his men there until 3 A.M. before finalizing the direction of the march for his unified force.

As crucial as it is to the understanding of what went wrong, the precise timing of the subsequent exchange of telegrams between Booker and Peacocke is difficult to ascertain. We do not know the distance that written messages were carried between headquarters and an available telegraph circuit. There is no evidence that either the volunteers or the British army had laid down cables for field telegraph; both Peacocke and Booker were relying at best on splicing into existing rail telegraph networks.[6] Nor can we know when the recipients turned their attention to telegraphed messages or how long they took to draft a response. Write-to-read times for telegrams between Booker and Peacocke on

June 2 seem to range widely between thirty minutes at the fastest, about forty-five on average, and from ninety minutes to two or even four hours at their most dilatory.[7]

1–2 A.M. In his official report Peacocke wrote, "About two o'clock I received a telegram from Col Booker, despatched before he was joined by Captain Akers informing me that he had given orders to attack the enemy at Fort Erie."[8] Peacocke later commented, "I was astonished at Col. Booker's undertaking to form a plan, but as I saw from the hour mentioned that the message was sent long before Captain Akers could have reached him, I made the remark 'No use answering that, Akers will set it all right when he arrives.'"[9]

Military engineers such as Akers enjoyed a more or less exalted status in nineteenth-century armies. They were regarded in most armies as an educated elite—the American national military academy at West Point, for example, was an engineering school.[10] When they were not constructing fortifications, bridges, and fieldworks or designing machines of war, engineers were often called upon to step in as adjutants, or intelligence and staff officers. They were the problem solvers and sages of the military arts in the modern industrial world of "big war sciences."[11] But even so, it was a strange oversight by Peacocke not to have sent a telegram explicitly countermanding Booker's order to advance. Routine military communication protocol requires redundant confirmation-negation; Peacocke *should have* responded to Booker's message. He had no guarantee that Akers was going to arrive at Booker's headquarters in time to stop the advance into Fort Erie.

The ninety-minute hiatus between the time Booker sent his message and when Peacocke claims he received it is suspiciously long. Perhaps Peacocke succumbed to a half-hour of needed sleep as he waited for reinforcements, there being nothing to do until their arrival. He might have dozed off before reading the message or without responding to it or he might have forgotten about it after he awoke. Whatever the true explanation, his failure to send an explicit message countermanding Booker's order triggered a chain reaction that concluded with a debacle on the battlefield later that day.

Dennis in the meantime had been pursuing a plan of his own. Earlier in the evening, at about 10:30 P.M., while he was still in command at Port Colborne, he had learned that the steam ferry, *International*, would not be coming as Peacocke had planned. Instead it had been sent into harbour on the Buffalo side, to keep it from being seized by the Fenian raiders.[12] The resourceful Dennis telegraphed Captain Lachlan McCallum in Dunnville, the owner of a steam tug, the *W.T. Robb*, and asked him to bring his vessel to Port Colborne.[13] The crusty McCallum, who had written to Macdonald in 1865 about his fantasy of converting the *Robb* into a war tug for carrying marines, responded to Dennis's telegram with enthusiasm.[14] He mobilized his Dunnville marines and steamed out for Port Colborne.

Dennis intended to load onto the *Robb* the gunners from the Welland Canal Field Battery, who without their artillery pieces were functioning as infantry. Dennis was determined to organize the mission as had been intended for the *International*, but now there would be a twist. Having seen no Fenians on his own forays and having believed Graham's misleading report, Dennis was convinced that the way into Fort Erie was open. He was chomping at the bit to advance when Booker arrived on the scene and took command.

It was very awkward—two lieutenant colonels, one only marginally senior. Dennis decided to put as much distance as he could between himself and his rival by taking personal command of the force going aboard the *Robb*. Here he would be the only ranking officer and in undisputed command. While Dennis waited for the vessel to arrive, he persuaded Booker to adopt his plan of advancing the brigade into Fort Erie by railway and flushing out the enemy; Dennis, meanwhile, would trap the retreating Fenians by chasing them down in the *Robb* and deploying the Welland gunners and marines along the bank of the

Niagara River. It was not a bad plan, and might have worked if only the Fenians *had* been retreating. Shortly after, as they awaited the arrival of the *Robb,* Captain Akers, RE, came into Port Colborne by train.

2–3 A.M. If there is a key to what went wrong on Limestone Ridge, then the first clue lies in the early hours of June 2, when Booker, Dennis, and Akers, advised by customs inspector Robert Graham, Frontier Police detective Charles Clarke,[15] and assistant route superintendent Robert Larmour,[16] made an extraordinary decision to change their British commander's plan.

Akers arrived in Port Colborne at approximately 1:30 A.M. to discover that Booker had taken command and that the troops appeared to be loaded upon a train ready to advance to Fort Erie.[17] Akers relayed to Booker and Dennis the orders from Peacocke: They were not to advance into Fort Erie on their own. They were instead to join with Peacocke's British regulars and other Canadian militia units at Stevensville. From there they would make a joint attack on the Fenians, who were believed to be at Black Creek. The *Robb* and its soldiers, by Peacocke's orders, were to be deployed as planned along the Niagara River to prevent the Fenians from retreating to the United States and to act as a floating messenger between Booker and Peacocke if necessary.

Booker and Dennis immediately disputed the orders, insisting to Akers that their intelligence was more current than Peacocke's. According to the two lieutenant colonels, the Fenians were at Frenchman's Creek, not Black Creek; Fort Erie was open, and they should take control of the town at once and proceed to attack the Fenians. As Booker in his statement to the Military Board of Inquiry asserted, "It appeared that Lieut. Col. Dennis and myself were in possession of later and more reliable information of the position of the enemy than Colonel Peacocke seemed to have had when Capt. Akers had left him at midnight."[18]

Captain Akers now took the initiative to devise a new plan. Although only a captain, he carried authority because he was a regular British army officer and a military engineer, and because Peacocke had dispatched him as his emissary. But the problem with nineteenth-century military engineers, according to former Sandhurst lecturer Paddy Griffith, "was that although they represented only one specialized branch in the art of war they were permitted to posture and parade as experts in the whole."[19]

As Akers later reported:

> I arranged a somewhat different plan of attack, subject of course, to Col Peacocke's approval. The plan was as follows—Lieut Col Booker to proceed by rail to Erie, with the greater part of his force, to arrive at Fort Erie at 8 A.M. Lt-Col Dennis and myself to go round the coast in a steam tug, taking a company of volunteer artillery to reconnoitre the shore between Fort Erie and Black Creek and to return to Fort Erie in time to meet Lt. Col Booker at 8. Should Col Peacocke approve of this he would march by the river road from Chippawa and make a combined attack with Lt. Col Booker at some point between Fort Erie and Black Creek, cutting off the enemy's retreat by the River; the tug to be employed cruising up and down the river, cutting off any boats that might attempt to escape and communicating between the forces advancing from Chippawa and Erie.[20]

At 3 A.M. Captain Akers telegraphed the proposed change of plan to Peacocke. Then without waiting for a reply, Akers decided to join Dennis on the *Robb*. Why Akers did not remain with Booker to assist him as a staff officer was never satisfactorily explained. Booker as brigade commander was left to manage a large unit on the move with almost no brigade staff. All the other officers at the scene had direct command responsibilities in their own battalions and could not be spared for duty on a brigade level. In this whole history, the only explanation ever offered by Akers for abandoning Booker was that he, Akers, "had no command or position with the voluntary force at Port Colborne."[21]

There was a sort of escape clause in the plan the three officers cooked up: Booker was not to adopt the new plan *unless* Peacocke approved the proposed changes. Otherwise Booker was to march to Stevensville as originally ordered. But that changed nothing of the *Robb*'s mission—either way it and the detachment of troops aboard under Dennis were headed for the Niagara River shoreline.

What Booker, Dennis, and Akers did appears to have been an extraordinary act of insubordination: Three junior officers unilaterally amended their commander's plan and then acted on it without his approval. This breach of military protocol did not go unnoticed. One journalist would remark, "Whether the three had an overflow of courage at Colborne before the hour of trial, or were only in their normal condition of heroes, held back and impatient of restraint, may never be known."[22] George T. Denison noted that Peacocke's plan had been "changed by his subordinates almost at the moment of execution. The three officers whom he had charged with the execution of his orders, including the staff officer who carried them, coolly forming themselves in a mimic council of war, aided by a customs officer, and unitedly deciding upon a plan which had previously shown to be absurd, a plan for cutting off the Fenian retreat to the east, but leaving the whole country open to them to the west, as well as uncovering the canal they were sent to protect ... The only way in which their conduct can be accounted for is, that they were so confident that Col. Peacocke would at once fall in with their plan of operation in lieu of his own, that they never, for one moment, calculated that his answer would be in the negative."[23]

3–5 A.M. Peacocke was understandably surprised and angered when he read Akers's telegram. His response, telegraphed back at 3:50 A.M., was unequivocal: "I have received your message of 3:00 A.M. I do not approve of it. Follow original plan. Acknowledge this."[24] He received a reply from Booker at 4:20 A.M.: "I will march on Stevensville as required."[25] When Peacocke's telegram countermanding the plan arrived, the *Robb* had already steamed out from Port Colborne with Dennis and Akers on board and it was too late to inform them of Peacocke's rejection of their plan.

The *Robb* arrived in Port Colborne shortly before 4 A.M. The men of the Welland Battery quickly scrambled onto the tug's deck where they joined the Dunnville Naval Brigade already on board.[26] The vessel departed as the sky began to lighten with the coming dawn, gliding through the calm morning waters of Lake Erie. Once they broke through the mist into open water, they saw no other sail or smoke column on the horizon. They were alone, a small band of seventy-one volunteer soldiers steaming at high speed toward the mouth of the Niagara River and their destiny.[27]

At about the same time that Booker's destination was finalized, the Fenian commander, O'Neill, began from near Black Creek his cross-country forced march southwest through a cedar swamp toward Limestone Ridge. It was as if O'Neill knew where Booker was headed before Booker did. This again supports the assertion that somebody leaked the contents of the messages between Peacocke and Booker to O'Neill or at least kept him apprised of the activity in Port Colborne and Chippawa. It is hard to imagine what else could have inspired him to dash so desperately fast toward Limestone Ridge that he was forced to dump wagonloads of precious ammunition and rifles along the way.

Key to resolving what went wrong that day is what exactly Booker understood his orders to be. According to the statement he submitted to the inquiry, Booker jotted down the plans as explained to him by Akers prior to his departure:

> Memo. Move at no later than 5.30–5 if bread be ready. Move to depot at Erie and wait till 7. If not communicated with before 7 move to Frenchman's Creek. If no by telegraph disembark at Ridgway and move to Stevensville at 9 to 9.30 A.M. Send pilot engine to communicate with Lieut Col Dennis at Erie and with telegrams.[28]

Booker repeatedly underscored two crucial points on the next page of his statement, punctuated by penned stress lines of *x*'s: *"Move no later than 5.30–5 if bread be ready xxx Disembark at Ridgeway and march to Stevensville at 9 to 9.30* A.M. *xxxx xxxx.*" Booker then proceeded to his account of the battle itself: "The bread ration having been secured the train left Port Colborne soon after 5 A.M. en route for Stevensville ..."[29]

Two decisions made by Booker on the eve of the battle would come under scrutiny later: his 5 A.M. departure and his choice of Ridgeway as the destination from which to begin his march to Stevensville. In his defence, Booker insisted that he was acting under Peacocke's explicit orders *as explained to him* by Captain Akers. In a June 7 report Akers partly corroborated Booker's assertions, stating he had instructed Booker that "Col Peacocke was to move on Stevensville so as to arrive there about 9:30 A.M; Lieut Col [Booker] to move along the railway to Ridgeway as far as the state of the railway would permit, and march from thence to meet Col Peacocke at Stevensville."[30]

Lieutenant Colonel Peacocke objected to Akers's report after the battle. According to Peacocke, the "plan was that the force present with me at Chippawa and that at Port Colborne were to meet at Stevensville between 10 A.M. and 11 A.M. the morning of the 2nd June. There was no discretion left to any one on that point, there was no alternative plan, and I saw Captain Akers make notes which I have no doubt he still has. I told him I should start at 6 o'clock. I could not reckon on being able to start earlier, as the expected reinforcement of 900 men was not expected before half past 4, and I wished to have a margin for accidents."[31]

Five months later, when testifying at the Dennis Inquiry, Akers would change his story and assume some of the blame for Booker's timing, stating, "I had not been able to ascertain the exact time at which Col Peacocke would start from Chippawa as he told me he would be detained till the arrival of reinforcements from St. Catharines or elsewhere. As far as I could make out he would leave Chippawa about six o'clock and *I therefore imagined* [my emphasis] that he would be at Stevensville at nine to half past nine, and gave instruction to Lt. Col Booker to meet him there at that time."[32]

George Denison in his history argued that the three officers, awed by the apparent currency of their own intelligence reports, assumed Peacocke would approve their new plan and therefore did not pay attention to the details of the original plan and later were unable to recall it accurately.[33] Unless a revelatory letter or diary is discovered in an attic, this discrepancy in Peacocke's and Akers's accounts of the timing of the intended junction at Stevensville may never be resolved.

We do know that about fifteen minutes after the *Robb* left, Booker received the telegram from Peacocke ordering him to abide by his original orders and proceed to Stevensville, and Booker replied, "I will march on Stevensville as required."[34]

Booker informed his officers that Ridgeway was now the final destination for the train and that they were to march from there to join Peacocke at Stevensville. Once again, despite the significance of the precise hour at which the forces were supposed to join together at Stevensville, Booker did not elicit testimony at the inquiry from either Gillmor of the QOR or Skinner of the Thirteenth Battalion as to the timetable he communicated to them that morning.

Booker was anxious to leave Port Colborne by 5 A.M. He was wound up and eager to position his troops so that the Fenians could not outflank them. As an auctioneer and merchant, Booker was sensitive to the logistics of transporting merchandise by rail. He was an entirely modern man, confident that steam technology would give him an edge on the battlefield. No doubt he had studied its success in several crucial campaigns of the recent American Civil War. In its grasp of modern mobile warfare doctrine, Booker's thinking was very sound; it was the ambition lurking behind it that was not.

5–6 A.M. The reinforcements Peacocke had been waiting for began to arrive in Chippawa at 4:30 A.M., but now the men required breakfast. According to his report, "The volunteers being unprovided with means of carrying provisions and of cooking them, had not been able to comply with an order I had sent the previous evening that they were to bring provisions in their haversacks."[35] Something as simple as a lack of haversacks became a huge problem in moving an army. Peacocke postponed his departure by an hour to 7 A.M. and telegraphed Booker, instructing him to delay his departure by an hour as well.[36] But Booker's brigade had left for Ridgeway at 5:15.[37] Peacocke's final telegram arrived at 5:20, five minutes too late.[38]

Denison argued that if Booker had "started at the proper time he would have received the message before he left. For even to have reached Stevensville at 9:30, it was not necessary for him to leave Port Colborne until six. He was at the battle ground, three miles from Stevensville at 7:30; and if not interrupted would have reached Stevensville at 8:30, about an hour earlier than Capt. Akers mentioned, and two hours before Colonel Peacocke's time of junction. This mistake of one hour led to his not receiving the message to delay, and therefore caused him to be really three hours too soon."[39]

Booker clung to the bitter end to his claim that he was ordered to "move no later than 5.30–5 if bread be ready."[40] In his statement to the inquiry, he insisted, "During the night at my request Major Skinner endeavoured to secure a bread ration for the men. Some biscuits and bread were obtained and that officer reported to me that the baker would prepare a batch of bread to be ready at (3) three A.M.[41] ... The bread ration having been secured, the train left Port Colborne soon after 5 A.M. en route for Stevensville."[42]

Witnesses not called by Booker to testify at the inquiry had a different story to tell. According to them, when Booker arrived in Port Colborne he arrogantly demanded that the reeve supply his troops with rations. The reeve asked for an official requisition and Booker haughtily replied, "No, I think the least the municipality can do is to provide us with rations."[43] Several more diplomatically skilled officers managed to procure some bread and cheese for the men's supper that evening.

A second transport from Toronto consisting of 125 men from the

Queen's Own Rifles was expected to arrive in Port Colborne, and those men would also have to be fed. After disembarking from the ferry *Toronto* at Port Dalhousie in the evening, they were immediately loaded onto a waiting train. There was no time for dinner, nor were any rations available.[44] The train was scheduled to arrive at Port Colborne at about 4 A.M., and the men had not been fed since leaving Toronto in the afternoon of the previous day.

At about 3 A.M. an officer called on Booker about arranging breakfast for all the men. According to one report, he found Booker seated with a dish of hot beefsteak before him. Booker replied to him, "I am very tired. Go see what you can get from the reeve or anyone in the village." The unnamed officer, accompanied by the quartermaster from the QOR, went to wake up the reeve, who, standing in his window, angrily sent them away. He told them, "You got all the bread I had hours ago."[45]

The officers managed to find rations of dried crackers and salted red herring, which were distributed to some of the men. The salted herring would trigger a raging thirst in all who ate it, but only a handful of men were issued with canteens to carry water.[46] Booker was taken to task for his testimony implying that he left Port Colborne at 5 A.M. because bread had been ordered at 3 and was presumably ready by 5. As one journalist would later point out, "As there was no bread to wait for, Booker left Colborne at [5:00] A.M. Twenty minutes afterwards the telegram arrived from Col. Peacocke ordering him not to move until 7."[47] Booker was just too eager to get into action.

His departure time was one issue. Another had to do with the route he chose. According to a map prepared by George T. Denison, Booker logically should have disembarked at Sherk's Crossing, one station before Ridgeway—a shorter and more direct route to Stevensville and, as ordered by Peacocke, farthest from the Fenian threat.[48] (See Regional Map.)

Again, Peacocke's and Booker's lack of suitable maps may account for the choice of Ridgeway as the disembarkation point for the brigade, but some suspect Booker had a different motive.[49] Ridgeway was the last and closest point before Fort Erie, where Booker could disembark for a planned junction with Peacocke. It also offered the best chance of a brush with the Fenians as they moved westwards from where he believed they were camped. If Booker found himself under attack by the Fenians before he joined up with the British, he could not be blamed for disobeying his orders and engaging the enemy, and if he was victorious the glory would be his alone. There could even be a knighthood in it for him.

One commentator has recently defended Booker, arguing that Stevensville was not directly accessible from Ridgeway because of a mile-long gap in the road. The only way to cross the gap was along a track through swampy ground. "The Ridge Road was the normal route between Ridgeway and Stevensville. The actual route was north of Ridge Road, west on Bertie Road and north again on Stevensville Road (about a half mile west of Ridge Road)."[50] But maps from the period (assuming they are accurate) show that there was a finished road running from Garrison Road to Stevensville—which crossed Ridge Road south of Bertie Road.[51] Thus the shortest way to Stevensville, even from Ridgeway, would have been to turn left on Garrison Road. There was no need to continue farther north up Ridge Road to Bertie Road and the Fenians.

Booker claimed that Captain Akers explicitly told him that Peacocke wanted him to disembark and march his soldiers from Ridgeway. Peacocke contested that assertion: "The only discretion left to the officer in command was as to the road he should follow. I had no map with me giving the roads and I could not therefore give him his route. However, aware of the danger attending all combined movements, I fully explained to Capt Akers the principle on which the march from Port Colborne should be conducted, tracing lines on my map between the different points as I alluded to them, which lines are still there with the distances marked on them obtained from guides I referred to at the time. I said, 'For instance, if he has any rolling stock on the railway he could run down towards Welland and then cut across to me, or he may take a direct line to Stevensville in N.E. direction, or he may go to, or part of the way to Ridgeway by rail and then turn off' but I remember adding, 'that will depend on his obtaining information that the country is clear in that direction' over and over again."[52]

The first detachment of the QOR, 356 men who had arrived in Port Colborne with Dennis the previous day at around 1 P.M., were lucky. They got both billets and meals.[53] The men of the Thirteenth Battalion from Hamilton were a little less lucky. They had been billeted first in Dunnville and had sat down to dinner when they were ordered back on the trains to proceed to Port Colborne at around 9 P.M. When they arrived at 11 P.M. no more billets were available, nor was there much to eat. It was probably for them that some cheese was procured and the last of the bread and the notorious salted red herring. One of the volunteers expressed his frustration by pinning a herring to the side of a railway car with his bayonet.[54] The men of the Thirteenth Battalion remained all night aboard the parked train.[55] The second detachment of QOR from Toronto, which arrived last, was the least lucky. The men had not eaten since their departure the previous afternoon and had spent a restless night on the train as it rumbled toward their destination. They pulled into Port Colborne at dawn, too late for many even to partake of the herring.[56]

William Tempest, the medical school student from Toronto who had left with the first transport without his fellow volunteers of the University College Rifles and had been forced to attach himself to the Trinity College Rifles, now rejoined his own unit and his friends, who had arrived just in the nick of time.[57]

The last thing that needed to be done was to supply the men with an adequate amount of ammunition. The men of the Queen's Own Rifles, except for Company 5, arrived with only five rounds of ammunition each. Booker now issued them an additional thirty rounds from his own stores.[58]

The two chaplains, Nathanael Burwash and David Inglis, had found themselves trapped in Brantford when the trains were cancelled. They attached themselves to Lieutenant Gibson and Captain Askin from Hamilton, who were also trying to get to their battalion. At around midnight, the two officers boarded a train bound for Port Colborne that was carrying a repair crew and rolls of telegraph wire, but the chaplains were told they were not allowed to join them. Only after the churchmen bribed the repair crew with five dollars were they given a place in a boxcar sitting on the coils of cable. They arrived in Port Colborne just in time to catch the troop train about to leave for Ridgeway.[59]

A single pilot engine led the way to ensure that the Fenians had not sabotaged the railway tracks during the night. The train that followed it, consisting of nine flatcars of troops and officers and a mail car with Skinner's horse, departed for Ridgeway at 5:15 A.M.[60] Booker had 841 militia officers and men: Queen's Own Rifles (481 officers and men);[61] Thirteenth Battalion (16 officers and 249 men); Caledonia Company (4 officers and 44 men); and York Rifle Company (3 officers and 44 men).[62] There were also two Frontier Constabulary detectives, along with an unknown number of armed customs inspectors, magistrates, and local constables, a few local volunteers and auxiliaries, the two chaplains, several armed civilians, and an unidentified journalist from the Toronto *Leader* (perhaps Canada's first war correspondent), all of whom would eventually attach themselves to Booker's column.[63]

They arrived at the railway station in the small village of Ridgeway at around 6 A.M.[64]

6–7 A.M. Sam Johnston had tracked the Fenians all through the night and into the morning. He galloped into Ridgeway just as the troop train rumbled into town. He eventually found Colonel Booker and informed him that he had sighted the Fenians approaching along Ridge Road about two and a half miles northeast of the village. Booker asked if they had artillery and Johnston replied they did not. Did they have cavalry?

Johnston said they had some mounted scouts but without saddles and swords. When he was asked how many men they had, Johnston ventured there were 1,500.[65] Booker asked if there was anyone present who could identify and vouch for Johnston. Peter Learn, the Justice of the Peace in Ridgeway who knew Johnston well, stepped forward and did so. Booker then asked Learn and his son Alanson to ride up Ridge Road and scout out if there were indeed any Fenians there.[66]

Sam Johnston had seen combat in the Civil War. He had joined the Fiftieth New York Volunteer Engineer Corps "Serrell's Engineers" in Grant's Army of the Potomac. He had fought in some of the Civil War's bloodiest battles, along the Rappahannock in Virginia in 1864–65 and later with Sheridan's cavalry in the Shenandoah Valley.[67] On his way into Ridgeway, Johnston noticed a dense pine thicket big enough to give cover for a battalion, and paralleled by a rail fence overlooking Ridge Road. To his experienced eye this was ideal ground upon which to ambush the approaching Fenians, and he had no hesitation in voicing his opinion to Booker. Johnston recalled later, "I spoke to him then and used these words: 'Why not ambush them?' He wore glasses and instead of looking through them, he looked over them, with the expression, 'Are you in command or me?'"[68] Johnston said that he was dismissed by Booker and, five minutes later, loud bugle calls sounded out, for sure alerting the Fenians on the road to the column's arrival.

Peter Learn and his son rode out along Ridge Road to the Fenian lines, received some fire, and turned back.[69] But by the time they returned, the brigade would have already marched out of Ridgeway. The Learns would confirm that the Fenians were just ahead of them, but Booker chose to ignore their report as well. Booker would later claim, "I made inquiries from the inhabitants as to their knowledge of the whereabouts of the enemy. The reports were contradictory and evidently unreliable."[70]

Thomas Kilvington, a private in Company 2, Thirteenth Battalion, was convinced that Booker deliberately headed toward the Fenians: "I think he wanted to gain a little glory by defeating the Fenians by himself, so we started out on a two-mile march and bumped into them."[71]

IT IS CONCEIVABLE that Booker deliberately set his column on the route to draw Fenian fire knowing that the insurgents were waiting for him close by, for he did not send out any scouts. Booker marched his entire force in column formation right up to the Fenians, preceded only by a forty-nine-man company armed with Spencer Rifles as an advance guard. A civilian who lived on Ridge Road later stated that the volunteers piled their greatcoats on the ground outside her cottage *before* firing had broken out.[72] W.W. Wilson, who was ten at the time, said that he and another boy were paid twenty-five cents each to pile knapsacks in the yard of Zachariah Teal's general store in Ridgeway after Booker ordered his men to divest themselves of them.[73] It is highly unlikely that the troops would have been ordered to jettison their greatcoats and knapsacks if they thought they were marching directly to Stevensville to join Peacocke's column.

Booker must have been anticipating going into battle *before* joining with Lieutenant Colonel Peacocke's column. It was common practice to unload packs and personal equipment in anticipation of a battle. Indeed, it was a source of anxiety for troops, especially for those on long campaigns who knew that if the battle did not go as planned they might not have an opportunity to collect their belongings again. Booker was obviously counting on a fight taking place near Ridgeway, where, after their presumed victory over the Fenians, his troops could pick up their coats and knapsacks at their leisure.

The brigade spent about an hour in Ridgeway, noisily detraining, unloading their supplies, and forming up for their march. When he failed to find any villager willing to volunteer a horse and wagon at his service, Booker foolishly ordered the remaining spare ammunition to be put on the train and sent back to Port Colborne with Larmour—another fatal error.[74] In the end, the Queen's Own Rifles, with the exception of the Spencer-armed Company 5, went into battle with thirty-five rounds each, while the other units had sixty.[75] Sergeant John Stoneman, the quartermaster, eventually did procure a wagon, but the ammunition had already left with the train. The wagon would trail the marching column, transporting a few scarce medical supplies (but no litters) and the two chaplains, David Inglis and Nathanael Burwash.[76]

The Queen's Own Rifles had had a surgeon and assistant surgeon appointed to the regiment a week before the battle: Dr. James Thorburn and Dr. Samuel P. May, respectively.[77] The Thirteenth Battalion was accompanied by its surgeon, Dr. Isaac Ryall, who carried a small medical bag with his father's surgical tools.[78] There were also an unspecified number of soldiers detailed as medical orderlies.[79]

Already at 7 A.M. it was clearly going to be a hot day. If any one thing stands out in the recollections of nearly all who fought on Limestone Ridge, it is how hot it was and how thirsty they all were. Stoneman recalled, "The day promised to become a scorcher. The soldiers wearing their greatcoats rolled, and in heavy scarlet tunics, made particularly for cold weather, panted and perspired and thirsted too. The heavy black shakoes were warm and uncomfortable."[80] (A shako is a felt-, leather-, and cardboard-lined headgear.)

Stoneman suggested that those men who had water bottles or canteens be allowed to fill them from the pumps at the station, but the officers overruled him. More than eight hundred men had to be mustered into columns in marching order along a narrow road and there was no time for each to go off for water. Stoneman then suggested that the men at least toss their heavy wool winter tunics into the wagon. He was overruled again for the same reason.[81] Thomas Kilvington recalled, "We had no supper or dinner the day before. And they wouldn't let us drink out of the streams, so we had no water. Anyway, we had no water bottles, and we had no medical supplies."[82]

Like many Canadians, Dr. N. Brewster, the village physician in Ridgeway, had served three years in the U.S. Army during the Civil

War. Upon learning that some of the troops had not eaten since the day before, he rallied some of the townspeople to bring food to the soldiers. Dr. Brewster would indignantly recall in 1911, "I never learned who was in fault, but surely someone blundered, that men were sent into battle without food in this part of the country."[83]

7 A.M. When Booker mounted Skinner's horse, he must have felt as if he were seated at destiny's gate. Eight hundred men were formed up in columns, steady and quiet, all their attention focused on him. Booker was at that moment, as one journalist later described him, "what he delighted to be, the observed of all observers."[84] Booker uttered his first battle command: "With ball cartridge—load!"[85]

Over half of the troops were under the age of twenty, some as young as fifteen.[86] Hearing this order as it resonated down the column was vividly remembered by many as a visceral moment of comprehension and dread.[87] With the loading of live ammunition, the seriousness of the thing upon which they were embarking was driven home to many for the first time. Half of them had never even practised firing with blank cartridges, let alone with live ammunition. Now they were expected to perform the highly complex and precise procedure of loading their weapons, and soon they would have to do it while under enemy fire.[88]

The Canadians carried a British Long Enfield 1853 pattern muzzle-loading percussion rifled-musket, weighing 9 lbs. 3 oz. with the bayonet or 8 lbs. 14 ¼ oz. without.[89] They loaded their weapons in seventeen precisely drilled stages, using paper cartridges that contained 65 grains of gunpowder and a huge thumb tip–sized 535 grain (about an ounce) .577-calibre lead bullet (or "ball," as it was still called). Biting open the gunpowder end of the paper cartridge (being toothless exempted one from military service), they carefully emptied the powder down the muzzle of their rifles, followed by the paper and then the bullet or sometimes the bullet still wrapped in the greased paper. They next drew a ramrod from its housing beneath the barrel of their rifle, and holding it gingerly between their thumb and forefinger, they carefully but firmly tamped down the paper and bullet on top of the powder charge. Then they would load a mercury-fulminate firing cap into a nipple beneath the hammer of the rifle lock.[90]

The Long Enfield rifle was 4 feet 7 inches in length—approximately chest-high to a soldier of average height in that period. It could not be reloaded on the move; the rifleman had to stand still. Nor could it be easily reloaded while the rifleman was lying down for cover; he had to stand up or at best kneel at an awkward angle to pour the powder down the muzzle. Reloading exposed the rifleman to enemy fire unless he was safely positioned behind cover, another reason why defenders would have tried their best to choose ground offering very little cover for an attacker.

A few exceptionally cool and super-skilled infantrymen were capable of cycling through this procedure as quickly as five times a minute—a shot and reload every twelve seconds.[91] Most, however, were considerably slower. Three shots a minute was considered optimal. A single missed stage or a break in the seventeen-step loading order could result in catastrophe. In the heat of battle soldiers were reported to have overloaded their rifles with several bullets, or to have forgotten to remove the ramrod from the barrel before firing it, a mistake so common that all veterans of Civil War combat were familiar with the strange "whizzing" sound of a fired ramrod in flight. Once the ramrod was lost, the weapon could not be reloaded.

Rifles often failed to fire: The average misfire rate for the percussion caps was sometimes as high as 25 percent. Improper loading accounted for another 9 percent of failures. And then there were accidents. For example, after being fired repeatedly, the barrel would get so hot that powder would flash as it was poured down the muzzle, rendering the rifle unusable until it cooled.[92]

Few of the Canadian volunteers had the training to handle their weapons competently. The Military Board of Inquiry later concluded that "a large proportion of the force had been for a very short time accustomed to bear arms; that a somewhat less proportion had not even been exercised with blank cartridge, and that practice with ball cartridge was by very many of the rank and File of that force to be entered upon for the first time in their lives on that day."[93]

Somewhat bizarrely, in the Canadian Volunteer Militia under British tutelage, the poorer a unit's performance during inspection, the lower its allotment of blank and ball ammunition to practise with. The "Requisition for Ammunition for Practice and Exercise" forms in Canada Archives from 1865 are rife with written comments from British army inspectors, such as "Inefficient in drill, recommend half the issue of the ammunition required by the company; Efficiency uncertain, no further allowance recommended at present; Recommend half the amount of ammunition required by this company: company very backward in drill; This company had improved very much lately in my opinion: 3 kegs of ball and the full allowance of blank should be issued at once."[94] Many of these forms were signed by Lieutenant Colonel Charles C. Villiers, the same bright officer who ordered that the Welland Canal Field Battery's guns be taken away and moved to Hamilton.[95]

It should be noted, however, that the use of live ammunition in training, in the form of "target practice," was an alien notion in that period. Military doctrine still called for coordinated massing of collective fire at close range as opposed to selective individual marksmanship at long range. Blank rounds were used in drilling the troops to quickly load and fire their weapons on command, and occasionally "ball" cartridges were used to give them the full experience of live fire. Individual "target practice" was a low priority, although the militia did sponsor off-duty marksmanship competitions.

The forty-nine men of QOR Company 5 who were armed with the state-of-the-art U.S.-made Spencer "repeating" rifles (nine short carbine versions and forty longer "Army" models) did not have to concern themselves with this complex loading procedure.[96] The Spencer fired seven self-contained brass cylinder cartridge bullets (similar to the modern bullet of today), which were inserted into a tubular magazine through the butt of the rifle while a lever below the trigger would advance a new bullet after every shot.

As both a breech-loader and a repeater, the Spencer Rifle was two generations ahead of the single-shot muzzleloaders almost everybody else carried that day—including the Fenians. The Spencer had a controversial recent history: It had been introduced into the U.S. Army only after Abraham Lincoln intervened personally to dismiss the sixty-six-year-old Chief of Ordinance Brigadier General James Ripley, nicknamed "Ripley Van Winkle" for his alleged intransigence to new technology. Ripley adhered to a school of military doctrine that opposed repeaters because they were thought to encourage troops to fire off their expensive ammunition too rapidly, increasing the volume of ammunition needed to be purchased, as well as increasing the cost of its transport (not only was there more of it, but also the metal cartridges were heavier than the old ball and paper cartridges). Repeaters also added weight to an individual infantryman's load on a battlefield, especially if he now needed to carry more ammo than usual. It was thought also that the habit of rapid fire further degraded the already discounted marksmanship of the average American soldier.[97]

Spencers were first used in battle on June 4, 1863, by Colonel Thomas John Wilder's brigade near Liberty, Tennessee. Wilder had bought a shipment at his own expense and deployed the weapons against the Confederate First Kentucky Cavalry. The rattled Confederates surrendered, commenting, "What kind of *Hell-fired* guns your men got?"[98] Soon the stories spread and Lincoln invited the weapon's designer, thirty-one-year-old Connecticut-born Christopher Spencer, to demonstrate the weapon for him in Washington. Lincoln and Spencer cheerfully blasted away with the rifle on a range at Treasury Park, and Ripley's fate was sealed.

As Ripley warned, there were problems with fire control when a limited number of Spencers were issued to troops. Soldiers had to be weaned off their initial propensity to exhaust their precious ammunition in a "mad minute." A year later at Gettysburg, where the casualty rates were as high as 20 percent, a highly disciplined veteran unit armed with repeaters was reported to have fired an average of thirty-two carefully aimed rounds per man over the course of the three-day battle.[99] That was the kind of firing discipline required of an infantryman armed with a Spencer.

There was another problem with the Spencer. According to a report later filed by Captain John Edwards, the officer who led Company 5 at Ridgeway, the complex repeater mechanism had a serious defect. If it misfired or jammed, it could not be loaded manually as a single-shot weapon through its breech, because when open, the breech was blocked by its extractor mechanism for the fired cartridge. To clear a misfired or jammed round required that the user be intimately familiar with the Spencer's delicate spring-loaded feeding mechanism, which had to be drawn out of its housing in the rifle butt and cleared from that end. The problem was compounded for the Canadians by the old surplus Civil War ammunition purchased for the rifle by the Militia Department. Rounds frequently fell short of their specified ranges or failed to fire at all. A militia staff officer commented on Edwards's report, "From personal observation, I know that the cartridges were hastily and carelessly made during the continuance of the American War."[100]

This sophisticated weapon was thrust into the hands of the men for the first time in their lives on the morning of June 1: "Most of them had never seen one before."[101] While they could now crank out seven shots in ten seconds, five times the rate of the most skilled soldier armed with a muzzleloader, what should have been an advantage became a disadvantage when they were issued only twenty-eight rounds of ammunition (four packages of seven rounds). Making matters worse, since the men were armed with state-of-the-art rifles, Booker decided that Company 5 should form the advance guard of the column.

FOR APPROXIMATELY FIVE CENTURIES following gunpowder's arrival in Europe from China, smoothbore muskets were basically inefficient weapons with which it was difficult to hit anything beyond one hundred yards. Defending troops were drilled to hold their ground and fire coordinated volleys at close range on command. Attacking troops were drilled to *take* fire while advancing to within short range of the defenders, unleashing a volley into the enemy ranks, and then launching a bayonet attack or sometimes just clubbing their enemy caveman style with their discharged muskets.

By the mid-1850s modern armies had replaced the smoothbore musket with one that had a series of twisting grooves incised inside the barrel called "rifling," thus the terms "rifled musket" or "rifle." These grooves would grip, spin, and guide the bullet (like a spinning American football) along the barrel with increased stability, accuracy, and a range four to five times that of the wobbly smoothbore ball. The increased range of the rifle had a profound effect on the front-line soldier. Against the smoothbore, an infantryman only needed to survive a one-hundred-yard dash through its optimum kill range, where the smoothbore was 80 percent accurate. But at two hundred yards the smoothbore's accuracy dropped to 65 percent, with almost one in every three shots missed. The rifle, on the other hand, easily doubled the 80 percent accuracy to a range of two hundred yards, while at one hundred yards it was tested at 100 percent accuracy—it was almost impossible to miss. And the *effective range* of the rifle was three to five times that of the smoothbore—five hundred yards—with *maximum ranges* approaching 1,200 yards, where the .57-calibre slug still could slam clean through two inches of pine board.

Armies did not easily adapt their tactics to the new rifles. Men were still drilled to advance in close-order ranks, touching elbow to elbow to guide their formation, bent forward as if advancing into a driving snowstorm, marching into volleys of massed concentrated fire. Now though, instead of having to survive the final one-hundred-yard charge, they had to advance through some five hundred yards of moderately effective fire, and charge the last two hundred yards through deadly accurate fire.[102] The best solution the U.S. Army could come up with in its new manuals on the eve of the Civil War was for troops to run faster, take bigger steps, and "breathe as much as possible through the nose, keeping the mouth closed. Experience has proved that, by conforming to this principle, a man can pass over a much longer distance, and with less fatigue."[103]

Defenders now had an unprecedented advantage. They basically had only to stand their ground, sheltered behind constructed breastworks, bullet screens, stone walls, or other improvised fortifications, exposing themselves only briefly to fire at attackers before ducking to reload. The attackers, on the other hand, advancing along open ground carefully chosen by the defenders, had to reload while exposed to enemy fire. At Cold Harbor in Virginia in 1864, ten thousand troops fell in *twenty minutes* in circumstances like these.

The Fenians were intimately acquainted with the catastrophic conditions of the Civil War battlefield; they were more than just veterans—they were survivors. Unlike the untested Canadian boys fearful for their reputations, the Fenian veterans had seen what happens on the battlefield; they were more concerned for their life and limb than for their pride. That is why the first things the Fenians seized upon landing in Canada were axes and saws, which they used to pull down fences and construct barricades. They built bullet screens as a matter of routine. They did so on the first day at Frenchman's Creek and then at Black Creek and now this morning along Bertie Road cutting across Ridge Road, facing Booker's advancing column. The Fenians suffered from no romantic illusions about battlefield glory and had no compunction about ducking under fire.

The amateur officers leading the Canadians had a theoretical understanding of the deadly new technology. The British had used the rifled barrel in Crimea in the 1850s and observed its effects in the Civil War.

But that was nowhere near the same as having *been* there. And as far as the volunteer rank and file, few had even an inkling of what the rifle was capable of, but they were about to find out.

7:25 A.M. At around 7 A.M., as if on parade, the Thirteenth Battalion unfurled its regimental colours—two flags borne by Ensigns Armstrong and Baker. Journalist Alexander Somerville, a former English mercenary who had fought in Spain, later sneered, "The Q.O. [R.] had no flag. And here, I repeat, that commanders of experience will not take flags into a wooded country upon a desultory campaign of bush fighting."[104]

With a bugle call, Booker's column with the colour party in the centre began its march up Ridge Road, ostensibly headed to Stevensville but actually marching straight toward the waiting Fenians.[105] Many of the villagers from Ridgeway followed the troops along the road as if on a holiday outing.[106]

From the Ridgeway railway station the column had approximately 1.4 miles to march northeast up Ridge Road to the intersection of Garrison Road.[107] At this intersection, if Booker had wanted to take the shortest route to Stevensville from Ridgeway, he would have turned west (left) onto Garrison Road, marched a little over a half mile, and then turned north (right) to go straight into Stevensville about three miles away. The longer Booker clung to Ridge Road, the farther it took him *away* from Stevensville and the closer to the waiting Fenians.

Booker arranged the column moving up Ridge Road in the following order: Captain Edwards leading QOR Company 5 as the advance guard; the rest of the QOR under the command of Major Gillmor and the York Rifles under Captain Davis in their support; the Thirteenth Battalion in reserve; and the Caledonia Company under Captain Jackson deployed in the rearguard of the marching column.[108] It has been assumed that Major Skinner was in command of the Thirteenth Battalion, but one source convincingly argues that Booker kept direct command of both the brigade and the battalion.[109] Booker rode in the centre of the column with the colour party acting as a visual point of reference for all the units in the field. Fifteen-year-old George C. Carlisle was one of the several bugle boys who would signal Booker's commands. Accompanying Booker was Major Gillmor, his brigade second-in-command who commanded in the field his own battalion of the QOR.[110]

Twenty-one-year-old Lance Corporal William Ellis, a chemistry student in QOR Company 9, "University Rifles," recalled later that as they approached the Fenian lines it seemed as though they were on a holiday stroll through the country: "It was a beautiful day—the trees were clothed with the tender, delicate foliage of early summer, and the fields were green with young crops."[111]

The column first spotted the Fenians at approximately 7:25 A.M.[112]

7:30 A.M. One remaining aspect of the timing of events remains to be dealt with. Lieutenant Colonel Peacocke in Chippawa had delayed his scheduled 6 A.M. departure for Stevensville to 7 A.M. He telegraphed Booker, ordering him to adjust his departure from Port Colborne by an hour accordingly. But the telegram did not arrive in Port Colborne until 5:20 A.M.—five minutes after Booker's train had left for Ridgeway.[113]

Captain McGrath, the general manager of the Welland line in Port Colborne, immediately recognized the significance of the message, and accompanied by another railway employee, Mr. Stovin, went off on a handcar toward Ridgeway with the message. About halfway there, they encountered Larmour's train on the way back from Ridgeway. McGrath returned with the train but ordered Stovin to continue on to Ridgeway on the handcar and deliver the message to Booker. He told him to carefully note the time of its delivery.[114]

Some sources insist that the message was delivered to Booker at 7:30 A.M., just as the battle was beginning. According to one source, Booker upon reading the message asked Frontier Detective Armstrong to ride out and deliver a reply to Peacocke. Booker said, "Tell him how I am situated."

Armstrong replied, "You must write it."

Booker began fumbling about in his pockets only to discover that he had neither paper nor pencil, and he told Armstrong again, "Tell him that." Armstrong again insisted that Booker's reply be put in writing. At this point a civilian by the name of Lawson offered Booker some paper and a pencil, although Armstrong would claim he offered the paper. Apparently Booker asked what time it was, and all three—Stovin, Lawson, and Armstrong—said "7:30." Armstrong, claiming to have seen the message, is quoted as stating that "7:30" was the only legible part of Booker's reply.[115]

Alfred Booker, however, later claimed that he did not get Peacocke's telegram until two hours later—at 9:30 A.M., when the battle was nearly over—and that he had written in his response "7:30" as the hour he had been attacked, and not as the time he had received the message.[116]

Lieutenant Colonel Peacocke disputed Booker's assertion, saying, "At about 11 o'clock, I received a few words from Lieut Col Booker written at 7.30 o'clock to the effect that he had *just received my telegram* [my emphasis], but that he was attacked in force by the enemy at a place 3 miles south of Stevensville."[117]

A month later Booker contradicted the story that he had had to be handed blank paper: "I wrote on the telegram I had just received, to the effect that the enemy had attacked us in force at 7:30 ..."[118] If we believe Booker, then it is marginally plausible, especially with Armstrong's claiming that Booker's scrawl was illegible except for the hour 7:30, that Peacocke was mistaken about what "7:30" referred to, confusing the hour of the reception of his telegraph by Booker with the hour he reported the attack had begun.

And there we are stuck. If Booker learned at 7:30 that Peacocke would be delayed by an hour, then his subsequent advance on the Fenians in full knowledge that there would be no support from Peacocke was reckless and irresponsible. If, however, he received the message only at 9:30, two hours into the battle as he claimed, then Booker is absolved and more of the blame begins to shift toward Peacocke.

There is certainly an inordinate time lag between the exchange of messages: Peacocke's 5:20 telegram took either two or four hours (7:30 or 9:30) to be delivered to Booker, depending upon whose version we believe. Similarly, Booker's response also took one and a half to three and a half hours to reach Peacocke (between ten and eleven o'clock),[119] again depending upon whom we believe. The message from Peacocke, we know, was taken in a handcar from Port Colborne up the railway line in pursuit of Booker. Did it take until 9:30 to be delivered on the field? Considering that there was a battle under way, perhaps. But if Booker received and responded to the message at 9:30, as he claims, then it took only ninety minutes, until 11 A.M., for Booker's response to be delivered by Armstrong on horseback all the way to Peacocke on his march from Chippawa—an unlikely scenario, as Armstrong would have had to ride a huge circle around the battle to reach him.

Then there is the question of whether, as reported, Booker had to ask somebody for a piece of paper to write his response or whether, as Booker claims, he wrote the response directly on the telegram he was handed. According to the journalist Somerville, Stovin told him later, "'It seems a strange thing to me that he sent away the telegram he had received; and still more so that after Armstrong was gone, he enquired of me where that telegram came from. He had not read Chippawa.' Squire Learn said of Booker then: 'If they have not got a fool for a commander, he is something worse.'"[120]

The original telegram sent by Peacocke and returned to him with Booker's scrawled response was never entered into evidence at the inquiry and has never surfaced since. Booker did not call any witnesses to testify as to the arrival time of the message, nor did he pose the question to Major Gillmor, to whom Booker claimed he showed the message upon its arrival at 9:30. In the end, Booker called no one to testify in his defence as to the hour the telegram from Peacocke was actually delivered.

In the histories of the battle published in 1866, Alexander Somerville and George T. Denison both concluded that Booker had received the telegram at 7:30 A.M., thereby condemning him, while Captain John A. Macdonald (no relation to the prime minister) in his 1910 history took Booker's word that it was at 9:30 A.M. This was also the conclusion of the Booker Inquiry, paradoxically chaired by George Denison.[121] The most equitable distribution of time between the delivery of the message from Port Colborne to Booker at Ridgeway, and then back to Peacocke on his march toward Stevensville, suggests that Booker did indeed receive the message at 7:30, when he still had time to disengage from the Fenians. Instead Booker ordered his men into battle.

SEVEN

Limestone Ridge, Morning, June 2, 1866

The battle began at 7:30 A.M., unfolding in the fields, orchards, copses, and woods flanking both sides of Ridge Road between Garrison Road on the south and Bertie Road 850 yards to the north.[1] (Bertie Road was then known as "the concession road" or "Split Rock Road.") From Garrison Road to Bertie Road, the terrain was intersected by five snake-rail fences delineating property lines. These fences presented a dangerous obstacle to the advancing Canadians while providing cover for the defending Fenians. The first lines of Fenian skirmishers were positioned on the south end of the battlefield inside a fence that ran along Garrison Road. Here on both sides of Ridge Road were open cultivated fields of young wheat, rye, and grass intersected by the fences, some of which were paralleled by a single file of excoriated trees, leafless and of dismal aspect.[2] A second line of Fenians was waiting in the north half of the battlefield, behind more fences and in several small apple tree orchards and groves of maple trees. Northward from Garrison Road the land sloped downward until about halfway to Bertie Road, where its slope turned upward again. The Canadians would have to fight their way down into a subtly depressed cauldron in the middle of the field before fighting their way upward. At the north end of the high ground, along Bertie Street, east of Ridge Road, the Fenians disassembled rail fences and constructed improvised slanting bullet screens as they had at Frenchman's Creek. (See Terrain Map.)

The terrain would have given the Fenians a distinct high-ground advantage over the Canadians pushing their way up from the south in any event, but the forested Limestone Ridge to the east of the road made the battlefield especially advantageous for the defenders. The ridge, a gentle slope almost indiscernible to the naked eye, rose approximately 50 feet parallel to the road about 150 to 200 yards on the right (east) of the fields across which the Canadians were advancing. Fenian troops took positions on top of this ridge, transforming Ridge Road and the fields on its east side into a crescent-shaped killing ground.[3]

While O'Neill himself would later claim he had six hundred men at the battle, it is likely he was understating his strength in the face of the Canadian force. Estimates of Fenian size based on their strength as reported at Frenchman's Creek often do not take into account the advance party of Fenians at Black Creek, who reunited with O'Neill's main army on their forced march to Limestone Ridge. The Fenian strength was closer to eight hundred men—approximately equal in size to the Canadian force advancing upon them. O'Neill himself reported in a message to Buffalo the night before the battle that he had 1,000 men, of whom he estimated only 750 to be fit for battle.[4]

The two hundred Ohio Fenians of the Eighteenth Regiment "Cleveland Rangers" and Nineteenth Regiment "Cincinnati Irish Republic Volunteers" under Lieutenant Colonel John Grace, a twenty-eight-year-old former captain in the 34th U.S. Ohio Volunteer Infantry, took up positions behind the hastily constructed fieldworks on the eastern flank of the battlefield along Bertie Street; while the one hundred men from the Buffalo Seventh Regiment under John Hoy took up positions in the open field on the western side of Ridge Road on the left flank of the Canadians.* In the centre behind them, approximately two to three hundred yards farther north of Bertie Street, O'Neill made his headquarters. Here he deployed the main Fenian force of about five hundred men, consisting of his own Thirteenth Regiment of Nashville, plus Fenians from Memphis, Tennessee, Terre Haute, Indiana, and New Orleans ("Louisiana Tigers"). The Seventeenth Fenian Regiment of Louisville, Kentucky, led by Lieutenant Colonel George Owen Starr, spread out along the crest of the tree-covered ridgeline and deployed skirmishers and scouts below to the southern bottom of the field near the Garrison Road fence.[5] From Garrison Road to the barricades on Bertie Street, the battlefield was approximately 850 yards in length—with O'Neill's main forces hanging back in the centre a further 200 to 300 yards north of that.[6] (See Fenian Positions Map.)

THE FENIAN SKIRMISHERS opened fire from behind the first fence along Garrison Road as the Canadians approached from the south along Ridge Road. The Fenians then quickly drew back behind the third fence and into the apple orchard as the Canadians scrambled over the fences, advancing across the open fields. Booker climbed down from the horse he was riding[7] and his orderly took charge of it.[8] He would remain dismounted for the remainder of the battle, with the consequent loss of mobility and a higher vantage point. (In theory, field officers in that era were expected to remain on their horses, despite the recent increase in musket range, but in practice nobody in their right mind begrudged his decision not to present himself as so obvious a target.)

Booker deployed the Queen's Own Rifles and the York Rifles in extended skirmishing lines across Garrison Road and into the fields

---

* It is unclear whether or not the Fenians built barricades along Bertie Road west of Ridge Road—there might have been a natural line of trees or a hillock screening their position.

ahead of them while keeping the Thirteenth Battalion and Caledonia Company in reserve, advancing cautiously in column formation up the centre along the road. It was a textbook deployment. The infantry companies could now be fed toward the front of the column, where they would be ordered as needed to extend in line out to the left or right or continue advancing up the centre on the road. (See Battle Map 1.)

The QOR were deployed to the front as follows: On the left (west) of the road, Company 1, backed by Company 4, swept west along Garrison Road before doubling back across the field to Ridge Road and taking positions on the right (east) side of it. Company 7, Educational Department, and Company 8, Trinity College Rifles (only a section, about twenty boys), remained on the far left (west) to wheel and advance through open ploughed fields.[9] The York Rifles were also deployed to the left in support of Company 8, Trinity College Rifles, which remained on the left throughout the battle.

On the right (east) side, the advance guard of Company 5 with Spencer Rifles led the attack, with Company 3 behind them and Company 2 to their rear right, backed by Company 6. They were soon joined by companies 1 and 4 returning from the left fields.[10] Eventually Company 7 was swung around from the left flank to the far right, coming near the rear of Company 5.[11]

At the centre, Company 9, University College Rifles, and Company 10, Highland Rifles, were held in reserve at first, followed by the Thirteenth Battalion and the Caledonia Company advancing along the road in column.[12] Later, companies 9 and 10 were deployed to skirmish on the right, then withdrawn to the rear, and then redeployed again to clear the ridge on the far right. That approximately was the movement of the troops in the first thirty to forty minutes of the battle.

Private A.G. Gilbert of Company 7 described what it meant to fight through terrain like that: "From their position they could see us long before we came up to them, as we had to march up to them over clean fields, and as little protected as the Cricket Field in Peterboro'. Another feature in their position was the fact that they arranged so that we had nothing but fences to go over from the beginning to the end, and well did they pepper us when climbing over. I have been told since that they raised the fences, in the direction our attack was made from, three rails each. At any rate, everyone noticed the extraordinary height of the fences, and you can imagine with sixty rounds of ammunition in our pouches, a bayonet hanging by your side, and a rifle loaded, capped and full cocked to take over those fences, was no little thing, and very tiresome work, but it had to be done, and we knocked down some rails, got through some, and climbed over others. This might on other occasions be not much, but exposed to a heavy fire from our active enemy, it is quite another thing."[13]

The Fenians were a dauntingly elusive enemy for the Canadians. Private McIntosh was acutely aware of the skill and wartime experience of the enemy: "It was easy to see that most of them were old soldiers of the American army by their perfect formation and the position they had taken up."[14] Private Thomas Kilvington, Thirteenth Battalion, was frustrated by not being able to take aim at the enemy: "Their breastworks were built of fence rails, sloping from the ground and banked with sods. The Fenians were cowards. They did not expose themselves long enough to take a good aim. We saw their heads behind the defences ducking up and down, and all their shots were going high."[15]

One of the Fenian officers, Captain John S. Mullen, a veteran who had been wounded in the battle of Missionary Ridge in Tennessee, recalled of the Canadians, "To most of us, who had been in the war, it was plain that fighting was new to them. They exposed themselves unnecessarily, which trained men never do. About all they could see of us was a line of flags, about the biggest display of green flags I ever saw, each with a sunburst on it, no harps."[16]

THE AMMUNITION the two sides unleashed on each other that day was a particularly nasty piece of ordnance. The Fenians' muskets fired a thumb-tip–sized .58-calibre 510-grain (one ounce) "Minié ball" (or "mini-ball," as it was pronounced by Americans). It was almost identical in weight to the large .577 ammunition carried by the Canadians.[17] Adopted by most modern armies by the mid-1850s, the Minié ball (which was not actually a ball but bullet shaped) was named for its designer, the French army captain Claude-Étienne Minié, who was seeking to solve a particular problem created by the introduction of rifled barrels. In order for the rifling to work, a ball had to fit tightly against the walls of the barrel, but it was difficult to insert this tight-fitting ammo down the muzzle when loading. The ball had to be literally hammered down the barrel, a time-consuming procedure unsuited for combat. To solve this problem, Minié designed the now-familiar lead cylindro-conoidal bullet with one major difference: It was hollowed out at its base. The hollow was key to producing a bullet that was marginally smaller than the diameter of the barrel and thus easily inserted down the muzzle. When the rifle was fired, gas from the discharge would fill the hollow base of the soft lead projectile and expand it, forcing it outwards tight against the twisting grooves of the barrel, which could now grip and guide it on its explosive path with increased range, power, and accuracy.[18]

There was an unintended side effect. When the hollow-based bullet hit something, it flattened out, or "mushroomed," into a jagged heavy-metal lump. The effect on the human body was devastating. The flattened slug left fist-sized exit wounds. A mere clip by the bullet across the top of the skull—a so-called "keyhole" wound—fragmented the bone and took half the skull away with it.[19] On impact, a flattened Minié ball shattered bone into a pink mist of tiny irreparable shards and splinters. Traces of rotting animal fat with which cartridges were greased were carried by the projectile into wounds, infecting them.

Amputation was the only known treatment for these kinds of wounds—preferably in the first twenty-four hours *before* infection set in. In 1866, medical science had not yet identified bacteria as the source of infection and therefore there was no theory of antisepsis. Surgical tools and operating surfaces were not routinely cleaned between amputations, water was not changed, and dressings were sometimes reused. "Laudable pus" was thought to be the lining of dead tissue expelled in a healing process and was encouraged to fester.[20] Infection and disease were believed to be caused by a bad smell—"effluvias" or "miasma"—and the only antiseptic measures taken consisted of opening windows to waft the smell away. In the American Civil War, soldiers had a better chance of surviving enemy fire than the care of their own surgeons.

At the end of the nineteenth century, international law prohibited the use in warfare of soft-nosed hollow point or any "bullets which expand or flatten easily in the human body."[21] The prohibition is in force to this day, when ostensibly only "clean" full metal-jacket, non-expanding, non-explosive types of small arms ammunition is permitted on the modern battlefield. But at Ridgeway in 1866, both sides viciously peppered each other with this ultra-lethal ammunition.

In Civil War photographs of casualties, one can occasionally see a corpse whose clothing is in a state of disarray, as if somebody had been going through his pockets. In fact the dying men did this to themselves as they tore away at their clothes to see if they had been "gut-shot."[22] Every soldier knew that after an initial minute of numbness, there was no more sure or painful way to die than to be shot through the abdomen or stomach. It was every soldier's worse nightmare.

WHEN THE FENIANS OPENED FIRE, the advance party of QOR Company 5 took the first volleys. The fifteen-year-old Fred McCallum recalled: "Suddenly while we were on rather high ground, in the middle of a wheat field, the Fenians opened fire on us. With this baptism we doubled up to the cover of a snake fence, and there we opened fire. Our officer told us to sight our rifles at 600 yards. Here the first casualty occurred."[23]

Private McIntosh wrote: "I remember there were several fields of long grass all wet with dew and several fences we had to jump before we got within range. At the last fence we were afraid they would open fire on us while jumping the fence but there being a little rise in the ground where the fence stood we all lay down and opened fire. It was here that Ensign McEachren fell—I believe the first. He was using a rifle and was a good shot, he got up on his knees to pull a rail out of the fence to get a better sight and was shot through the body."[24]

Thirty-five-year-old Ensign Malcolm McEachren, the Sunday school teacher and a recent convert to the Wesleyan Methodists, had led his section up to the fence. He took a direct hit through his abdomen. McEachren cried out, "I am shot!" and then slumped to the ground on a broad flat stone near the fence.[25]

Captain J. Edwards at first decided it was too dangerous to move the wounded McEachren under fire and called out, "Surgeons to the front."[26] The battalion assistant surgeon, Dr. Samuel P. May of QOR Company 7, ran forward to the skirmish line, waving his hat and sword and then throwing it down as a signal to the Fenians that he was a non-combatant.[27] But firing continued unabated, the Fenians probably not having seen the doctor's signal.[28]

McEachren's sword and belt were removed from his body and laid against a corner of the fence.[29] After examining the wound, Dr. May ordered McEachren to be carried to a nearby cabin on the other side of Ridge Road. Seventeen-year-old George A. Mackenzie and his company of Thirteenth Battalion soldiers were formed up in reserve on the road, nervously waiting to be deployed, when Captain Edwards and several QOR soldiers rushed toward them bearing McEachren off the field. As they passed, one of the waiting soldiers crumpled and fainted after catching sight of the gaping wound in McEachren's stomach.[30] They were only ten minutes into the battle.

Captain Edwards, tears streaming from his eyes, asked the two chaplains, David Inglis and Nathanael Burwash, to attend to the dying ensign inside the cabin.[31] McEachren, who remained conscious, dictated to Edwards a farewell message to his wife, Margaret. Inglis later wrote in a letter to the *Globe,* "Dr. May was in attendance, but a glance at the wound shewed that it was mortal, and it fell to me to inform him of that fact. He received the intelligence as a Christian soldier, informing me that his faith rested in the Lord Jesus Christ."[32]

Fred McCallum, who helped carry McEachren off the field, heard the Wesleyan ensign utter his last words: "Jesus, I have often dreamt of dying thus."[33] Burwash would write in a letter a week later that when the dying McEachren discovered that Burwash was a Methodist minister, he "threw his cold arms, all blood, around my neck" and whispered, "Pray that I may have brighter evidence."[34]

For the young Wesleyan minister who had been at a crossroads in his faith, it was a seminal moment of assurance as to the possibility of vital religious experience. For the rest of his life, in lessons and sermons, Nathanael Burwash would frequently refer to the "witness of the Spirit" and the necessity for its conscious acuity as he had experienced it while tending to the dying McEachren on Limestone Ridge.[35]

Malcolm McEachren died twenty minutes after being shot.[36]

While technically the Canadian militia was still a British colonial force, and would remain so for another twelve months, in reality it had developed into an indigenous modern national military since the Militia Act of 1855. It was administrated, led, and manned by Canadians, now only awaiting the stamp of Confederation and the inevitable departure of the British army. Ensign Malcolm McEachren is the modern Canadian army's first soldier and officer to be killed in action.[37]

THE CANADIANS FOUGHT that day for approximately two hours, advancing up Ridge Road, along the open fields flanking it, and through the forested ridge on their right. The column of companies pushing up the road were deployed one by one into skirmishing order, some holding the centre while others were sent off into the fields to relieve the first line of companies. The combatants' reminiscences of the battle are contradictory and distorted by the heat of action and by the distance that separated them from other units. They often did not see each other and did not know what was happening on other parts of the battlefield. One thing, however, is patently clear. The Canadians were moving forward, and their steady advance gave them the impression that they had the Fenians on the run.

But the Canadians had been fighting only the Fenian skirmishers at their first line of defence behind the barricades on Bertie Road. They had not yet encountered the main battle group, consisting of approximately five hundred men, waiting patiently about three hundred yards north of Bertie Road. The Fenians were not retreating but rather luring the Canadians into effective range. The Fenians were fighting the way they had fought in the Civil War, drawing their enemy forward across open ground that they had first chosen and prepared.

Company 5, after losing Ensign McEachren, began to return fire with their Spencers. The inexperienced riflemen fired off their meagre twenty-eight rounds of defective ammunition in about five or ten minutes.[38] Now Company 5 needed covering fire under which to retire for more ammunition (had there been any) while another unit advanced into their place.

The battle began to break apart into four distinct sectors: the farm fields on the left side of the road, the road itself in the centre, the fenced fields and orchards on the right side of the road, and the forested Limestone Ridge that loomed over the battlefield to the right. Booker and the colour party, consisting of the two flags carried by ensigns and the buglers, advanced in the centre on or close to Ridge Road. Booker, unhorsed, had to rely on verbal reports from Skinner and Gillmor, who themselves also had a limited view of the battlefield. Nobody really knew what was happening on the field next to him. Nor did the men have clear sight forward.

For historians attempting to reconstruct what happened, it is as if the Battle of Ridgeway unfolded in four different places in four different time zones. As George T. Denison later wrote, "The chapter on the Battle of Ridgeway gave me more trouble than all the others united.

The accounts were so conflicting that I almost gave up in despair."[39] Another lamented, "The Q.O.[R] companies interchanged and relieved each other, or without being in each case, relieved, fell back, making a column of reserve. The order in which this was done cannot be distinctly traced, as few of the Q.O. officers or men, agree in giving the same statement."[40]

In the open fields to the right of the road below the ridge, the Queen's Own Rifles called out for "more ammunition" and Gillmor asked Booker to relieve the QOR.[41] The time of the request is difficult to determine. Every participant's sense of time was distorted. Alexander Muir testified before the Board of Inquiry that forty-five minutes had passed since the fighting began when the Queen's Own Rifles companies, one by one, exhausted their supply.[42] Skinner testified that just ten minutes had elapsed after the firing began and McEachren was wounded, when Booker said, "Major Skinner, you will skirmish with the right wing."

The green-uniformed QOR fought as independent rifle companies, darting from cover to cover as they advanced over the fields through the rail fences, bushes, and orchards, but the scarlet-clad infantry of the Thirteenth were now deployed openly in ranks in line formation, advancing erect, rifles at ready as if on a parade ground.[43] O'Neill later said, "When they advanced in line of battle in their red uniforms they presented a beautiful appearance. It was one of the prettiest sights I ever witnessed. The line was well formed and their advance was brave."[44] O'Neill in fact had hardly spotted the green-uniformed QOR companies, remarking that "the red uniform appeared to me the most conspicuous on the field."[45]

For the Fenians this would have been their seminal moment. After all the decades of seething rebellion, the years of planning and talk, they believed the moment had finally arrived when they were coming face to face, musket to musket, with the hated symbol of the British Empire: the redcoats. Fenian Captain Mullen recalled, "At the sight of the English redcoats some of our fellows got mad to get at them."[46]

THE FIGHTING BECAME HEAVIEST in the apple orchard just south of the Jim N. Angur barn and small house, the "brick house" as it became known, on the southeast corner of Bertie and Ridge roads.[47] Jim was one of the sons of Henry Angur, whose house stood farther north up Ridge Road, where O'Neill had made his headquarters. QOR Company 6 cleared the apple orchard and broke into the grounds of the Jim Angur farm, taking cover behind his barn. To their right, about fifty yards to the north, were the Fenian barricades strung out along Bertie Road to the east of the Angur farm. Acting as the right wing of the Thirteenth Battalion, companies 1, 2, and 3, under Major Skinner and Battalion Adjutant Captain John Henery, a former sergeant major of the Coldstream Guards, now advanced through the orchard. The Fenians fired volley after volley through the apple trees. QOR Company 6, positioned behind the barn, found itself trapped in the crossfire between the Thirteenth behind and the Fenians in front.[48] It was hot, smoky, and brutal going. This was before the introduction of "smokeless" powder, and the men were engulfed in clouds of sticky gun smoke, their faces stained black and blue.* Taking the fierce recoil from their rifles, round after round, the men's arms and shoulders were bruised a deep purple, their uniforms soaked in sweat and caked with dark powder-residue.[49]

The three Hamilton companies advanced slowly through the apple orchard, relieving the QOR between them and the Fenian barricade on Bertie Road.[50] Blown loose by volleys of Fenian bullets, soft white flower petals rained down on the men from the apple trees as they fought their way through the orchard.[51] George A. Mackenzie of the Thirteenth Battalion recalled: "When we had reached an orchard we were ordered to lie down. It was not pleasant to hear the bullets clipping the leaves from the apple boughs above us."[52] Andrew McIntosh remembered: "The firing soon became general; it is not a pleasant sound to hear the

* Smokeless powder (*pyrocellulose*), or *Poudre B.*, had been developed by the French only in 1884.

bullets whistling around you, but you get used to it. About the coolest thing I saw that day was one of our men sit up on his knees light a match and then light his pipe and go on with his firing."[53] Lieutenant Percy Gore Routh, a twenty-five-year-old store clerk from Hamilton, led Company 4 of the Thirteenth Battalion. Routh had a twenty-seven-year-old wife and earned $750 a year. He and his brother together supported his fifty-six-year-old widowed mother.[54] Chaplain Burwash described Routh as "a rarely handsome young man with a musical voice and a winsome face, his scarlet uniform fitting like a glove on his lithe and elegant form. In appearance he seemed better fitted for a gay festival than for the trying work which lay just before him."[55]

Routh ardently led his men forward into the Fenian volleys. His superior officers would later remark on his "gallant and soldierly demeanour."[56] Seventeen-year-old George Mackenzie, who was under Routh's command, was less impressed. Some sixty years later, he would recall, "As we advanced through the fields the officer in command of the company, Lieut. Percy Routh, manifested a keen enjoyment at the prospect of getting into the fight. At one time he fairly leaped into the air with an exclamation of delight. I did not share his enthusiasm. Poor Routh! It was not long before a Fenian bullet passed through one of his lungs."[57]

Routh had first been dinged lightly in his hip by a spent bullet. He laughed it off, gamely shouting out, "I will not run. I will die first."[58] As the Fenian rounds rained down on them, his men dropped to the ground for cover. Routh raised himself high, standing in front of his huddled men. Fearlessly he turned his back to the Fenians—almost taunting them to test his invincibility—and facing his own men began rallying them to go forward into action. A Minié ball smashed into his back just below his left shoulder blade, tore downward through his left lung and heart muscle, and exited about an inch below his left nipple, leaving a gaping, ragged hole in his chest. Routh folded to the ground, dark pulmonic blood frothing out of the hole in the breast of his finely tailored scarlet uniform.[59]

A nearby farmhouse had been commandeered to shelter the wounded, and Routh was carried roughly into the house and laid out on the floor on a blanket. A plaster was applied to seal off the sucking air and blood bubbling through his open chest wound. Nobody believed Routh could survive. Abandoned for dead, he lay in the farmhouse in his blood-soaked uniform for thirty hours before he was found still alive.[60] The Hamilton *Evening Times* reported his death later that day, and three days later the *Globe* was still reporting him as dead.[61] Routh survived his wound but was disabled for the rest of his life.[62] Mackenzie recalled, "For many weeks he lay between life and death. He pulled through, but I doubt if he ever completely recovered his health. He died a comparatively young man."[63]

The three companies of the Thirteenth finally broke out of the orchard and advanced upon the Fenian barricades skirting the south side of Bertie Road. The Fenians withdrew about 150 yards north across Bertie Road and took cover in another orchard farther upslope. There they formed a new skirmishing line between the advancing Canadians and their main battle group still waiting farther to the north.[64] Skinner deployed Company 1 (Captain Grant, Lieutenant Gibson, Ensign Mackenzie) to hold the abandoned barricades along Bertie Road to his right. He ordered Company 3 (Lieutenant Ferguson, Ensign Armstrong) to the left side of Ridge Road, advancing them approximately fifty yards beyond the northwest corner of Bertie Road.[65] From their new positions, the Fenians now began firing volleys onto the Angur farmstead.

At the Angur farm, Skinner with Company 2 (Captain Watson and Lieutenant Sewell) took control of the grounds around the brick house overlooking the southeast corner of Bertie and Ridge roads. With Fenian rounds pelting down on them, the men crashed through the garden gates and one of the soldiers forced the padlock on the back door.[66] The company took cover inside the house, firing from its front doorway and windows at the Fenians in the orchard about 150 yards away.[67] Here Skinner and Company 2 dug in to hold the crossroads while waiting for the rest of the companies to advance from behind them in support.[68]

O'Neill himself offered only a bare-bones recollection of the battle to this point: "The skirmishing was kept up over half an hour, when perceiving the enemy flanking me on both sides, and not being able to draw out his centre which was partially protected by thick timber, I fell back a few hundred yards and formed a new line."[69]

So far the Canadians were performing outstandingly in the face of heavy enemy fire. They appeared to have driven the Fenians back and, according to O'Neill, were flanking him *on both sides*. O'Neill also said he could not draw out the centre. In other words, the centre on Ridge Road was lagging behind the left and right wings in the fields, which were now threatening to outflank him. O'Neill drew his men back north of Bertie Road and formed new lines closer to his main force.

Booker and his colour party, along with Gillmor, were managing the battle from a position near the road 150 yards south of the brick house. Clustered around them were the Queen's Own Rifles companies who had retired to the column from the field after having been relieved or run out of ammunition.

Farther to their rear were the last three redcoat companies of the Thirteenth Battalion held in reserve (companies 4, 5, and 6), still waiting for the order to deploy. (See Battle Map 2.) Finally these last reserves received the order to advance and extend into battle. At this point, many witnesses recall hearing the QOR men at the centre cheering at what they thought was the arrival of the British army to relieve them.[70] This cheering broke out at approximately 9:30 A.M. and marks, in the recollections of many, the point at which suddenly and inexplicably things began to go catastrophically wrong.

9:30 A.M. On the far left (west, or O'Neill's far-right flank) the going was easy. The QOR Trinity College Rifles and the Thirteenth Battalion York Rifles had moved halfway through the last field south of Bertie Road without taking any heavy fire.[71] The Fenian skirmishers facing them wheeled back to the east, crossed Ridge Road north of Bertie Road, and rejoined their main battle group near O'Neill's headquarters.

In the meantime Company 3, Thirteenth Battalion, pushed forward diagonally across Bertie Road northwest from the brick house across the intersection, eventually taking cover in a small orchard belonging to a farmer by the name of Stoneman. They were accompanied by a section from QOR Company 6 led by Lieutenant Campbell and Ensign McLean, which had been fighting from behind the barn on Angur's farm.[72] They too advanced across the intersection approximately fifty to seventy-five yards into the Stoneman orchard north of Bertie Road to the west of Ridge Road. Together, Company 3, Thirteenth Battalion, and a section from QOR Company 6 would have been the Canadian units that advanced farthest on the left and on the centre flanks of the battlefield.

Now we turn to the ridge on the far right flank, to QOR Company 9, University Rifles, and Company 10, Highlanders. The Fenian plan to ambush the Canadians in a crossfire from the ridgeline on the right failed when the Fenians opened fire too early and revealed their positions on the ridge. Booker ordered Gillmor to clear the ridge[73] and Gillmor sent in the University Rifles and the Highlanders.[74] The Highlanders under Captain John Gardner moved out from their position behind a schoolhouse on Garrison Road.[75] From where the University Rifles began their advance is unclear, but it appears that they led, with the Highlanders coming up behind them in support. The Highlanders fought through the woods to the rear and east of the University Rifles until, between them, they forced the Fenians off the ridge, pushing them north toward their lines and across Bertie Road. The Highlanders came off the ridge to take positions on the south side of the road on the far right of the battlefield, to the far right of Company 1 of the Thirteenth, which had fought up from the centre and was now holding the abandoned Fenian barricade.[76] But the University Rifles did not stop. They just kept going straight, charging across Bertie Road in the direction of O'Neill's waiting main battle group.

QOR Company 9 consisted of twenty-eight college boys from the University of Toronto.[77] Their officer-professors who formed the company and recruited them—Captain Croft and Lieutenant Cherriman—never arrived to lead the boys into battle. Neither did their ensign, Adam Crooks, a Toronto Q.C. (Crooks would later become the Ontario minister of education in Premier Oliver Mowat's Cabinet),[78] although one source reports that Crooks had resigned from the company in 1865 and had been replaced by Sergeant W.C. Campbell.[79] According to another source, the officers were "detained in Toronto in consequence of their academic duties."[80] One wonders what these academic duties were, considering that most students had already written their exams and had gone home while the university had waived exams for those students who reported for combat.[81] Yet another source claims that "Captain Croft was not permitted to go to the front in June, 1866, as he desired to do, and was assigned duties at headquarters in Toronto,"[82] while the *Globe* reported that Croft had been put in charge of recruiting in Toronto and that Cherriman had gone to the front but only after the fighting was over.[83] At the last minute, an inexperienced officer-cadet who had only received his ensign's rank in March, George Y. Whitney from Company 8, Trinity College Rifles, was re-assigned to lead Company 9, University Rifles, into combat, a task he would fulfill with distinction.[84]

When ordered to clear Limestone Ridge, University College students Corporal William Ellis, privates Malcolm McKenzie and John Mewburn, and medical student William Tempest, along with the other college boys of Company 9, found themselves fighting the Fenians through thick bush and forest along the ridgeline. Malcolm McKenzie, the farmer's boy from Zorra who had leased his land and borrowed money to pursue a college education in Toronto, fell first in the company, shot dead through the heart during the fight in the woods. The company fought all the way through the forest, and with the Highlanders broke out into an open field just south of Bertie Road, outflanking the Fenian defenders strung out along the road, who were shooting at the main force of the Canadians advancing through the fields and the apple orchard.

The Fenians, finding themselves now in a crossfire between the Thirteenth Battalion moving up from the apple orchard in the centre and the Highlanders and University Rifles coming along the ridge from their left, abandoned their barricades and fell back into the fields and orchards north of the road, as described earlier. The University Rifles followed them recklessly across Bertie Road, past their abandoned barricade, and into the fields to the north, leaving the rest of their brigade behind. The QOR Company 9, University Rifles, would advance the farthest on the field that day against the Fenians.

William Ellis, later a chemistry professor at the University of Toronto, recalled: "We then crossed a road, where the Fenians had made a barricade of fence rails, and entered a field of young wheat, studded at intervals with black stumps."[85] The company fought through the field, dashing from stump to stump, dropping to their stomachs as Fenian bullets kicked up dust and wood splinters. They had advanced so far ahead of the rest of the brigade and so close to the Fenians that they were beginning to come under fire from their own troops: "Here we were a good deal annoyed by the fire of some of our own friends, who, not knowing our whereabouts, were firing into the wood from behind us. Sergeant Bryce—now the Rev. Professor Bryce, of Winnipeg—had taken a post behind a fine, thick maple tree. Before long it became doubtful which side of the tree was the safest, and Bryce settled it by saying, 'I'd rather be hit before than behind,' and deliberately placed himself in front of the tree."[86]

Without realizing it, the twenty-eight boys from the University Rifles were coming up alone onto the positions of the main Fenian force. One fenced field separated the boys from a massive force of insurgents coiled for a counterattack. As they began to climb over the fence into this last field, eager to get at the Fenians, Ellis recalled, "We heard the bugle sounding the retire. Whitney gave the word to us, and called back those who had crossed the fence. When we turned our backs on the Fenians, we had not the faintest suspicion of defeat. We had, up to the moment when we got the order to retire, steadily driven the Fenians before us, but we could see them in greatly superior numbers."[87] By now the withdrawing Fenians had joined with their main battle group. The twenty-eight college boys were only one field away from the regrouped force of some eight hundred Fenians. Only they stood between the insurgents and their own brigade behind them when suddenly they heard the bugle call to retire.

WHEN THE BUGLE SOUNDED, Major Skinner and his three companies of the Thirteenth and elements of QOR Company 6 were in the thick of a firefight around the brick Angur house. An officer from the QOR was positioned behind a corner of the barn, firing rifles that several of his men behind him were loading and passing to him one after the other.[88] Skinner and Captain Henery moved up and down the lines at the crossroads, encouraging their men by patting them on the shoulders with, "Good boys, take steady aim; do not throw away your fire; do not expose yourself needlessly."[89] Skinner later testified at the inquiry:

> Someone on the left of the road called out, "Don't you hear the bugle?" I said, "No. What does it say?" The reply I got was, "Retreat." I then looked around to the rear for the first time since we came out, and I saw our men at the right running in. I then heard someone on my left say, "Why, they are preparing to receive cavalry." I looked around and said, "Where is the cavalry?" implying that I saw none.[90]

Fighting on the far-left flank in the fields, Captain Davis of the York Rifles also testified:

> I heard a bugle call which my sergeant said was "the retire." He said that it was a mistake, that it was "the Advance" that was meant. In

> a few minutes "the advance" was sounded, and I took my company over the fence behind which they were lying and told them to get to the next one as soon as they could. When about half way across the field "the Retire" was again sounded, followed by "the double." I looked along the line of skirmishers and saw them firing and retiring, and a good many running in. We retired, the men firing occasionally, until we reached the Garrison Road.[91]

Captain Henery had traversed over to the left side of Ridge Road near the crossroads and the brick house during the firefight. He testified:

> There was then a cry of "Cavalry!" from my right rear. I was on the road with the left of No. 2 Company on the line of skirmishers. I looked and saw two or three horses, and cried out that there was no cavalry. I heard no bugle blow the "retire." When I looked around I saw both red and green coats running to the rear from the line of skirmishers, in order, but not firing.[92]

The official history of what went wrong at Ridgeway would be the one that was simplest to explain to the broadest spectrum of the public, the clients, and the patrons of the impending state. The story told is that somewhere to the front of the advancing reserves and Booker's colour party, somebody saw two or three Fenian scouts on horseback and cried out "Cavalry." The alarm made its way through the ranks down the road until it reached Booker and Gillmor, who were approximately 150 yards south of the crossroads. Booker had taken cover behind a barn and was unable to see up the road from his position or view the field of battle.[93] He blindly shouted out, "Look out for cavalry!" and Gillmor then gave the order to form a square, the standard defensive formation against a cavalry charge, in which infantry drew into a tight full or three-sided square, some kneeling, some standing, bristling with bayonets intended to impale any enemy riders and their horses who got too close.[94]

According to Alfred Booker's statement:

> Cries of "Cavalry" and "Look out for cavalry" came down the road. I then observed men doubling down the hill. In the next few moments events succeeded each other very rapidly. As the cry came down the road, directions were given the reserves on the road to "Form square." At this crisis the fire of the enemy came heavily to our right flank, as well as into the front and rear of our force in advance. I saw nothing to justify the first impression that we were to be attacked by cavalry. I gave the word to "Re-form column," with the view of deploying, when to my surprise I found the rear of the reserve which had formed part of the square had dissipated, and moving down the road. Major Gillmor came and reported to me that the enemy was bringing up his reserves. I asked him how he knew. He replied that he saw them himself. I then inquired, "In what shape?" when he replied, "In column—in mass of column." I then ordered to retire. But the confusion had become a panic.[95]

Journalist Alexander Somerville, who had frequently covered the activities of the Thirteenth Battalion for Hamilton newspapers, would later write of Booker: "It had been his custom on field days, and Hamilton holidays, to follow the call of *skirmishers retire* with *form square*; *prepare to receive cavalry*. My old note-books written when looking on, bear that record, so do the memories of his men.[96] Perhaps, in this hour of his mental prostration he reverted to the old rotation of movements learned from a book and gave the order to the bugler *form square*. Charity would rather believe that he made that mistake in forgetfulness, than that his vision of cavalry, crossing a variety of fences, five and six feet high, in pursuit of the retiring skirmishers, whom he had called in, led to the formation of a square."[97]

Indeed, as the Booker Inquiry concluded, the notion of Fenian cavalry or, for that matter, any cavalry charging across that terrain was absurd.[98] It was the reaction of an inexperienced amateur officer who had read too many boyish romances of lance- and sword-wielding cavalry charges of long ago and not enough recent literature on just how cavalry had been transformed into scouts and mobile infantry armed with rifled carbines who now dismounted before proceeding to fight on foot.

AS THE MEN FIXED BAYONETS and came into a tight three-sided square in the middle of the road, the Fenian riflemen opened fire from their covered positions into the densely packed formation, which presented a tantalizing target. Private Christopher Alderson of QOR Company 7, Educational Department, was shot through the heart while in the square or attempting to enter it.[99] He fell dead in the road. The thirty-eight-year-old Alderson was a recently married messenger whose wife and her nine-year-old son from a previous marriage were left destitute by his death.[100]

Booker realized his error and ordered the men to be redeployed into their previous column formation. As they were manoeuvring under heavy fire back into a column on the road, skirmishers falling back from the front came ploughing through them. The two groups collided, creating a confused mass of men, some dropping under Fenian fire while penned in by snake fences and a low stone wall on the eastern side. A witness later recalled, "A heavy volley struck the column, and I heard a sound which I took to be that of men falling. The column swayed backwards, as I supposed, from the effects of the fire."[101]

Booker panicked and sounded the "retire." In the confusion, the manoeuvring ranks rapidly degenerated into a retreat as Fenian rounds rained down on them. Booker tried to regain control and sounded "reform column" and "advance" when they were hit by another Fenian volley. A childless married labourer, Private William Smith, fell dead.[102] Booker was now completely unnerved. He again sounded the "retire" but now added the urgent signal, "the double." This became a desperate call to retreat: Everyone run for your life!

The Fenians, seeing the Canadian lines wavering, now began to press their advantage and, fixing bayonets, formed up to counterattack. They advanced downslope, firing volleys into the confused mass of men below them. The Canadian lines on the road buckled as the dead and wounded began to fall around them.

The Court of Inquiry later concluded that Booker had committed an error but did his best to correct it. It criticized him, however, in that to believe "the idle rumour that the enemy's force was partly composed of cavalry in a country where such an arm could be of scarcely any value in attack, or to assume, even for a moment, that a mounted corps which he could not see was advancing at such a rate as to render it necessary to give the words of caution which he used, was ill-judged, and was the first act which gave rise to the disorganization of his force, which then followed."[103]

The inquiry concluded:

> The officer in command (apparently hesitating as to whether he should advance or retreat) unfortunately gave the order to retire, and the bugles having taken it up at the advanced posts of the attack, our force began to fall back; and notwithstanding the exertions of the officers, who in every case shown in the evidence before the Court behaved in a very steady and energetic manner to rally their broken ranks, the column had retreated too far in the direction of Ridgeway before the advanced parties had all came in to render this possible.[104]

The court laid the blame for the debacle on the skirmishers fighting to the front of Booker's column, who, they concluded, cried out "cavalry" upon spotting a few Fenian horsemen. At least, that was the official "look out for cavalry" version that the inquiry settled on. What really happened was slightly different.

THE FIRST PROBLEM with the official version of events is found in Major Skinner's testimony. Skinner was leading the skirmishers and insisted that the cry of cavalry did not come from them: "I then heard someone on my left say, 'Why, they are preparing to receive cavalry.' I looked around and said, 'Where is the cavalry?' implying that I saw none."[105]

Captain Henery, on the left wing of the skirmishers, also testified: "There was then a cry of 'Cavalry!' from my right *rear*. I was on the road with the left of No. 2 Company on the line of skirmishers. I looked and saw two or three horses, and cried out that there was no cavalry."[106]

Their testimony suggests that the cry of "cavalry" came from somebody in Booker's column, not from the skirmishers in the front as alleged, or from somewhere in between the column and the skirmishers, possibly from the other section of QOR Company 6, which had remained on the grounds of the Angur farm and was now retiring back to the column at the centre. (The other section of QOR Company 6 had advanced with Thirteenth Battalion Company 3 into the Stoneman orchard.)

Another problem is the issue of when precisely the bugle signalled the order to "retire." Ensign Maclean, for example, said he heard it *before* the cry of "cavalry." Fighting in QOR Company 6, Maclean testified:

> I saw the Fenians advancing down the road. They were pushing forward their skirmishers and were advancing, as I thought, in a heavy column of companies. They continued their advance, and we received an order to retire. We then retired as skirmishers usually do in closing in on their supports. We came out, but found no support to close upon, and reached the open space where there was a large body of men formed into square. After reaching this open space I heard a cry of "Cavalry" but saw none. I heard a cheer from our square, and from some cause the rear of the square seemed to turn and go down the road. The square now seemed to dissolve, and the men formed a confused mixture of red and green down the road to Ridgeway.[107]

Frontier Police detective Charles Clarke likewise testified that several horses suddenly appeared on the crest of Ridge Road north of the crossroads. He heard the order "Prepare for cavalry" and saw the men form into a square. Then he said:

> A body of red-coats were coming around a curve in the road about two hundred yards in rear of the square. The Queen's Own and those of the Thirteenth began to cheer, supposing them to belong to the 47th Regiment [British army regular redcoats] coming to their relief. As soon as we ascertained that they were not the 47th, we supposed that

> they were two companies of the Thirteenth who had been driven in by main force, and the result was that we became panic-stricken, and we all broke.[108]

It is interesting to compare the views of the two senior commanders in the field—Booker and Gillmor—as reflected in the reports they sent shortly after the battle, before they had much time to think about it. Booker wrote on the evening after the battle:

> A cry of Cavalry from the front, and the retreat of a number of men in our centre on the reserves, caused me to form a square and prepare for Cavalry. This mistake originated from relieved skirmishers doubling back. I immediately reformed column and endeavoured to deploy to the right. A panic here seized our men and I could not bring them again to the front.[109]

Major Gillmor wrote on June 6:

> As my skirmishers were coming in, Col. Booker gave me the command to prepare for Cavalry which I obeyed, but failing to see Cavalry I reformed Column and ordered the two leading Companies of Queens Own to extend and drive back the enemy then fearfully near us; this was done in splendid style, I had then necessarily to retire the rest of Column consisting of Hamilton Volunteers and one or two companies of Queen's Own; while retiring they observed the left wing of Hamilton Volunteers advancing, and imagined it the advance of the 16th and 47th cheered; on which the wing turned and ran and a scene of confusion ensued.[110]

Arthur James Moody, a seventeen-year-old private in the Queen's Own Rifles, wrote in a recently discovered diary entry for June 2:

> Oh, that awful Square! Men falling all around us thick and fast with no chance to protect themselves. The order to reform for action was given but even the stern command of Major Gillmor and the officers could

> not prevent the terrible confusion which followed. When hark! What is that cry? A line of red coats is seen thro the trees some distance back. The cry is "The 47th Regulars." Hats fly up with loud hurrahs. Men are frantic with wild excitement and joy that the day is not lost thro their mistake. No use trying to reform! No use trying to regain command of the men. The excitement is too great, too wild to be brought under control. Many are coolly and independently firing at the Fenians, thus keeping them in check. A few start for the redcoated line, others follow. When it seems impossible to prevent it the whole body of 600 men retire to gain help from the supposed 'Regulars'. Lo! Phantom like it retreats and is lost sight of. Where is it? There is no one to answer. It was a terrible delusion. It was only the rear guard of our own brigade drawn up in line with fixed bayonets awaiting the order to advance or retire.[111]

There is even a possibility that the cheer reported by witnesses was actually coming from the Fenians as they counterattacked. Captain Gardner, commanding QOR Company 10 on the far front of the right flank at Bertie Road, testified:

> We continued here engaged with the enemy for some time, until we heard some cheering on our left front, along the enemy's line. I thought it was our men cheering and making a dash on the enemy. I then ordered my men to get over the fence and cross the field to the left, in the direction from which the cheering came. As soon as we came to the opening commanding a view of the field, we perceived that it was the Fenians who had cheered, and were advancing in large numbers towards our forces.[112]

In his history of the battle, Somerville argued that it was not the cry of cavalry that triggered the panic, but the bugle calls to retire. Somerville maintained that O'Neill at first thought the bugle call to retire was a trick to lure him back toward the Canadian lines. Perhaps as O'Neill was probing the Canadian lines, he and several scouts might have ridden out on horseback toward the crest of Ridge Road. O'Neill would have observed the Canadians wavering. In response, the veteran Fenians now launched a well-timed and massive counterattack that would drive the Canadians back.[113]

The irony is that the Canadian ranks broke in the middle rear, not at the front closest to the enemy. The skirmishers testified that when they were overwhelmed by the advancing Fenians and began to fall back, they discovered that Booker and the reserves behind them were gone. Skinner testified:

> I looked around and said, "Where is the cavalry?" implying that I saw none. I then ran across the road to the left and saw that the men were all running as fast as they could to the rear. I ran for a barn and remained there a few moments to get breath, and then ran for another fence. I saw a few of our men behind me, and the enemy pursuing them. Two of our men were shot here, Stewart [Stuart] and Powell.
>
> I then made for the road where we had previously deployed, expecting to find the reserve there. I found none. Our skirmishers were then comprising [*sic*] men of all of our companies, mixed with those in green. I suppose there were about 150 red coats and about 30 or 40 in green. I then asked for the commanding officer, but got no answer. I then asked for Col. Booker, and one man in the crowd cried out, "He is off, three miles ahead." I do not know who it was that said so. I then called for Major Gillmor, and got no reply.[114]

PRIOR TO LAUNCHING THEIR COUNTERATTACK, the Fenians had regrouped into a tight formation. It was at this juncture that most of the Canadian casualties were inflicted. The Fenians fired rapid volleys into the advancing Canadians. Not only were the Fenians experienced and cool under fire, but they were also highly skilled riflemen, able to reload their weapons so quickly that many of the Canadians would later be convinced that the Fenians were all armed with repeating rifles.[115] The Canadians found themselves caught in a hailstorm of Minié balls pouring down on them from the Fenian lines.

The hollow lead Minié ball travelled at a relatively slow subsonic velocity—950 feet per second.[116] The enormous .58-calibre bullet tumbled as it flew, its hollow base emitting a dull whistling sound. It was like getting hit by a combination sledgehammer and power saw flying at 647 miles per hour. The wounds inflicted were frequently described as "crushing" and "tearing."

The heavy round was clumsy in how it did its damage. If a bullet hit on the sharp nose-end of its tumble—and as long as it passed through soft tissue—it could bore its way cleanly through human flesh, leaving a neat quarter-sized tunnel wound. The wound would take forever to heal, if at all. Post–Civil-War–era photographs show veterans some fifteen years after the war standing before a mirror and passing coat-hanger wires through unhealed hollow tunnels traversing their torsos.[117] But if the Minié ball hit something harder—muscle, tendon, cartilage, or bone—or if it hit on the flat side of its tumble, not only did it "mushroom" and inflict huge, ugly gaping wounds, but also the misshapen chunk of lead erratically bounced and tumbled about inside the body, ripping and crushing everything in its path.

The Minié ball was at its worst when it hit bone dead on. It inflicted what was called a "compound comminuted fracture": The bone was shattered into minuscule razor-sharp shards that were often blown out through the exit wound, tearing and slicing flesh along the exit path and sometimes exposing the jagged stump of the bone. There was no splinting or reconstructing a bone injury like that. The victim was lucky if he got to keep his deformed limb. At one point surgeons experimented with keeping the limb intact by clearing away the remaining bone grist in the gap of the bone in a procedure known as "resection," but the resulting flipper-like boneless limbs drove men so mad that they often asked for them to be amputated later.

The men Skinner mentioned in his report, Stuart and Powell, who were hit near the Angur barn, fared better than most of the wounded. Nineteen-year-old Private James Stuart, a grocery clerk in Hamilton, was shot through the clavicle in his shoulder, with the bullet deflecting up into his neck and exiting harmlessly behind his left ear. Stuart was evacuated to a hospital in St. Catharines on June 3. Remarkably, he was back at work in the grocery store ten weeks later.[118] Twenty-three-year-old Private John George Powell of Company 3, Thirteenth Battalion, was a coach-maker. He was hit in the back of the leg just above the knee and felt the bullet smash into his bone and lodge there.[119] The bullet remained in Powell's leg and he was permanently disabled.[120]

As there were no stretchers to carry the wounded to safety, doors were torn down from their hinges and used to carry some of the wounded away.[121] A small field hospital was set up in a log house where a local resident, Mrs. Jaboc Danner, and her young granddaughter, Georgina Beam, tended to the wounded.[122] At one point as the little girl was rushing a bucket of water to some thirsty soldiers, a bullet zinged through it. Georgina was reported to be completely unfazed, only saying, "Mother, the pail is leaking; it won't hold water."[123]

Many of the farm families were caught up in the battle. Mary Mellisa Teal, a three-year-old orphan taken in by her grandmother and aunts, would later recall huddling with her baby cousin on the bedroom floor as bullets riddled the walls of their log cabin. Her young aunts eventually rushed the children across the back fields to safety, but not before Mary caught a glimpse of a dead or wounded soldier on the ground near their porch. The family's widowed matriarch, Phebe Teal, chose to remain at the house and is reputed to have joined in the fighting because, according to her grandson, "the old lady was the only one who knew how to handle a muzzle-loader."[124]

Men were hit standing in the square and in the fields as they were retreating. It was during the retreat on the left flank that Percy Routh was shot as he attempted to rally his men. James Johnson of Bradford was a civilian but came out to fight just the same that day. Unable to find a rifle, he armed himself with an old sword and joined Booker's column looking more like a Fenian than a soldier. Johnson was near Routh when he was shot and helped another soldier to carry him into a house.[125]

It was also here in the retreat that seventeen-year-old George Mackenzie, the college student serving in the Thirteenth who earlier had not been particularly impressed with Routh's martial enthusiasm, was also hit by a Minié ball. Mackenzie was seventy-seven years old when in 1926 he described the incident to a reporter from the Hamilton *Spectator*: "I was retiring, with the tide of men flowing in the wrong direction, and was carrying my rifle in my left hand. Suddenly the rifle flew from my hand and my arm swung helpless at my side. A bullet had passed clean through my arm between the shoulder and the elbow, shattering the bone; 'a compound comminuted fracture,' as I afterwards learned to call it."[126]

In the records of the military board of compensation archived in Ottawa is an application written by Mackenzie with leaden Victorian formality and dating from four months after the battle:

> I have the honour to request that you will be pleased to forward to the proper authorities this, my application, for compensation for wound received in action with the enemy at Lime Ridge on June 2, 1866. A bullet struck my left arm near the elbow joint causing [compound comminuted] fracture and great laceration of flesh, from the effect of which I was ill for more than two months, and I am still unable to extend the arm, or to make free use of it, it being considerably deformed from the effects of this injury and will never be restored as it was before the wound.[127]

The words "compound comminuted" are carefully inserted in Mackenzie's own hand. The military medical board found his wound "equal to the loss of the arm."[128] Despite his horrific wound, Mackenzie returned to his studies at Trinity College in Toronto that September.

Corporal Francis Lackey, of QOR Company 2, a twenty-six-year-old shoemaker from Toronto, fared much worse. With unusual frankness a newspaper article reported: "The ball had passed into his head through the upper jaw, breaking three of the front teeth and the bone of the palate, and lodging near the base of the brain. The ball was of a conical shape and very much bruised by striking against the bones of the head. Much difficulty was experienced in breathing, and there was a considerable loss of blood."[129] Corporal Lackey died two days later, leaving his twenty-six-year-old wife destitute.[130] Sergeant Hugh Matheson of QOR Company 2, an assistant pharmacist in his father's York Street drugstore, was shot through the knee and hospitalized at St. Catharines. The wound became infected and on Friday Matheson's leg was amputated. It did not help—Matheson died three days later, attended on by his brother and sister.[131]

The worst casualties were inflicted on Company 9, University College Rifles, which advanced the farthest that day and took the brunt of the Fenian counterattack. Some eight hundred Fenians rolled over the twenty-eight university students from Toronto.

Ensign Whitney had become aware that his company was alone in the field and assumed that the bugle call to retire was a summons to rejoin the rest of the battalion. None of the men thought that anything was wrong on the battlefield, other than that they had advanced too far ahead of the rest of the column. But as they withdrew, they realized to their horror that the entire Fenian army was following them, firing massive volleys into their small group.[132]

The University College Rifles doubled back southwest, toward the crossroads of Bertie and Ridge roads. When they arrived there, they found themselves alone. The rest of the brigade had withdrawn toward Ridgeway. The boys now took up positions at the crossroads and attempted to return fire from behind the fences. It was hopeless.[133]

Private Edgar J. Paul, a nineteen-year-old student, was shot in the back of his leg, the Minié ball tearing a two-and-a-half-inch wound through his thigh muscle. His wound was declared "slight" but would not heal. In 1880 it was still causing pain and disabling him.[134] Private Rupert Kingsford, a seventeen-year-old student on a scholarship at University College, was shot in the leg just below his knee joint and taken prisoner by the Fenians. Private Ephrain G. Patterson, a twenty-year-old student with an annual scholarship of thirty-five dollars, was shot through the muscle of his forearm. William Vandermissen was gravely wounded in the groin. John Harriman Mewburn, twenty-one years old, from Stamford, Ontario, also a scholarship student at University College, died in Fenian custody several hours later under unclear circumstances. According to George Denison, Mewburn was "struck by a rifle bullet on the temple, which fractured the inner plate, and produced delirium and convulsions. He was made prisoner by the enemy, robbed, and very roughly if not cruelly treated by them. His hands were bound behind him and he was thrown on his face, but at the earnest request of a wounded comrade, M. Rupert Kingsford, he was turned on his back, and his hands unbound half an hour before he died."[135] Other sources report Mewburn's dying of heatstroke.[136] Mewburn's body was thrown into a kitchen at the back of a house on Ridge Road, along with that of a dead Fenian.

Chemistry student William Ellis and medical student William Tempest saw a massive wave of Fenians coming at them from the north. They made a dash back over the snake fences and into Bertie Road, running to the intersection at Ridge Road. When they got there, they realized that the rest of their column had vanished down the road to Ridgeway. They were cut off. Ellis described what happened next: "In the cross road Tempest was next to me. Just after firing a shot he rose to his feet. He was a very tall fellow, and presented a conspicuous mark above the fence. Next moment I heard the sound of a dull, heavy blow, and saw him fall forward on his face. I ran to his side and found a small, round hole in his forehead. He had been shot through the head, and the bullet, after penetrating the brain, had broken the bone at the back of the skull. Of course he died instantly. As soon as I saw that nothing more could be done for him, I looked about me and found that I was alone on the road."[137]

Ellis decided to run for cover in the brick house on the corner. As he approached it, he saw troops in dark uniforms in the orchard and assumed they were Queen's Own. They were Fenians. Ellis realized his mistake too late and was captured. He was taken into the house and put under guard.[138] That the Fenians were in the orchard and holding the Angur house by the time Ellis reached it indicates just how far the University Rifles had advanced that day before turning back. The University Rifles suffered three killed and four wounded—the highest casualty rate of any unit in the battle.[139]

QOR Company 10, Highlanders, who were supporting the University Rifles on the ridge but only advanced as far as Bertie Road, did not hear the bugle call to retire. Alexander Muir recalled that they saw the advancing lines of the Thirteenth Battalion suddenly waver and then observed a large formation of Fenians sweeping down from north of Bertie Road.

As the brigade began to retreat, the Highlanders from their positions fired two or three volleys into the Fenian flank to cover the retreat of their comrades below. Muir observed the flank pull back toward its centre. The Highlanders split into two sections—the left section under Captain Gardner took the field below while the section on the right followed Lieutenant Gibson and his Hamilton company, retiring back along the ridge. Sergeant Bain on the ridge above observed the Fenians massing for another attack and shouted down to the left section of the Highlanders in the field below to get out. They traversed the fields and joined the retreating column on Ridge Road. The right section with Muir turned back the way they came and withdrew over the ridge. When they emerged on Garrison Road they saw to their surprise the brigade falling back down Ridge Road toward Ridgeway. The Fenians by then were occupying the same position where QOR Company 5 had sighted the enemy for the first time. Muir estimated their number to be at six to seven hundred.[140]

The Highlanders fought their way back to the crossroads of Garrison and Ridge roads, and taking up positions behind the fences there, they opened up several volleys against the oncoming Fenians. They were the last to withdraw from the field.[141] Colour Sergeant Forbes McHardy and

Private John White were wounded on Garrison Road in the final stand by the Highlanders before leaving the field.[142] McHardy was wounded in his arm, the bullet ripping "downwards, backwards, and inwards through the biceps and emerging two inches above internal condyle" near his elbow.[143] He was twenty-eight years old and unmarried, an eight-hundred-dollar-a-year store clerk in Toronto. Private John White was also wounded in the arm, but more severely. His arm had to be amputated.[144]

AFTER UNLEASHING SEVERAL deadly rolling volleys, the Fenians charged the Canadians with fixed bayonets. John O'Neill laconically reported, "We gave them a volley and then charged them, driving them nearly three miles through the town of Ridgeway. In their hasty retreat, they threw away knapsacks, guns and everything that was likely to retard their speed."[145]

For centuries the bayonet charge has often been a decisive moment in combat between men with firearms. With the development of the percussion cap, the rate of fire increased while rifling increased the range and accuracy, so that gradually bayonet wounds became rare by the mid-nineteenth century. Bayonet charges did not, however: They became almost a form of psychological warfare. As Paddy Griffith explains, "A bayonet charge could be highly effective even without any bayonet actually touching an enemy soldier, let alone killing him. One hundred per cent of the casualties might be caused by musketry, yet the bayonet could still be the instrument of victory. This was because its purpose was not to kill soldiers but to disorganize regiments and win ground. It was the flourish of the bayonet and the determination in the eyes of its owner that on some occasions produced shock."[146]

Nothing in the Canadians' drill, in their officers' training school curriculum, or in their lives could have prepared them to face a bayonet charge—and certainly not the savage one that the Irish Fenians unleashed. Their charge must have been a fearsome sight and sound, one experienced over two thousand years by dozens of conscript armies facing a wild rebel Celtic charge. From the Roman Legions at Telamon in 225 B.C. to "Butcher Billy" Duke of Cumberland's redcoats at Culloden in 1746, men recalled the horrifying corkscrew sensation that went up their spines upon hearing the shrieking war cry of charging Celts rolling toward them, what the Romans described as a "wild tumult of sound ... weird discordant music ... an immense and dreadful din ... the whole army shouting their war-cries at the same time ... it seemed that not only the soldiers but all the country round had got a voice and caught up the cry."[147] *That* was what broke the elite Coldstream Guards at Fontonay in 1745 and set them running like jackrabbits in the face of the screaming Irish Wild Geese, the one rare time that the Celtic charge did not end with the Celts cut down like wheat as they were at Telamon and Culloden by the powerful Roman and British war machines. And then there was Limestone Ridge, where the courageous but inexperienced Canadian farm boys and shop clerks crumbled when they were charged by the Irish veterans. A simple, fundamental factor made all the difference: their lack of seasoning in combat. The Fenians rushed forward with fixed bayonets, charging headlong and barefoot-crazy, howling the "rebel yell" and *"Erin go bragh!"* ("Ireland Forever").[148] O'Neill would later say, "It was my opportunity and just at the psychological moment I gave the order to charge. My men gave the old Union yell and some southern vets gave the Rebel yell, Yi-Yi-Yi in the well-remembered high key and you know the result."[149]

Fenian Captain Mullen recalled, "We ran fast, many of us being barefoot after the march the night before, but they ran faster, a confused crowd of red and dark green, throwing away their muskets, knapsacks and overcoats. We pursued them for three miles, into the town of Ridgeway, and found the place deserted by all save one man. Their dead and wounded lay along the road and in the fields."[150]

It should be noted, however, that the Fenian impression that the Canadians abandoned their knapsacks and overcoats in their panic arises from the order given by Booker *before* the battle for the troops to divest themselves of these items. Obviously, all the items would have been arranged together neatly at a single location, thus one is left questioning the veracity of the scarce Fenian observations on the battle.

THE RETREAT WAS BOTH bloody and chaotic, and its history became a rancorous blame game, with the Queen's Own Rifles denouncing the Thirteenth Battalion skirmishers as "Scarlet Runners" while the Thirteenth nicknamed the QOR "Quickest Outta Ridgeway." In the end, nobody was sure which came first, the cheering at the sight of the appearance of redcoats in the mistaken belief that they were British regulars and then the panic when it turned out they were not, or the sight of horsemen and the call to form a square, along with the rout after the Fenians charged.

At the inquiry Major Gillmor, the QOR commander, testified that the square came first, then the Fenian volley followed by the appearance of the redcoat relief, and as a result, only then the cheering and panic: "I then saw some men in red, whom I believe were the left wing of the Thirteenth, and whom these men, I suppose, took to be reinforcements. When these men in red heard the cheer they broke and retired. Then the whole column became disorganized."[151]

Reverend Inglis testified that he saw green-uniformed men retreating first: "A small number of men (about 25 or 30) broke from the ranks and ran down the road, leaving the remainder standing mostly faced to the rear. These men were all dressed in green. Immediately behind those that were running away came from six to eight in red coats, who ran after the others down the road ... This retreat continued, with the red and green mixed together."[152]

It makes sense that if anyone mistook the Thirteenth for British regulars and began to withdraw from the field, it would have been the QOR at the centre, many of whom had already fallen back to the reserves, having used up their ammunition. Troops from the Thirteenth

A Welland Railway locomotive that transported volunteers to the front during the Fenian Raid.

There are no known photographs of the battle, but American artists produced colour lithographs celebrating a Fenian victory over the "redcoats." The Fenians are portrayed wearing green, while the Canadians are in red. In reality the Fenians wore blue U.S. Army tunics, Confederate grey, and civilian clothes, while half of the Canadians wore the "rifle-green" QOR uniform. Lithograph by Major C. Donahue and D. Egan, Sage Sons & Co, Buffalo, New York, 1869. (See ridgewaybattle.org for a colour version.)

"The Battle of Ridgeway, C.W. June 2, 1866." Part of the caption reads, "Much credit is due to the Fenian soldiers and Col. O'Neill for their gallantry in defeating over three times their number." Lithograph by Thomas Kelly, New York, 1870.

This 1866 illustration printed in *Leslie's Weekly* was more accurate in its depiction of the battle.

"The Queen's Own Rifles in engagement with Fenians." Although the ferocity of the fight at the "brick house" and Fenian barricade is accurately portrayed, the final fight for the house was undertaken by the 13th Battalion, not the QOR. Illustration by A. Wynn-Clark for Simpson's Confederation Jubilee Series, 1927.

The Angur "brick house" today, on the corner of Ridge and Bertie Road in Ridgeway.

The north wall of the brick house is still marked by Fenian rifle bullet hits from the 1866 battle.

Toronto volunteer militia drilling in a "square" formation used to defend against cavalry charges.

QOR Company 10 (Highlanders) in Stratford several days after the battle.

Top, Left: Alfred Booker, Jr., prominent Hamilton auctioneer and volunteer Lieutenant Colonel of the 13th Battalion. He aggressively sought overall command of the Canadian brigade and led it into disaster at Ridgeway.
Above: Alfred Booker in his uniformed splendour during a visit to Montreal in 1862. It was said of the ambitious Booker, "He delighted to be, the observed of all observers."
Middle, Left: Wealthy Hamilton chinaware merchant and volunteer Major James Atchison Skinner, second in command of the 13th Battalion. Many officers believed that he should have been in command instead of Booker. After the battle Skinner made his move.
Left: University of Toronto chemistry professor and volunteer Captain Henry Holmes Croft, enthusiastic founder and commanding officer of the University College rifle company. When the Fenian invasion came, the college boys went out to die, while Croft stayed behind safely in Toronto.

Top, Left: "Wesleyan Ensign" Malcolm McEachren, Sunday school teacher and store clerk, the modern Canadian army's first soldier and officer to be killed in action.
Top, Right: Corporal Francis Lackey, a Toronto shoemaker, died from horrific wounds sustained on Limestone Ridge.
Bottom, Right: Lance Corporal Mark Defries, a Toronto beer brewery maltster, killed in action.

Left: Private John Harriman Mewburn, a university student from QOR Company 9, killed in action.
Right: Sergeant Hugh Matheson, an assistant pharmacist from Toronto, lost a leg at Ridgeway and died three days later.

Left: Lieutenant Percy Gore Routh commanded Company 4 of the 13th Battalion. Some of his men were not impressed with his enthusiasm for battle. Gravely wounded, Routh was abandoned for dead in a hut on the battlefield.
Right: Private William Fairbanks Tempest, a med student serving in QOR Company 9, "University Rifles," killed in the Fenian counterattack. In the weeks before the battle, he had premonitions of his death.

Left, Top: The deadly thumb tip–sized .58-calibre lead "Minié ball" ammunition, named for its designer Claude-Étienne Minié. The familiar bullet-shaped slug featured a hollow base intended for more efficient muzzle loading, but the hollow also caused a deadly unintended side effect.

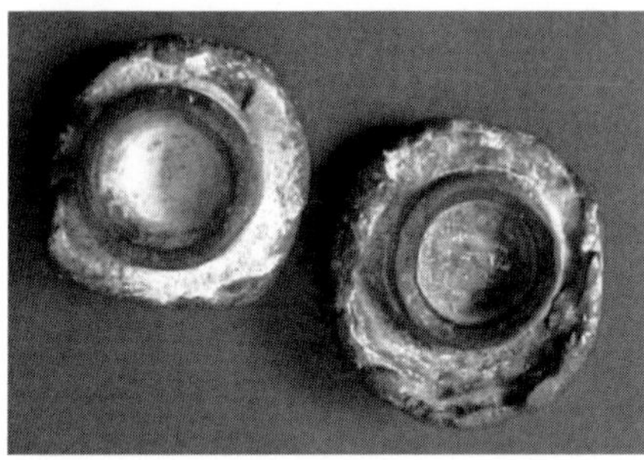

Left: When the Minié ball hit flesh, muscle, or bone, it "mushroomed," inflicting horrendous wounds comparable to those caused by modern hollow-point bullets. The use of expanding bullets in conventional warfare was outlawed by international law in 1899, too late for the men who fought at Ridgeway.

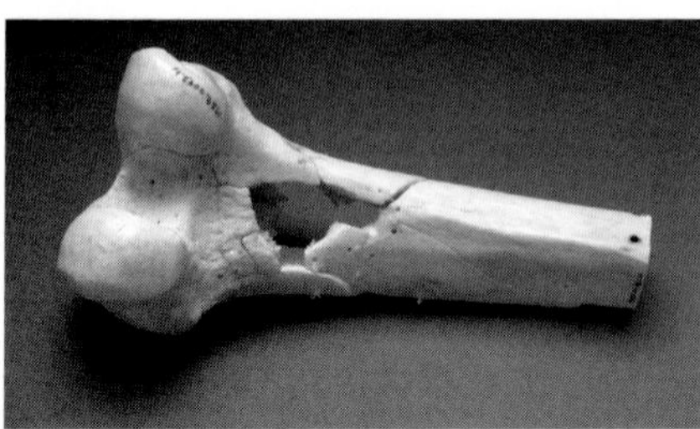

Human distal femur shot with a Minié ball causing an irreparable "compound comminuted fracture." Amputation was the only treatment available.

Skull showing "keyhole" gunshot trauma from a graze by a Minié ball.

Battalion would not likely have mistaken the identity of their own companies. It is also here at the centre that one of the more shameful episodes told of the panic that had occurred: the trampling of Captain Boustead by retreating men.

Captain James B. Boustead was a thirty-three-year-old Toronto wholesale trader, in command of QOR Company 3. Under his command the company had advanced resolutely behind Company 5, and soon after Company 5 had run out of ammunition for their Spencers and retired, Boustead led Company 3 forward in their place through the apple orchard before his company came to be relieved in turn. Company 3 then fell back toward the centre behind Booker's command as other companies passed it to take the field forward.

When the Fenian bayonet charge uncoiled and all the companies were trapped in the road between the fields and fences, many became unnerved and panicked. Once they began to run, their minds numbed with fear and herd instinct, nothing could stop them. Boustead was knocked down and trampled so severely that he would need hospitalization.[153] Private Isaac Greensides dashed into the path of the Fenian charge, slung the unconscious Boustead over his shoulder, and carried him off to safety.[154]

As the rout unfolded, Lieutenant Colonel Booker was overheard to say, "Oh God! What is this?" He made several attempts to stop the running men.[155] He ran to the rear on foot (to the front of the retreat), and waving his sword, urged the men to turn back: "For God sake, men, don't make cowards of yourselves."[156] At some point he mounted his horse and rode off after his retreating men, attempting to get ahead of them and turn them back.[157] To the skirmishers in the front ranks of the battle, Booker must have appeared as if he were fleeing in fear and leaving them behind.

Booker dismounted again and gave his horse back to his orderly. Lieutenant Arthurs of the QOR then mounted it and also made an attempt to turn the retreating men back at revolver point. Shortly afterward Booker took back his horse again and rode back and forth in his futile attempt to rally the troops.[158]

One of the last to be hit was Ensign William Fahey of QOR Company 1, who was wounded in the knee. He was carried to one of the houses near Ridge Road and left there to be captured by the Fenians.[159] He remained disabled for eighteen months.[160]

The rattle and pop of rifle fire was easily heard in the village of Ridgeway. Upon hearing the familiar sound, Dr. Brewster, who had served as a surgeon in the U.S. Army in the Civil War, decided to set out for the battlefield. He gathered up what was left of his military surgical kit: instruments, bandages, adhesive plaster, chloroform, a canteen full of whiskey and another of water. Brewster would later recollect:

> Just at the bend of the road to the north of the village, I met such a mixed and confused mass, as I have never seen elsewhere before or since. Soldiers and citizens, men, women and children, on foot and in all varieties of vehicles, with horses, cattle, sheep and pigs, all mingled together, and all hurrying along the road south. It brought to my mind Russel's [*sic*] description of Bull Run.*
>
> I saw two soldiers without guns, running, and close behind them an officer with revolver in hand, crying halt, and firing in the air occasionally, but running as fast as he could, and close behind him, more soldiers running.[161]

Some of the volunteers escaped into the side roads and bushes, but most made their way as far as the railway station in Ridgeway. From there, they began following the railway tracks westward, back toward Port Colborne. Booker rode with his men but eventually gave his horse to a wounded man.[162]

---

* William Russell was *The Times* correspondent in the United States during the Civil War and witnessed the panicked retreat of Union troops intermingled with civilian onlookers and dignitaries from Washington, DC, at the Battle of Bull Run–Manassas in June 1861, the war's first major battle.

AT 12 P.M. AN URGENT TELEGRAM from an unidentified party in Port Colborne reported:

> I have just had a talk with one of the Toronto volunteer officers in Port Colborne office. He reports Queen's Own obliged to fall back for want of support leaving their dead and wounded behind. Reinforcements are being hurried forward. The information is strictly private and will not be given to the public by us unless authorized by Gen. John Michel [commander of British forces in Canada].[163]

At 12:15 P.M. Robert Larmour telegraphed C.J. Brydges from Port Colborne.[164] Larmour told the Grand Trunk Railway managing director and confidential aide-de-camp to John A. Macdonald[165] that he was returning to Ridgeway with two flatcars of militiamen and a load of ammunition. An hour later Larmour would see the Elephant, the green and red thing hurtling through the shimmering heat waves toward him.

At 1:30 P.M., Isaac Buchanan in Hamilton, the former commander of the Thirteenth Battalion, telegraphed Sir John Michel, already suggesting who might have blundered:

> Telegraph from Port Colborne says that for want of support our volunteers are retreating disastrously. There must have been a want of experienced officers and ignorance of locality.[166]

The pointing of fingers had begun within three hours of the battle. Within six hours, the cover-up would begin. At 4 P.M. the following telegram began circulating on the military communications net:

> In a private message to [illegible] the following paragraph occurs, "Volunteers badly beaten at Fort Erie left many dead and wounded on the field." I have suppressed this paragraph and sent on the business part of the message.[167]

THE UNIDENTIFIED JOURNALIST from the Toronto *Leader* was caught up in the retreat and asked by one of the medical orderlies to help him with the wounded. He found himself with several wounded soldiers in Hoffman's Tavern, which had been made into a makeshift hospital when the Fenians overran his position. Several Fenians burst into the tavern and, assuming he was the owner, began to demand alcohol. He managed to find some rye whiskey in the basement.

The journalist and a volunteer attempted to give aid to the wounded men, among them Private Charles Lugsdin from QOR Company 4, who was gravely wounded through the lungs and shoulder. A Fenian officer eventually chased the drinking Fenians out of the tavern and took the volunteer orderly prisoner. The journalist protested his being left alone with all the wounded and the Fenian officer assigned to him one of his own men to help.

As the Fenians were approaching, James Johnson, the civilian armed with a sword who had helped Percy Routh off the field into a house, took Routh's watch, which had been hanging out of his pocket by its chain, and attempted to secrete it in the fireplace but was unsuccessful. Convinced that Routh was dead, Johnson hid the watch in his boot, intending to save it from being taken by the Fenians. As a civilian he found it easy to slip across the Fenian lines.[168]

The journalist in the meantime went out into the field. Approximately one hundred yards from Hoffman's Tavern he found Lance Corporal Mark Defries from QOR Company 3, a maltster in his brother's brewery, lying face down near a fence, shot through the back but still conscious: "He knew that he was dying. He requested me to take a ring from his finger and send it with a message to a young lady in Toronto. He also requested me to take his watch and send it to his father, whose address he gave me. This I attempted to do, but he could not endure to be touched. He told me it would do to take it after he was dead."[169]

In another farmhouse, the journalist found two severely wounded volunteers, Private W.H. Vandersmissen from the University Rifles, shot through the groin, and Corporal Francis Lackey from QOR Company 2, shot through the mouth. After doing everything he could for the two wounded men, the journalist then found a Fenian officer, a Major McDonnell, who gave him a written pass to move around the Fenian positions. The journalist returned to help the dying Defries but discovered that his body had been moved. He found Defries dead in a back room at the tavern. When he attempted to remove Defries's watch he found that it was now gone, presumably stolen.

In several houses in the area, the journalist found numerous wounded soldiers. In one house he found Private John Harriman Mewburn in a state of convulsions, suffering from either heatstroke and dehydration or from a blunt trauma wound to his head. Mewburn would soon die. In the same house he found Rupert Kingsford, also a student from Company 9, wounded in the leg and lying on a lounge but "remarkably cheerful." A Fenian by the name of John Gerrahty from Cincinnati was brought in, accidentally wounded in the side by one of his comrades. A crucifix was held before him for as long as he could see. He died thirteen minutes later. Outside, the journalist came upon a Queen's Own soldier lying in the road, shot dead through the head (probably Tempest), and a Fenian badly wounded in the hip, who was being aided by three of his comrades.

A pall of smoke hung over the battlefield as the dry grass along the slopes of the ridge was ignited by smouldering scraps of cartridge wadding fired from the rifles. Henry Teal, a local farmer, hitched a plough to several horses and, at the risk of losing them to the Fenians, ploughed a series of furrows around the field to prevent the fire from spreading.[170]

Dr. Brewster arrived on the battlefield in the last minutes of the fight and circled around to the rear of the Fenian lines. He identified himself as a former U.S. Army surgeon and was allowed by the Fenians to move about, freely aiding both Fenian and Canadian wounded. Observing several Fenians in the uniform of the U.S. Army, Brewster was told by a Fenian captain that he had not taken off his uniform since the war ended. Brewster scolded him that "it was time he did, as this was no place for it, and that I thought too highly of that uniform to see it worn in such a cause, as I had myself worn it for three years."[171] Brewster collected a list of names of Canadian and Fenian casualties he found in the vicinity. He later lost the list but recalled that it consisted of twenty-six names, including two Canadian and four Fenian dead.[172]

By now the Fenians were returning from Ridgeway and regrouping at the corners of Garrison and Ridge roads. On a slight rise across the road from the tavern, a Fenian green flag with a golden sunburst was fluttering. A Fenian officer advised the journalist that two injured volunteers were lying in the road toward Ridgeway. The journalist asked for some men to help carry the injured away, but before any could be assigned, a bugle signal was given and the insurgents began moving east along Garrison Road back toward Fort Erie. The journalist found himself alone with a volunteer from the QOR who was wounded in the wrist (probably Private Copp, QOR Company 5). The two of them were unable to move the two men in the road. The men appeared to be suffering from heatstroke; the journalist gave them some water and, using greatcoats he found abandoned in the field, built a small tent to shelter them from the sun.[173]

Private W.R. Hines of QOR Company 8 was taken prisoner. A Fenian officer seized his rifle, swore that it would never be used again against the Irish, and smashed its butt down against a boulder. The cocked and loaded weapon discharged, the bullet hitting the Fenian officer in the throat and exiting out the back of his head, killing him instantly. He was the last of the six or eight Fenians believed to have been killed in the battle of Limestone Ridge.[174]

Private George Mackenzie, whose arm had been shattered by a Minié ball, was helped off the field by two men during the retreat. But upon crossing the railway tracks in Ridgeway, he could go no farther and took shelter in an abandoned house. Private Alfred Powis remained with Mackenzie, laying him out on a bed in one of the bedrooms.

Eventually they heard the Fenians entering the town, and Powis climbed a ladder to an attic loft and hid. Too weak to follow him, Mackenzie remained below in the bed. He later recounted what happened next: "A rough fellow appeared at the door of the room where I lay. He started to see a red-coated youngster upon the bed, and exclaimed, 'You are my prisoner.' I was in no position to gainsay him, so I feebly assented. I soon discovered that I need fear no violence from my captors. They crowded into the room, rough-looking fellows in civilian dress, with the exception of a few, but all thoroughly armed, and looked on me with curiosity, some of them with compassion. One man, calling a friend to his assistance, undertook to tend to my wounded arm."[175]

After the Fenians had left, Mackenzie remained in the house, with Powis tending to him. Powis shot a chicken with his revolver and made a failed attempt to cook it, with Mackenzie complaining it was too tough to eat. They remained there all night until the owners returned in the morning. Mackenzie was then carried to a train, transported to Port Colborne, and subsequently hospitalized for six weeks in St. Catharines. His arm remained misshapen for the rest of his life.[176]

John O'Neill found Lieutenant Percy Routh lying on the floor of a cabin with his horrific chest wound, abandoned for dead. The Fenian commander, according to Routh, was concerned that Routh's sword and belt were causing him discomfort and tenderly removed them. Routh offered to surrender his sword to O'Neill, who refused to accept it, saying, "No, I will not take it; its possession may be a solace to you. I will leave it by your side."

Routh replied, "Thank you but some one less kind may come and take it." O'Neill carefully hid the sword under Routh's blanket before bidding him farewell.[177]

Dr. Brewster recalled: "Very few of the inhabitants of the village remained in their homes, but went with the crowd, and so gave the Fenians full liberty; but they took very little from the houses, chiefly handkerchiefs, stockings and little items to keep as souvenirs."[178]

In his history of the battle, Denison would conclude, "The Fenians, except in so far as they were wrong in invading a peaceful country, in carrying on an unjustifiable war, behaved remarkably well to the inhabitants ... They have been called plunderers, robbers and marauders, yet, no matter how unwilling we may be to admit it, the positive fact remains, that they stole but a few valuables, that they destroyed, comparatively speaking, little or nothing and that they committed no outrages on the inhabitants but treated every one with unvarying courtesy. On taking a number of ... prisoners they treated them with the greatest kindness, putting the officers under their parole and returning them their side arms ..."[179] Limestone Ridge may have been the first modern battle fought by Canadians, but it was probably the last one fought with Old World gallantry.

The Toronto *Leader* journalist all that afternoon attempted to find a horse and wagon to evacuate the wounded, but most of the locals had fled, driving their horses away. Calling on different houses in the area, he found more wounded volunteers sheltered in them. Eventually he found a horse and returned to Port Colborne in the late afternoon, reporting the presence of abandoned wounded at Ridgeway. A number of volunteer physicians—Dr. Clark of St. Catharines, Dr. Eraser of Fonthill, Dr. Downie and Dr. Allen of Brantford—immediately rushed by wagon to Ridgeway. They arrived there in the evening and began rendering aid to the wounded, who would be evacuated by train the next morning. Behind them came a team of surgeons and physicians from the Toronto area. News of the battle reached Toronto within several hours and at 1 P.M. eight physicians immediately left by railway for Port Colborne, where they arrived at 9 P.M. Among the volunteer physicians was Dr. Tempest, who upon arriving at the scene learned that his son William had been killed.[180] All the years of hope for the medical partnership so carefully planned by father and son were in an instant struck down dead in a road on Limestone Ridge. It would break Dr. Tempest's heart.[181]

In the evening the journalist returned with the doctors from Port

Colborne to collect the dead, departing at dawn the next morning. He subsequently wrote: "We arrived at Port Colborne with our melancholy burden, about six o'clock A.M. on the 3rd. I may mention that two of the wounded men, whom I left alive in the afternoon, were dead when we returned in evening. Thus terminated the day of horrors. God grant that it may never be my lot to relate similar experiences."[182]

The immediate toll that morning at Limestone Ridge was seven volunteers killed and twenty-eight wounded. Two more would die of their wounds over the next forty-eight hours, bringing the total of men killed in action to nine. The dead were all from the Queen's Own Rifles. Of the twenty-eight wounded, twenty were from the Toronto Queen's Own Rifles, six from the Hamilton Battalion, and two from the York Rifles.[183] Somewhere between six and eight Fenians are believed to have been killed—the number is difficult to fix, as villagers buried some while the Fenians evacuated other casualties, and some later died of their wounds in the United States.[184] One of the Fenian casualties would be mistaken for a Queen's Own, brought back to Toronto, and laid out for the funeral in a casket draped with the Union Jack before somebody noticed the mistake.[185] Over the next few weeks the number of dead nearly doubled as several more succumbed to their wounds and to disease contracted during the campaign.

As the Fenians marched back toward the Niagara River, flush in their victory, the "day of horrors" for the seventy-one men and seven officers under Lieutenant Colonel Dennis and aboard the *W.T. Robb* at Fort Erie was only about to begin.

EIGHT

The Stand at Fort Erie, Afternoon, June 2, 1866

On the morning of Saturday, June 2, as Booker was embattled on Limestone Ridge, back in Toronto Major George T. Denison, the impatient young attorney and commander of the Governor General's Body Guard, was waiting at the docks with his fifty-five-horse cavalry troop. The departure of the steam ferry *Toronto* had been delayed to complete the loading of supplies for the front. Since the Fenian landing early Friday morning, Denison had been relentlessly lobbying the incompetent General George Napier, commander of British forces in Canada West, to deploy Denison's cavalrymen.[1]

Years later Denison would write, "The idea never entered my head that the authorities would send infantry without any cavalry whatever. I should have known that infantry officers would probably forget all about the cavalry, but I must confess I never thought of such a thing. I do not blame myself for not foreseeing this, for I was still a young man, only twenty-six, and I had not then that confidence in the average stupidity of officials which, through long experience, I have since acquired."[2]

Late on Friday afternoon, Denison had finally received orders to mobilize his men and join Peacocke's forces. Denison transferred his outstanding law cases to his partners and ordered his cavalry to gather at the exhibition grounds that night. At dawn on June 2, they rode down to the Toronto docks.[3] The ferry finally steamed out at 8 A.M., bound for Port Dalhousie thirty miles across Lake Ontario.[4] Booker by now was in the heat of battle at Ridgeway.

Denison had requested Spencer Rifles from the Militia Department but was turned down.[5] He complained, "I had to take my corps on a campaign without the carbines I had asked for, but with revolvers for which we had only some four or five ten-year-old paper cartridges for each. We did not know whether they would go off or not. We had no haversacks, no water bottles, no nose bags. Some of us had small tin cups fastened on our saddles. We had no canteens or knives or forks, or cooking utensils of any kind, or valises. We had no clothes except those on our backs (I had an extra flannel shirt and one pair of socks in the small wallets in front of my saddle). We had no tents and no blankets."[6]

On board the ferry Denison requisitioned from the supplies a container of hardtack biscuits and distributed one to each of his men. He recalled, "Some wags bored holes in them, hung them around their necks and wore them as medals."[7]

Denison arrived at Port Dalhousie near noon, was ferried by train to Port Robinson, and from there rode to Chippawa, pacing his horses so as not to tire them out before the end of the day. In Chippawa he received news that Booker had fought the Fenians and had been driven off the field. Denison rode on to catch up with Peacocke's column that had departed that morning.

THAT MORNING, Lieutenant Colonel George Peacocke, the British commander of the Niagara campaign, after having telegraphed Booker orders to delay his advance by at least an hour, arranged breakfast for his arriving reinforcements. At about 7 A.M. after everyone had been fed, Peacocke left from Chippawa with a mixed force of from sixteen to seventeen hundred British regular troops and Canadian volunteers and six artillery pieces. They marched toward Stevensville, where he planned to meet Booker's brigade at 11 A.M.[8]

Peacocke still had only his ten-mile-to-an-inch–scale postal map of Canada West, which showed post offices and mail routes but indicated neither roads nor terrain. John Kirkpatrick, the reeve of Chippawa, had a detailed county map, but he assumed that Peacocke had a superior military map and did not think of offering him his own. Peacocke found himself relying on several anonymous locals who led him on a circuitous route much longer than necessary.[9] Instead of advancing from Chippawa directly south along Sodom Road to Stevensville, a distance of about seven miles, the guides took Peacocke along a meandering road that followed the Niagara River to Black Creek, a distance of eleven miles—four miles farther than necessary. The guides claimed that Sodom Road was impassable to Peacocke's artillery. In fact the road was in better condition than the river road. Denison, who rode down it several hours later that day, reported, "Strange to say, along this road we met scores of vehicles of every description belonging to people of the neighbourhood, who had by this time discovered that the Sodom Road was the best way home, and were using it to get back."[10] Denison suggested that the guides feared that the Fenians might move up from Black Creek into Chippawa along the river road and were acting in what they thought was Peacocke's best military interest.[11] Journalist Alexander Somerville, on the other hand, argued that the guides were leading the troops along the river road to ensure that their own property along the route was cleared of Fenians and protected from looting, or perhaps the guides were even Fenian sympathizers.[12] In the end the choice of this river route was never adequately explained. Peacocke himself merely stated in his report, "Guides took us by a road much longer than necessary."[13]

At 11 A.M., when Peacocke had originally anticipated joining with Booker in Stevensville, he was still some three miles away.[14] According to him it was at this time that he was delivered the message from Booker that he had engaged the Fenians alone. Peacocke insisted that the message was written at 7:30 A.M. (Booker claimed the message had been written at 9:30 A.M., reporting that he made contact with the enemy at 7:30 A.M.)[15] Peacocke added, "At the same time I received information that he had retired on Ridgeway."[16]

With the receipt of the message Peacocke knew of Booker's retreat and the approximate location of the Fenian army: about six miles away to the southwest toward Ridgeway, between him and Booker's retreating force. Yet Peacocke chose not to pursue the Fenians or come to Booker's aid at this critical moment. According to Denison, "Saturday the 2nd June was the first really hot day of the season, there was hardly a breath of wind stirring and the heat of the sun was excessive. The men were all warmly clad, and it being the first hot day, they suffered far more seriously from it than if they had become inured to it by a succession of warm weather. After marching some miles the men began to fall out from fatigue and exhaustion caused by the heat, the regulars suffered more and fell out to a greater extent than the volunteers, on account of being heavily loaded with knapsacks."[17]

Ironically, the men of the British army, being better equipped than the Canadians, were suffering more because of the weight of their kit. One Canadian volunteer who marched with Peacocke's column, Barlow Cumberland, later recalled how the roadside was strewn with British infantrymen prostrated from heat exhaustion. One British soldier, Corporal Carrington, died from heatstroke—the only known British casualty in Canada West during the Fenian Raid.[18]

Cumberland recalled, "Our men in the unaccustomed weight of heavy shakoes, close buttoned thick tunics, and with military overcoats over their shoulders and heavy leather ammunition pouches which banged on their buttocks at every step, suffered much from the speed and the heat. Their thirst was insatiable and being without water bottles they would drop out of the ranks to lap up the water in the ditches alongside the roads only to be still more overheated by running up to take their places in the ranks again ... Our men suffered most from their feet. The volunteers were marching in their own usual civilian, every-day city shoes, many with high heels and narrow toes, quite unfitted for a forced march on a hot day over hardened ruts, made slippery by dust, on a sun-baked country road."[19]

Rather than advancing farther, Peacocke now marched the men inland to a small crossroads called "New Germany" (near the corner of the present Sodom and Netherby roads), a mile and a half short of Stevensville.[20] There Peacocke halted at noon to rest and feed the men and, inexplicably, planned to spend the night there![21] Cumberland recalled how, while the Fenians were sweeping through Ridgeway, Peacocke's men concerned themselves with foraging for lunch at nearby farms and pricking and sponging their blistered feet under the shade of trees. Peacocke's column sat at New Germany doing absolutely nothing for the next five hours while the Fenians regrouped and turned back toward Fort Erie.

It was only at 4 P.M., after receiving intelligence that the Fenians were returning to Fort Erie, that Peacocke began rousing his men to march again.[22] It took him nearly an hour and a half to raise his footsore men, who had expected to spend the night, to pack up what they needed and leave what they did not, and to re-form into columns to begin the march toward Fort Erie.[23] Just as Peacocke was leaving at 5:30 P.M., Denison galloped in on Sodom Road with his troop of cavalry. Peacocke ordered him to ride out in front of the marching column as an advance guard. Denison was frustrated by having now to pace his cavalry at an infantryman's speed, recalling, "This was the regular rule for the guidance of an advance guard, and I can remember how I began to chafe almost at once at not being able to push on. I felt that there was no reason why I should not go on until I struck the enemy's pickets, for I knew I could easily fall back if overmatched."[24]

They had covered a distance of nine miles when it began to turn to dusk.[25] At that point they were marching east along Bowen Road toward the Niagara River and were inland three miles short of Fort Erie when they came upon a narrow portion of the road where woods came up to the edges on both sides—potentially a point for an ambush. On the road ahead of them they spotted a party of men whom they thought might be Fenians. As the cavalry rode forward, the men melted away into the woods. The horsemen followed them into the forest, but failing light forced them to turn back. With darkness descending upon them, Peacocke decided to halt the column in its current formation and pass the night with the men sleeping on their arms in the road.[26]

Peacocke's decisions to hold his reinforcements on the train in Clifton the night before, to delay his march from Chippawa by an hour in order to serve breakfast, to follow the guides on the meandering river road, to spend the afternoon camped at New Germany, to put off until 5:30 the departure for Fort Erie, and now his decision to halt about three miles short of Fort Erie, were later blamed for the Fenian escape and even the disaster at Limestone Ridge and Fort Erie.[27] As a British army officer, Peacocke was beyond the reproach of Canadian authorities or the reach of local journalists. His official reports do not broach the issue, and if his superiors in the British army questioned his march that day, no record of the inquiry apparently survived in the archives.

As the men bedded down in the road for the night, wild rumours began to trickle into the camp. The news of the retreat of Booker's column at Ridgeway was true enough, but they began to hear reports that the men of the Welland Canal Field Battery and Dunnville Naval Brigade, who had departed Port Colborne in the morning aboard the *Robb,* had been massacred in Fort Erie that afternoon with only four survivors remaining. According to the rumours, two thousand more Fenians had crossed into Canada from Buffalo.[28]

IT WAS AFTER 3 A.M. on Sunday, June 3, as Denison was inspecting the encampment, that he heard somebody approach him in the darkness and ask, "Is that you George?"

Denison would recall: "I stopped, and a man came up whom I could not recognize. He was dressed in the common clothes of a labouring man, and had a close fitting old cloth cap pulled down over his head, a red woollen scarf around his neck, a large pair of heavy moustaches and a wild, hunted look about the eyes. He shook hands with me and said: 'Do you not know me?' I knew there was something familiar, but I could not place him."[29]

Denison finally recognized the voice and realized that the dishevelled man standing before him had shaved off his luxurious mutton-chop Dundreary sidewhiskers: It was Lieutenant Colonel John Stoughton Dennis, the commander of the *Robb* expedition.

Dennis was in a frightfully disordered state. Denison recalled: "I shall never forget how it startled me; I knew he had gone away in command of the Queen's Own. I knew they had been defeated with heavy loss, but we had only heard wild rumours, and seeing the commanding officer coming into camp disguised, with his whiskers shaved off and looking altogether most wretched, the thought flashed through my mind as to what had become of all my comrades and friends who had been under his command."[30]

When Denison asked what had happened, Dennis replied that he had landed his men in Fort Erie in the afternoon. He said, "I heard the Fenians were coming and I formed up to meet them. Suddenly a large force of Fenians appeared on our flank on the hill and fired upon us. The volunteers behaved badly; they fired one volley and then broke and ran. I ran down the river and into a house and back into a stable and hid in the hay in the loft for some hours. I was not discovered, and when I got an opportunity I disguised myself as you see and came across through the woods till I came upon the pickets of your force."[31]

George Denison was most disturbed that Dennis "could not give me any information whatever as to what had happened to his men."[32]

WHAT HAPPENED TO DENNIS and his men was more complex a story than the one he had blurted out upon his arrival at Peacocke's camp. The Military Court of Inquiry into the Battle of Fort Erie was held in secret several months after the battle, and the Canadian government would hold back for years the transcript of testimony given there; not even Members of Parliament were allowed access.[33] Unlike the record of the Booker Inquiry, the transcript of the testimony, even when no longer classified, was forgotten and overlooked to this day: A single handwritten version, not even a microfilm copy, is available in the archives in Ottawa.[34] Although at some point in the subsequent century the transcript became available to historians, most were unaware of its existence and never referred to it.[35] What follows is based on the 350-page transcript of that inquiry.

After leaving Port Colborne near dawn on the morning of June 2, the *Robb* steamed along Lake Erie toward Buffalo through calm waters with no other ships in sight.[36] Approximately seventy-one men and eight officers were aboard.[37] The 128-foot, 180-tonne steam-powered vessel, christened the *W.T. Robb* after its captain and McCallum's close friend, Walter Tyrie Robb, was considered to be one of the fastest on the Great Lakes.[38] It was manned by nineteen men and three officers (Captain Lachlan McCallum, Lieutenant Walter T. Robb, and Second Lieutenant Angus Macdonald) of the Dunnville Naval Brigade of marines.

At Port Colborne they had taken aboard Lieutenant Colonel Dennis and Captain Charles Akers, Royal Engineers, along with the men of Welland Canal Field Battery, consisting of fifty-one gunners and NCOs, British Royal Artillery bombardier Sergeant James McCracken, and three officers (Captain Richard Saunders King, MD, and Lieutenants Adam K. Scholfield and Charles Nimmo [Nemmo]). With their field artillery locked up by the British in Hamilton, half of the Welland gunners were armed with standard-issue Long-Enfield rifles, but the other half carried obsolete smoothbore Victoria carbines.[39] While the Victoria's twenty-six-inch smoothbore .733-calibre barrel weighed a hefty seven pounds nine ounces, it was paradoxically intended to be a cavalry carbine. Its short barrel, however, resulted in agonizing recoil and flash and flame that frightened even the most hardened warhorse. It had an effective range of only three hundred yards at best. The British army stopped issuing the weapon in 1853, and the surplus carbines ended up being supplied to the Canadian Volunteer Militia during the *Trent* Crisis.[40]

The *Robb* expedition has often been portrayed as a hare-brained scheme devised by Dennis after Booker relieved him of his command in Port Colborne, but Peacocke had initiated the plan long before Booker arrived on the scene.[41] When Peacocke sent his midnight telegram informing Booker and Dennis that he was sending Akers to them, he also reconfirmed his original 5 P.M. order that an armed party be sent if a vessel could be found.[42] Dennis arranged for the *Robb* to come when he learned that the *International*, which Peacocke had requested earlier in the day, was not coming. What *was* hare-brained, however, was his decision to take personal command of the mission. Peacocke later stated that Akers and Dennis "should never" have gone aboard, but reserved most of his condemnation for Akers:

> Capt Akers and Col. Dennis *should never have left Port Colborne.* To the former I had explained thoroughly that I wished to prevent all possibility of the Fenians meeting Booker singly, and I had desired him to remain and make himself useful at Port Colborne.[43] [Emphasis in original.]

Dennis's thinking, like Booker's, was driven by unbridled ambition and a determination to take advantage of this rare opportunity to cap his business and social achievements with an act of prowess on the battlefield. Knighthoods were made of such stuff.

When the *Robb* steamed past Buffalo it was daylight, and those on board saw huge crowds gathered along the American shore observing the unfolding action. The troops were ordered to conceal themselves below deck so as not to alarm U.S. authorities and not to tip off the Fenians that the tug had armed men aboard.[44] As they slipped into the mouth of the Niagara River and steamed by the village of Fort Erie at around 6 A.M., it appeared to be deserted.[45] After it passed the village, the *Robb* was pulled to by the U.S. Navy gunship U.S.S. *Michigan* near Black Rock. The *Michigan*'s captain, Commander Bryson, informed Dennis that the Fenians had abandoned their camp on Frenchman's Creek in the middle of the night.[46]

The *Robb* continued north down the Niagara River, past the former Fenian encampment, steaming as far as Black Creek, but saw no sign of the enemy. Docking near Black Creek, the troops learned that the Fenians had moved westward toward Ridge Road. Dennis dispatched a message to Peacocke informing him of this and turned the *Robb* back up the river to the B&LH Railroad terminal in Fort Erie where, according to their improvised plan, he was to meet Booker's brigade.[47] Booker, of course, was not coming.

It was now around 8:00 or 8:30 A.M. If a wind had been blowing in the right direction or if the sound had been reflected against a low cloud cover, the men of the *Robb* might have heard the gunfire from Limestone Ridge seven miles away. But on this clear, windless morning, they heard nothing, and Dennis assumed that Booker must not have received approval from Peacocke for their new plan of action and had marched to Stevensville instead. Dennis was on his own.

Dennis ordered the *Robb* to put in at the main wharf near the centre of Fort Erie. This was a densely built and busy town with its wharves, hotels, taverns, warehouses, and customs offices. A street grid of about twenty-five city blocks of mostly clapboard buildings rose upward from the river on a steep slope toward a crest about 250 yards away before levelling out into farm fields and orchards to the west. Front Street

(Niagara Boulevard today) ran along the shore, dividing the docks and railway track on one side from the line of buildings on the other. Front Street ran to Lake Erie on the southern end and the ruins of the old fort beyond. From there, the road turned inland and climbed uphill, merging with Garrison Road leading to Ridgeway. (See Fort Erie Battle Map.)

At about 9 A.M. Dennis landed the Welland Canal Field Battery and the Dunnville Naval Brigade, who cautiously took up positions on the Fort Erie wharf. The village loomed above them from the riverside along the slopes of the hill, eerily devoid of the hundreds of travellers, railway and ferry workers, merchants, farmers, and revenue and customs officials who normally crowded Fort Erie's narrow streets. No smoke was seen coming from any of the chimneys, and some of the houses stood with their doors broken open and their gates torn down.

"The telegraph wires were strewn on the ground and a stillness, almost like death prevailed," Welland Battery Corporal Stephen Beatty later recalled.[48]

Captain King, the commander of the Welland Battery, cautiously led his gunners into the village. The troops moved through the streets in close order, without sending out skirmishers to feel their way forward. Entering a house he thought was empty, King found a man in bed under blankets, pretending to be asleep. When King ordered him out of bed he discovered that the man, who gave his name as Daniel Drummond, was clothed and armed with a handgun. Drummond was arrested and escorted back to the wharf. The jittery troops almost shot a disabled man riding into the village when they mistook his crutch for a rifle.[49]

Once they realized Canadian troops were on the scene, villagers began to come out of hiding and reported the whereabouts of suspected Fenians. Approximately eleven suspicious men were flushed out and arrested by the patrols.[50] The prisoners were herded into the schoolhouse and town hall. Legal formalities were strictly adhered to, with time taken to swear in special constables to take charge of the prisoners.

Seven men from the Naval Brigade were posted to the schoolhouse to guard the prisoners.[51]

As the heat began to take hold of the day, the men were ordered to pile their heavy greatcoats in the Customs Station House. Dennis split his forces into two sections: One section (left) under Captain Akers and Lieutenant Nimmo or Scholfield was to move north through Fort Erie along the ridge of the hilltop and out into the forests and fields paralleling the Niagara River. The other section (right) under Captain King was to march closer to the riverbank. The two sections were to converge about five miles north of Fort Erie, some two miles before Black Creek.[52]

Dennis re-embarked upon the *Robb* with Captain McCallum and Lieutenant Macdonald and the rest of the Naval Brigade, and steamed down the river, keeping ahead of the inland columns and landing additional patrols along the river road.[53] Dennis so far was doing an outstanding job of taking control of the Canadian side of the Niagara River.

Akers and his troops made their way north through the outskirts of town and across farms and fields, along the way arresting anyone found to be suspicious. Eventually they arrived at the abandoned Fenian camp at Frenchman's Creek. The camp was in a field just under an acre in size and strewn with abandoned food, ammunition cartridges, and bent and smashed rifles. In the middle of the field they found a pyre of approximately one hundred burnt rifles. Seeing weapons glistening in shallow water, some of the men jumped in to retrieve them. Akers urged the men to stay together and not delay their march by retrieving souvenir rifles they could not use.[54]

Stephen Beatty, the volunteer who had to abandon his gristmill, recalled, "The men suffered greatly from the heat which was intense. There was not a drinking cup in the whole company whereby thirst could be quenched if water could be got. All farmhouses were deserted until the arrival at Mr. Percy Becums, that gentleman supplied us with fresh milk and buttermilk as long as the supply lasted and then we had to resort to water."[55]

Dennis, in the meantime, observed the shore from the *Robb*'s deck through a telescope or field glasses as the vessel drifted up the river.[56] At one point he spotted some ten armed men and landed a "boats crew" of eight marines under Lieutenant Angus Macdonald to capture them. Macdonald complained that there was a barn nearby, and that Fenians could be inside waiting to ambush them. In the end Macdonald captured four of the men and sent them down to the small boat to wait for the *Robb*'s return from Black Creek. Dennis continued to make his way along the river, landing troops to scour woods or arrest any armed men he spotted from the deck of the *Robb*.[57]

Eventually Akers's section reunited with Captain King's, which had taken approximately ten prisoners. Before they reached Black Creek, the *Robb* arrived and the Welland Battery and its prisoners were brought aboard in small boats.[58] According to Dennis, the prisoners reported that the Fenians had fought a battle and had been "utterly dispersed." At about 11 A.M. Dennis had glimpsed Lieutenant Colonel Peacocke's struggling column as it turned inland near Black Creek, and he had no reason to disbelieve the reports of the Fenian defeat.[59] Akers testified, "My general impression from what I had seen and heard on shore was that the Fenians were disheartened and would get away as soon as they could ... The report at Black Creek was to the effect that the Fenians had been thrashed, so much so that the men of the artillery began cheering."[60] A fatal assumption was made for a second time over the last twelve hours that the Fenians had no fight left in them and would now be easy prey.

It was approximately between 3 and 4 P.M. when Dennis decided to return to Fort Erie and billet his men there for the night.[61] Sometime between 4 and 5 the *Robb* steamed back into the town with thirty to forty prisoners in its hold.[62] Dennis had sufficient time during the day to take down the names and particulars of twenty prisoners, whose names he inscribed later in the margin of his report.[63]

The men still had not been fed since the previous night. Stephen Beatty's recollections of the mission are punctuated with comments on the hunger all the men felt throughout the day. At one point he commented, "In that respect officers and men shared alike."[64] Beatty did not know that some of the officers on the trip back to Fort Erie had enjoyed a leisurely lunch in the captain's cabin out of sight of their hungry men.[65]

ONCE THE *ROBB* WAS TIED UP to the Niagara River railway wharf at Fort Erie, the troops were formed up on the dock and Dr. Kempson, the village reeve, began writing billet tickets and handing them out to the men.[66] The prisoners were disembarked from the *Robb* and taken to join the prisoners held in the schoolhouse, with the intention of transporting them to the Welland jail.[67] Dennis and Akers in the meantime went into a store to find paper on which to compose telegrams to various authorities.[68] Akers was to take their messages to the telegraph station in the B&LH Railway terminal. Dennis was still composing his telegrams on the counter of the store when suddenly Akers, as evidently was his habit, inexplicably rode off on his own in a buggy toward the railway station before Dennis could hand his messages to him.[69]

About two miles outside of Fort Erie, Lewis Palmer, a retired British army captain in his seventies and a veteran of the War of 1812 and the 1837 Rebellion, was smoking in the door of his house near Garrison Road when he suddenly observed the glistening in the sun of rifles and bayonets approaching on the road from the west.[70] Palmer at first assumed that these were Canadian or British troops, but as they came closer he realized they were Fenians. He quickly mounted his horse and galloped into town to give warning.[71]

Numerous people were now streaming into Fort Erie with news that the Fenians were coming. Captain King was standing on Front Street when Clara Kempson, the reeve's young wife, came running down in a fright to inform him that a rider had just galloped up to her house and collapsed in exhaustion. He had told her that a huge force of Fenians had defeated the volunteers at Ridgeway and was now approaching the town from Garrison Road. Captain King dismissed the report as a rumour, saying to her, "Stuff woman, I don't believe it."[72] Clara ran off toward the dock to find her husband.

There were numerous civilians thronged among the troops on the dock. One of them, Edwin Thomas, a Fort Erie resident, later testified, "I met the Reeve's wife in a fright running down towards the wharf. She hailed me and told me the Fenians had whipped the British and were coming to burn and plunder the village. I told her straight it was a false rumour, that if they had whipped the British they would not be likely to be falling back on Fort Erie."[73]

On his way to the railway station Akers also heard from a panicked passerby that there had been a battle in the morning and that the Canadian volunteers had been "driven out." Akers also did not believe the report. He had arrived at the railway terminal in his buggy and had gone in to see whether he could establish a telegraphic link with Peacocke when he heard that troops were coming down Garrison Road from the west.

Akers cautiously climbed up a ladder along the side of the terminal to get a better look. He saw in the distance a huge swaggering army with horses and wagons coming toward him down Garrison Road. At first he thought it was British artillery, but as the force drew nearer Akers began to make out their varied uniforms and realized that he was looking at nearly eight hundred Fenians barrelling straight toward the town. Akers claimed that he jumped into his buggy and began riding back toward Fort Erie to give warning but that advancing Fenian skirmishers poured across Garrison Road in front of him and cut him off. He now turned around and escaped by taking his buggy to Port Colborne on a road skirting Lake Erie. He would arrive there safely at about seven that evening.[74]

Lewis Palmer in the meantime rode into town and down to the dock, where he found Captain King and told him that the Fenians were about fifteen minutes from the town.[75] King asked how many there were. Palmer replied there were four or five hundred as near as he could judge.[76] Shortly afterward another man arrived in a buggy carrying the same warning, and then a third horseman galloped in—the estimates varied between 450 to 800, but all agreed that the enemy was advancing from Garrison Road and would be there in less than ten to fifteen minutes.[77]

King by now was convinced of the veracity of the reports and, unable to find Dennis, ordered the prisoners to be taken from the schoolhouse and put aboard the *Robb* on "the double."[78] A debate broke out about what to do next. Several civilians urged King to withdraw his men to the *Robb* and escape or risk being "cut to pieces"[79] or "all shot down."[80] Kempson urged the troops to defend the town, saying, "I would show a little resistance." The retired Captain Palmer argued that with so few men it would be no use to resist a force as large as the one coming at them.[81] Still unable to find Dennis anywhere, King ordered the troops to get back aboard the *Robb*.[82]

Sylvester Graham, a resident of Fort Erie, in the meantime encountered Dennis in the street and told him that a rider had come into town warning of the approaching Fenians.[83] Dennis asked Graham to show him from where the Fenians were advancing, and the two men jogged westward up Bertie Road toward the crest of the hill that arched its way through the town north to south. Graham pointed out a barn on the horizon on a hillcrest near where Garrison Road was, about a half mile away. Dennis later did not say whether he had brought the telescope or field glasses he had aboard the *Robb* when he went into town; very likely he had not, as he was not expecting to engage the Fenians any time soon, but in his final statement to the Court of Inquiry five months later, Dennis nonetheless claimed:

> We then and there saw the Fenians standing on the hill near the barn. I judged their number at about 150. They were stationary and seemed to be only partly armed. They did not to my view present any formidable

> appearance and I took them to be the remnant of the invading force of the Fenians on the retreat with our troops in pursuit. This was consistent with the reports which were prevalent in the village that afternoon and to which I had heard no contradiction, which were that our troops had met the Fenians out in the country and had beaten them and that the latter were flying in all directions. I at once concluded that I should not be justified in embarking my force small as it was and leaving the village defenceless and placing no obstacle in the way of their escape by the Ferry Steamer which at this time was making her regular trips across from Fort Erie to Black Rock and I returned to the dock and took measures accordingly. I was at the time fully under the impression that the men I had seen as before stated about 150 in number composed all that was left of the Fenian invading force.[84]

In this statement of October 27, made in the final days of the Court of Inquiry, Dennis was desperately attempting to exculpate himself after days of damning testimony, and his assertions contradicted other earlier statements he had made as to where he first saw the Fenian force. It is only one of the many inconsistencies that would emerge in the inquiry, challenging the veracity of his original report written shortly after the battle on June 4.

In that report Dennis claimed, for example:

> Having in the meantime made up my mind to send the prisoners by the tug to Welland gaol, I had them brought down and embarked there in charge of the Reeve when the alarm was given that the Fenians were entering the town in force. In fact the first messenger had hardly delivered the news when a second came in to say that they were within quarter of a mile coming down the street along the river. I went over from the pier to satisfy myself and saw them in numbers, as I judged, about 150 advancing upon the street indicated.

Already a half mile separates where Dennis said he first saw the Fenians in his June report, "coming down the street along the river," from where he said he saw them in his October statement, "standing on the hill near the barn" half a mile away. Dennis continued in his June report:

> Supposing them to be of the material, and of the same miserable character physically as the prisoners we had been taking all day, I thought the detachment I had with the boat, even if we had to resort to the bayonet, sufficient for them, and concluded that my duty lay in making a stand against them.

In his June report, Dennis claimed he gave orders to put the prisoners aboard the *Robb* and placed himself in command at the dock when the Fenians were first seen:

> I first took the precaution to put the prisoners under hatches and then advancing to meet the enemy about 150 yards, drew up my little command across the street. As they came within about 200 yards they opened fire on us, when my detachment, by order fired a volley from each of the companies, upon which a severe flank fire was opened on us from the West, and on looking in the direction, I observed *for the first time* [my emphasis], two considerable bodies of the enemy running in a northerly parallel with the river evidently with the intention of cutting us off, and getting possession of both of us and the steamer at the same time."[85]

According to his report, Dennis did not see the enemy on his western flank (on the hillside) until after he ordered the first volley to be fired, when he suddenly came under surprise fire on his flank. Dennis continued:

> I therefore concluded that my duty lay in saving the prisoners we had on board and preventing the enemy from getting possession of the vessel, which I know, and he probably knew also, was his only means of escape, and I therefore ordered the captain to cast off and get in the stream, and ordered my men to retreat and to do the best they could to get away, each man for himself. During this time a heavy fire was kept

> up on us both in front and flank, and I had the grief of seeing several of my men fall.

Dennis claimed that he retreated with his men down Front Street "under a heavy though comparatively ineffective fire" and that against his advice some of his men took shelter in the village post office. As for himself, Dennis reported:

> I turned into the premises of a friend in the lower part of the village where I lay concealed ... I dressed in disguise furnished by my friends and then came out and remained in the village till nightfall, when I got through the lines, and struck across the country in search of Colonel Peacocke—finding his camp at about five miles back of Fort Erie, arriving there at three o'clock A.M. ... On my return I was able to learn, for the first time, something of the casualties in the affair of the previous evening.[86]

This fable spun by Dennis would become the official story of what transpired in Fort Erie, as the testimony of other witnesses ended up being classified. The true story is rather different.

ACCORDING TO THIS TESTIMONY, while Dennis was preparing to send a telegram in one of the stores in town, and reports of the imminent Fenian approach arrived one after another, Captains King and McCallum were in command on the docks.[87] It is unclear who ordered the prisoners to be transferred from the schoolhouse to the *Robb*—Dennis claimed it was he but other witnesses stated it was King who gave the order.[88]

King ordered his gunners to climb back aboard to the safety of the *Robb*.[89] Some of the troops were plainly frightened, having heard that the approaching Fenians outnumbered them by at least ten to one.[90] Private Samuel Cormick nervously asked Captain McCallum, "Are the Fenians coming?" McCallum replied, "They say so."[91] The men were relieved to return to the safety of the tug.

Shortly afterward, Dennis arrived on the empty wharf to discover that the men had reboarded the vessel without his orders. To their horror, Dennis angrily ordered King to disembark the Welland Battery back onto the dock and told McCallum likewise to disembark all the men he could spare from his Naval Brigade.[92] King and McCallum argued with Dennis that it would be wiser to remain on board, cast off into stream, and assess the size of the approaching Fenian force. If the situation proved manageable, they could then land the troops again to deal with the enemy; if not, they could remain safely offshore, blocking the Fenians from escaping over the river to Buffalo until Peacocke's forces arrived.[93]

Dennis angrily stamped his foot and reminded King and McCallum that he was in command.[94] He dismissed their objections, declaring that they had come here to face the Fenians and that the force headed toward them was in retreat and probably being pursued by Peacocke's column close behind. They should check the Fenian retreat long enough for Peacocke to catch and overrun them.[95]

King had no alternative but to order his reluctant men to come off the *Robb* and fall in on the dock, saying to them, "It is hard boys but we will do our duty."[96]

After Dennis ordered that McCallum disembark as many of his Naval Brigade as possible, leaving behind only a crew sufficient to man the *Robb* and guard the prisoners, many of the marines protested. But McCallum urged them on, saying that if any harm came to the Welland Battery, the men of the Naval Brigade would be branded cowards if they remained aboard the *Robb*.[97] Grudgingly, the marines joined the Welland Battery forming up on the dock. McCallum attempted to keep as many of his men as possible safely aboard the ship. He posted two men to guard the cabin door, but Dennis countermanded the order, saying one man was sufficient, and had the other join the rest of the company on the dock.[98] Captain McCallum joined his men on shore, leaving Lieutenant Robb in command of the vessel.

IN HIS STATEMENT to the Court of Inquiry, Dennis insisted that none of this happened:

> On my return to the dock I stated my intention to Capts King and McCallum, neither of whom either there or at any other time made any objection or counter proposition. During my absence as remarked, a few of the Battery, I should think about four or five not more, had gone onto the boat, the remainder of the corps was on the dock as I had left it. I called them to join those on the dock which they did ... The officers and men of both companies responded as it seemed to me with cheerfulness and alacrity.[99]

During the inquiry, Dennis attempted to elicit testimony in support of his assertion that the men had "cheerfully" followed his command and that neither King nor McCallum had objected to his plan to make a stand in Fort Erie. He never managed to elicit the testimony he sought.

Dennis claimed that neither the Welland Battery nor the Naval Brigade was sufficiently familiar with infantry drill and that he ordered the Welland Battery drill instructor, Sergeant McCracken, the veteran British bombardier, to adapt artillery drill commands to those of infantry.[100] Confused, McCracken asked Dennis to clarify what he meant, at which point Dennis snapped back, "You will know what I mean by the orders I give you."[101]

A number of civilians were running around on the wharf and in the streets near it, some fleeing from the scene while others were running toward it to watch. A small crowd of curious onlookers, including William Ives, a librarian from the Young Men's Association in Buffalo, tagged along with the troops. Ives had come across on the ferry in the morning with his young son to see the action unfolding in Fort Erie.[102]

Events unfolded in a matter of minutes—as one witness said, "The whole thing happened very suddenly, quicker than we could tell it."[103] Several hundred Fenians suddenly appeared about six hundred yards away, approaching from the south along Front Street. Some of the troops on the dock could also see Fenians trickling in along the ridge of the hill above the town. The size of the Fenian army was swelling before their eyes.[104] Civilians who had crowded around the soldiers now dashed for safety—some like Ives and his son ran toward the dock and huddled behind the piles of lumber, railway ties, and cordwood.[105] Others ran north along Front Street away from the approaching Fenians, while still others climbed into rowboats and hastily crossed over to Buffalo.[106] On the American side, thousands of picnicking spectators—almost all Fenian supporters—gathered on the riverbank to watch and cheer.[107]

Dennis now gave the order for the troops to leave the dock and take a position on Front Street facing south to meet the Fenians in the road.[108] Almost as an afterthought he sent Captain McCallum back to the boat with orders for Lieutenant Robb to prevent under any circumstances the capture of the vessel and rescue of the prisoners by the Fenians.[109] After giving the order, McCallum returned, rejoining his company of marines marching with the Welland Battery.

The Canadians advanced toward the Fenians. The terrain and street grid where the battle took place remain almost exactly the same today as they were then, although none of the buildings have survived.

The men had marched south about fifty yards up Front Street as far as a grove of weeping willow trees (the grove is still there) near the City Hotel, just short of Bertie Street, when Lieutenant Robb, with his elevated view from the bridge of the tug, observed a line of Fenians rise up on the crest of the hill above the town to the west of them. Robb shouted out a warning to Captain McCallum on the shore, "Old man they are flanking you."

"I know that," McCallum replied, waving his hand.[110]

Several roads that led down the hill through the town toward Front Street began filling up with Fenians as well. With Front Street screened from the hill behind it by a line of storefronts, Dennis could not see what was happening above him unless he stepped into one of the hillside roads. Bertie Road was about fifteen yards in front of him and offered that opportunity. The Fenians were about four hundred yards away when, suddenly, more Fenians poured into Front Street from the side streets in front of Dennis. (See Fort Erie Battle Map.)

Just before it came to the intersection of Front and Bertie streets, the column was ordered to halt near the City Hotel and the small grove of willow trees. Dennis Sullivan, one of the British privates from the Royal Canadian Rifles stationed on lookout in Fort Erie, who had been captured and paroled by the Fenians the previous day, accompanied the troops in the street. He "took the liberty," he testified, to warn Dennis that the Fenians above them were outflanking them. Dennis at first paid no heed. When Sullivan warned him a second time, Dennis asked, "What is the best to do?"

Sullivan replied, "Flank them before we should be flanked."[111]

Dennis's claim to the inquiry that he had seen the Fenians on the hillside for the first time only when they opened fire on him was patently false. Everyone saw them, including him.

Dennis ordered the men to turn and march back about one hundred yards north along Front, past the *Robb* still docked at the wharf, toward Murray Street and the stores and workshops that stood on its corner.[112] Rather than remain behind the screen of buildings between the Fenians on the hill and his men on Front Street, Dennis stupidly marched his men into the open intersection at Murray Street, exposing them to the enemy on two flanks simultaneously: to the force coming down the hill from the west and to the one advancing along Front Street from the south. They were about to be caught in a Fenian pincer.

As the volunteers fell into the intersection, they saw the Fenians forming up on the road above them about three hundred yards away.[113] The volunteers were deployed across the intersection in an L-shaped formation at right angles to each other: the Welland Canal Field Battery across Murray Street in two sections facing uphill to the west, and the Dunnville Naval Brigade on their left, across Front Street facing south.[114]

As the volunteers came to a halt at the intersection, a silence fell over the scene. There they stood: five officers and sixty-eight men, a third of them armed with obsolete smoothbore muskets, about to be attacked on two sides by nearly eight hundred Fenian insurgents.

The Fenians on the hill edged forward down Murray Street. They must have been a frightening sight, with their rifles and bayonets gleaming, their sunburst flag borne above them, its dark green appearing black against the bright afternoon sky. Gunner William Clarke, who had only joined the battery the day before, would later recall in a letter to a fellow gunner, "Do you remember the muzzles of those guns pointed at us by the enemy as he came down the hill, and do you remember the black flag that was fluttering in the air, my, but it was fierce."[115]

ALMOST AT THE SAME TIME the Fenians on the southern flank began to close in along Front Street, and the Canadians anxiously waited for the order to open fire. None came.[116] Sergeant McCracken later testified, "I turned around watching to see if orders were given and I saw Lt. Col Dennis standing between the left flank of the Battery and the Naval Brigade. I thought according to his manner that he appeared to be very much confused. I then spoke to Capt King, and asked him, if we were to stand there and be shot down without receiving any word of command."[117]

When the Fenians were 150 yards away, Captain McCallum could wait no longer and gave the order to fire, but it was immediately countermanded by Dennis: "Not yet Captain, not yet."[118]

McCallum angrily turned to Dennis and growled, "Are you going to let the men be shot down like Stoughton bottles?"*[119]

Dennis did not have time to reply. A woman suddenly ran into the

* The phrase referred to "Stoughton's Great Cordial Elixir" from pre-Revolutionary times, which was shipped to North America in heavy stoneware bottles that were recycled for storing liquids or filled with sand and used as doorstops or heated as foot warmers. To "stand like a Stoughton bottle" came to mean to sit or stand around silently and apathetically.

street between the columns. Gunner Patrick Roach shouted to her to get out of the way or she would be shot. She scurried around the corner, behind the men, and ran north along Front Street.[120]

Then a single shot was fired from the Fenians on the hill. The heavy round whizzed over the men's heads and thudded into the road behind them, kicking up a cloud of dirt.[121]

It was at this moment that many suddenly heard Captain McCallum shout out, "Where the hell are you going?"[122]

Not all who heard him were sure who McCallum was swearing at. But Gunner Roach testified that he saw Dennis running away in a stooped position along the sidewalk on Front Street toward the north, not far behind the fleeing woman.[123] Numerous other men and officers testified to seeing, immediately after the first shot was fired, Dennis running away from them, stooped low, loping away down the sidewalk and along a fence holding his undrawn sword by the scabbard in his left hand.[124]

Dennis in his final statement to the Court of Inquiry insisted that McCallum was yelling at his own poorly drilled men when he shouted, "Where the hell are you going?" In both his initial report and his final statement, he claimed that it was he who gave the orders to fire and that he remained at the intersection with the men under fire.[125] The preponderance of the testimony, however, has him running away after the first shot.

As Dennis ran off and the Fenian formation in the road above the Canadians continued to grow in size, one of the men commented that it would be better to be aboard the tug, at which point Captain King drew his revolver and threatened to shoot any man who broke ranks.[126] A second shot was fired by the Fenians, which was immediately followed by a heavy volley. Then the Fenian army lurched forward and charged at the Canadians. Captains King and McCallum gave the order for "independent firing" or "every man for himself," telling the men to "do the best you can."[127] King shouted, "Fire. Give it to them boys!"[128] The Canadians fired a return volley.

As the charging Fenians were now about a hundred yards away, only a few of the more skilled Canadians had time to reload and fire a second volley.[129] The rest were lucky even to reload. Although no orders had been given them, the Canadians withdrew in relatively ordered ranks from the exposed Murray Street intersection and pulled back behind the corner about twenty yards farther north on Front Street, putting the buildings lining the street between themselves and the Fenians on the hill.[130] They were still exposed, however, to the Fenians on Front Street. As one civilian witness replied when asked if the Canadians fell back in an orderly manner, "Yes, they were in good order—a good mark to shoot at."[131]

From their falling back position some managed to reload and fire again at what must have been a wall of Fenians.[132] Yet the density of the Fenian ranks also made them easy to hit—three Fenians were shot down by the retreating Canadians, one of them a mounted officer, Colonel Michael Bailey of Buffalo, who was shot through the chest. [133] Although he survived the wound at first, he succumbed to complications related to it, dying in Buffalo on January 16, 1868.[134] (Some sources state that Bailey had been shot by the Canadians while riding down under a white flag to invite them to surrender. While this is not mentioned in the inquiry testimony, had it happened, it is unlikely that it would have been admitted to by the Canadians.)[135]

It was now too late to return to the *Robb*. Only after the Fenians had taken over the position close to the *Robb*, the one previously occupied by the Canadians, did the tug cast off and back out stern first into the river.[136] The men on board the ship opened fire from the deck, hoping to slow the Fenian advance.[137] It was of little help.

As the Fenians continued to fire, Gunner Fergus Scholfield, a twenty-two-year-old butcher employed by his uncle, was first among the Canadians to be hit. A Minié ball struck him in the left leg below the knee, shattering his bone. The next day Dr. Kempson would amputate Scholfield's leg three inches below the knee.[138] The preponderance of leg wounds at Limestone Ridge and Fort Erie had to do with the propensity of experienced combatants to routinely aim low to compensate for the upward recoil of the rifle.

THE CANADIANS ATTEMPTED to return fire as they fell back down Front Street, but it was hopeless. The stand was over probably in a minute, if not less. As hundreds of Fenians began to pour volley after volley into the Canadian ranks they came apart and scattered. Some men led by Captain King took cover behind piles of lumber and railway ties. Others turned and ran for their lives, heading north down Front Street, along it, and then inland away from the Fenians. Many of those who ran in this direction testified that they saw Dennis jogging some forty yards ahead of them in the distance.[139]

Near the dock, Captain King was hit in the leg just above the ankle, his bone shattered. He collapsed to the ground, crying out, "Good God boys, I'm done."[140] Some of King's men helped him to the wharf. He remained prone on the ground and fired his revolver two or three times from behind the lumber before a Fenian round knocked it from his hand.[141] The much larger Fenian force pushed down on the handful of Canadians hunkered down on the dock with their backs to the river. The Canadians fought on stubbornly, led by Captain King, his foot folded up just above the ankle and stuffed into his boot like a rag; there was no bone left—it had been completely destroyed. As a physician, King must have had a sickeningly acute understanding of his wound.

The clutch of Canadians simply did not have enough time to reload when they were overrun. There had been thousands of bayonet charges in the American Civil War, but because of the lethal range of the new rifles, few bayonet wounds. The bayonet charge had become a psychological tactic intended to break the spirit of opposing ranks, exactly as it had done a few hours earlier on Limestone Ridge.[142] But as the wall of Fenians closed in on them, one of the besieged Canadians thrust his bayonet deep into an advancing Fenian's chest, just below his neck.[143] This must have horrified everyone. Few of even the most battle-hardened Fenians would have ever witnessed an actual bayonet wound—or even had much bayonet drill. Being struck by flying bullets was one thing, but being impaled by cold-edged steel was something primitive and viscerally different. The combatants must have gasped at the unusual sight of the bayonetted Fenian. How exactly the incident ended is not clear from the testimony, but in the next few seconds the Fenians halted, thought again about their bayonet advance, and probably prepared to unload a final volley on the Canadians remaining on the dock. The besieged volunteers chose wisely to surrender instead without further resistance.

Captain King in the meantime rolled himself along the dock and splashed over into the river below. He clung to the piles underneath in the hope of avoiding capture. In the bright sunlight of that June afternoon, the water must have been as crystal clear as it is today, the current sucking a crimson cloud from King's leg wound. He was easy to spot. The Fenians fished him out and took him prisoner.[144] He was laid out on the dock in the hot sun, light wisps of steam rising from his cold, soaked uniform. King asked someone to slash his left trouser leg open and to cut through his boot to the toe. This revealed a compound comminuted fracture two inches above his ankle. His foot hung to his leg by a gristly strip of bloodied flesh. King was fading fast from shock, cold, and loss of blood and began to slip into unconsciousness.[145]

A friend of King's was miraculously at the scene in Fort Erie: Retired Captain Whitney rushed over to Buffalo and secured the services of a surgeon, Julius F. Minor, a professor of surgery in the medical school at the University of Buffalo. Whitney and Minor, after securing a pass from the U.S. Army, returned to Fort Erie in a small skiff and found King barely clinging to life. After securing permission from the Fenians to evacuate King, they laid him out on the bottom of the boat and crossed back to Buffalo. King's leg was amputated below the knee the next day. Both King and the Canadian government commended the American surgeon for his bravery in coming to the aid of King in the face of popular pro-Fenian sentiments in Buffalo.

THE REMAINING CANADIANS ran north along Front Street and into the yards and gardens of the town, firing as best they could at the pursuing Fenians behind them. Thirty-two-year-old Gunner Robert Jordan Thomas managed to get into the fields near a water tank at the northern outskirts of town. There he managed to fire his rifle for the first time at a Fenian closing in on him. A return round tore the shoulder strap from Thomas's uniform. Thomas reloaded and fired again at the Fenian, who now was only some seventy yards away. Thomas could not tell if he hit him, but when the smoke cleared the Fenian was gone. Thomas reloaded and turned toward a group of Fenians flanking him on higher ground. He fired in their direction. Before he could reload, he was shot through the thigh. Luckily the bullet passed through his flesh. Thomas now ran through the garden gate of the last house on the outskirts of town, which was owned by Edwin Thomas (no relation.) Gunner Thomas had a twenty-four-year-old wife, three children, a dependent sister, and a seventy-year-old mother, all waiting for him at home. He was determined to survive.[146]

The owner's son, nineteen-year-old George, took Thomas into the house and hid him and his rifle. He lay still in the attic, his wound undressed, hoping the Fenians would not find him.[147]

Thomas was not the first soldier to seek shelter in the house. A minute or two before him, George had admitted another escaping soldier. Gunner John Greybiel had come rushing through the door without his rifle and terrified. He tore straight up the stairs to the second floor. There he found several civilians closeted in a room, trying to stay out of the line of fire. Greybiel asked them to exchange an overcoat with him, which they were reluctant to do. George suggested that Greybiel hide in the wardrobe but he refused, saying the Fenians would find him there for sure. He wandered into the hallway, stripped off his uniform, entered an empty bedroom, climbed into bed, and pulled up the covers. George picked up Greybiel's crumpled uniform from the floor and hid it. After about fifteen minutes, the owner, Edwin Thomas, appeared. Edwin was annoyed by the presence of escaping soldiers in his house and told Greybiel he must leave.[148] Greybiel was forced to climb out of bed and get dressed. He left the house by the back door, escaping across the fields toward Peacocke's lines, which he safely reached that night.[149] The lightly wounded Thomas evaded capture as well, either remaining hidden in the house or making his way alone to Peacocke's camp.

Not all the Canadians escaped that easily. The men trapped on the dock surrendered quickly and were taken prisoner. But farther in town, the Canadians engaged the Fenians in fierce house-to-house fighting, firing from behind street corners and telegraph poles, over garden fences and woodpiles, through doorways and windows, crashing through front doors and out the back, yard by yard, and block by block through the town.[150] It was Canada's first and, hopefully, last street battle at home.

Eventually a small group with Lieutenant Nimmo found themselves near the two-storey wood frame "Lewis House" attached to the village post office at the north end of Front Street (between Lavinia and Catherine streets today). Seeing other men piling into the house, Nimmo followed. It was not a good idea—the woefully thin wood frame and clapboard walls were no defence against rifle bullets—especially at close range.

Captain McCallum, who was running down Front Street at that moment, paused and shouted, "Nimmo, for God's sake keep out of that house or you will all be murdered."

Nimmo called back, "I [will] hold the house. I might as well be killed there as anywhere else."

Before continuing down the road, McCallum urged Nimmo one more time, "Come out and get the boys out."[151] They did not listen.

McCallum, several of his men, and some gunners continued along the river shore closely pursued by the Fenians. Eventually their pursuers overtook them. McCallum drew his revolver and squeezed off three shots but missed every time.[152] The Fenians shouted, "Get the bloody officer." One of them fired two shots at McCallum with his handgun from about ten feet away. He also missed.[153] Before he could take a third shot, William Calback, a marine in McCallum's company and a veteran of the Civil War, lunged forward, thrusting his bayonet through the Fenian's throat and out the spine at the back of his neck, pinning him to a fence post. Even the salty-tongued McCallum was shocked by the sight. He later recalled that Calback muttered, "Pretty hot here, cap!" as he withdrew his bayonet, releasing the pinned Fenian to slip to the ground.

McCallum later explained almost apologetically, "Kilback [*sic*] had been through the American War."[154]

The pursuing Fenians backed off while the *Robb*, which had been flanking McCallum's escape along the riverbank, lowered a boat to shore and brought McCallum and his party of escaping men safely back aboard.[155] Other retreating soldiers ran through the back roads and fields, some eventually reaching Lieutenant Colonel Peacocke's column after dark while others simply walked all night to their homes in Dunnville and Port Robinson, leaving the chaos behind them. The Fenians did not pursue them far beyond the town limits.

About fourteen men and two officers—Lieutenants Nimmo and Macdonald—found themselves trapped in the Lewis House and surrounded by Fenians.[156] They fired at the Fenians through the doorway and from the windows on the second floor. When a Fenian attempted to force his way through the narrow doorway, he was killed with a bayonet thrust.[157] Considering how extraordinarily rare bayonet wounds were by 1866, that three Fenians were bayonetted to death is indicative of just how savage the close-order fighting was. On the Canadian side, Nelson Bush, a mariner from the Naval Brigade, also received a bayonet wound to the chest but not so grave as to prevent him from being on duty the next morning.[158] Eventually the door was bolted shut, trapping several soldiers on the outside as they attempted to gain entry. The Fenians quickly captured them.[159]

Stephen Beatty had earlier blindly followed another soldier into the house and had run up the stairs to the second floor. He found himself in a smoke-filled room with Lieutenant Macdonald and six other men who were firing down at the Fenians below. More men were firing from the other rooms.[160]

The Fenians took cover behind woodpiles, fences, and neighbouring buildings and began peppering the house at close range from all sides.[161] The bullets pierced the clapboard siding like cardboard, sending glass and wood chips flying through the house. The rooms filled with clouds of plaster dust so thick that those inside could not see each other.[162] George Denison, who inspected the house the next day, reported, "The walls were perfectly riddled, one small room having some 32 bullet holes through it ..."[163] Remarkably, nobody inside was hit.

The Fenians smashed in the window frames on the ground floor, the breaking glass making what Beatty described as "a hideous sound."[164] They then threatened to set the building on fire if the Canadians did not immediately surrender.[165] The men were running out of ammunition and Lieutenant Macdonald decided it was futile to resist further. He handed his white pocket handkerchief to Private Abraham Thewlis and ordered him to go out into the yard and offer their surrender to the Fenians.[166]

The Fenians were angry—especially at the cost to them of the stubborn and futile resistance by the Canadians in the Lewis House. Several of them threatened to shoot the prisoners, but with the arrival of O'Neill on the scene that notion was quickly squelched. The Fenians did submit the men to a tongue-lashing, reserving the worst of their curses for those prisoners who by their brogue revealed themselves to be Irish.[167] When the prisoners were marched into Front Street, a huge cheer rose up from thousands of spectators on the American side of the Niagara River.[168]

Despite the ten-to-one odds, in Fort Erie the Canadians had killed nine Fenians and wounded fourteen with none killed from their own ranks.[169] The total Canadian losses were five wounded (not including the light bayonet wound suffered by Nelson Bush). In addition to those already described, Gunner John Bradley, a twenty-eight-year-old married carriage trimmer with an infant daughter and a six-year-old orphaned niece in his care, was shot in the leg during the opening volley on Front Street, the bullet shattering his right femur. Dr. Kempson amputated Bradley's leg above the knee the next day.[170] Gunner John Harbison was initially less severely wounded in the tibia.[171] His wound, however, became infected and he faced a possible amputation.

THIRTY-SEVEN CANADIANS were captured, including some of the wounded men who were put in Dr. Kempson's care or evacuated to Buffalo as Captain King had been.[172] The rest were marched south out of town toward the ruins of the fort. On the way, the prisoners heard gunfire and hoped it was Peacocke's column arriving to rescue them.[173] In fact it was the *Robb* on her way back to Port Colborne with fifty-seven prisoners in her hold. On board were Captain McCallum, Lieutenant Robb, two men from the Naval Brigade, and thirteen from the Welland Battery—the rest were missing, wounded, or taken prisoner. As the *Robb* passed Fort Erie, the two sides exchanged fire. Several shots smashed into the wheelhouse but nobody was hit. The *Robb* arrived in Port Colborne at 6:30 P.M.[174]

The captured Canadians, hot and sunburned, collapsed on the grass around the old fort. Several Fenians brought them water from Lake Erie while one of the guards cursed his solicitous comrades for not serving the guards before the prisoners.[175] The Fenians shared a small ration of raw bacon and soda crackers with the prisoners, the first meal many had had since the night before.[176] As the sun went down and the temperature dropped, it became damp and chilly. O'Neill allowed a small squad of prisoners to return to the customs house at the dock and bring back the greatcoats the men had stored there in the morning, but they found the doors locked and were unable to gain entry. By midnight the ground was as damp with dew as if a rain had fallen.[177]

Some stayed alert and watched for an opportunity to escape, which never came. The rest of the exhausted men slept. Stephen Beatty, now among the prisoners, recalled, "We had to content ourselves to take things as they come and settled down for the night. My pillow was a stone and the canopy of Heaven my blanket."[178]

LIEUTENANT COLONEL John Stoughton Dennis had been last seen running along Front Street about forty to fifty yards in front of his men. Shortly after, he vanished from sight. Upon reaching the northern outskirts of the town, Dennis came upon the Edwin Thomas house, the same house two other soldiers had previously hidden themselves in.[179] George, the owner's son, saw Dennis go around to the back of the house and hide in the hayloft of the stable behind it.[180]

Since Edwin Thomas was already annoyed that his son had taken escaping soldiers into the house, George did not tell his father about Dennis. The Fenians had searched the house twice, but not thoroughly—none of the soldiers hiding on the premises were found. On the day before the battle, on the dock, Edwin Thomas had asked Dr. Kempson to introduce him to the commanding officer and then invited Dennis to visit his home. Now as Thomas was preparing to sit down to dinner, his wife suddenly announced that Lieutenant Colonel Dennis was going "to dine" with them.[181] Thomas found Dennis sitting at the dinner table in civilian clothing. At the Court of Inquiry, Thomas was not asked about the subject of the dinner conversation that evening.

At about 2 A.M., Thomas escorted Dennis through the dark of night across the Fenian lines and then directed him toward Lieutenant Colonel Peacocke's forces on Bertie Road.[182] Dennis wore a workman's jacket, a red woollen scarf, and a rough cloth cap. To complete his disguise, he shaved off his luxurious Dundreary sidewhiskers. He arrived at Peacocke's position about an hour later, where he encountered George T. Denison.[183]

At about the same time, O'Neill realized that no further Fenian reinforcements or supplies were going to get across the river from Buffalo through the U.S. naval blockade and that British and Canadian reinforcements were ready to close in on him from all sides. He decided to attempt a withdrawal of his entire force across the river to Buffalo and the safety of U.S. territory.

At about 2:30 A.M. Stephen Beatty and the rest of the prisoners in the ruins of Fort Erie were awakened and marched back into town to the wharfs. There Beatty witnessed the Fenian army boarding a waiting barge towed by a steam tug. Between 700 and 850 insurgents were aboard the huge barge.[184] O'Neill told the Canadians they were free to go. He bade them goodbye, said he hoped that they would treat their Fenian prisoners as well as they had been treated, and with a rifle volley salute, the barge was towed off toward Buffalo.[185] As it floated into the middle of the Niagara River, the U.S. gunboat *Harrison* darted in and intercepted it. The *Harrison* was shortly joined by the U.S.S. *Michigan*. The Fenians, including O'Neill, were all arrested. The barge was tied to the *Michigan,* becoming a floating prison for the next two days.

It was over. At dawn most of the released prisoners left for their homes on foot, but Stephen Beatty and three others, Corporals James S. Boyle and Villroy McKee, along with Gunner Jacob Garner, decided to stay behind. They first headed for the fort to see if the Fenians had left behind anything of value. On the way they came across an old man standing at his front gate. They told him they were hungry, and after apologizing that his wife was still not up to cook them a hot breakfast, he invited them in for a breakfast of fresh milk, cold roast beef, and bread and butter. Except for the meagre ration provided by their captors, the three men had not eaten for nearly forty hours. When Beatty offered to pay for the meal the old man refused, saying he knew what it meant to be a soldier, having served with the Duke of Wellington in the Peninsular Campaign. It was a poignant meeting of a Napoleonic warrior with Canada's first modern soldiers.

When they had finished eating, the men returned to the road toward the ruins but were too late in their quest for Fenian loot. A single horse-drawn wagon with two men in it was returning from the old fort loaded with everything of value that the Fenians had abandoned. Beatty and his companions stopped the wagon and each took a Springfield rifle from it. McKee also took a U.S. Army snare drum. Satisfied with their take, the men returned to the town. They called at one of the hotels and asked the owner if they could store their captured rifles there.

Restless and unable to come down from the experience of the last two days, Beatty and McKee decided to take a stroll along Front Street. There they encountered Lieutenant Adam Scholfield from the Welland Battery, who told Beatty that Dr. Kempson was looking for him. Beatty was unable to find Kempson. Later he learned that Kempson had wanted him to assist with the leg amputations he was performing that morning on Gunners Scholfield and Bradley. Fortunately for Beatty, that was one experience that never became part of his memory of that day.

At around 6 A.M. Denison's cavalry rode into town. Denison briefly questioned Beatty and McKee and then put them on guard duty in front of a feed store. Several acquaintances approached Beatty with strange looks on their faces. Apparently, soldiers who had escaped from the town earlier had reported him dead. Strangers approached the two gunners, shaking their hands, clapping them on the back, and praising them for their courage. After standing guard for an hour, Beatty and McKee were relieved and ordered to go to a hotel where they were finally served a hot breakfast. "We relished it," Beatty recalled.

At 9 A.M. a column of troops under Colonel Lowry entered the town. Beatty and McKee in the meantime had made themselves comfortable sprawling in the armchairs of the hotel lobby with a fruitcake and two bottles of wine that a townswoman had presented to them. It was sweet: They had survived. Forty-eight hours earlier Beatty had opened his gristmill for its first day of business. Two days later he was lucky to be alive. Now *that* was something to pray for, eat and drink to.

Stephen Beatty recalled that it was 10 A.M. when they settled down for their fourth meal that morning: "Then we had dinner, so we didn't fare as badly as on the previous day."[186]

This is what one part of Canada was like that Sunday morning of June 3, 1866.

PART 3
The Hidden History

Booker's Run

The rifles flashed, the balls go by:
The Queen's Own fled with groan and cry.
"Good Lord" I'd give the world that I
Were safe at home, said Booker.

He spurred for shelter here and there,
He wheeled and galloped to the rear,
Till every loyal Volunteer
Was shaking in his boots with fear.

Then turning quick he fled the place;
He wished, he said, to change his base.
His soldiers joined him in the race.
And all went off at railroad pace.

Helter skelter, oh/he/ho,
Higgledy/piggledy, there they go,
Swords and guns, away they throw,
The Queen's and Colonel Booker.

Oh, never say the Indian breed
Bear off the palm for wind and speed,
What darky Chief could take the lead
From loyal Colonel Booker?

Bid bring them out by day or night,
The gallant Queen's, equipped for fight.
With Colonel John O'Neill in sight,
Amidst a ridge of bayonets bright.

Then give the word and, oh/he/ho,
See how they'll fly the Irish foe,
See how they'll play the heel and toe,
The Queen's and Colonel Booker.

DRINKING SONG,
PEACOCKE'S SIXTEENTH BEDFORDSHIRE REGIMENT[1]

NINE

Booker's Run, June–July 1866

As the men from the *Robb* and the Fenians were about to do battle in Fort Erie, Lieutenant Colonel Alfred Booker's brigade was limping toward Port Colborne until Robert Larmour came upon it in his train. It took Larmour two trips to shuttle the broken red and green battalions back to Port Colborne. Booker and Major Gillmor, the commanding officer of the Queen's Own Rifles, rode on the second train, arriving at approximately 3 P.M.

The first thing Booker did on his return was to go to the customs house, find pen, ink, and paper, and then sit down to compose his report.[1] In it he made many of the claims described in the previous chapters. Booker then asked Gillmor to review it. Asked a month later before the Court of Inquiry if he concurred with the report, Gillmor stated, "Yes, the general tenor of the report was correct and I assented to it."[2]

As to what precisely went wrong, Booker's explanation that evening was, "A cry of Cavalry from the front, and the retreat of a number of men in our centre on the reserves, caused me to form a square and prepare for Cavalry. This mistake originated from relieved skirmishers doubling back. I immediately reformed column and endeavoured to deploy to the right. A panic here seized our men and I could not bring them again to the front. I regret to say we have lost several valuable officers and men. I estimate the strength of the enemy as greater than ours; and from the rapid firing, they were evidently armed with repeating rifles."[3]

THAT EVENING BOOKER was still commanding officer of the Port Colborne garrison, in direct command of his brigade and of his Hamilton battalion, and of all the other newly arriving battalions and companies deployed in the wake of the news from the battle. But nobody could get in to see him. Booker was apparently descending into some kind of nervous breakdown. This is really no great surprise. Booker was an auctioneer, not a soldier. He had never commanded a brigade, not even in exercises or on parade. His military service had been a matter of brass bands, parades, and evening balls. Canada had not seen combat since 1838, and military service was rose-tinted with soldier-boy naïveté. The snap and zip of bullets, the shattered bones and blood, the muttered dying prayers—the dead—he had conceived none of it in his *Boys' Life* adventure-magazine imagination. Some had taken their baptism in combat more gracefully than others. Major Gillmor had remained cool in the eye of the battle while leading his battalion. He prefaced his report with a bloodied humility, saying: "As I had never seen a shot fired before in action, my opinion can be taken for what it is worth ..."[4] The pompous Booker, on the other hand, had been thrown off balance by his initiation. And in the evening, as the magnitude and significance of the disaster under his command began to dawn on him, he came undone.

Major George Gray with the Twenty-Second Battalion Oxford Rifles arrived in Port Colborne at 6 P.M. as part of several reinforcements rushed to the region. Booker was nowhere to be seen. Gray reported the front-line garrison to be "in a state of confusion."[5] There were no provisions, no billets, no blankets, and most important, no orders. To his dismay Gray discovered that the railway line in the direction of Ridgeway and Fort Erie was dangerously unprotected. He deployed his troops to patrol the tracks while another officer went off to find Booker. Gray reported that after considerable delay, the officer "returned and stated that he had seen Col. Booker—that he could get nothing satisfactory from him."[6]

At around 7 P.M. British army engineer Captain Charles Akers drove into Port Colborne at the reins of his commandeered carriage, having escaped the attack on Fort Erie by minutes. Akers's arrival caused Booker to unravel completely: He threw himself at Akers, begging him for help. Akers promptly began putting the garrison in order. For the next few hours he and Booker were closeted together in the telegraph office, composing reams of messages to their field commanders and superiors in Toronto and Chippawa.

According to Akers's report, "The garrison was in the greatest state of confusion ... No arrangements had been made for obtaining either provisions or ammunition, for securing the post from attack, or further offensive operations. I rendered what assistance I could to Colonel Booker, who appeared quite overcome with fatigue and anxiety. He begged me to undertake all necessary arrangements, and later in the evening requested me to take the command out of his hands. Finding this was also the wish of the other Volunteer officers of superior rank to myself, I telegraphed for instructions, and was desired ... to take the command."[7]

When they emerged from the telegraph office late that night, Booker had been relieved of command not only of the brigade at Port Colborne as he had requested, but also of his own Thirteenth Battalion. Captain Akers was now acting brigade commander, whereas Major Skinner would take command of the Thirteenth Battalion. Booker would later claim that this was all a misunderstanding, that he had asked only to be relieved of the brigade and placed under a British officer while still retaining his own command of the Thirteenth Battalion.[8]

Before leaving the telegraph office and collapsing into much-needed sleep, Booker was said to have sent one more message that would tarnish his reputation forever. He would be accused of sending a telegram to Toronto stating that the Thirteenth Battalion was demoralized and unfit for duty.[9]

While newly arriving units from Oxford County and London took up positions in Port Colborne, the tired men of the Thirteenth and Queen's Own Rifles were fed and bedded down in a schoolhouse. Rumours began to filter in from refugees arriving from Fort Erie that the Fenians had massacred the garrison there. As the men began falling into a worried yet exhausted sleep, one of them began to read aloud from the 121st, 124th, and 125th Psalms: "I will lift up mine eyes to the hills from whence cometh my help ... The sun shall not smite thee by day, nor the moon by night ... If it had not been the Lord, who was on our side, when men rose up against us ... Blessed be the Lord, who hath not given us as a prey to their teeth ..."[10]

AT 3 A.M., after having been already awakened once to a false alarm, the troops were again awakened to reports that the Fenians were returning to Ridgeway. Nobody knew that O'Neill at that moment was loading his men into a barge for a crossing back to Buffalo. Only when the garrison was formed up at the train station platform did some of the senior officers realize that Booker had been relieved and that Akers had taken his place.[11] In Booker's absence, Major Skinner took a position at the head of the Thirteenth Battalion while Major Gillmor gave a short speech to his Queen's Own, bolstering their morale for the fight ahead. The two battalions were joined by two more of the newly arrived reinforcements and local Home Guard formations.

As the 5 A.M. departure time approached, unit by unit they boarded the freight cars: the Twenty-Second Battalion Oxford Rifles, the Seventh Battalion "Prince Arthur's Own" from London, two companies of St. Catharines Home Guard, including several veterans of the War of 1812, along with the exhausted Queen's Own Rifles and the York and Caledonia companies.[12] But when the train lurched forward toward Ridgeway, the Thirteenth Battalion to their shock realized they were being left behind. As the rest of the brigade went off, presumably to win back their honour in another fight with the Fenians, the Thirteenth were told they were to stay behind with the women and children and guard the town. Some of the men began to weep in shame at the insult they had just been dealt.[13]

Booker might have been forgiven for his ambition, for his bungling on the battlefield, even for his embarrassing breakdown in the wake of the retreat, but for having reported the men demoralized and unfit for duty, for that humiliation, he would not be forgiven. The irony is that while Booker was guilty of many of the accusations described, it is unclear whether he singled out the Thirteenth as being unfit. In his report to the Court of Inquiry a month later, Booker claimed, "When at Port Colborne I reported that the Thirteenth and Queen's Own were alike tired and hungry, and that if it were possible they should have a day's rest, and that those volunteers who had arrived during the day of the 2nd of June at Port Colborne should be sent forward first ... It was not by my wish that the Thirteenth were detained at Port Colborne on that morning of the 3rd June, while the Queen's Own were ordered to march on to Fort Erie. I was anxious that both should be thoroughly refreshed, and I felt regret that the companions of the day previous should be separated, as they were equally able to proceed."[14]

Akers in his own report typically wrote nothing that would enlighten us as to why he chose the Thirteenth Battalion to remain in Port Colborne, and except for Booker's one report, none of the telegrams sent from Port Colborne that evening have surfaced.

AFTER THE TRAIN returned to Ridgeway station at about 6 A.M. and disembarked the troops, they began the same hot and thirsty march up Ridge Road. There are no reports or accounts that mention the physicians who had arrived in the area, the searches for wounded in the farmhouses, or their evacuation back to Port Colborne by the same train that had brought the column in that morning. Perhaps the wounded were kept out of sight until the men had marched by.

The march back to Limestone Ridge must have been strange for the men who had fought there the day before. Lieutenant Stinson of QOR Company 4 recalled, "It was a lovely Sabbath morning, and many a thought and prayer strayed homeward for those dear relations and friends, who that day would meet in God's sanctuaries, to implore the protection of Heaven upon our little band. The men marched on in silence only interrupted by the bugle of the commanding officer calling us frequently to halt."[15]

Except for a few scraps of litter, broken fences, and trampled crops, the men would have seen few traces of the previous day's battle, the field appearing as serene as on any other June Sunday morning. As soon as the Fenians had left Ridgeway on Saturday afternoon to return to Fort Erie, hundreds of locals descended on the battlefield and picked it clean of every rifle, belt, greatcoat, pack, or anything else of possible value. They even cut the "IRA"-emblazoned brass buttons from the tunics of dead Fenians for souvenirs before they buried them and charged the township for the service. (Eight Fenians were said to have been interred in the fields and orchards of Limestone Ridge.)[16] The inhabitants of the Niagara region were later called upon by customs collectors, who seized looted Fenian rifles because they had been "imported" into the province without payment of duty. Notice was given two days after the battle in a newspaper article entitled "A Hint to Owners of Fenian Trophies" that "all arms and *materiel* abandoned by the enemy is liable to be taken possession of ... as legitimate property of the Government."[17]

The column never got to fight the Fenians again. They marched east on Garrison Road into Fort Erie to meet with the other units advancing into the town. To their surprise they were met by a reserve bordering on hostility from some townspeople that morning. The town had changed hands four times in the last forty-eight hours and its inhabitants were edgy; who was to say that tomorrow the Fenians would not return?

One hotel owner, "paroled'" by the Fenians during their occupation of the town, refused to serve breakfast to the soldiers on the grounds that the Fenians had reserved it the evening before.[18] A correspondent for the Hamilton *Evening Times* commented on the villagers' demeanour: "One would imagine that the fighting had taken place between two opposing forces of foreigners on neutral ground entirely."[19] Border towns, of course, are like that.

MOST OF THE WOUNDED were transferred to an improvised general hospital set up in the St. Catharines town hall. Physicians and surgeons and volunteer nurses rushed to the scene, as did family members. Citizen committees collected medical supplies. A few of the more gravely wounded, like Percy Routh, who had been abandoned for dead on a blanket on the floor in a pool of his own blood for thirty hours, could not be moved immediately. Routh was cared for at Ridgeway by Dr. Billings, a surgeon from Hamilton, who was summoned there by telegram by his family.[20] When the Thirteenth Battalion surgeon, Dr. Ryall, appeared on the scene to look in on Routh, Routh's brother angrily turned him away.[21]

James Johnson, the civilian who was convinced that Routh was dead and had hidden Routh's watch in his boot, telegraphed on Monday the Hamilton *Evening Times* from his home in Brantford, asking them to contact Routh's family in Hamilton and return his watch. He was surprised to learn Routh was alive. Routh and his watch were reunited.[22]

The dead, all members of Toronto's Queen's Own Rifles, were taken by train to Port Colborne where a field hospital had been set up for the wounded pending their transfer to St. Catharines. Adam Wright, a student from QOR Company 9, volunteered as an orderly to help with the wounded. He was tending to them when the bodies of the dead were brought in and laid out in an out-building. Wright was asked to help identify his killed fellow students from the University Rifles. He recalled, "I went out, and entered a building. On one side was a row of nine roughly made tables. On these were nine bodies stripped to the waist. The heads and upper parts of the bodies had been washed and there was every evidence that they had been laid with a kindly and cleanly care which has always seemed to me remarkable since it had been done by perfect strangers.

"On the first table was McKenzie with placid face, which, although it had lost expression to some extent, looked to me at first sight, like one alive but sleeping. His round shoulders and broad chest were creamy white in colour, not unpleasant to behold, had it not been for that horrid, ragged bullet hole over his heart.

"Passing by the second body, unknown to me, I found Mewburn lying on the third table with face twisted and features contorted as if he had died in agony. From what we could learn it seemed probable that he died in a convulsion brought on by a blow on the side of his head behind the ear."[23]

Wright recalled that Mewburn had a beautiful singing voice and that one of his favourite songs was *Dulce et Decorum est pro patria mori* ("It is sweet and fitting to die for one's country.") Wright thought to himself as he gazed at Mewburn's body, "Poor boy! You surely died for your country as you used to sing, but I am at present unable to appreciate the *dulce.*"

After passing two other unknown bodies, Wright came to the sixth table on which lay Tempest. "There was the bullet hole in his forehead, which seemed not so large or ragged as that on McKenzie's chest. There was therefore not so much disfigurement as one would expect. The face looked fairly natural, but the entire absence of that beautiful rosy colour which was so marked in his face, changed its appearance greatly. That scene has remained with me, clear and vivid as it was on that Sunday ..."

Wright, who was a U of T professor when he wrote those recollections in 1921, reported that Dr. Tempest came over that afternoon and seemed to be full of hope that his son might be seriously wounded but still alive. Wright said he did not know what Tempest had been told, but that he "at once brought him out to the 'chamber of death.' When he caught sight of his boy his anguish was terrible to behold."

The dead were redressed in their uniforms and furnished with plain pine caskets, their names written in chalk on the lids, and then forwarded to Port Dalhousie where they were to be loaded into the same ferry that had brought them there: *City of Toronto*.[24] The ferry had steamed over from Toronto in the afternoon of Sunday, June 3, with instructions to bring back the dead and wounded. It carried supplies donated by Torontonians, and many family members went on the crossing to find their wounded sons and relations. The scene at Port Dalhousie was disheartening. One of the wounded refused to be carried in a litter and insisted on walking but then sank to the ground and was borne aboard by several persons. A wounded soldier too weak to speak smiled when he saw his father and weakly held out his hand to him, while another seriously wounded boy, at the sight of his mother bursting into tears, assured her, "That's nothing mother."[25]

Around 10 P.M. the returning ferry passed by the clanking buoys bobbing off the Toronto Islands and slipped into the bay with its melancholy cargo. As it approached the wharf at the bottom of Yonge Street, the slow toll of church bells in the city could be heard. To those aboard the ship it seemed as if the entire populace had assembled on the water's edge to greet them. As one witness reported, "Lanterns held here and there at intervals gave a weird vastness to the crowd and, although they did not reveal all its proportions, gave some idea of its wonderful extent."[26]

As the wounded came off the vessel, the murmuring crowd parted. They fell silent and bared their heads as the wounded passed by. The lightly wounded came first and were put into cabs lined up at the docks and taken to their homes; the more severely wounded came on litters; and last of all came the dead. The witness to this scene later observed, "The funeral was an imposing spectacle; but this night's reception of the dead had in it some elements of solemnity and grandeur which could not be introduced into the funeral."[27]

The body of fallen university student John Mewburn remained at St. Catharines for burial near his home at Stamford. The bodies of University of Toronto students Malcolm McKenzie and William Tempest were brought back to Toronto and borne to University College. They were laid out in the reading room in open caskets, the boys still dressed in their soiled and bloodied uniforms as they were found on the field. Faculty and students filled the room to the doors while Professor Croft stood vigil over the boys with tears streaming down his face.[28]

No satisfactory explanation has survived for why Croft and his fellow officer Professor John Cherriman had not gone to Ridgeway with their boys. There were the two contradictory reports: first, that Croft was ordered to remain in Toronto for an assignment at headquarters and, second, that urgent "academic duties" kept him and Cherriman away.[29] Other alternatives remained unspoken. The bumbling professors might have been kept away on purpose, on the assumption that they would have done more damage on the field of battle than away from it. Or perhaps, knowing their own limitations, they themselves chose to stay away. At least one young soldier calculated that his life was more expendable than some others, writing matter-of-factly to his father four days after the battle that the Queen's Own consisted of "some of the most substantial men in Toronto and whom it would be hard to replace; [and] University Company, whose members if killed could scarcely make a void in the Country, for they have not yet taken positions in the battle of life."[30]

On Monday the fallen of the Queen's Own Rifles were laid out in the drill shed where the public lined up for blocks to pay their respects. On Tuesday, all business in Toronto ceased for the funeral, which was conducted with patriotic sermons, dignitaries in attendance, and all the Victorian pomp and circumstance the moment called for. The burials took place at St. James Cemetery and the graves were later moved to the Winchester Street Necropolis in Toronto's Cabbagetown. (Malcolm McKenzie was buried in Woodstock.)[31]

The funeral program printed in all the newspapers included the name of Private Henry Anderson among the dead.[32] The next day his name would vanish from the list. At the funeral those who knew Anderson could not recognize the body in the Union Jack–draped casket. It was not Anderson! Eventually it was determined that it was a Fenian casualty, his clothing so soaked in sweat and blood, and so caked in dust and gunpowder, that he had been mistaken for the missing QOR private. The Fenian corpse was quickly whisked away, most likely to the Potter's field.[33] A week later, police in Dundas arrested a man they suspected might be a Fenian. He turned out to be Anderson, who had deserted during the battle. When Gillmor was telegraphed for instructions on what to do with the prisoner, he replied, "Turn him loose again—we don't want him here."[34]

Several days later on June 13, a smaller funeral was held for the two men who had subsequently died of their wounds: Sergeant Matheson and Corporal Lackey. The city again remained shuttered for the day.

BACK IN PORT COLBORNE that Sunday morning after the battle, a Welland Railway train was waiting at the platform for the wounded evacuated from Ridgeway to be transferred to it and transported to the improvised hospital in St. Catharines. The loading was supervised by the railway's general manager, Captain McGrath, himself in command of a railway infantry company. According to McGrath, Booker suddenly appeared on the platform that morning carrying his cloak, belt, and sword slung over his shoulder. Upon seeing McGrath, Booker began to nag him incoherently about the train's departure time. Booker said he urgently needed to get to St. Catharines, from where he hoped to catch a connection home to Hamilton. He wanted the train to leave "special."

McGrath told Booker they must wait until the wounded and sick were loaded aboard the train. Booker inexplicably shouted out, "Hold my cloak! What shall we do? We are attacked, hold my cloak."

"I cannot hold your cloak, Sir, I have other business to attend to, some of these men about the platform can hold it," McGrath responded.

"Take my sword, hold my sword," Booker insisted.

"Really, Sir, I have no time to hold your sword, I am busy," McGrath replied, according to his account.[35]

Booker eventually boarded the train, but his continued odd behaviour was noted at several railway stations as Booker journeyed home to Hamilton.

That same Sunday morning in Hamilton, Alexander Somerville, the fifty-five-year-old freelance journalist for *The Spectator* and the *Evening Times*, boarded a train bound for St. Catharines with hospital supplies and then continuing on to Port Colborne with provisions for the garrison there. Just ten minutes west of Grimsby, at 2 P.M., Booker's and Somerville's trains heading in opposite directions passed each other.[36] Ten minutes later the two men's lives became linked to each other forever.

When Somerville stopped at Grimsby in his train, he was surprised to hear from platform workers that Booker had been there just ten minutes earlier. At first, the only conclusion Somerville could reach was that Booker was on his way to Hamilton to organize relief and provisions for his battalion.[37]

The farther Somerville travelled that afternoon down the railway line toward Port Colborne, the more "whispers of something wrong about Colonel Booker passed at the different halting places."[38] That was how Somerville first came into the story of Colonel Booker's disgrace. While hundreds of journalists from New York and across Canada were rushing toward the story, many, if not all of them, must have heard the rumours of Booker's run. That Somerville was *the one* to report the story became something more than ordinary coincidence simply because of Somerville's extraordinary past.

ALEXANDER SOMERVILLE was born in Scotland in 1811 during the last years of the Napoleonic Wars, the eleventh child, and the eighth to survive, of a landless agricultural labourer.[39] When he died seventy-four years later in a woodshed behind a ramshackle boarding house on York Street in Toronto, *The New York Times* published an eighty-five-line obituary headlined, "'The Whistler at the Plough': Death of Alexander Somerville After a Life of Vicissitudes."[40] The Toronto *Globe* in its even longer obituary, "Close of a Checkered and Eventful Career," noted that among Somerville's ancestors was "a reputed witch."[41]

There are no words to describe adequately the deprivation that shaped Somerville as a youth or the enormity of the catastrophic depression in Britain that followed the end of the Napoleonic Wars, when Somerville was raised. He was, however, taught to read and write and sent to school at the late age of eight before embarking on what promised to be an endless cycle of casual labour as a ploughboy, cowherd, sawyer, drainer, quarryman, harbour construction worker, and nursery gardener. Working frequently in Edinburgh during the late 1820s, he became a diligent reader of as many of that city's newspapers as he could lay his hands on. During this period Somerville witnessed the Reform Act* rioting and developed a more than casual interest in the politics of the time.[42]

In the winter of 1831, facing unemployment, the opinionated twenty-year-old Somerville enlisted in the Second Royal North British Dragoons—the "Scots Greys."[43] In the continued civil unrest over the Reform Act, his unit was put on alert and dispatched to the industrial city of Birmingham. Somerville, himself an opponent of radical reform, wrote a letter to the editor of the Birmingham *Weekly Dispatch* urging moderation among Reformers and claiming that many among the soldiers in his regiment were pro-Reform. He assured readers that "the Scots Greys would not fire on a peaceful gathering."[44]

---

* The Reform Act promised to modernize parliamentary constituencies in Britain. Simply explained, it threatened the power of the landed aristocracy to control a large number of seats in Parliament by creating new ridings in densely populated urban centres. The problem was how to get the old Parliament to pass this legislation; thus the rioting.

Somerville's officers wanted to know who these soldiers were who "would not fire," and when he declined to reveal their identities, he was convicted on trumped-up charges of insubordination for refusing when ordered to mount a wild horse. The sentence, to be carried out immediately, was typical of the British army in 1832: two hundred lashes from a cat-o'-nine-tails. After one hundred lashes, the commanding officer halted the flogging on account of Somerville's youth.

Somerville's punishment became a national *cause célèbre*. Reformers made it a symbol of everything that was wrong with the old Tory order and an argument for why reform was so much needed.[45] The case was debated in Parliament as nationwide petitions poured in for the young soldier's release from further military service.[46] Somerville's commanding officer was officially reprimanded by the king's authority and, although not abolished, military flogging was significantly reduced. Somerville gained the reputation, albeit somewhat inaccurately, as "the last soldier to be flogged in the British army."[47] Subscriptions from sympathizers brought Somerville a sum sufficient, with money still left over, to buy his way out of the British army after only nine months of service.

After a brief visit home to Scotland where he had hoped to woo an early love of his life, the rejected and broken-hearted Somerville moved to London where he proceeded to lose all his money. Next he fell into a radical revolutionary plot to kidnap the king and queen and Prime Minister Viscount Melbourne and immediately denounced the conspirators, becoming briefly one of those spies that the English would come to detest so vehemently.[48]

Now not only was Somerville broke, but also his life was in danger, and so in 1835 he enlisted in the mercenary British Auxiliary Legion that was fighting in a brutal civil war in Spain. The British government tacitly approved the legion, which backed Queen Isabella II in a dynastic war against the Carlist rebels and their Basque allies. It was a horrifically dirty little war in the way Spanish civil wars tend to be. A quarter of the ten thousand men of the legion died from disease or combat.

The Carlists took no prisoners. Any British Legionnaires captured were slowly tortured to death. Six months after having arrived, Somerville was one of only 250 survivors of his original 800-man unit of Highlanders.[49]

Somerville was promoted to the rank of colour sergeant and was wounded twice, once heavily when he was shot in the arm on March 16, 1837, in the storming of Oriamendi fortress near San Sebastián in the heart of Spain's Basque country. The ball remained lodged in his arm for the rest of his life. Somerville was commended for his leadership and bravery, and upon recovering from his wound, he mustered out in 1837 with two years' unspent pay in his pocket. He returned to Glasgow where he wrote an account of his recent adventures. His *History of the British Legion* was published in 1839 and launched Somerville's career as a writer, pamphleteer, activist, and journalist.[50]

By the late 1830s the Chartist movement, named for its *People's Charter* listing demands for democratic reform, had moved to the forefront of radical politics in Britain. Somerville emerged as a moderating voice, urging the Chartists to ratchet down their radical stance in his *Dissuasive Warning to the People on Street Warfare* (1839). He became a supporter of Richard Cobden's Anti–Corn Law League, championing Cobden as the rational reform alternative to Chartist radicalism. When Cobden was returned to Parliament as an MP from Greater Manchester in 1841, Somerville became his agricultural adviser.

Somerville was a prolific commentator on political issues, often writing for working-class readers under the pseudonym "One Who Whistles at the Plough" on the subject of the "bread tax," the protectionist Corn Laws that enriched the landed proprietors but kept farmhands hungry. In 1852, a collection of his articles was reprinted under his own name in a book entitled *The Whistler at the Plough*. From then on he would use the moniker as his signature byline beneath his name.[51]

In 1841, Somerville married sixteen-year-old Emma Binks, a girl he had known since she was nine, the daughter of a family in London that had befriended him and whom he had frequently visited.[52] He and Emma would have six children: a daughter and five sons; a seventh child died a month after birth.[53]

During the 1840s Somerville wrote on the plight of Irish farm tenants in *A Cry from Ireland* (1843). In 1847–48 he travelled extensively through Ireland as a correspondent for the *Manchester Examiner*, and with an artist for the *Illustrated London News*, he dispatched shockingly honest and compassionate accounts of the suffering of Irish peasants at the height of the famine.[54] His pamphlets, newspaper articles, and books were often quoted in parliamentary debates by prime ministers: Robert Peel, John Russell, and Viscount Palmerston. Moving constantly between London, Liverpool, Edinburgh, and Dublin, Somerville wrote on the potato blight, the freedom of the seas, reciprocity, and trade guilds.

His collected articles published as books were bestsellers: *On the Economy of Revolution, With Warning on Street Warfare* (1843); *Free Trade and the League: A Biographic History* (1848); *The O'Connor Land Scheme Examined* (1848). Somerville also wrote a series of popular fictional pseudo-biographies—*Paul Swainston* (1839), *Jerry Queen the Toy Maker* (1840), and *Eliza Greenwood* (1841)—works that, according to Somerville, influenced both Charles Dickens and William Makepeace Thackeray.[55] He was a consultant on British banking to visiting American bankers and worked as a press agent on Fleet Street, lobbying publications to carry articles favouring the repeal of the Corn Laws. When he was thirty-six, ill with fever and convinced he was dying, he wrote for his infant son James probably his best-known work, *The Autobiography of a Working Man* (1848).

Somerville recovered, but things began to go wrong for him. When in 1852 Cobden became one of the founders of the Peace League opposed to Britain's going to war with Russia in Crimea, Somerville turned against him. Some of his writing became shrill with disillusion: *Cobdenic Policy, the Internal Enemy of England* (1854); *Working Man's*

Witness Against London's Literary Infidels (1857); *Biography of the League Leader* (1857); *Bowring, Cobden and China* (1857).

Cobden and his powerful allies struck back, sabotaging Somerville's career, blacklisting him from publication, and driving him into financial ruin. Somerville tried desperately to recover, writing articles on a wide range of topics, including trade unions, electromagnetism, witchcraft, and folk customs, and returning briefly to Scotland to act as an editor in Edinburgh. In 1857, under the pressure of continued failure, Somerville had a nervous breakdown and was hospitalized in St. Bartholomew's Hospital in London.[56]

Exhausted, bankrupt, and defeated, Somerville took his family to Canada for a new start, landing in Quebec with his wife and six children in August 1858. In Quebec there was a robust community of Scottish editors publishing anglophone newspapers, and Somerville was welcomed by them and quickly found employment. But eleven months later disaster struck again: His wife, Emma, died of tuberculosis, leaving Somerville alone to care for their six children.

Somerville left his younger children in Quebec City, where they were given room and board in exchange for their labour, while he slowly drifted west with his older sons. Along the way he wrote newspaper articles and pamphlets on Canada, which because of his unfamiliarity with the country and its customs and politics did not always get a good reception. In 1860 he moved to Brockville, then to Perth, and then to Arnprior. The next year he drifted on through Kingston to Windsor and Detroit, then back to Brantford, sending out along the way his "Whistler at the Plough" reports on those communities to papers in the British Empire as far away as New Zealand.[57]

When the *Canada Illustrated News* was founded in Hamilton in 1862, Somerville landed a job as its first editor. Settling in Hamilton, he wrote and published *Canada, a Battle Ground: About a Kingdom in America* (1862), an apocalyptic treatise on the Civil War–era tensions between the United States and Britain and what might happen if war came to Canada. But in December 1863, when the *Canada Illustrated News* was moved by its new owners to Toronto, Somerville chose to remain in Hamilton, where he was frequently freelancing for *The Spectator* and the *Evening Times*. By now his younger children had joined him, but the family continued to struggle in abject poverty. Somerville wrote Isaac Buchanan on January 1, 1864, pleading for cast-off clothing for his older sons, which apparently Buchanan sent him.[58]

Somerville still cut an impressive figure: tall, boisterous, and portly, with long hair just touching his shoulders and a silk hat. In the streets and parlours of Hamilton he was above all reputed to be the "last soldier to be flogged in the British army."[59] Somerville often wrote about military matters, and as former soldiers do, he drifted into friendships and associations with soldiers in Hamilton, occasionally writing in *The Spectator* and the *Evening Times* about the activities of the Thirteenth Battalion. He became a fixture at Thirteenth Battalion parades, balls, and exercises and was acquainted with many of its officers and men. When the Fenian invasion began, Somerville, like hundreds of fellow journalists, rushed to the scene to cover it. That is how he ended up on the train to Port Colborne riding in the wake of Booker's bizarre behaviour.

THE CLOSER SOMERVILLE approached his destination, the more stories he heard about Booker with every station the train stopped at. When he finally arrived at the garrison that evening, Somerville was swarmed by both men and officers of the Thirteenth, still stinging from the shame of having been left behind earlier that morning. They rushed to the familiar Somerville and denounced Booker as an incompetent and a coward who had galloped away when the tide of battle turned.

Somerville was not actually the first to report on Booker's disgrace. On Monday, June 4, the Hamilton *Evening Times* reprinted a short story by another reporter from the Toronto *Leader,* probably the same one who had found himself on the battlefield, blaming both Booker *and* the Thirteenth for the disaster:

> The Queen's Own blame Col. Booker very much for cowardice. It is said that when the Queen's Own found the Fenians in force in the woods they retreated and upon observing Booker's men they cheered. Booker thought the Fenians cheered and that the Queen's Own were defeated. He put spurs to his horse and retreated before his men who stampeded. Had this error not occurred the Fenians would have been badly handled. He has resigned or been dismissed since.[60]

The foot soldiers' grapevine was already abuzz with a new moniker for the Thirteenth: "The Scarlet Runners."[61]

Somerville's story of Booker's bumbling and disgrace appeared in the Wednesday, June 6, edition of the *Hamilton Spectator* and included quotes from some of the soldiers, such as:

> Sir, do you see where the setting sun is, over yonder, red among the trees? Well, when we had got the bugle order to retire, and were falling back, the first thing we saw of Booker was his figure on horseback, a mile and half ahead on the top of a ridge. We and the Rifles between him and the enemy.

Somerville quoted an unnamed officer saying,

> It was not alone his misconduct in misdirecting the Battalions under his command in action, or his wretched poltroonery in deserting his command, but this morning when the 13th, in common with the Queen's Rifles and other Volunteer forces at Port Colborne, were ordered out to march towards Ridgeway and Fort Erie, Booker reported the Battalion demoralized and unfit for duty. The only demoralization of the Battalion was in himself.

A soldier pleaded in Somerville's report, "You cannot shield him from the contempt and indignation of the Toronto's Queen's Rifles, and the 13th of Hamilton, whom he sent on to be slaughtered, threw into confusion by bugle calls which only an imbecile could have ordered, and then basely deserted." Somerville understood perfectly the ramifications of making accusations in print against a prominent figure like Alfred Booker, but he was also acutely aware of his role as a journalist and of an underlying professional code of ethics. He prefaced his article by stating: "If the reputation of only this gentleman was in the issue, his faults might be glossed over, and his mistakes of Saturday attributed to the other officers and three hundred men of the battalion who nobly did their duty. This would be in journalism, a crime; to society an unpardonable offence. The other course is to write the truth, even though the reputation of a citizen volunteer officer, hitherto esteemed as without reproach, should be irretrievably blasted."[62] Somerville added that his investigation had "been careful in research, in collecting and collating evidence. And no inducement under heaven would lead me to write what I do not believe to be true."[63]

Despite the appearance of the *Leader* article and the risk of being scooped by other journalists, Somerville did not dispatch his story to *The Spectator* until Tuesday, which then published it on Wednesday.[64] It was perhaps Booker's decision to return to Port Colborne on Monday night and his attempt to retake command of the Thirteenth that spurred the old crusading reformer in Somerville to take pen in hand to defend the rank and file of the battalion. He believed injustice was being perpetrated by a socially privileged incompetent, who was pompously protecting his own reputation while ordinary men died by his errors. As Somerville wrote in his history of Ridgeway, "My life has been a battle, and my battle has been the rights of man."[65]

After his return to Hamilton on Sunday evening, Booker awakened Monday morning as if from a nightmare. He must have read the newspaper reports that morning on the fortuitous conclusion of events and regretted his rash decision to abandon his battalion. He bathed, shaved, breakfasted, put on a clean uniform, and got back on the train that afternoon, arriving at his battalion headquarters in Port Colborne on Monday evening.

On Tuesday, June 5, the Hamilton *Evening Times* carried a short report from Somerville in Port Colborne about Booker's return the night before: "Lieut. Col. Booker arrived there at 6 o'clock last evening to the surprise of most persons there. No sentry or other men met the Col., and the battalion was not on hand when he reached the barracks, else there might have been a demonstration; as it was there was some hissing."[66]

Once in Port Colborne, Booker telegraphed Colonel Lowry, the new commander of forces on the Niagara Frontier, saying, "I am waiting for orders." Colonel Villiers, who by then had replaced Captain Akers as the brigade commander at Port Colborne, asked Lowry for instructions. Lowry replied to Villiers, "What does Booker mean?"[67]

Booker lobbied hard to be reinstated in his command of the Thirteenth. Lowry referred the matter to Major General Napier, senior commander in Canada West headquartered in Toronto. Napier urged the officers of the Thirteenth in Port Colborne to acquiesce in writing to Booker's reinstatement. The response from most of them was to threaten to resign immediately if Booker were reappointed. Left stripped of his field commands, Booker was sent home in disgrace, but for the time being he retained his appointment as the overall commander of militia in the Hamilton district.

IN THE ENSUING WEEKS, other newspapers picked up Somerville's reports and a noisy debate began to snowball as to who was to blame for the disaster at Ridgeway. Peacocke received his fair share of blame for failing to arrive on time to aid Booker, while some papers came to the defence of Booker. The issues of timing and orders and miscommunication between the commanders in the field, all described in the previous chapters, were discussed by the media in excruciating detail.[68] But the "best story," the one that sold the most papers, was the one of Booker's "imbecility" and cowardice, and it just kept getting bigger and bigger with every passing day.

Somerville always claimed that he never accused Booker of cowardice, only of emotional instability and incompetence. Somerville wrote, "I do not attribute Colonel Booker's incapacity to cowardice, but to an unbalanced judgement, nervous temperament, and non-acquaintance with any military elements, except those suitable to a holiday parade. Were every day a Queen's birthday, the Colonel might have continued to be what he was, and what he delighted to be, the observed of all observers."[69]

By June 12, *The New York Times* was commenting on Somerville's reports, and the story began to pick up momentum when the *Globe* reprinted *The New York Times* story on its front page, including this passage:

> That Col. Booker lost his head on this his first occasion of smelling gunpowder cannot be doubted; and the moral is, that it is very risky to entrust troops, however enthusiastic and full of pluck, to the command of a mere pipe-clay soldier, who because he had studied somewhat of the theory of military tactics, believed himself capable of leading on his men to certain victory. Booker had been for some years an auctioneer in Hamilton, and excelled in the art of "going-going-gone"—an individual particularly remarkable for the possession of a large amount of self-esteem, the positive *funk* which he displayed is by no means a marvellous thing in the opinion of those who have long known him.[70]

Seeing his name now completely besmirched in the press, Booker went to Ottawa, where he lobbied for a Military Court of Inquiry to clear his name. On June 16 the Hamilton *Evening Times* reported: "In reply to earnest solicitations made by Lieut. Col. Booker, on his late visit to the Capital, intimation was received from the Government, that the movements of the troops in the late 'campaign' before Fort Erie would be made the subject of an official investigation. Col. Booker, we understand, hopes to relieve himself of some proportions of the charges and condemnations that have been promiscuously heaped upon him."[71]

Gilbert McMicken, the Canada West secret service chief, was in Port Colborne on the day the Hamilton *Evening Times* ran that story, and he must have read it as the paper was shipped and distributed to the troops stationed there.[72] Perhaps some alcohol had been consumed before McMicken sat down to scrawl a long and rambling memorandum to John A. Macdonald that same day. It contained discourses on McMicken's mother, on prayer and English grammar, a report on the cost of damages to his home while billeting volunteers, as well as intelligence assessments and political and personal advice. It was cryptic and familiar, a four-page cross-written letter in two different-coloured inks in a scrawl daunting to decipher.

One particular passage in McMicken's strange letter, however, must have made the minister of militia and Attorney General cringe: "Booker is perhaps not so much to blame after all and I question whether the 13th are to blame at all ... Booker did the best he could, the best he knew how. Who sent an auctioneer to fight *in command?* Not Booker! Suppose someone in authority sent General Napier to auction off goods ... he most assuredly would make a sad mess of it. What would you, what would anybody else say of it? *Several* have said of Booker, any fool might have done better. Just so ... Who sent Booker to fight? And that's it in a nutshell."[73]

Indeed, if Booker was an incompetent coward, then how did he come to command a brigade at the moment of Canada's need? *Who* had sent him to fight? For his own political security and future in the brewing scandal, Macdonald needed Booker's reputation repaired and protected, or he would have to explain how this incompetent officer had risen to command on his watch.

McMicken would quickly change his mind about both Booker and Dennis. Two days later, on June 18, McMicken travelled to Buffalo and spent two hours by the bedside of Captain King, who was recuperating from the amputation of his lower leg. In a memo labelled both "private and confidential"—a rare double classification among the thousands of pages of secret service correspondence—McMicken wrote to Macdonald on June 23, "I snatch a few moments to write you in this way my now conviction of the grossest incompetence displayed by Booker and Dennis in the late Erie and Ridgeway affair. The latter worse by far than the former."[74]

According to McMicken, Dennis "exhibited the greatest poltroonery and cowardice ... ran and hid himself leaving the poor Welland fellows to be murdered ... Dennis turned up some day or two after with his whiskers shaved off. As to Booker he absolutely lost all presence of mind and it is true absolutely that he ran away."[75]

Thus three weeks after the battle and ten days before the first of the inquiries would begin, Macdonald had been informed of the worst of the accusations and rumours and assured by his secret service chief that they were true.

THREE DAYS LATER, the Adjutant General of Militia, Patrick L. MacDougall, issued explicit instructions stipulating the mandate of the inquiry. A Military Court of Inquiry was akin to a preliminary hearing to examine evidence and determine whether a more formal court martial was called for. Its conduct was less formal than that of a full court martial and could be as adversarial as authorities chose to make it. The purpose, according to MacDougall's instructions to the judges, was to give Booker "the opportunity of disproving the unfavourable imputations which have been cast upon him in the public prints. You will therefore be pleased to take all evidence which may be produced before the Court by Col. Booker and you will also endeavour to produce all the evidence which may tend to elucidate the truth. The opinion of the Court of Enquiry must of course be based on and sustained by such evidence *only as is embodied in the written proceedings* [my emphasis]."[76]

In other words, the judges were told to make sure that nothing discreditable to Booker slipped into the written record. (Into the "Q & A," as it would be termed today.) As the Hamilton *Evening Times* later complained, the examination of witnesses "was conducted with a caution even exceeding the usual red-tape formality of government enquiries. The replies of such witnesses were rigorously restricted to direct bearing upon the questions carefully framed and propounded by the Court, and causal departures from the strict letter were neither permitted or taken down in the reports."[77]

When on July 3 the Court of Inquiry into "the circumstances connected with the late engagement at Lime Ridge" convened in the Royal Hotel on James Street in Hamilton, it sat for only one day and was closed to the public and the press. To the outrage of the officers and men of the Thirteenth, it was even closed to them, unless they were called as witnesses—and the only person authorized to call witnesses was Colonel Alfred Booker, who was also the only one to argue and present evidence. It was a one-sided process: There would be no cross-examination, except by the three officers sitting on the board, and only if they cared to do so—and they rarely did.[78]

How the recently promoted twenty-six-year-old Lieutenant Colonel George T. Denison was selected to preside over the Board of Inquiry is not entirely clear. Denison was an attorney, which certainly qualified him for the job. Both Denison and one of his fellow board members, Lieutenant Colonel G.K. Chisholm, commanding officer of the Oakville Rifle Company, had just been mentioned by Colonel Lowry of the British army, the commander of forces on the Niagara Frontier, in his dispatches to Canada's Adjutant General of Militia, British army Colonel Patrick L. MacDougall.[79] The third member of the court was Lieutenant Colonel James Shanly, commander of the Seventh Battalion, London.[80]

As much as the press was dissatisfied with the closed proceedings, it generally decided to wait until the Court had published its report before lashing out. In the meantime, the Hamilton *Evening Times,* despite

Somerville's protests, stopped publishing further reports of Booker's alleged misconduct. The social crusader in Somerville flickered to life once more. He began selling his own printed broadsheets in the streets of Hamilton without waiting for the Court's findings.[81]

Back in June, three days after the battle, Somerville had secured a deal with Thomas and Richard White, the proprietors of the Hamilton *Spectator*, to publish a "quickie" book on the battle. It was to be rushed into print at the end of June, but now as the misdeeds of Booker became a major part of the story, Somerville wanted to wait until the inquiry had been held and its report released before completing his book. The publishers were not happy with the delay; they were banking on cashing in on the public's interest, which by midsummer was beginning to show signs of waning.[82]

The officers of the Thirteenth Battalion, who saw in Somerville their champion and had been giving him access to their men, meetings, and correspondence, offered to guarantee the cost of the book's printing if Somerville would wait for the report. Lieutenant Colonel Skinner, Captain Askin, and Lieutenant Gibson formed a committee to oversee the payment of the advance to the printer and to coordinate the book's completion and release. To his infinite regret, Somerville agreed to their offer.[83]

On July 26, Macdonald stood before the legislature and announced that he had reviewed the inquiry's report and that it concluded Booker had acted "in a most soldierly and praiseworthy manner."[84] The report and its full transcripts of the coached witness testimony were released to the public on August 3, and newspapers printed the full text of its carefully orchestrated proceedings. The Court declared that while Booker had made an understandable mistake when forming the square, otherwise "there is not the slightest foundation for the unfavourable imputations cast upon him in the public prints, and most improperly circulated through that channel ... at no period of that day could want of personal coolness be imputed to Lieut. Col. Booker." In its most barefaced lie, the report concluded, "The Court lastly finds that the whole of the wounded and sick were brought with the retreating column and that it reached Port Colborne ..."[85]

Some of the witness testimony about Booker's precise location in battle and his actions during the retreat had been doctored, according to Somerville: "The Court made several answers into one; thereby placing Booker where he was not."[86] The reaction to the report from the press was predictable: "thoroughly whitewashed";[87] "made no effort to ascertain the truth."[88]

FROM LATE JULY through early September, four books on the Battle of Ridgeway would come to be published. The rambling and often satirical *History of the Fenian Invasion of Canada,* with its illustrations of drunken, simian Irish Fenians, was published under the pseudonym Doscen Gauust; useless as a history, it was a diatribe against Catholics. The Chewett Company's collection of previously published newspaper reports, entitled *The Fenian Raid at Fort Erie,* was only as accurate as the press reports it reprinted.

George T. Denison's *The Fenian Raid on Fort Erie with an Account of the Battle of Ridgeway*, published in early August, was the only one of the three that could be considered an attempt at researched history, despite his obviously too-close-for-comfort role in the events. Denison of course concurred with most of the findings of the Court of Inquiry that he presided over, but as we saw in a previous chapter, not with all the testimony submitted there—particularly on the issue of when Booker actually received Peacocke's telegram ordering him to delay his departure for Ridgeway. Denison condemned Booker in his account, concluding that he had received the order at 7:30 A.M. and not, as Booker insisted, at 9:30 A.M.[89] In all other respects, Denison's history was kind to Booker. According to Denison's description of the retreat, "A large body of red coats and green, fighting gallantly, slowly and sullenly retired, covering the retreat, and holding the Fenians at bay."[90] Much of Denison's focus was on defending the conduct and reputation of Lieutenant Colonel Peacocke under whose command he had served. In any case, in his book

Denison made no reference to the inquiry, submitting his manuscript for publication perhaps before he had any authority to refer directly to the inquiry transcripts and its report.

ONLY SOMERVILLE'S 128-page pamphlet book now remained to be published. The text of his book had been partially printed on half-sheets of eight pages, which, when folded together, would produce the finished book. Some of the half-sheets were left sequentially blank so that once the inquiry had released its report and Denison had published his awaited book, Somerville could insert at the last minute a response and additional information from Denison's work.[91] The last ten pages consisted of recent corrections to the earlier, already-printed pages.[92]

As Somerville worked through August to complete his book, he discovered to his dismay that the committee of officers—in particular Skinner and Askin—had become a shadow editorial board and were insisting that Booker's disgrace become the central theme of the book, something that Somerville claimed had never been his intention.[93]

Obviously, the unsatisfactory conclusion of the Booker Inquiry was driving both the officers and their men to want the final word. As the Hamilton *Evening Times* editorialized, "The finding of the Court of Enquiry in Col. Booker's favour amounts to a verdict of 'guilty' against the Thirteenth Battalion ... The announcement in the House by the Attorney General, that the Commission had completely exonerated Colonel Booker from blame, was received with cheers. That errors were committed in the short campaign, by raw troops who had never been before under fire, is perhaps no more than might naturally have been expected. If that is not taking the blame clear off Col. Booker, and putting it down heavily on the men, then we confess to a most inadequate comprehension of the meaning of words ..."[94]

There was more at stake than just the reputation of the battalion. Booker was claiming that he had actually resigned from command of the Thirteenth Battalion on May 12, long before the Fenian crisis, and that his resignation had not been accepted in time for the Fenian Raid.[95] He insisted that his removal from battalion command was merely the routine acceptance of an already accomplished fact. As the Hamilton *Evening Times* pointed out, Booker had not resigned, nor had he been removed from his more senior position as overall commander of the Hamilton district. Along with all the other militia units in the district, the Thirteenth remained under Booker's overall authority. The paper warned, "Mark that he says he *has no intention* of resuming the command. But he *may have* such an intention next week, for all we know ... the common talk among the officers and men of the Battalion is, that they will believe in Col. Booker's resignation, of *all and every* official command over or connection with them, when they see it in the *Gazette*. And it is not the resignation by him of *one* commission only, but of *two,* which is required to do away with all deceptive arrangements of the difficulty."[96]

On August 14 the Hamilton *Evening Times* announced correctly that Booker was closing his business in Hamilton and moving to Montreal. But the next day, at Booker's insistence, it ran a retraction of the story. The notion that Booker was remaining in Hamilton can only have redoubled the determination of the Thirteenth Battalion to get their final word in on Booker's conduct.

Somerville in the meantime was becoming frustrated with Skinner and Askin's meddling. Skinner had lined up witnesses for Somerville to interview, who were alleging all sorts of misdeeds by Booker. Somerville found some of them completely unreliable and refused to include their allegations in the book. He was forced to travel to Skinner's home in Woodstock with the proofs of the most recent additions to the half-sheets and to fight and argue with him line by line over the final text. He managed to remove some of the assertions he felt were untrue or unreliable, but in the editorial give-and-take with his patrons, he admitted that some objectionable statements remained.[97]

When the two thousand copies of Somerville's *Narrative of the Fenian*

Invasion were finally published on September 26, Booker's disgrace was made utterly complete. Booker was portrayed as a scheming, pompous, ambitious, and incompetent social climber who, as he approached the field of battle, became increasingly scared and confused. He was said to have mistaken cows for Fenian cavalry, to have led his men blindly into slaughter, and to have ridden off in panic, leaving behind his dying and wounded men on the field. He is shown succumbing to a nervous breakdown after the battle and, as a final indignity, slandering his own rank and file. Perhaps the most damning line from the book was to be found at the climax of the battle, when Booker ordered the retreat. Somerville wrote: "He seemed to have decided, so far as, in a condition of imbecility and nervous prostration, he could decide anything, to retreat from the field of action."[98]

Despite the meddling of Skinner and Askin, Somerville made no mention of their role when the book was published. No doubt Somerville wanted no repetition of the kind of treatment he had received in Britain when he had opposed Cobden. And of course, he could ill afford to lose whatever the book might earn as he continued to exist on the margins of poverty as a single parent of six children.

Somerville's book administered the *coup de grâce* to Alfred Booker's crumbling reputation. Nobody was really satisfied with this outcome and no one was redeemed in any meaningful way, not Booker, not Somerville, and neither the officers nor the men of the Thirteenth.

Talk of the battle faded away in the summer and stopped entirely toward the end of August, but there would be no end to Booker's disgrace. On August 25, MacDougall reviewed on horseback the men of the Queen's Own Rifles, and when the men broke out into a cheer, it startled the horse. The *Grand River Sachem* gleefully reported, "Colonel MacDougall rode the horse Col. Booker had at Lime ridge, and it was noticed that at the first cheer he bolted off with the Adjutant-General."[99]

Late in the autumn, sixteen-year-old George Mackenzie, whose arm had been shattered at the elbow and who had been dressed down by Booker on the morning of the muster for asking if he had time to get breakfast, ran into his former commanding officer in downtown Hamilton. Mackenzie recalled, "I was convalescent and able to go about with my arm in a sling, walking one day on James Street I saw Colonel Booker sitting by himself in the portico of the Royal hotel. The last time he had spoken to me he had administered a sharp rebuke. Now he came forward eagerly and shook me warmly by the hand. He was greatly changed. As I remember, he looked shrunken and ill. His habitual smartness of appearance had gone. His dress looked negligent, even slovenly. His deep humiliation had bitten into his soul and he was a broken man."[100]

Shortly afterward Alfred Booker closed his business, sold his house, and moved to Montreal, never to return to Hamilton again.

FOR THE NEXT YEAR and eight months the affair nagged at Somerville's pride and conscience until he could take it no longer. On April 14, 1868, he sent Booker a "private and confidential" memorandum describing the role Skinner and other officers had had in the publication of the book. While full of complaints against Skinner, Somerville's letter offered only a marginal disavowal of his book's contents.

Somerville began by declaring, "Matter not approved by me was printed. Because an over-ruling *animus* among certain of the officers of the 13th (not all), hostile to Colonel Booker, and blind to fair play, constrained me to allow the matter of the last 60 pages of the Narrative to go forth as it did."[101] From those pages, however, Somerville explicitly disavowed only two items: a story about Booker's mistaking cows for Fenian horsemen on the eve of the battle, and Booker's comment on "dismounting Skinner" from his horse. Those episodes, Somerville said, came from Captain Askin, who had acted in pure spite and should be regarded as unreliable.[102]

Somerville then described in lurid detail all the "libels" he had *not* put into the book. Dissecting the evidence in each allegation, he insisted that he fought with Skinner to maintain the book's journalistic integrity. He was chiefly preoccupied, however, with a description of how his book was financed and printed, and included affidavits from the printers. He wrote about issues irrelevant to the veracity of the book: royalties, print runs, fees, and other matters. Somerville complained that Skinner had accused him of obtaining confidential battalion telegrams surreptitiously, to which he said Skinner had actually given him access; and of betraying confidences when revealing conversations between officers, to which Somerville said Skinner made him unconditionally privy. Somerville's review of his sources actually has the effect of increasing the credibility of some of the passages in his book where the reader wonders *how could he know that,* unless he saw the telegrams or was privy to conversations between the officers. Well, he *did* see them and he *was* privy. As a prominent outsider with a reputation, Somerville gained the kind of trust that a socially superior insider like George Denison would never have been able to elicit from junior officers. Somerville always had an eye-level view of his subjects, whatever their class—he was a chameleon of a social historian.

Some of Somerville's memorandum would have been humorous had its subject not been so tragic. After describing how he hated the pamphlet published in his name, Somerville went on to write, "It is known to Adjutant General MacDougall, to whom I gave one, as to every newspaper editor who had them from my hand in Montreal, that I desired them not to accept all that was said of Col. Booker as exact truths or as if given on my own authority."[103]

What Somerville really wanted, he said, was to "stand absolved before the country of having, as the historian of the 'Fenian Invasion of Canada, 1866,' intentionally and unnecessarily injured the reputation of Colonel Booker."[104] Frustratingly, Somerville insisted that nobody, not even the most severe of Booker's accusers, had charged him of cowardice but only of "nervous excitability. Other inferences may have been drawn from the different published accounts."[105] Perhaps most frustrating of all was Somerville's salutation to Booker: "Dear Sir, I commit this Memorandum to your care. You have my permission to do with it what you think best, except to publish it without my knowledge."[106]

In the summer of 1870, as the newly completed Volunteers Monument near Queen's Park was about to be dedicated to the fallen at Ridgeway, a letter from Somerville was printed in the Montreal *Gazette* repeating, without naming the guilty parties, some of the allegations he had made in his confidential memorandum. In this letter Somerville stated that he had been "grievously misled" by "one corrupted source in Hamilton," that he regretted anything he had done to contribute to the damage to Booker's reputation, and that he hoped Booker would be invited to attend the dedication ceremony.

The *Globe* acidly commented, "Confession, we are told, is good for the soul ... but confession to be salutary ought to be complete ... The whole conspiracy must come out. Who, then was the man that 'grievously misled' Mr. Somerville? Who is the 'one corrupted source in Hamilton'?"[107]

Then in November 1870 Napier came to the defence of Booker, writing an open letter in the press in which he said he hoped some of the volunteer officers from 1866 would be decorated, "and I shall be very glad to see Colonel Booker's name amongst the recipients, as I never for one moment doubted his courage in the field, *however,* much I regretted he did not completely best the Fenians at Ridgeway ... it is a well known fact that he left Port Colborne *long before* the hour named by Colonel Peacocke, and had it not been for the unfortunate alarm about cavalry he would have defeated them."[108]

Poor Booker must have been apoplectic. Right to the end he wasn't getting a break—not even from his defenders. Nobody was getting his story right! He was forever stuck with Denison's conclusion: "This mistake of one hour led to his not receiving the message to delay, and therefore caused him to be really three hours too soon."[109] Booker wrote a letter to the editor in response, thanking Napier "for his good opinion of me," but adding, "I beg leave, nevertheless, to call in question the accuracy of the General's information to the effect that 'it is a well known fact that he (Col. Booker) left Port Colborne *long before* the hour named by Colonel Peacocke.' The public of Canada have, to some extent shared this impression with General Napier."[110]

Booker made his case once more, this time in the pages of the *Globe*, that he had been ordered to leave Port Colborne at "5 o'clock, if possible, but no later than 5:30 under all circumstances—rations or no rations." He explained that he received "during the engagement" the telegram from Peacocke about his own delayed departure too late to stop the advance into the Fenian ambush. As for the issue of the Fenian cavalry and his ordering a square to be formed, Booker remained mute, having always admitted he had made a mistake.

Less than a year later Booker was dead. It had all been too much for him. He became "suddenly ill"—sometimes a euphemism for suicide. He died of unspecified causes at the relatively young age of forty-seven on September 27, 1871, and was buried in Montreal with military honours that did not extend beyond his burial day.[111]

The irony of Alfred Booker's tragic story is that his bungling at Limestone Ridge probably saved more men than it killed. Having advanced that far in the battle, believing that they had been pushing the Fenians back and taking the field from them, the men were particularly bitter that Booker had botched the last phase of what they were sure was going to be an imminent victory. But had Booker not lost control, had the men not retreated, had they pushed on farther, low in ammunition, advancing uphill, into the waiting centre wing of the Fenian force, now concentrated at twice the size it had been in the previous ninety minutes, sitting behind improvised cover on top of all its spare ammunition ... what a massacre *that* would have been! Although they did not know it, for most of the boys on Limestone Ridge that morning, Booker's incompetence was the luckiest break of their lives.

ALEXANDER SOMERVILLE continued to struggle in his attempts to escape destitution and ruin. Shortly after Confederation, under the sponsorship of D'Arcy McGee, he authored a guide for immigrants to Canada and began planning his return to England as an immigration agent. But in the early hours of April 7, 1868, when McGee went home to his Sparks Street boarding house after a late-night parliamentary debate and was fumbling with the lock on his front door, an assassin stepped out from the shadows behind him and shot him dead. A tailor, Patrick Whelan, either a Fenian or a sympathizer, was charged, convicted, and hanged for the murder under circumstances still debated by historians.[112]

When Somerville claimed his payment for the work he had done for McGee, he was told that McGee had "made no appropriation out of which the amount could be paid." Despite Macdonald's endorsement, Somerville remained unpaid, although a small pension was granted to him in 1876 for his work.[113]

As Somerville's children grew up and became independent, most left for other parts of the Empire and to the United States. Two sons enrolled in the British army overseas, while another became a stage designer in New York. Somerville remained alone, drifting among Hamilton, Montreal, and Toronto, eking out a meagre income by writing articles on Canada for English newspapers and living in a shelter maintained by the St. Andrew's Society in Montreal. There Somerville undertook his last crusade: defending the reputation of and caring for the dying William Scott, an impoverished fellow inmate of the shelter and the disputed nephew of the celebrated author Sir Walter Scott.[114] In those years, Somerville struggled to get a government post of some kind or sponsorship for a pamphlet but was unsuccessful, except for a contract in 1877 to rewrite the *Emigrant's Guide*.[115]

In 1874 Somerville moved to Toronto after finding work as editor of the Anglican *Church Herald*, to which he was contributing numerous articles. For a time he could afford to take a room in the upscale City Hotel on Front and Simcoe streets. He listed himself in the Toronto

City Directory as "writer in English, Welsh, Irish and Scottish Journals, books, magazines, cyclopedias."[116] Most of his writings in this period, however, were anonymous dispatches to newspapers. Somerville's luck was all bad. The *Church Herald* merged with a New York publication and moved its editorial offices to the United States, leaving Somerville, now in his late sixties, unemployed and with no income other than his minuscule pension.[117] By now Somerville was a three-hundred-pound hulk living in a single room in the City Hotel, which he shared with a mouse he fed by hand. He sent out thousands of articles to collect minute royalties and carried on a stream of correspondence to which he often attached tiny clippings of his previous publications. His life became a daily struggle to earn sufficient income to pay for postage. Eventually his room, and even his bed, were piled so full of newspapers, manuscripts, notebooks, clippings, and letters that he turned to sleeping on the floor rolled up in a sheet or blanket. Just one small pile of paper, his memoirs, was estimated to consist of some five thousand pages. In 1880 he could no longer afford the City Hotel and moved into a dilapidated boarding house at 106 York Street, in the heart of what was then Toronto's red-light district and skid row. Eventually he could not afford or perhaps abide living in the cramped room, and in 1883 he dragged five trunks jammed full of his notes and manuscripts into a woodshed adjoining the house. He lived there summer and winter, despite the landlady's protests, for the next two years.[118]

On June 17, 1885, Somerville, who had been ill for some time, died in the woodshed to which he had retreated, stubbornly refusing in his last days any attempt to have him moved indoors. He had given his trunks of manuscripts to somebody for safekeeping a few months earlier, but the person never came forward after his death. Despite many searches, the last by a Yale historian as recently as the 1960s, and then my own, the papers were never found. Although there were claims that papers were turned over to the Canadian government for safekeeping shortly after Somerville's death, Canada Archives has no record of them in its collections.[119]

Alexander Somerville was buried on Friday, June 19, by the St. Andrew's Society on their grounds at the Toronto Necropolis, in an unmarked grave that is still easily found today beneath a twin-stemmed tree overlooking the Don Valley. There the musket ball that took flight in 1837 in Spain and painfully lodged itself in his arm finally came to rest. There it remains today under the roar of traffic from the nearby Don Valley Parkway, louder in Somerville's eternal sleep than the din of any battle or rebellious tumult he had witnessed in his life.

TEN

The Dennis Inquiry, August–December 1866

Approximately ten thousand Fenians had answered the call and arrived on the border with Quebec and Ontario that June. Some five thousand were mustered in the Buffalo area, facing three thousand British regulars, artillery, and Canadian militia in Chippawa and Fort Erie.[1] The United States intervened, just as Secretary of State William Seward and President Andrew Johnson had promised the British they would. The Fenian insurgents were quickly taken into custody, their leaders hauled into federal court and charged with violation of the Neutrality Act and just as quickly released with no further prosecution. The thousands of rank-and-file Fenians assembled on the border were given paid railway passage home courtesy of the the U.S. War Department after giving their parole to stay clear of Canada.[2]

In the first three days of the Fenian invasion, some twenty-two thousand volunteers reported for duty throughout Canada West and

Canada East to fight the "Finnegans," as they were popularly called.[3] Some volunteers reported from as far away as New Orleans. A group of fifty-six Canadians who had abandoned their jobs in Chicago and arrived in Toronto on June 5 were met at the railway station by the mayor and aldermen, cheering crowds, and two companies of infantry as a guard of honour. The "Chicago Volunteers" were celebrated from one end of the province to the other.[4]

The Six Nations sent fifty Delaware and Cayuga warriors in buckskin, feathers, and war paint, who were armed with flintlock muzzleloaders; the warriors were led by William Montour from Willow Grove near Hagersville and Caledonia. They reported for duty on June 2, at the Thirteenth Battalion's James Street drill shed in Hamilton, with hard rations of dried corn and rabbit jerky. The warriors had heard Canada was invaded by *yaluk wanduk/Del* (savage people from far off) whose name they pronounced "Feen-yince."[5]

Another two hundred First Nations warriors assembled at the Dunnville station on June 2 and telegraphed a request to Major General Napier for Enfield rifles. They received no response. In the evening Captain Akers, by then in command at Port Colborne, endorsed the request to Napier for the rifles but also received no reply. The Six Nations chief, W.J. Simcoe Kerr, wrote the Militia Department later, "I was at the place Ridgeway where the fight with the Fenians took place and am prepared to say that had the 200 Indians I commanded been there on Saturday, not only would the lives of the Volunteers been saved but some slight disgrace which attended the expedition prevented."[6]

Kerr was offended by the government's reluctance to issue the warriors with arms. The attitude of the colonial authorities had radically changed since the War of 1812, when Natives were welcomed and recognized as independent allied nations in the war against the United States. Now, after fifty-four years of peace during which the warriors were not needed, and with the ascendency of mid-Victorian racism, a different attitude prevailed. The chief felt compelled to remind the Militia

Department that if they were unwilling to issue the warriors with rifles, the Six Nations were prepared to buy them, for "they have property to guard as well as the white men and it seems strange that they should not be placed in a position to guard it."[7]

There were even American citizens reporting for duty in the defence of Canada. At Oil Springs in Lambton County near Sarnia, a third of a volunteer infantry company consisted of Pennsylvania oilmen led by Captain Read, a lawyer, and Lieutenant Robert Mathison, a printer.[8]

It was an entirely different invasion in Lower Canada, one that its historian, Hereward Senior, described as being "over before it began."[9] The Fenian Right (East) Wing of the Irish Republican Army[10] under West Point graduate Fenian General Samuel B. Spears ("General Whiskey") invaded just east of Lake Champlain from Vermont into Missisquoi County, Quebec, on June 7, but was hampered not only by the U.S. Army, but also by a lack of troops and supplies, and was forced to withdraw from Canadian territory.

The only combat took place at Pigeon Hill on June 9, when Crown forces and artillery pulled up in front of approximately two hundred Fenians still lingering in Canada. When the Fenians opened fire, a troop of cavalry—the Royal Guides, or Governor General's Body Guard for Lower Canada, elite members of the Montreal Hunt Club—charged the barricades and smacked the Fenians with the flat of their swords, herding them across the border into the arms of the waiting U.S. Army, who seized and disarmed them. It may have been the first and last cavalry charge on Canadian soil. There were no casualties on either side.[11]

ON JUNE 15 Macdonald wrote to the Executive Council, "As all apprehensions of a recurrence of Fenian Raids seem to have passed away for the time being, and as the gallant volunteers on active service are suffering from their absence from their homes and vocations—the force can without hazard to the safety of the province be greatly reduced."[12] On the same day, the Toronto *Globe* began advertising "cheap excursions" to Fort Erie by the *City of Toronto* and Erie-Niagara Railway so that many may "avail themselves of this opportunity to visit a place historic before, but having a peculiar attraction now."[13]

As Canadians settled down into the last dog days of summer, it appeared as if Lieutenant Colonel John Stoughton Dennis had not only escaped the Fenians on the night of June 2 in Fort Erie, but also any public or press scrutiny. No accusations or rumours bubbled up about Dennis in the Canadian newspapers throughout the summer while Booker's and Peacocke's errors and misdeeds were endlessly debated.

In the days after the battle at Fort Erie, Dennis had been appointed "brigade major" (chief of staff) to Colonel Lowry, the British commander of forces on the Niagara Frontier—a notable honour. Dennis was mentioned in dispatches by Lowry, who wrote on June 18 that Dennis had "proved himself admirable in matter of detail and has been most active and useful to me here. He has special talent for the performance of staff duties and as there has been a force of about 3,000 volunteers on this Frontier, his capacity in that respect has been well tested."[14]

McMicken's confidential memo to Macdonald describing Dennis's "poltroonery and cowardice" was filed away and not acted upon. On June 24 and 25, Dennis survived what must have been the most dangerous moment for his reputation. Newspapers across Canada published a series of official reports released by the government from key commanders in the field during the operation. Included among them was Dennis's own account of how he drew up his "little command" in Fort Erie and made a courageous stand with his men but, being outnumbered by the Fenians, was forced to order them to retreat and to conceal himself until he could fight another day.

Running near the end of these documents was a short report from the *Robb*'s captain, Lachlan McCallum. It had been written at Dennis's request and addressed to him. In it McCallum refrained from describing the ground combat and only reported on the movement of the *Robb*, referring to Dennis only once: "On Saturday last, 2nd June between the hours of 2 and 4 P.M.[15] *after your departure* [my emphasis], I retreated down the river under a galling fire ..."[16]

The term "after your departure" had not caught anybody's attention, and Dennis must have felt tremendously relieved that the press did not catch the scent of disgrace. McMicken and Macdonald, however, knew precisely how pointed that phrase was, as did all the men who were under Dennis's command that day in Fort Erie.

Three days later, in military parlance, "the stuff hit the fan." Adjutant General of Militia Patrick L. MacDougall received in Ottawa a letter from the *Robb*'s salty captain. McCallum was outraged by what he had read in Dennis's published report. In his letter McCallum accused Dennis of ordering his men ashore "against the judgments of all the Officers under his command," resulting in four brave men's being made "cripples for life besides exposing the lives of all his command to no effect except the shooting of a few Fenians." Furthermore, McCallum wrote, Dennis halted his command at a point when they were exposed to fire from both Fenian flanks, and despite having time to retreat to the *Robb*, he recklessly did not. Dennis countermanded orders that McCallum had given to open fire on the enemy and then "departed from his command before a gun was fired leaving us in that painful position ..."[17]

On July 4, *The New York Times* reprinted a story from the Detroit *Advertiser*, "Heroism of an English Colonel," that alleged Dennis had stripped off his uniform and hidden naked in a hayloft, and that he nervously cut himself twice while shaving off his whiskers to disguise himself.[18] Dennis must have felt the sharks circling him, but the press in Canada was chewing on Booker and Peacocke and did not bite on the Dennis story just yet.

On July 17, Dennis sent Colonel William Smith Durie, the Assistant Adjutant-General of Militia in Canada West, an eight-page letter refuting the accusations, with five appended affidavits from Fort Erie citizens attesting to his version of events.[19] It almost did the trick. On August 16, General Sir John Michel, the commander-in-chief of British troops in Canada, wrote MacDougall that he saw no reason for further investigation into Dennis's conduct and added, "I think that Cap. McCallum might be desired to be more careful in making charges such as these he had advanced."[20] There must have been a collective sigh of relief that McCallum's allegations could now be put away quietly, especially since criticism of the government's performance during the Fenian crisis was dying down. Nobody wanted to stir up any new revelations or scandals.

It was not going to be that easy. Artillery Captain Dr. Richard King had recovered from the amputation of his leg sufficiently to depart Buffalo for his home in Port Robinson. Nothing would make for a better mid-Victorian summer picnic festival in Welland County than to proudly welcome home a hero. On August 9 thousands of citizens and dignitaries flocked to King's homecoming on foot, in carriages, on horseback, and by train. The Welland Railway ran special trains and charged half-price for the tickets. Flags and bunting were hung everywhere. So many communities along the canal wanted to participate that a route was organized for a flotilla of yachts that would take King down the system, stopping at various points for receptions and for people to view him on the deck. He was surrounded by a military guard of honour while a brass band played "Home Again." Gun batteries fired salutes as he passed.[21]

Newspaper reporters poured into the area, prepared for once to write a "good news" story on a hero's homecoming. Along the way at the various stops, dignitaries, civil officials, MPPs, and even Toronto's mayor, Francis Medcalf, assembled to greet Captain King. Everywhere King went there stood huge arches across the span of which was written, "Welcome to our brave captain."[22]

As the yacht arrived at its final destination of Port Robinson, King was borne off the deck to a waiting carriage in which sat MPP T.C. Street. From the carriage, King was to review and address his brave men of the Welland Canal Field Battery assembled in their ranks before him. One version of what happened next, printed in the *Globe,* was that

King said "he was an Irishman by birth, but a Canadian by adoption, and we will defend Canada to the last. But said he, I thank the Fenians for this (raising his leg, of which the stump from a little below the knee remained). He hoped he should have enough or a piece of a leg left to lead them against the Fenians again ... The material is in Canada to drive these Fenians out of the country if they came again. There is not better material for fighting than the men of Canada."[23]

Without naming Dennis, the *Globe* reported only a single discordant note in the speech: "Dr. King complained bitterly of the management of the commander ... He said they could have done better than they did but for the way in which they were commanded."[24]

The other version of Captain King's speech was contained in a less circumspect report from a different newspaper, a clipping of which was attached to a letter Colonel Durie received from Dennis four days later, in which he complained: "Capt. King is there stated to have applied the following language to me—'We were commanded by a coward. I allude to Colonel Dennis who is a coward and a paltry one' and again, further on, 'What did that coward, that poltrooney scoundrel Dennis say ... etc.'"[25]

Dennis now demanded a Court of Inquiry just like Booker's and that Captain King be ordered to retract his comments or be charged with conduct unbecoming an officer for making such remarks in public about a superior officer while addressing a military force. In the wake of the cries of "whitewash" following publication of the findings of the Booker Inquiry, this new development was not at all welcome. There was no way that Dennis could be given a similar cleansing to the one that had exonerated Booker. Durie forwarded the letter to MacDougall in Ottawa, noting on it "that an error of judgement which may be attributed to Lt. Col Dennis—is one thing—cowardice—another."[26]

Durie was convinced that "Capt. King was not warranted in making use of the language alluded to from all the information I can learn. Beg to suggest that Captain King be called upon to substantiate or at once withdraw and apologize for the ... language."[27]

"Beg" was a good choice of words: The chances of Durie's and MacDougall's dragging the one-legged hero before a court martial for his choice of language without raising a stink in the press were slim to none. MacDougall's letter to Captain King was no doubt diplomatic and full of hope. Possibly it contained the suggestion that the press might have exaggerated King's remarks and that the captain might be disposed to assure everyone that he would not accuse Lieutenant Colonel Dennis of cowardice. Perhaps he misspoke in the excitement of his return home and the press was exaggerating his remarks.

Captain King's defiant response to MacDougall's letter dashed any such hopes:

> The report of my speech as contained in enclosed printed slip ... is substantially correct so far as concerns the application of the words "Poltroon" and "coward" to Colonel Dennis. In reply I beg leave to state that the words above underlined were applied by me to Colonel Dennis on the field of battle at Fort Erie when that officer was in the act of deserting his post and I have no doubt in the excitement at Port Robinson on the occasion of my landing, I repeated the charges.[28]

General Michel was clearly frustrated. There must have been a marshalling of opinion as to how to silence King, including a proposal to court-martial him. On September 6, on the back of King's reply, Michel penned:

> I think that it will be impossible to maintain discipline in the volunteer force if junior officers are to be allowed to [discourse/denounce] at public receptions their superiors for their conduct when in command. Some allowance must of course be made for the particular circumstances of Captain King's case, but he has had ample time since his recovery to make his charges against Lt. Col. Dennis if he was so disposed and not having done so I can entertain but an opinion namely that they are not capable of being substantiated. I think a letter should be written to Captain King reprimanding him for the objectionable

> course he has adopted expressing to him at the same time my deep regret that a regard for the interests of the service oblige me to convey such a communication of my disapproval to be made to an officer who has suffered so severely as he has in action and expressing a hope that on having the impropriety of his conduct clearly pointed out to him he will see the necessity for making every reparation in his power to the feelings of Lt. Col Dennis.[29]

Everything humanly and bureaucratically possible to avoid another Court of Inquiry into yet another officer's command was being done.

Dennis in the meantime had got wind that George Denison was about to publish in August his history of the Fenian invasion. He invited Denison to visit him in his Toronto offices to discuss its contents. The two men had a long history. Denison had known Dennis, his senior by nineteen years, since his childhood. Dennis had been a junior officer in Denison's father's cavalry troop, where, according to George Denison, he did not distinguish himself. He would later describe Dennis as "useless as a soldier."[30]

When, at the time of the invasion, Denison heard from Peacocke how Dennis and Akers took off on their own mission, he impetuously burst out that they both should be arrested. According to Denison, Peacocke replied, "Dennis is not a soldier and did not know any better, and he is a volunteer officer and it would look as if I was trying to make a scapegoat of him to save myself."[31] Denison felt that as a result of Peacocke's discretion, the British officer himself had now become a scapegoat for the Fenian escape from Fort Erie. It offended Denison's acute sense of officer class propriety.

Dennis begged Denison to defend his reputation in his upcoming book. Dennis reminded him that they were old friends, brother officers, and perhaps he also reminded him that they were fellow gentlemen who should stand by one another. Denison claims he replied that he must "write an honest, true book or not write one at all." According to Denison in his 1901 memoir, he was later visited by an unnamed emissary who likewise urged him to defend Dennis's conduct. Denison framed the dilemma as a question of defending Peacocke's reputation rather than necessarily condemning that of Dennis, and indeed his history includes a chapter dedicated to Peacocke's conduct.[32]

Denison's *The Fenian Raid on Fort Erie* was only mildly critical of Dennis compared with the accusations from McCallum and King. Like all the other historians—including Somerville—Denison essentially accepted Dennis's version as contained in his official report. Denison questioned Dennis's judgment in undertaking the *Robb* mission, unfairly characterizing it as the product of his ambition and overlooking the fact that it was Peacocke who, while not having ordered Dennis to accompany the mission, had ordered a patrol boat to be deployed on the Niagara River. The hare-brained scheme was not Dennis's alone, as Denison and others portrayed it. Denison did not otherwise challenge in his book Dennis's account of what happened in Fort Erie.

Denison in his memoir claimed that after the publication of his history in 1866, Dennis never spoke to him again.[33] He neglects to mention the most likely reason for the snub: Denison was appointed to preside over the "Court of Inquiry into the Circumstance of the Engagement at Fort Erie"—the Dennis Inquiry! Its proceedings would be so secret that even in his memoir in 1901, Denison makes no mention of them, claiming instead that the publication of his book ruptured his relations with Dennis, rather than what he would do to him while presiding over the inquiry.

GEORGE DENISON'S fellow judges were Lieutenant Colonels James Shanly of the Seventh Battalion, London, and Silas Fairbanks of the Oshawa Rifles (William Tempest's uncle). The process would be more adversarial than the Booker Inquiry. Its purpose was broader: to determine whether "Captain King and Captain McCallum or both of them, had any charges to prefer against Lieutenant Colonel Dennis, in reference to his conduct as commanding officer at Fort Erie."[34]

Fenian Secretary of War and former U.S. Army General Thomas W. Sweeny. "Fighting Tom" lost his arm at age seventeen in the Mexican–American War. During the Civil War he would ride his horse into battle holding the reins in his mouth and his sword in his left hand. It was Sweeny who drew up the Fenian invasion plan.

Fenian General John O'Neill of Tennessee led the invasion at Fort Erie and commanded the IRA at Ridgeway. A former captain in the U.S. Cavalry, O'Neill was a specialist in anti-guerrilla warfare during the Civil War.

"Colonel O'Neill addressing his troops." Irish Catholics and rebels were often portrayed in Victorian-era British illustrations as dark-skinned "European Negros" or drunken simian brutes with ape-like noses and jaws. Although some historians claim that colonial Canadian press was innocent of this tendency, these illustrations prove otherwise. From a pamphlet published in Hamilton in 1866 by Doscen Gauust (a pseudonym), *History of the Fenian Invasion of Canada.*

"Shooting Niagara: The Invasion of Great Britain via Canada." American anti-Fenian press also portrayed Irish Americans with simian features as in this 1876 newspaper cartoon by Thomas Nast.

J.S. Dennis in later life as Canada's first deputy minister of the Interior Department. Photo from the 1870s.

Volunteer naval Captain Lachlan McCallum, commanding officer of the Dunnville Naval Brigade, owner and builder of the *W.T. Robb*. Photo taken in 1868.

Captain Dr. Richard Saunders King, M.D., volunteer commanding officer of the Welland Field Artillery Battery assigned to the *Robb* on its mission to Fort Erie. Stripped of their artillery by the British Army, the gunners fought with rifles and obsolete carbine muskets. King would never forgive Dennis for Fort Erie or for the loss of his leg in the futile but heroic stand.

Naval Lieutenant Walter Tyrie Robb, captain of the *W.T. Robb,* which was named for him by Lachlan McCallum.

The only known photo of the *W.T. Robb,* reputed to be the fastest vessel on the Great Lakes in the 1860s. McCallum dreamt of outfitting it with guns.

What might be among Canada's rarest military decorations, the Welland County–minted silver "Fort Erie Medal" was issued to the men who made the stand there. The British Imperial War Office subsequently endorsed the unusual decoration. Image from *The Canadian Antiquarian and Numismatic Journal*, 1874.

Looking west on the corner of present day Murray Street and Niagara Boulevard in Fort Erie, where the forgotten battle took place. Fenian invaders advanced from the hilltop in the background and up Niagara Boulevard.

A view of the same corners looking south on Niagara Boulevard toward where the left wing of the Fenian army advanced on the Canadians. The river is further to the left of the photo. Dennis foolishly ordered the men to take position in the middle of the street corners, exposing them to heavy fire from both flanks of Fenians.

The Lewis House and post office in Fort Erie where some of the Canadians took cover and found themselves under siege. Photo from the 1860s.

Top, Left: Alexander Somerville, shortly before his death in Toronto in 1885. His reporting of what happened at Ridgeway was driven by what he perceived as an injustice against the men of the 13th Batallion. Somerville wrote, "My life has been a battle, and my battle has been the rights of man."
Right: Volunteer Major George T. Denison III, twenty-six-year-old Toronto attorney, City Council alderman, pamphleteer, Canadian defence policy critic, wartime agent of the Confederate Secret Service in Canada, and commanding officer of his family-founded troop of cavalry, which is still active today. Denison would not only preside as a judge on the Military Courts of Inquiry into Ridgeway and Fort Erie, he would also write a history of the battle.
Bottom, Left: Denison as a Lieutenant Colonel in the 1880s, after winning a prize from Tsar Alexander II of Russia for authoring a history of cavalry, still considered a definitive work by some. In his time he was known as "the watchdog of the British Empire" and the "Teddy Roosevelt of Canada." Denison also served as a Toronto Police Court judge until shortly before his death in 1926, but in life the one thing he wanted most eluded him, and today he is almost entirely unknown to Canadians.

On June 3, when the Fenians attempted to return to Buffalo in a barge across the Niagara River, they were intercepted by the U.S. Navy and towed and tied to the *Michigan,* where they were held prisoner for several days. Illustration from *Harper's Weekly,* 1866.

A few surviving veterans march on Decoration Day in Niagara Falls in the mid-1920s. Some Canadian communities, especially those in the Niagara region where the Fenian Raids took place, still commemorate the day at local military war graves.

The Canadian Volunteers Monument at Queen's Park in Toronto, the city's oldest standing public monument. Erected in 1871, it was the site of the first memorial day ceremonies, beginning with the anniversary of Ridgeway in June, 1890. For decades the event was known as Decoration Day, when as many as thirty thousand people gathered to cover the monument in flowers in remembrance of Canada's fallen soldiers. In 1931 an act of Parliament moved the event to November 11 and renamed it Remembrance Day, excluding the Ridgeway casualties from any further official memorial commemoration.

A young rifleman from the QOR stands watch at Malcolm McEachren's grave in Toronto in 2009, during the dedication ceremony of new gravestones for the fallen of Ridgeway. Without official recognition from Veterans Affairs Canada, the Ontario resting places of the soldiers killed at Ridgeway are neglected and cared for by only the private efforts of the regiment in which they served.

King and McCallum were to prepare a list of charges, call witnesses, and present evidence, whereas Dennis would defend himself by calling his own witnesses. Each of the parties could cross-examine witnesses. While more balanced and adversarial in its procedures than the Booker Inquiry, the proceedings of the Dennis Inquiry were closed to the press and public and the inquiry's very existence was kept quiet until it was over.

The charges preferred by King and McCallum, here in an abbreviated but verbatim form, were:

1. Utter disregard for the lives and safety of the officers and men;
2. Recklessness in uselessly landing men and marching them along an exposed road, and then posting them in a most dangerous position;
3. Neglect to give orders for a retreat, and directing that no order to fire should be given;
4. Disgrace in the face of the enemy in order to secure his personal safety, desertion of his command and leaving it without orders of any kind;
5. Knowingly rendering in his official report a false account of events. Specifically, falsely claiming that, having advanced to meet the enemy at Fort Erie on June 2, in order to save the prisoners then on board the *Robb* and prevent the enemy from obtaining possession of that vessel, he ordered the Captain of that vessel to cast off and get into the stream, and ordered his men do the best they could to get away, each man for himself, when in reality he did not give such orders, and had at the time of which he alleges he gave them, deserted his command;
6. Misconduct for doing all of the above resulting in the subsequent escape of the Fenians.[35]

Unlike the one-day Booker Inquiry, the Dennis Inquiry began on September 22 in Fort Erie and, with several adjournments, continued for six weeks until a verdict on the charges was delivered on November 8. Captain King was still too weak to be in Court daily and after the first day was replaced at the prosecution table by Captain John Verner, his co-founder of the Welland Canal Field Battery. Verner and McCallum presented twenty-five witnesses and Dennis twenty-one witnesses, on whose collective testimony the chapter describing the battle is based.

As the inquiry was winding down in November, Dennis was sniped at again from a different angle. At least one newspaper was prepared to break with the discreet silence maintained by most of the others and so offered a glimpse of the scuttlebutt going the rounds. During the trial of a Fenian prisoner in Toronto, a prosecution witness claimed that he was the only one in Fort Erie who had not run away. The *Irish Canadian* gleefully reported his cross-examination:

> Q: Come now, were you not hiding in a pig pen that day? (Laughter)
> A: Yes, I did hide in a pig pen that day because they would have killed me; and Colonel Dennis also hid in the pen with me. (Laughter)[36]

The thrust and parry of argument in the Dennis Inquiry could fill a volume on its own. One of the highlights, perhaps, occurred when Denison, as presiding judge, was himself called upon as a witness by McCallum and Verner to testify about Dennis's condition upon his arrival in Peacocke's camp; and Denison was asked too about his statements in his recently published book. Dennis, however, managed to exclude most of Denison's testimony on the grounds that it referred to matters relating to events *after* the engagement in question.[37]

In his cross-examinations, Dennis questioned the relationship between Captain McCallum and witnesses from the Dunnville Naval Brigade, some of whom were McCallum's relatives and many of whom were in his employ. Captain King and his supporters were accused of intimidating witnesses from the Welland Battery who might have testified on Dennis's behalf, of attempting to prevent one witness, Private Thomas, from travelling to testify at the inquiry by detaining him, and of harassing a visiting officer, Captain Wallace, who was gathering evidence in Port Robinson on Dennis's behalf.[38]

In the end, the verdict, despite the evidence contained in the testimony, was "not guilty on all counts." However, George Denison, always the maverick, spoiled a perfect broth by dissenting from his two fellow judges on two charges, in which he voted "guilty": Charge 2, recklessness in uselessly landing men and marching them along an exposed road, and posting them in a most dangerous position; and Charge 3, neglecting to give orders for a retreat (with the exception of directing that no order to fire should be given).[39]

But there was more. Denison had also wanted to abstain from voting on the most serious charge, Charge 4, "Disgrace in the face of the enemy in order to secure his personal safety and desertion of his command." Denison wanted to abstain because "the evidence is so conflicting," but in the end his abstention was struck out and withdrawn, there being no procedural provisions for abstentions; a "not guilty" vote to the count was entered. His original abstaining notation, however, survives in the archived transcripts.[40]

The text of the charges, the verdicts, and Denison's dissent (but not his attempted abstention on the charges of cowardice), followed by comments from General Michel on Dennis's acquittal, along with condemnation of Wallace's intimidation and Thomas's arrest, was published in newspapers on December 17 in the hush of winter. There was little or no comment in the press.[41] The 356 pages of transcripts, unlike those from the Booker Inquiry, were not made public. The whole thing passed unnoticed and quietly went away, exactly as the authorities had hoped it would.

In the summer of 1867, Captain Lachlan McCallum was elected to Canada's first federal Parliament, and in November he made a futile attempt to have the transcripts of the Dennis Inquiry released to the public. The debate fills five Hansard-sized pages, with the Minister of Militia George-Étienne Cartier arguing: "The evidence taken before that court referred to personal and private matters, which should not be made public without very grave reasons." Macdonald concurred: "Col. Dennis was tried by a court, consisting of three officers and three gentlemen for Ontario, and they had acquitted him. Bringing down evidence now could do no good ... it was inexpedient and against the interests of the volunteer and militia organization to grant this motion."[42] The transcript remained secret, and eventually its very existence was forgotten. Fort Erie became a footnote in histories of the Fenian Raid and the Battle of Ridgeway.

WHEREAS BOOKER WAS BROKEN by the events of June 2, John Stoughton Dennis prospered. Three years later, a *New York Times* headline would report, "Narrow Escape of Colonel Dennis," but it was not referring to Fort Erie.[43] Dennis had been appointed as a surveyor of the Red River Settlement in Manitoba. When rebellious Metis under Louis Riel obstructed his surveys, Dennis had the Lieutenant Governor–designate in the territory appoint him as his "Lieutenant and a conservator of the peace"; he was authorized "to raise, organise, arm, equip and provision a sufficient force ... to attack, arrest, disarm or disperse" those in arms, and "to assault, fire upon, pull down or break into any fort, house, stronghold or other place in which the said armed men may be found."[44]

The "Lieutenant and conservator of the peace" began forming his own militia army. When the Metis threatened to surround the army, Dennis ran off, leaving his men behind without pay or protection.[45] One of Dennis's captured men, a surveyor and Orangeman named Thomas Scott, was executed on Riel's watch, leading to a popular call in anglophone Canada for Riel's execution. Riel was eventually hanged in 1885 after his second rebellion, an event that divided Canadians and is still characterized as an act of martyrdom by many, especially by francophone, Metis, and First Nations peoples.

Yet John Stoughton Dennis remained a consummate survivor: Not even this new disgrace could stop his career. In 1871 he was appointed Surveyor General of Dominion Lands in the West and in 1878 became the first deputy minister of Canada's Interior Department. In 1882 he was raised to British chivalry with a C.M.G., Companion of St. Michael and St. George.[46] He died in July 1885, and remained active to the end—both the man and his reputation—the ultimate moving-target-survivor-subscriber.

DENISON PROSPERED TOO. The twenty-six-year-old commander of the Governor General's Horse Guard, Toronto attorney, alderman, Confederate secret service agent, twice-presiding military judge, and author of *Canada: Is She Prepared for War? The National Defences,* and *The Fenian Raid* would write and do a lot more in his long life. His biographer, Carl Berger, pointed out: "Of all the public figures of his generation he alone left behind three volumes of autobiography."[47] These were *Soldiering in Canada* (1901); *The Struggle for Imperial Unity* (1909); and *Recollections of a Police Magistrate* (1920).

Between 1866 and 1925, when not visiting and corresponding with former Confederate generals, including Robert E. Lee, Denison wrote *Modern Cavalry: Its Organization, Armament, and Employment in War* (1868); he unsuccessfully ran for Parliament and served briefly as an immigration commissioner in England before returning to write *A History of Cavalry from the Earliest Time with Lessons for the Future* (1877), which won a prestigious cash award from Russia's Tsar Alexander II and is today still considered the definitive work on the history of cavalry.[48]

In 1868 in Ottawa, Denison fell in with five other young men who felt disillusioned with Canadian politics and shared a fear and suspicion of the United States. Growing in number, they eventually became known as the "Twelve Apostles," a lobby group that for a time considered forming itself into Canada's third party.[49] Many of the Apostles later went on to back Denison when he became known as "the watchdog of the British Empire," leading the Canada First movement and becoming a principal in the Imperial Federation League and the British Empire League, as well as a spokesman for the descendants of the United Empire Loyalists.[50]

In 1877, at the invitation of Ontario's premier, Oliver Mowat, Denison took the post of Toronto's Police Magistrate. In the next forty-four years as a Criminal Court judge, George Denison—"the Beak," as he was known—ran an assembly-line courtroom; it was not uncommon for him, according to one source, to dispose of 250 cases in a two-hour morning while he himself dubiously claimed that he had presided over nearly 650,000 cases in his career.[51] Nonetheless, a Toronto crime reporter noted that in Denison's court, "I have known a man to stand up in the dock, enter a plea of guilty to a series of crimes, and be on his way to serve a five-year term at the penitentiary, all in six minutes."[52]

Denison published an autobiography in which he revealed his cavalryman's approach to the law: "I never follow precedents unless they agree with my view"[53] and "I depend upon an intuitive feeling as to a man's guilt or innocence and not to weighing and balancing the evidence. I depend upon this feeling *in spite* of evidence."[54] As Denison explained, "I never allow a point of law to be raised. This is a court of justice, not a court of law."[55] One of his friends observed, "He wears a helmet in court and sits with spurs on."[56]

An American journalist called Denison the "[Teddy] Roosevelt of Canada."[57] Roosevelt, after having led his mounted infantry, the Rough Riders, in the legendary charge up San Juan Hill in the Spanish–American War, praised Denison's book on cavalry as "the best I have read on the subject."[58] But unlike Roosevelt, Denison would never lead a cavalry charge on a San Juan Hill. While the "Fighting Denisons" produced over a dozen officers (and even an admiral of the British navy) who fought their way through every conflict over the next ninety years, from the Red River and the Nile to Europe and Korea, George Denison ironically remained the quirky savant of Canada's military with whom nobody was completely comfortable. While honoured by the Tsar of

Russia, the one thing he wanted most, recognition at home and a permanent military command in Canada's army, eluded him. He was just too much of a maverick.

George T. Denison III died on June 6, 1925, shortly after his retirement from the bench. He was buried at St. John's-on-the-Humber, the private family cemetery secreted today between crack houses and outlaw biker clubs in the Jane Street–Weston Road triangle of Toronto. His cenotaph stands in a command position over the many other distinguished ranks of the Denisons interred there. When in 1901 Denison wrote about the aftermath of the Battle of Ridgeway, saying, "The striking feature to me was the falsification of history that was taking place all around me," he made no mention of his own role in that falsification as the presiding officer of the two Courts of Inquiry that whitewashed the history clean from our national memory.[59] George T. Denison was both a historian and an anti-historian, no less and no more than Somerville had been. Both succumbed to their opposing passions that blinded them as objective historians—Denison for galloping on horseback in defence of the old order, and Somerville for blindly charging, pen in hand, in defence of the new one. After Somerville published his history in September 1866, for the next thirty years little would be published anywhere about Ridgeway other than in Irish journalist James McCarroll's 1868 documentary novel, *Ridgeway: An Historical Romance of the Fenian Invasion of Canada.* Everything known and said of Ridgeway, along with the falsifications and cover-ups that took place in the twelve weeks after the battle, was set, sealed, and frozen like a viral brew, awaiting revival in its imperfect and partly falsified form sometime in the future.

THE TRIALS OF FORTY of the captured Fenian prisoners began in Toronto on October 6, 1866, and dragged on until January 29, 1867, followed by appeals. The prisoners were charged in regular criminal court with the capital offence of "Levying War" under the Lawless Aggressions Act of Upper Canada, which Macdonald had extended to Lower Canada on

June 8. The law was specially tooled to include the death penalty provisions of treason, charges that otherwise would have been diplomatically problematic to bring against former British subjects who were naturalized as American citizens.[60] At first the press eagerly followed the trials, but after the first few defendants were convicted, the public's interest waned.[61]

The secret agreement cobbled together between British envoy William Frederick Adolphus Bruce and Secretary of State Seward would apply to American Fenians captured at Fort Erie. Within days of the battle it was clear to everyone but the public that U.S. citizens convicted in Canada would never be executed. Back on June 11, Bruce reminded Canada's Governor General Lord Monck that "the future relations of Canada [with the United States] and its deliverance from any chance of becoming a battlefield of Fenianism will depend in a great measure on the tact and temper with which this question of the prisoners is managed."[62] On June 13, Bruce had counselled the Foreign Office, "Let the prisoners be tried by the ordinary forms of law, and let these trials be postponed as long as possible in order to allow the present excitement to abate. If possible no blood should be shed."[63] Almost everyone, ranging from the Foreign Office in Britain to the colonial authorities in Canada, was in agreement. Twenty-two of the accused were found guilty and several were sentenced to death, but nobody in charge wanted martyrs or vengeance and the death sentences were commuted to twenty years' hard labour or life imprisonment in Kingston Penitentiary. None of the convicted Fenians served the full sentence. Except for one who died in prison, they were all quietly released between 1869 and 1872, with the last, David Whalen, emerging on July 26, 1872.[64]

In 1867 the Fenians in Ireland attempted a mass uprising that was quickly snuffed out. This was followed by dramatic prison breaks, dynamite bombings, murders, and assassinations in Ireland and then Britain. In Canada, habeas corpus was again suspended in November 1867 after renewed fears of a Fenian invasion, and was used after D'Arcy McGee's assassination in 1868 to detain twenty-five suspects.[65] In the United

States, John O'Neill was elected to head the Fenian Brotherhood. Two more Fenian raids of Canada would be undertaken—both led by O'Neill. On May 25, 1870, O'Neill led six hundred men and a cannon across the border from Vermont into Quebec and was quickly and efficiently repulsed. Six Fenians were killed with no casualties on the Canadian side. He tried again in 1871 in Manitoba, where the Fenians failed in their hope to unite with Louis Riel's Metis rebels. At Manitoba, O'Neill's force totalled only thirty-five men.

By the 1880s a new generation of Fenians had targeted the British directly in London with a series of bombings and assassination plots, including one against Queen Victoria. The Special Branch of the London Metropolitan Police was formed to deal with them, a permanent domestic intelligence agency that the British had so long resisted establishing. In Canada the Toronto Police were called out in February 1883 to guard the Parliament Buildings in Ottawa against threatened Fenian bombings. The bombings never came and in May the Toronto cops were sent home.

The last Fenian Convention was held in November 1885. There were 132 Fenians in attendance.[66] Fenianism was moving to Britain and Ireland, often with diminishing direct American participation or in a more radical form, under a different name—the *Clan-na-Gael*. Later, the Irish Republican Army—the IRA—would take up the struggle. The last reports of Fenian threats against Canada came in April 1900, when three Irish nationalists acting in support of the Boers in the South African War detonated a dynamite charge on Lock No. 24 of the Welland Canal in an attempt to damage the canal and flood the Niagara countryside. Although they were described as Fenians, that was impossible; the American Fenian Brotherhood had vanished in 1886.[67] Eventually three Irish Americans linked to a shadowy factional Napper Tandy Club of the *Clan-na-Gael* in Brooklyn, New York, were arrested in Thornwald, tried, and sentenced to life imprisonment in Kingston Penitentiary.[68]

By then General John O'Neill was long dead. In 1871, after his last failed raid, he settled in Holt County, Nebraska, where he organized a settlement of Fenian families that eventually became the town of O'Neill, officially declared by the Governor in 1969 as "The Irish Capital of Nebraska," and where today the Battle of Ridgeway is remembered on June 2 in a way that it is not in Canada.[69] O'Neill, Nebraska, claims the world's largest permanent shamrock, made of Irish green–coloured concrete embedded in the surface of the town's main intersection.[70]

John O'Neill died on January 8, 1878, at the comparatively young age of forty-four, and was buried in Omaha, Nebraska.[71] On October 28, 1919, the exiled president of the newly founded Irish Republic, Éamon De Valera, made a pilgrimage to Omaha's Holy Sepulcher Cemetery to attend the dedication of a monument to "General John O'Neill: Hero of Ridgeway." E.H. Whelan, chairman of the monument committee, concluded his dedication address by declaring, "Only heroes do what O'Neill did on June 2, 1866, at Ridgeway. Only heroes lead forlorn hopes ..."[72]

John O'Neill's heroism at Ridgeway was far more easily and gracefully recognized than that of the Canadian soldiers who fought him. Recognition for them was going to be a slower and more difficult process in the decades following the battle, as uphill as the terrain they fought and died on.

THE BATTLES AT LIMESTONE RIDGE and Fort Erie left in their wake that summer thirteen dead (seven killed in action, two dead of wounds, and four from disease) and seventy-two wounded, injured, or felled by sickness. In early 1867, the Militia Department calculated pension allocations of twenty cents a day here and there, the lump sum payments for loss of limbs, and the doctors' fees for amputating them, arriving at a total of $15,986.02, or $426,826.73 in current dollars. Of that sum, $4,960.50 ($132,445.35 today) would have been pensions, paid annually to the wounded and to the families of the dead.

The highest compensation payments were awarded to the officers Percy Routh, who had been disgracefully abandoned for dead, and Dr. King, who claimed a loss of income of two to three thousand dollars a year as a physician and surgeon. They received a lump sum payment of $1,029.30 ($27,482.31 in current dollars) and a pension for life of $400 ($10,680) a year.[73] From there it went downhill. Wounded men who were hospitalized were granted a third of their missed wages—in the nineteenth century, a meagre thing for labourers and clerks to begin with. Whether a pension was added depended upon whether the wounded had lost a limb or was permanently disabled. The loss of an arm or leg garnered privates a pension of thirty cents a day or roughly $3,000 a year in today's dollars, plus a one-time lump sum payment of $50 ($1,335). As an officer's widow, McEachren's destitute wife received an annual pension of $184, plus $28 for each of her children, the boys until the age of eighteen, the girls until twenty-one. Corporal Lackey's widow received a pension of $146, whereas the destitute widows of privates received $110 ($2,937). The Militia Department, while paying the widow of Private Christopher Alderson her $110 pension, refused any payments for her seven-year-old son, as he was from her previous marriage. Medical expenses were paid but were frequently a subject of dispute between the physicians and the Militia Department, which frequently challenged the billing.[74]

In the following year the Militia Department listed an additional sixteen dead from disease contracted in service and thirty-one more wounded or sick, including a female civilian shot by accident, all adding another $8,000 to the cost.

The total casualties in the Fenian Campaign of 1866 are 31 dead (including 2 from disease in Canada East) and 103 wounded or sick.[75]

ELEVEN

Ridgeway Forgotten, 1867–1890

Everyone who went to Limestone Ridge that June 2 was somehow transformed by it. Even the two chaplains were pushed to the far edges of Christian charity and tolerance. The Presbyterian reverend Dr. David Inglis, for example, found in the Battle of Ridgeway confirmation in the struggle for the supremacy of Protestantism in the emerging nation of Canada.

On December 6, 1866, Inglis gave a Thanksgiving sermon at his McNab Street church in Hamilton entitled "Righteousness Exalteth a Nation," a reference to Proverbs 14:34, "Righteousness exalteth a nation; but sin is a reproach to any people." Inglis argued that Limestone Ridge was a Protestant Armageddon in the face of unholy Fenian Catholicism, reminding his parishioners that the Catholic and Greek Orthodox "communions have so overshadowed the great and glorious truths of the gospel by their errors and superstitions, that as systems we can only designate them as anti-Christian rather than Christian."[1]

Inglis preached: "The expected confederation of the British North American Provinces gives bright promise of a nation growing up here which shall occupy a high place in the future annals of civilization ... What is to be our national character? On what do we rest as our security for national permanence and prosperity? Not surely on our extensive national resources, or on our facilities for making them available, or the energy and enterprise of our people. Not even on our much cherished relation to the British Throne, though this is a tower of strength to us."

Only in its commitment to Protestantism can Canada be safe, Inglis concluded. "It is becoming far too common a thing to say that Canada with its immense frontier cannot be defended—that in the event of war between Great Britain and the United States we are powerless to defend ourselves." But have we forgotten the history of Protestant Switzerland, which stands independent next to more powerful and often hostile Catholic neighbours, asked Inglis, or the recent victory of underdog Protestant Prussia against the more powerful Catholic Austria?

"If we possess and maintain that righteousness which exalteth a nation, then no power shall be suffered to prevail against us," declared Inglis. "Let Canada flourish by the preaching of the word."[2] For Inglis, "the word" was exclusively Protestant and its colour was Orange.

Inglis went on to teach "systematic theology" at Knox College in Toronto before becoming the pastor of the Reformed Church in Brooklyn Heights, New York, in 1872. He died there in 1877.

The young Methodist chaplain Nathanael Burwash took home a different lesson. Limestone Ridge became the crossroads of his faith. The dying Ensign McEachren's last words to him, "Pray that I may have brighter evidence," were a Methodist transfiguration of Burwash's doubts in his faith. For the rest of his life, as Burwash became chancellor and dean of Victoria College at the University of Toronto, he would often lecture on the fundamental theology of Methodism in the "witness of the Spirit" and the necessity for its conscious awareness as he had experienced it while ministering to the dying Wesleyan ensign on the battlefield.[3] Nathanael Burwash died on March 31, 1918, and Victoria College's Burwash Hall today is named in his memory.

THE CRISIS TESTED Canadian commitment to fundamental principles of liberty and justice at the very moment that the nation was taking its first breaths. John A. Macdonald put Canada under a war measures or anti-terrorist act—the Habeas Corpus Suspension Act (1866)—which was fully enacted on June 8 and valid for a year. It allowed for the detention without appeal and right to bail of persons captured by the armed forces or militia, or arrested on a warrant issued by any two magistrates on charges of acts against the state. But the suspension of civil rights in any particular case could extend longer than fourteen days only if explicitly authorized by the Cabinet, and arrests were to be based on evidence of specific acts perpetrated, not mere membership in a Fenian circle.[4] Nevertheless, local magistrates abused their power, issuing warrants on the mere "suspicion" of Fenianism.[5] All sorts of old scores were settled, and accusations overwhelmingly fell on Catholics.[6] Throughout the cities and countryside, there was a spate of arrests of "suspicious persons" and of those against whom denunciations for Fenianism were sworn.[7]

One Welland-area resident recalled, "It is said that in remote Irish settlements of Canada there were parties who were in sympathy with the Fenian movement and who were expected to acquire the property of their neighbours if the invasion was a success. In York County (Toronto) there were known to be at least two Fenian head-centres and much secrecy was observed in the movements of these people. Quantities of pikes were said to be stored in the houses of members of the organizations."[8]

Zealous Orangemen in Toronto accused Catholics of disloyalty and of harbouring Fenians among them.[9] In west Toronto, constables and fifty members of a Home Guard, with signatures signed by two alderman-magistrates, raided the premises of an Irish Catholic baker name McGuire, chopping down his doors with an axe, destroying his bread wagon, and ransacking his premises before taking him away without a warrant.[10] In Hamilton a tavern on Market Square was raided and its proprietor, John Harkins, and two others arrested on suspicion of "disloyal proclivities and sympathy with the Fenian invasion scheme ... A search of the premises discovered a loaded rifle and a bayonet, a six shooter, a U.S. knapsack, and sixty rounds of rifle cartridge."[11] Some newspapers editorialized, "It is to be hoped that we shall not be troubled with any whining, babyish complaints about 'infringing the liberty of the subject' in this crisis. Reports from many quarters agree to the effect that Fenians in the hundreds, if not in thousands, are quietly stealing into Canada."[12]

In Montreal D'Arcy McGee whipped up a gathering of Home Guard with dark talk about settling scores, which was gleefully reported in St. Catharines:

> On then, with the good work of the civic guard! Separate forever the loyal men from the disaffected and the vicious—the wheat from the chaff. Take and keep an accurate record of every man who refuses to defend the city, and when this thing is all over—as over it will be in a week; or a fortnight at farthest—as God is over us all, we will weed the scoundrels out of our city. (Cheers, and cries of "that's the talk.")[13]

A delegation of prominent Catholics fearing impending arrest approached Macdonald on June 14 with a request to post bail in advance on their good conduct and promise to appear if called. Macdonald responded that he had no authority to issue bail if no charges were laid against them, and if they were, then the Habeas Corpus Suspension Act prohibited him from then issuing it.[14]

Yet as historian Brian Jenkins recently observed, Friedrich Engels, no admirer of the British Empire and married to Lizzy Burns, a Fenian,[15] had declared, "England is unquestionably the freest—that is the least unfree—country in the world, North America not excepted."[16] Despite the popular sentiment among some of Canada's Protestant anglophones in support of a ruthless war on Fenianism and its "Papist" cells at home, Macdonald to his credit quickly put an end to the abuses. On June 21, he warned and instructed Crown attorneys in Canada West, "There is a great deal of uneasiness among the Irish Roman Catholic population in consequence of some of these hasty and ill-judged arrests, and, I must ask you, should any such case arise in your County to intervene actively for the protection of the arrested party and to report the circumstances to me without delay."[17]

Privately Macdonald wrote, "This is a country of law and we cannot go beyond the law ... The consequence of allowing illiterate magistrates to arrest every man they chose to suspect (and that would be, in rural districts, every Roman Catholic) would be to drive all that class out of the Country, to ruin many a respectable family by forcing them to sacrifice their property, and to swell the ranks of the Fenian organization."[18]

The Fenian Raid was a salient moment in Canada's political culture and in the troubled history of the relations between its Irish Catholic and Protestant citizens. The loyalty of Irish (and French) Catholics in Canada had been tested—and they did not rise up in aid of the invaders to the extent that both the Fenians and the Orangemen had hoped for. This, along with Macdonald's care to ensure that suspension of habeas corpus did not bludgeon the rights of Irish Catholics in Canada despite several weeks of attempts to do precisely that, was the beginning of the integration of Irish Catholics into an increasingly pluralistic anglophone-Canadian society.[19] Irish Catholics in Canada proved to have as strong a claim to loyalty as anybody else, and while decades more hostility between the faiths remained, their loyalty en masse would not be questioned again.

It made perfect sense. Of the fifty-eight Fenians captured on the Niagara Frontier and confined to the Toronto jail after Ridgeway, a full third were Protestants (nineteen, with one prisoner claiming no religious affiliation).[20] The invasion had been a republican thing—not a Catholic one.

LISTED AT FIRST among the wounded, Alexander Muir from QOR Company 10, Highlanders, was fortunate to be injured in a fall instead of wounded by a Minié ball.[21] During the advance he had dislocated his left shoulder when he fell from a fence while under fire. By the time the Highlanders arrived at the intersection of Garrison and Ridge roads, Muir was firing his rifle with only one arm by bracing it on a fence.

Muir was thirty-six years old, a Toronto schoolteacher and principal, a prominent Orangeman and the president of the Highlanders civil organization.[22] He had a nineteen-year-old wife, Mary Alice, whom he had recently married after his first wife had died, and three children from his first marriage.[23] In October 1867, Muir made a last-minute entry into a poetry contest sponsored by the Caledonia Society in Montreal to celebrate the new nation's founding. His second prize–winning entry was set to music and became the Queen's Own Rifles' regimental hymn and anglophone Canada's unofficial anthem, "The Maple Leaf Forever."

According to popular history, Muir was inspired to write the song by a maple leaf's falling from a tree in front of his house in the autumn of 1867. The house, "Maple Cottage," and the maple tree on 62 Laing Street at the corner of Memory Lane in Toronto's Leslieville neighbourhood are designated as an Ontario Heritage Property. In the 1930s the Orange Order installed a plaque on the tree attesting to the house's and the tree's historic significance and then replaced the plaque in 1958. Officiating at the 1958 ceremony was Leslie H. Saunders, the chairman of the Toronto Historical Board at the time and the Grand Master of the Orange Association.[24]

There were a couple of problems with this designation. First, the house was only constructed in 1873, five years after the song was written, and second, Muir never lived there, a fact acknowledged by the Ontario Conservation Review Board in 1992. The board decided to retain the designation just the same because of the building's link to "oral tradition" and its role as a vital reminder of a community's past cultural totems.[25]

The legend of the maple tree was spun in the 1900s by publisher John Ross Robertson, the author of *Landmarks of Toronto,* who apparently heard the story from Muir's widow[26] and from George Leslie (after whom the Leslieville neighbourhood is named). Leslie claimed to have been there with Muir when a maple leaf alighted on his sleeve. According to Leslie, he said, "There Muir! There's your text! The maple leaf is the emblem of Canada! Build your poem on that."[27] Nobody really knows for sure exactly what inspired Muir to write his song.[28]

The song became popular only in anglophone Canada, as it celebrated the British heritage, which, Muir wrote, "joined in love together, The Thistle, Shamrock, Rose entwine, The Maple Leaf forever!" but pointedly neglected the fleur-de-lys. Muir also neglected to secure a copyright for the song with its rising popularity, and when Abraham and Samuel Nordheimer published the lyrics in 1871, Muir was not paid any royalties.[29]

In February 1878, Muir's battalion, the Queen's Own Rifles, adopted as their regimental insignia a large maple leaf subsuming a smaller crown in its folds.[30]

"The Maple Leaf Forever" underwent numerous revisions, including one in 1997 by the CBC, which sponsored a contest for a version less offensive to francophone sensibilities.[31] The politically correct version, with the appropriate references to the fleur-de-lys, debuted in its first full orchestral treatment on June 27, 1997, at a concert by the Toronto Symphony Orchestra. It has rarely been heard since.[32]

THE FENIAN INVASION of Canada not only tested its people's courage and commitment to justice but also the nation's capacity to defend itself. By deploying twenty-two thousand troops within a few days, Canadians acquired a new sense of self-confidence. The experience of actual combat also led to some positive change. No more Spencer Rifles were purchased by the militia but instead the muzzleloaders were replaced by single-shot breech-loading rifles, technically one generation less advanced but more reliable. In the immediate aftermath of the experience at Ridgeway, the militia purchased new weapons, knapsacks, canteens, field surgeries, and gunboats and introduced training camps for privates, not just officers. New regulations and manuals were published containing "Hints on Skirmishing" that reminded soldiers: "When skirmishing, men should remember that in the field an enemy will be opposed to them, whose business is to keep himself as much as possible under cover at the same time he fires upon them whenever they expose themselves. Two lines of skirmishers opposed to each other on smooth ground and keeping their lines properly dressed, are never seen in a real fight."[33] All these improvements and reforms put the Volunteer Militia on the path to gradually becoming a partner to a full-time professional army, which was to be established in 1883.[34]

The railroad builders who had supported Confederation as a way of financing in the east an interprovincial rail system now added the national defence imperative to their promotion of the railway. An epic poem by J.T. Breeze, commissioned by the Grand Trunk Railway in 1867, included these lines:

> These powers can roll two thousand noble men
> To brave the bullets of the foe again
> Its rapid trains and quick machinery,
> Will guide our boys to meet the foemen free—
> Two thousand soldiers, with a stubborn heart,
> Would daunt Feniana and bid foes depart ...
> Beware ye fools misguided by those knaves,
> That gave your fellows ignominious graves—
> Be counselled now, if human life be sweet,
> Remembering Ridgeway's miserable retreat;
> Our generous country did benignly save
> Those captured then from a dishonoured grave![35]

The poem is ambiguous as to precisely *whose* retreat Freeze is referring to. Less ambiguous was the British army drinking song "Booker's

Run," according to which Canadians not only lost at Limestone Ridge, but also ran at "railroad pace."[36] The Fenians had a drinking song of their own celebrating Booker:

The Queen's Own Regiment was their name,
From fair Toronto town they came
To put the Irish all to shame,
The Queen's and Colonel Booker.

What fury fills each loyal mind
No volunteer would stay behind,
They flung their red flag to the wind,
"Harrah, my boys," said Booker.

Now helter, skelter, Ohio,
See how they pay that "heel and toe,"
See how they run from their Irish foe,
The Queen's and Colonel Booker![37]

The QOR, unable to shake the nickname "Quickest Outta Ridgeway," were horrified to be associated with Booker, and the blame sometimes fell on the men of his Thirteenth as well, now saddled with the nickname "Scarlet Runners." Reverend David Inglis became an impartial arbitrator in the dispute between the two regiments, attesting to the courage and the errors of both the "scarlet and the green" in a letter to the *Globe* and in his testimony at the Booker Inquiry.[38] Just the same, in 1923 the Queen's Own Rifles applied for Ridgeway to be added to their official battle honours on their regimental colours, arguing that they had displayed tactical acuity by withdrawing from the field when they did. According to military historian Brian Reid, "The regiment was told in no uncertain terms never to raise the matter again."[39]

MANY DEVELOPMENTS CONSPIRED to obliterate the memory of Ridgeway from the nation's consciousness. The disaster at Limestone

Ridge was not a shining exemplar of military prowess suitable for a national founding myth, despite the heroism of the rank and file. To whom the Canadians lost was significant. Defeat at the hands of the Celtic Fenians carried an extra measure of shame in the context of centuries of British propaganda about Irish rebels. In the nineteenth century the race-conscious Victorians frequently portrayed the Irish rebels as inferior, dark-skinned simian brutes, as "European Negroes" who were inevitably Catholic.[40] This transformation of the Irish rebel into a "Celtic Frankenstein," as historian Lewis P. Curtis termed it, had deep roots going back to the English conquest of Ireland and the subsequent traumas of the Reformation and Counter-Reformation in European civilization.[41] The Fenians were, and often still are, portrayed as a farcical, superstitious, brawling, whoring, drunken mob. Fenian General John O'Neill is referred to by historians even today as "General" (in quotes),[42] as is Thomas Sweeny, who planned the invasion, as "Secretary of War," as if such Fenian ranks and designations were patently comic and ridiculous.[43] For upright, square-jawed "white" Anglo-Saxon Protestant soldiers to take a beating of the kind they took at Ridgeway from an Irish American "rabble" was a shame that bit deeply and was best not spoken of once the dead had been buried and the wounded hidden.

Nor does the Battle of Ridgeway distinguish itself in general military history, where the prominence of a battle often has to do with its tactical or strategic novelty or its butcher's bill. There was nothing novel about how Ridgeway was fought, and its casualties were comparatively light. By 1900 the Canadian casualty rates from the South African War easily overshadowed those of Ridgeway, and those of the subsequent two World Wars guaranteed Ridgeway's relative insignificance even in the context of Canada's short military history.

Furthermore, the battle at Ridgeway did not resolve the Fenian threat: The 1866 raids were followed by the assassination of D'Arcy McGee by a suspected Fenian sympathizer, the parliamentary dynamite panics, and more Fenian raids in the early 1870s. The raids never passed into history because it took so long for them to pass from politics.

The "Veterans of '66" were not just a reminder of the debacle but a fiscal and jurisdictional burden as well, and as such they were thrown back and forth like a hot potato between Ottawa and Ontario. Whose responsibility are pre-Confederation militia veterans? asked legislators. That of the province that had founded and maintained the militias at the time of their service or of the new Dominion government, which now had exclusive jurisdiction over national defence and the military? Or were they Britian's responsibility as a former colonial militia? Nobody wanted the fiscal responsibility.[44]

Then there was late-Victorian reform liberalism with a shade of political correctness remarkably reminiscent of today's, which skewed discussions on awarding a medal and land grants to militia volunteers who had participated in the expedition against the Metis in 1885. As the *Globe* editorialized, "There would have been some sense in bestowing a medal for the Ridgeway and Pigeon Hill affairs, in which Canadian troops repulsed a foreign marauder; but a decoration for the Northwest, where the enemy consisted of a handful of fellow-subjects driven to despair by the misconduct of our own officials, was almost as much out of place as a decoration would be for British soldiers whose duty had obliged them to take part in an Irish eviction or in the massacre of Peterloo."[45] Somerville could not have written it with more liberal reform gusto had he still been alive. To award decorations to one generation of militia volunteers but not another was problematic. Political dilemmas of that kind are most easily resolved through silence and inaction, respectively the sworn enemies of history and progress.

There was another issue. Following Confederation a three-decades-long hostility arose to what historians today call the "militia myth": That volunteer citizen soldiers can effectively defend Canada without the British, as some alleged they did in the War of 1812 and the Fenian Raids. Between 1870 and 1900, Canadian defence doctrine was shaped in a bitter rivalry between proponents of a permanent, standing modern professional army, which Canada would finally form by 1883, and a decreasing number of supporters of the volunteer citizen army, who shared the traditional English suspicion of standing armies at home and who argued that Canada's militia system alone was sufficient to defend it. This debate occurred during economic downturns and in a period in which popular opinion in Canada no longer regarded the United States as a threat. Canada's militia was ignored in this climate.[46]

IF ALL THESE FACTORS were not enough to obscure the memory of Ridgeway, then there was one more: the vision of Canada the volunteers were defending on that June day. While many historians agree that Ridgeway was where we first fought for the ideal of an indigenous Canadian "national" homeland as opposed to the British Empire, not everyone in the decades following Confederation agreed on exactly what that "nation" was or its constitutional nature. The virulence of that debate also contributed to the historical amnesia into which Ridgeway would descend.

On July 1, 1870, the Volunteers Monument, sponsored and paid for by Toronto citizens, was dedicated on the University of Toronto campus near Queen's Park. The inscription on the monument reads "Campaign June 1866. Honour the brave who died for their country." The date of the dedication ceremony was a month after the fourth anniversary of Ridgeway and coincided with Canada Dominion Day.

Some ten thousand people attended the dedication, during which Governor General Sir John Young, Baron Lisgar declared it a memorial to "the brave men who ran the greatest risk and made the greatest sacrifice which mortal man can make in defence of the principles of generous independence and orderly freedom, which are embodied in the name and auspices of the Dominion of Canada."[47] The Governor General identified the fallen of Ridgeway as the embodiment of Canadian nationhood, which was soon to include Manitoba, British Columbia, and Prince

Edward Island in addition to the original partners of 1867: Ontario, Quebec, Nova Scotia, and New Brunswick. Indeed, the Volunteer Militia marching song in the summer of 1869, as this time border tensions with the United States rose in the Pacific, now went like this:

> Come, boys, let's sing a song, for the day it won't be long
> When united to our country we will be.
> Then the Maple Leaf entwined and the Beaver combined
> With old England's flag shall float upon the sea.
>
> Tramp, tramp, tramp, the New Dominion
> Now is knocking at the door,
> So goodbye dear Uncle Sam as we do not care a clam
> For your Greenback or your bunkum any more.[48]

The *Globe*'s report on the dedication of the monument was a rare instance of Ridgeway's being mentioned in its pages in the decades following the battle. Ridgeway was not commemorated in the newspaper's pages in June 1867, a year after the battle, nor on the fifth anniversary in 1871; nor on the tenth in 1876; nor on the twentieth in 1886; and in none of the years in between. This long period of silence was as odd as Ridgeway's later sudden restoration to public discourse and memory in 1890, twenty-four years after the battle.

After Confederation in 1867, the government in Ottawa led for the next twenty-five years by John A. Macdonald (except for the interruption from 1873 to 1878) became our "nation builder," shepherding territories to provincial status and persuading remaining colonies into the national dream called "Canada." The original partners of 1867, including the two highly diverse cultural and political communities of Ontario and Quebec, individually now had less to do with that process.

That Confederation was followed by two decades of disputes over provincial rights between the government in Ottawa and Oliver Mowat's Reform-Liberal Ontario provincial government in Toronto is not a subject entirely forgotten in Canadian history.[49] What is forgotten is how bitter these disputes were and how intense they became by 1883, when they resulted in what was known as the "Rat Portage War," a bloodless "proto–civil war" in which Ottawa-sponsored Manitoba constables and Mowat's Ontario police began escalating their use of force by arresting each other's chiefs and inspectors in a territorial dispute and breaking each other out of jail.[50] "Civil war" was precisely the term Mowat used in the Ontario legislature in describing what he feared might happen in the face of Ottawa's obstinacy on the issue of where the Manitoba-Ontario boundary lay.[51] It was also in that same year, 1883, that Ottawa finally established a permanent, national "regular" army.

This made the Battle of Ridgeway the last battle fought by the developing semi-autonomous Upper Canadian political community, which before Confederation maintained its own direct link to Britain through the office of the Lieutenant-Governor. When in 1867 Upper Canada was subsumed into the federal province of Ontario, Ottawa emerged as an uninvited interloper in that relationship. Moreover, Ridgeway had already been fought in two places simultaneously: the colonial dual-cultural United Province of Canada formed in 1841, about which few "Ontarians" at the time gave a damn, and a monocultural anglophone Protestant Upper Canada, about which they cared passionately. (As I once heard said recently, "Canada West was a postal address, but Upper Canada was a people.") The Canada they sang about in "Tramp, Tramp, Tramp" as they marched to Ridgeway was not the same Canada we sing about and "stand on guard" for today.

When in 1872 Oliver Mowat resigned as a judge and returned to provincial politics, he told voters he did so because Ontario had to fight once more not only for liberty and "responsible government" but also against the tyranny of Ottawa.[52] Mowat's claim is an odd one to generations of Canadians today who have been taught in school that liberty and "responsible government" came to Canada shortly after the Rebellions of 1837 and the *Durham Report*, which led to the merging of

Upper and Lower Canada in 1841 and the waning of the power of the Family Compact.

At its simplest, the issue between Mowat and Ottawa was which level of government is supreme in Canada—the provincial or the federal. Mowat claimed that Ontario had inherited provincial sovereignty from Upper Canada's direct pre-Confederation relationship with Britain, when there was no interlocutory level of government between Toronto and the Crown in London. In an argument familiar to that of Quebec separatists today, Mowat argued that the federal government in Ottawa was a joint agent of the sovereign provinces in a "compact" between them, in which unspecified provincial powers were delegated to an administrative centre in Ottawa through the British North America (BNA) Act but no provincial sovereignty itself had been surrendered, as it was thought indivisible in British constitutional doctrine. Ottawa was a shared servant to the provinces, according to Mowat, and not the other way around. This was a dangerously similar argument to the one put forward by the southern states on the eve of the American Civil War, as it left open the option for a state or province to "reclaim" its sovereignty and leave at will from the jointly contracted Union or from Confederation, as Quebec sometimes contemplates doing.

This was not Macdonald's view. All sovereignty, according to Macdonald, had always been vested in the British Crown and never in the provinces. After Confederation, Ottawa argued that federal and provincial *powers* were indeed divided between Ottawa and the provinces by the BNA Act, but *sovereignty* itself had remained vested as always in the Crown, which in turn now delegated its privileges to Ottawa, as symbolized to this day by the image of the Queen of England on Canadian coinage.[53]

FOR TWENTY-FIVE YEARS following Confederation, these issues polarized Canadians not only between Ottawa and Ontario but within Ontario itself, where the 1837 Radical Reform–led rebellion had been put down by the Tories, who emphasized their victory with a public double-hanging near the corner of Church and King streets in Toronto. It was unclear precisely how the volunteer militiamen who played a key role in the crisis of 1837–38, and again in 1866, were situated in the ideologically fuzzy spectrum between opposition and loyalty or liberty and tyranny. This question manifested itself in Ontario legislative debates from the 1870s to the 1890s, politicizing the issue of compensating the Volunteer Militia at a time when Mowat was claiming liberty as the motive for his fight with Ottawa. The provincial Tory Opposition baited Mowat's Reformers by sponsoring bills to give additional recognition to the militia volunteers of 1837 who had fought to defend the Tory Family Compact from the Radical Reform rebels. The debate was a complicated one: Mowat, who had himself served in the militia that suppressed the rebellion, now lauded the rebels as the champions of liberty. In 1885, almost fifty years after the rebellion, the debate would take this tenor: Who is to be commended, the militia volunteers of 1837 who turned out to defend the tyranny of the Tory Family Compact or the rebels who fought for liberty as it was understood at the time in England? Who were the patriots and who the lawless rebels? Those resisting the tyrannical Family Compact that rejected constitutional reforms adopted in England or the Reformers who strove to bring the new British democratic values to Canada in the face of local tyrants? Who were the *real* lawless rebels in our bosom, William Lyon Mackenzie's radicals, who hardly did any damage in 1837, or the Tory opponents of the *Rebellion Losses Bill*, who burned down the Parliament Buildings in Montreal in 1849?[54]

During these debates George Ross, Mowat's minister of education, commented on an amendment to a bill recognizing the heroism of the 1837 volunteers, but added commendations for the Reform struggle as well. Ross framed his comments in the context of home rule and suggested that the 1837 Rebellion was a struggle for provincial rights, saying to the legislature: "It says what should be said concerning those who stood up for the Government of the day, and also for those who believe that they were fighting for Provincial rights and privileges ... But there are those who were not volunteers in 1837–38 who have risked their lives in defence of British institutions, and for the interests of the Dominion of Canada. If I remember correctly, there was trouble in 1866 and those who were called out then loyally obeyed the call, and their services are worthy of recognition."[55]

The question of who to recognize—who were the "real" patriots—was still being debated in 1892, fifty-five years after the rebellion, when again a motion was raised to further financially recognize somehow the volunteers of 1837, of whom there were hardly any left! Again opponents asked a politically loaded question: "If the hon. Member wanted to reward the volunteer militia of this country why did he pass over the volunteers of 1866?"[56]

THE DEPTH, BITTERNESS, and longevity of this Tory vs. Reform polarity puts into question how Canadian history was practised at the turn of the century. In Ontario throughout most of the Victorian era, some schools simply did not teach recent Canadian history at all. Until 1896 when George M. Wrong began to teach it at the University of Toronto, the school did not teach Canadian history past 1815 for fear of "injuring older reputations."[57] By the early twentieth century it was professionally a dangerous thing to question the Reform version of Canadian history, despite their claim to liberty. When in 1908 William Dawson LeSueur submitted what has been called "the first truly critical biography written in Canada"[58] of William Lyon Mackenzie, which challenged the traditional Reform version of the rebellion's place in Canadian history, a cabal of Liberal-Reform hard-liners, including the future prime minister of Canada, William Lyon Mackenzie King (the rebel's grandson),[59] seized the manuscript and were stopped from destroying it only by a Supreme Court of Canada decision in 1911.[60] They still managed subsequently to ensure that its contents and author were so thoroughly silenced by a new series of court orders[61] that the LeSueur history could only be published in 1979—118 years after its subject's death.[62]

"After 1833, our history is controversial," commented Clarence M. Warner, the president of the Ontario Historical Society, in 1916. "Many of the events of these years, when clear, calm judgment was absent on the part of people in control of the affairs of State and of those in Opposition, are today given us in books, pamphlets, newspapers and other documents, and someday the unbiased story will probably be told."[63]

Covered up and falsified in a series of inquiries, newspaper editorials, and histories penned by interested parties, and politicized by the subsequent militia debate and the provincial rights clashes, the Battle of Ridgeway became a blank spot in Canadian history, caught in a historical acoustic shadow, perceptible to some but not others. The men who fought there were left on the fringes of Canada's national historical narrative. Even their marching song, "Tramp, Tramp, Tramp," had been appropriated by 1910, serving as an angry labour hymn for Joe Hill and the radical "wobblies," the Industrial Workers of the World (IWW):

Cross the street a sign I read, "Work for Jesus," so it said.
Here's a chance for me, you bet I'll surely try.
So I knelt down on the floor till my knees were red and sore;
At mealtime the preacher sadly said:

Tramp, tramp, tramp, keep on a-tramping,
There is nothing a-doing here for you.
If I catch you round again, you will wear the mullen chain,
Keep on tramping, that's the best thing you can do. [64]

TWELVE

Memory and Remembrance, 1890–2010

Ridgeway of course was not entirely erased from our memory. In November 2009 the Queen's Own Rifles regiment held a church parade and a march from the corner of Bloor and Jarvis streets down Parliament Street and through Toronto's Cabbagetown to a dedication ceremony of new gravestones paid for by private donations raised by the regiment for the Ridgeway dead buried in the Necropolis.[1] The Queen's Own Rifles that I saw that Sunday morning were a multicultural mix of bright teenage boys and girls, led by young men and women, some with service ribbons from Somalia, the Balkans, and Afghanistan, which undermined the popular notion of our militia today as "weekend warriors." In the church nave, I overheard the elders telling the youngsters how they were there to commemorate the regiment's "first officer, sergeant, corporal, and privates" killed in action. At the service in the cemetery, a retired Queen's Own legionnaire of Second World War vintage reverently placed on the gravestones the original bugle that had sounded at Ridgeway and then snapped a digital photograph of it. Limestone Ridge calls for commemoration as deeply as does Ypres, Ortona, or Kapyong, and as sadly as will Kandahar.

The memory of Ridgeway lived on among those Canadians who cared to remember. First, regardless of the *Globe*'s silence and although the newspaper gradually became Canada's national "paper of record," it was by no means the only paper in the country; and second, Toronto, although Ontario's capital, was far from being the only political and cultural community capable of sustaining memory. While the Queen's Own Rifles were encouraged by Ottawa to forget adding Ridgeway to their battle honours, University College dedicated a memorial window in its East Hall to the fallen students who served in its ranks. In their communities, the Welland Canal Field Battery and Dunnville Naval Brigade were memorialized and honoured annually near the anniversary of the battle, as they still are to this day.[2] On October 25, 1866, in Port Robinson, two thousand people gathered to watch the presentation of engraved swords to Captains McCallum and King.[3] "The women of Dunnville" presented the Dunnville Naval Brigade with battle colours on a purple background with a crown and anchor in a garland of maple leaves. A grant of one hundred acres of land was given to each of the four wounded men by Welland County, which also struck silver medals to be awarded to every volunteer who served in the *Robb* expedition and made the stand at Fort Erie.[4] The medal depicted on one side a field gun with the inscription "Fort Erie, June 2, 1866," and on the obverse, "Presented by the County of Welland." When the Welland County Council learned that they had violated military protocols by issuing the medal, they appealed to the Imperial War Office to recognize their act. Permission was granted for the men to wear the medal.[5] As early as 1874, *The Canadian Antiquarian and Numismatic Journal* correctly predicted that the medal would be among Canada's rarest.[6]

In Hamilton, the Thirteenth Battalion faced an uphill battle to defend their reputation and pride since the day they were left behind in Port Colborne while their comrades marched back to Ridgeway. Unlike the Toronto *Globe,* the Hamilton *Spectator* on the tenth anniversary of the battle ran a story, entitled "The Anniversary of Ridgeway: A Sketch of the Fray: What the Hamilton Boys Did."[7] But after that, it too joined the subsequent silence for the next twenty-five years, as nobody wanted either Ridgeway's burden or its flawed heritage in these times of provincial controversy.

By the 1890s, however, Mowat had taken his fight with Ottawa as far as it could go. By then politics and industrialization had trumped constitutional law and parochial patriotism as Macdonald's National Policy protective tariffs contributed to the rapid urbanization of Ontario. Reform's urban liberals until then had depended upon their "electoral infantry," as constitutional historian Paul Romney called the agrarian populists, but now their power began to wane when U.S. western grain production and Macdonald's Pacific railway triggered a severe agricultural crisis in Ontario. The balance of power shifted to the rising middle class in urban industrialized constituencies for whom a centralized state offered more opportunity than a sovereign Ontario.[8]

In 1896, after having embraced over the last ten years both Ontario Irish and French Catholics in their call for "home rule,"[9] the Reformers surrendered and endorsed the National Policy but went on to carry Liberal Wilfrid Laurier to the Prime Minister's office. A new era had clearly begun, and the controversies that had plagued the recognition of the Veterans of '66 waned. It became safe to talk about Ridgeway—Ontario's battle—without it's being a hornet's nest of politicized collateral issues. That is how Ridgeway, which was systematically forgotten in the 1870s and 1880s, began to be recognized and revived in the early 1890s.

IN MAY 1890, after nearly two and a half decades of silence, a short paragraph in the *Globe,* "Ridgeway Remembered," reported that the veterans of the battle had "taken the matter in hand" and would meet for the first time in public on the twenty-fourth anniversary of the battle to lay flowers and wreaths at the Canadian Volunteers Monument near Queen's Park.[10] Captain B. Mercer Adams, who had commanded QOR Company 6, Upper Canada College Rifles, or "The Babies," addressed a crowd gathered at the monument, saying, "The bloodshed at Ridgeway was the martyr-seed of a nation. Out of it came that impulse which drew the various Provinces together, and however discordant may be the question we have yet to face, we hope that the bonds that unite us as a people may be still more firmly riveted and that each passing year shall see our beloved Canada rise to greater things."[11]

The *Globe* described the occasion under the headline "Our Decoration Day" and promised that from now on the day would be commemorated annually.[12] The next year in Hamilton, it was reported that the Ridgeway veterans of the Thirteenth Battalion had come together for a reunion for the first time in twenty-five years.[13] The national memorialization of Ridgeway had begun and would now unfold from about 1890 to 1925, resulting in a thirty-five-year renaissance of acknowledgments, awards, speeches, ceremonies, reminiscences, and published accounts, some sponsored by regional historical societies.

In Toronto on June 2, 1891, the twenty-fifth anniversary of the battle, thirty thousand people gathered at the Volunteers Monument. Spectators climbed up on the scaffolding of the newly constructed Parliament Buildings, onto lumber piled up at the site, and into the trees of the park. Schoolchildren covered the monument in wreaths and leafy plants, some bearing the names of those killed at Ridgeway. Not a practice followed in Britain at the time, this was a gesture adopted from the United States where, after the Civil War, flowers were laid on military graves in May on national Memorial Day, or Decoration Day, as it was also known. Toronto's militia regiments, along with 450 boys from the public school drill corps carrying muskets and accompanied by 30 Toronto Police constables, escorted several hundred Veterans of '66 from the drill shed at Simcoe Street along a route packed with 50,000 spectators.[14] The "decoration" of the monument by Toronto's schoolchildren became an annual ritual. It was the beginning of Canada's remembrance day.[15]

Decoration Day would eventually encompass the remembrance of those who died in the Northwest Rebellion[16] and later the South African War, with the first joint remembrance ceremony held in June 1903.[17] By the 1920s the day included, or more aptly was subsumed by, the remembrance of the mass casualties of the Great War. Until 1931, Decoration Day was Canada's national memorial day, held in late May or early June.[18] It is still commemorated today in some of the Ontario rural communities that witnessed the Fenian Raids or saw their sons die or be broken in them. In 2010 the town of Dunnville held its 113th annual Decoration Day on June 6,[19] while Caledonia held its own on May 30.[20]

IN ITS COVERAGE of the anniversary of the Battle of Ridgeway in 1891, the *Globe* ran four full-page columns, including a recapitulation of the history of the Fenian invasion. The sacrifice of the "Varsity Company"—as the University Rifles were called by then—was singled out for recognition. Colonel William Otter, the former Queen's Own Rifles adjutant and now Canada's deputy adjutant general, spoke of "homage to the gallant militiamen who fell in the defence of our common country." One of Premier Mowat's ministers, John Morison Gibson, MPP for Hamilton, spoke next of the heroism and sacrifice. Gibson had served as a lieutenant at Limestone Ridge in Company 1, Thirteenth Battalion, which held the abandoned Fenian barricades along Bertie Road to the right of the Angur brick house. In his speech, Gibson nudged Otter on the question of Ridgeway's casualties falling for "our common country." Gibson remained a passionate proponent of "home rule" for Ontario and reminded everybody that day, "It is unfortunate that there is divided authority, education being in the hands of the Province and the militia in the care of the Dominion. There may be difficulty in arranging concurrent action, but no doubt it will be overcome."[21]

Colonel George Denison spoke last and hinted at the lingering question of loyalty. "In the past Canada had not shown so much of that spirit of reverence for her dead as one might wish, but within the last three or four years it has steadily grown. Very seldom now was it said that we should not speak of loyalty, although there are still wandering professors who say that loyalty is out of fashion. Canadians felt that they had a country and were they to allow Canada to go under they would blush with shame when looking at the monument which told of men who died for Canada. It would have to come down ... Let them not be untrue to the dead. The country which does not honor its noble dead deserves to sink into oblivion."[22]

Throughout the 1890s, during debates about awarding volunteer troops who fought in the Red River and Northwest rebellions, the question was still frequently raised: Why not the volunteers in the Fenian invasions of 1866 and 1870? By the end of the decade, the fact that the volunteers in 1866 might have fought for a different Canada than those in 1870 began to matter less and then not at all as Canadians were called upon to volunteer once again—this time in 1899 to fight in the South African War in which 284 would die.

By 1895 the Veterans of '66 Association had organized a national petition for the recognition of all the volunteers who served during the Fenian Raids.[23] On June 2, 1896, the *Globe* commemorated the thirtieth anniversary of the battle, commenting, "It is to the everlasting discredit of the Tory Government of Canada that outside of their empty thanks, which cost nothing but printers' ink, not a single man who participated in it, except those who were wounded, have got a tittle of recompense, or even a memento for their services up to the present day ... The survivors have yet a hope but if that tardy recognition ever comes it will come from a Liberal and patriotic Government and not from a band of boodle-mongers whose life-long history connects them with selfishness and a policy of personal aggrandizement at the expense of the country."[24]

Eleven days later Wilfrid Laurier led the Liberal Party to electoral victory over the Conservatives, ushering in a new era for Canada, as well as for its relationship with its rebellious province of Ontario. The next year fifty thousand spectators gathered for Decoration Day as the Veterans of '66 marched by in review to the Volunteers Monument.

In January 1899, in response to the petition, Britain authorized a Canadian General Service Medal for veterans of the 1866 and 1870 Fenian Raids and the 1870 Red River Rebellion. Anybody who was on active service in the field, had served as a guard at any point when an attack from the enemy was expected, or had been detailed for some specific service or duty was eligible for the medal upon applying for it—it was not issued automatically. There were 15,300 of these medals issued to Canadians with their individual names and units engraved on the rim. (Another 1,368 were claimed by British veterans.)[25] The medal was issued by Britain just in time for the call on Canada to help in the upcoming South African War. The Canadian federal government acquiesced to the British medal but added nothing of its own for the veterans of Ridgeway as it did in the case of the Red River Expedition and Northwest Rebellion, whose veterans were granted 160 acres of Crown land, whereas those who fought in South Africa would get 320 acres.[26] In the end, in 1901 the province of Ontario undertook to grant its Fenian Raid veterans 160 acres of provincial land if they applied for it.[27]

For some, the medal thirty-four years after the event came just in the nick of time. Isaac Greensides, who had carried under fire the trampled Captain Boustead away from the Fenian charge, was on his deathbed when a delegation of the Veterans of '66 Association came by and pinned the medal to his pillow. He was buried with it a few days later.[28] Booker and Dennis never got their medals, having died by then, and neither did Major James Atchison Skinner, who took Booker's place—he had died at his home in Woodstock on Christmas Eve in 1894.[29] After Booker's resignation-dismissal, Skinner remained in command of the Thirteenth Battalion for the next twenty years and was succeeded in 1886 by John Gibson, Mowat's ally in his struggles for "home rule" for Ontario. Skinner was also elected to the provincial legislature as a Reform MPP in South Oxford in 1874 and 1878.

The influence of former combatants from Ridgeway in the Ontario and Canadian governments, in the nation's military, institutions, businesses, churches, culture, and press, was extensive and has nowhere near been adequately studied. Captain James Boustead, for example, went into the life and fire insurance business, became an alderman in Toronto and chairman of the Water Works Committee, and is credited with reforming Toronto's fire department and establishing the city's first modern fire alarm system. QOR adjutant Captain William Otter led Canadian troops in the South African War, rose to the rank of general, and became in 1908 the first Canadian-born chief of the general staff, the head of the Canadian army. During the First World War he came out of retirement to oversee the internment of "enemy nationals" resident in Canada. He died in 1929. His grandson is Desmond Morton, one of Canada's prominent military historians.

On January 25, 1900, approximately ninety surviving veterans of the Thirteenth Battalion assembled in the armoury on James Street to receive their medals. For many this was to be their redemption from the humiliation of thirty-four years earlier, when they were left standing in Port Colborne in the first dawn light after the battle, watching the troop train depart with all those who fought at Ridgeway, except for themselves. The first to receive his medal was Colonel John Morison Gibson, Ontario Attorney General at the time and recently retired commanding officer of the battalion. Mrs. J.V. Teetzel, the mayor's wife, pinned the medal to Gibson's chest. Gibson's wife awarded the medal to the next recipient, Lieutenant Colonel H. Moore; Mrs. Mason, the wife of Major J.J. Mason, awarded the medal to Captain Dr. Isaac Ryall, the surgeon; and so it went down the ranks of the ninety men as each of the wives and daughters and mothers awarded a medal to each of the men on the drill floor, one by one.[30]

While the medals and recognition might have healed some hurt pride, the process of historical restoration was incomplete. The public events were accompanied by newspaper articles on the histories of the battle and on the units who fought in it. Over the next two decades, witnesses and veterans of the battle began publishing their recollections in popular magazines and historical journals and in papers presented at historical society talks.[31] But these fragmentary sources were never assembled or collated in any new comprehensive history of the battle other than the one authored by Captain John A. Macdonald in 1910. His book, *Troublous Times in Canada: The History of the Fenian Raids of 1866 and 1870,* would be the last on the battle for more than a century to follow. It added nothing new, but lamented how "it is a strange fact that Canadian authors and historians do not seem to have fully realized the gravity of the situation that then existed, as the event has been passed over by them with the barest possible mention. Thus the people of the present generation know very little of the Fenian troubles of 1866 and 1870, and the great mass of the young Canadian boys and girls who are being educated in our Public Schools and Colleges are in total ignorance of the grave danger which cast dark shadows over this fair and prosperous Dominion in those stormy days."[32] Nothing has changed since then.

In the early 1900s, mention of "Decoration Day" began to fade from the newspapers. By 1903 the commemoration coverage in the *Globe* was reduced once again to a small paragraph, and by 1907 the event had been moved to the privacy of the cemeteries where the fallen were buried. It was no longer the public event it had been in the 1890s and gradually became disconnected from June 2 and moved closer to Victoria Day in May. After years of peace following the South African War, the Great War of 1914–18 sadly revived Decoration Day as Canada's national memorial day.

In 1916, on the fiftieth anniversary of Ridgeway, the cornerstone for a monument was laid at a five-acre site on the Garrison Road end of the battlefield, approximately where the schoolhouse stood and where the ridge began its rise toward the north. In 1921 the site was made a National Historic Battlefield to be administrated by Parks Canada with a cairn to mark the spot. One of the surviving cabins that was used during the battle as a field hospital was relocated to the site. Farther down the road in the town of Ridgeway are a battlefield museum and Fort Erie's historical archives. The battlefield itself, east of Ridge Road between Garrison and Bertie roads, until very recently had remained untouched, although the orchards had long disappeared, but it is now facing extinction under creeping housing developments. The Angur "brick house" still stands on the corner of Ridge and Bertie roads, with a few unrepaired hits from Minié balls visible in its north exterior wall.

With time, the veterans, participants, and witnesses were all scattered in many different directions. Robert Larmour remained with the Grand Trunk Railway for the rest of his working life, stationed at first in Stratford and later at the railway's corporate headquarters in London, Ontario. In 1885 Larmour was issued a patent for his design of a "Portable Shield for Skirmishers." A light-steel contraption, it was described by Larmour as a "portable rifle-pit," designed to be carried across battlefields and periodically set up on the ground while the soldier was shooting. It was never adopted by the military.[33]

The eleven-year-old farm boy E.A. Cruikshank, whose father on the morning of the invasion sent him to drive their horses to safety, joined the Canadian army, rose to the rank of brigadier general, and in the 1920s became a prominent military historian and member of the Historic Sites and Monuments Board of Canada. In 1925 he authored an important short article on the battle, which was published by the Welland County Historical Society.

The whiskey smuggler Sam Johnston—the "Paul Revere of Canada"—became a customs inspector and then went west to seek his fortune. When in the 1920s interest in Ridgeway was revived, reporters found Johnston, a grizzled old man with a dog, mining for gold at Rock Creek, British Columbia, and newspapers told his story for one last time.[34]

In 1887 Thomas Conlon, whose timber scow had been seized at Lower Black Rock by the Fenian advance party for their crossing, ran as a Reform candidate in the federal election. He lost to a Conservative in an avalanche of "dirty trick" accusations, which included the charge that he had "supplied" the Fenians with vessels to invade Canada.[35]

George C. Carlisle, Booker's fifteen-year-old bugle boy, survived Ridgeway without a scratch, rose to the rank of lieutenant colonel, bought a ranch in Crossfields, Alberta, and lived prosperously to the age of seventy-eight until he was struck dead by a taxicab in New York City in April 1929.[36]

The reeve of Fort Erie, Dr. Peter Tertius Kempson, lost his brave young wife, Clara, and moved as a widower to Metuchen, New Jersey. His claim to fame in the United States is that he became in 1876 the second husband of the widowed Julie Hart Beers, a leading nineteenth-century American landscape painter.[37] Dr. Kempson died in 1890.

Gunner Fergus Scholfield, the twenty-two-year-old apprentice butcher who lost his leg at Fort Erie, found work for the next thirty-five years as a lighthouse keeper, married, had three children, and survived two of them, dying at the age of eighty-one on January 8, 1925.[38]

Eighteen of the Trinity College students in QOR Company 8 were ordained as Anglican ministers.[39]

In 1872, artillery Captain Dr. Richard King, MD, ran as a Conservative candidate in Thorold for federal Parliament but lost to the Reformer William Thompson.[40] King remained in command of the Welland Canal Field Battery until his death on August 2, 1885, upon which the battery headquarters was first moved to Port Colborne, and later to St. Catharines, and then disbanded.[41]

It was not just those who fought at Ridgeway whose lives were transformed by the battle. Professor Croft's absence from Ridgeway became the subject of viral innuendo of the kind for which university departments are notorious. For the rest of his life, these acidic rumours ate away at his reputation and he was reported to suffer as a result from an increasing number of nervous afflictions.[42] There were darker rumours. When Croft died in 1883 at the age of sixty-three, Daniel Wilson, the president of University College, cryptically noted in his journal Croft's "wretched failing—I always blamed the Volunteering movement into which 'Captain Croft' threw himself with all heartiest zeal; and in its camp life was exposed to temptations, which home unhappily offered then no influence to counteract."[43]

Dr. Tempest never got over arriving at Ridgeway after the battle to discover his son had been killed. William's death broke Tempest and devastated the family. His medical practice in which his son was about to join him came apart, his health and mental state deteriorated, and he died in Toronto five years later, on August 9, 1871, leaving his wife, Hannah, to care for their three daughters and two sons on a single life insurance payout of one thousand dollars. Reduced to crushing poverty, Hannah Tempest petitioned the Militia Department for a pension of four hundred dollars, arguing that had William completed medical school and not been killed, the family would have been solvent and the father never would have died as early as he did. Neighbours, an MP, and several officers from the QOR wrote the minister of militia in support of Hannah's petition, describing the punishing physician's workload that killed Dr. Tempest and the family's dire financial condition, but the petition was shuffled back and forth for over a year. Apparently Dr. Tempest, in 1866, could not bear to apply for compensation for the loss of his son. Had he, it would have been granted, but now it was too late; the deadline had passed. There were no provisions in the regulations for such payment to be made to a widowed mother without a special Act of Parliament enacted. Dr. Tempest probably could not imagine asking for payment for the death of his son, and some of the wounded men themselves did not file for compensation either. It was not in their character or the austere, proud nature of mid-century Upper Canadians, many of whom perceived applying for financial compensation for war wounds and lost family members as a form of begging for charity and alms. In the end, a pension of $250 annually was granted to Hannah Tempest.[44] The family and its name then vanished from the historical record, another casualty of war.

As I sat in a History Department office in Jorgenson Hall at Ryerson University, reviewing digital images of letters I had photographed in the archives, I came to read that the shattered and bankrupt Tempest family gave as their last known address a squalid rooming house on Gerrard East near Yonge Street in Toronto, roughly in the same spot where I was now sitting and where this passage was being written. Some of the Ryerson historians claim to hear strange ghostly murmuring when working late at night in the Jorgenson building. Maybe dead ground can come back and haunt us the way dead people do.

After the Dennis Inquiry verdict, the disillusioned Captain Lachlan McCallum resigned his commission in the Dunnville Naval Brigade in protest. Nobody was capable of making the brigade what he had, and the unit was disbanded on December 29, 1866.[45] McCallum, in the days when one could do that, was elected as a Conservative member for the riding of Monck to both provincial and federal parliaments. In Parliament he failed to persuade the government to release the transcripts of the Dennis Inquiry. He was appointed to the Senate in 1887 and died on January 13, 1903.

On June 5, 1868, McCallum's lifelong friend Walter Tyrie Robb, for whom the war tug had been named, took the *Robb* into Long Point Bay on Lake Erie, where he met his brother James B. Robb, the captain of the tug *Jessie*. Mooring their two vessels in the bay, they took a smaller sailboat out into open water to do some fishing. They never returned. When they were about two miles out, they were hit by a sudden squall and were drowned.[46] After that McCallum probably could not stand the sight of the *Robb*. He sold the tug two years later, and the vessel was refitted to tow lumber between Toronto and Prescott. When a depression hit the lumber business, the *Robb* was converted into an excursion boat, towing between Toronto and Niagara a schooner full of tourists and a brass band.

The *Robb* survived this way until 1891, when she finally outlived her usefulness and was stripped bare of her fittings and engine and towed to Victoria Park in Toronto, an amusement park in the Beaches at the east end of the city. Moored to the water's edge, she was used as a changing house for bathers. Later the old war tug was beached as a breakwater next to a pier to create a beach expansion. Eventually Victoria Park closed down and the *Robb* was abandoned to rot in the sand like a whale carcass. One night her decks were set afire and she burned down to the hull. When the Toronto R.C. Harris Water Treatment Plant was built at the site in the 1930s, the beach at Victoria Park was closed and waves began to reclaim the charred skeletal remains of the *Robb*, driving her below the sand and water until finally, in 1943, she slipped beneath the surface, where she rests to this day.[47]

ON JUNE 1, 1930, eight surviving Ridgeway veterans in their eighties marched in St. Catharines in the last Decoration Day parade there as passing aircraft scattered poppies over them like the soft petals of the apple blossoms that had rained down on both the living and the dead in the orchards at Limestone Ridge sixty-four year earlier.[48] After that they came no more.

On November 9, 1936, the Hamilton *Spectator* noted that "the last but one" of the remaining Fenian Raid veterans from the Thirteenth Battalion, Thomas Kilvington, had died. Allan Land, ninety-two years old, was the only one left standing of the "boys" from Hamilton.[49]

Following the First World War, Decoration Day in late May or early June had continued to be Canada's national memorial day for all veterans until an Act of Parliament in 1931 transformed November 11, Armistice Day, into "Remembrance Day" while Thanksgiving Day was moved back a month to October.[50] The Ridgeway veterans were forgotten and excluded from the new Remembrance Day, the honour being extended by Veterans Affairs Canada only as far back as to those who fought in the South African War.[51] At this writing, the fallen of Ridgeway are not listed in Canada's National Books of Remembrance and their graves remain forgotten and uncared for by the government, abandoned without National War Grave status.[52]

IN THE EARLY 1930S when *Globe and Mail* columnist Frank Jones was a boy growing up in Toronto, he met a grizzled old man who had fought on Limestone Ridge with the Queen's Own Rifles as an eighteen-year-old. In his boyish curiosity and enthusiasm, Jones pestered the man for years to tell him about the battle he had fought in, but the old soldier would always fall silent and shake his head, refusing to say anything. No matter how much Jones asked him, the man never said a word about the battle, until one day he showed Jones his Fenian Raid medal and muttered a single sentence, the only thing he would ever say to him about being on Limestone Ridge. Frank Jones was deeply disappointed by what he heard and did not understand the old man's stubborn, tight-lipped reticence until years later when it all became crystal clear to him on a hilltop in Italy in 1943.

The old man had said, "It was a hot day and I was thirsty."[53]

For more on the Battle of Ridgeway and the Fenian Raids visit
www.ridgewaybattle.org

NOTES

SOURCE ABBREVIATIONS

ARCAT	Archives of the Roman Catholic Archdiocese of Toronto
CTA	City of Toronto Archives
DCB	Dictionary of Canadian Biography Online (http://www.biographi.ca)
DFUSCF	Despatches from U.S. Consuls in Fort Erie Canada, 1865–1906, Records of the Foreign Service Posts of the Department of State, 1788–1964, RG84 (National Archives Microfilm Publication T465, Roll 1), National Archives at College Park, College Park, MD (NARA)
DFUSCT	Despatches from U.S. Consuls in Toronto, Canada 1864–1906, United States Consular Records for Toronto, Records of the Foreign Service Posts of the Department of State, 1788–1964, RG84 (National Archives Microfilm Publication T491, Roll 1), College Park, MD (NARA)
FEHM	Fort Erie Historical Museum, Ridgeway
FRSR	Fenian Raid Service Records, Adjutant General's Office, United Canada, Pensions and Land Grants, RG9 IC5; Vols. 30–32. *Compensation of Injuries, Wounds, etc., Received on Active Service Fenian Raids 1866–1868*, Library and Archives of Canada (LAC)
LAC	Library and Archives of Canada
LBCC	Letter Books of the Chief Constable 1859–1921, RG9/Fond 38 Toronto Police Service, Series 90, City of Toronto Archives (CTA)
MRFR	Miscellaneous Records Relating to the Fenian Raids, British Military and Naval Records "C" Series, Miscellaneous Records

	RG8-1, Vol. 1672 [Microfilm Reels C-4299 to C-4300], LAC
NA/PRO	National Archives, U.K., former Public Records Office
NARA	National Archives and Records Administration
UCAVC	United Church Archives formerly at Victoria College
WDR	War Department Reports 1863–1872, Division of the Atlantic, Department of the East, RG 393: Records of the U.S. Army Continental Commands, 1817–1940, Inventory Identifier 1428, National Archives Building, Washington, DC (NARA)

EPIGRAPHS

1. Ken Burns, "The Universe of Battle," *The Civil War,* Episode 5, Florentine Films–PBS, 1990.
2. Charles D. Ross, *Acoustic Shadows in the Civil War,* Acoustical Society of America 136th Meeting, Lay Language Papers, Norfolk, VA, October 13, 1998, http://www.acoustics.org/press/136th/ross.htm [retrieved Dec. 21, 2008]. See also, Charles D. Ross, *Civil War Acoustic Shadows,* Shippensburg, PA: Whitemane Books, 2001.
3. *Globe,* June 3, 1891.
4. Olga Berggolts, inscription at the Piskaryovskoye Memorial Cemetery to the victims of the Leningrad Blockade 1941–1944.

PREFACE: RIDGEWAY IN THE ACOUSTIC SHADOW OF HISTORY

1. Robert Larmour, "With Booker's Column" [Part 1] *The Canadian Magazine,* Vol. 10, No. 2 (Dec. 1897), [Part 2] *The Canadian Magazine,* Vol. 10, No. 3 (Jan. 1898).
2. Randall M. Miller, "Mr. Lincoln's T-Mail: The Untold Story of How Abraham Lincoln Used the Telegraph to Win the Civil War," *Library Journal,* Vol. 131, No. 20 (2006) (thanks to Justin Lamoureux); Tom Standage, *The Victorian Internet: The Remarkable Story of the Telegraph and the Nineteenth Century's On-line Pioneers,* New York: Berkeley Books, 1999.
3. [s.n.], "Robert Larmour," *History of the Country of Middlesex Canada*, Toronto: W.A. & C.L. Goodspeed, 1889, p. 884.
4. Larmour, [Part 2] p. 229.
5. While the "regular" permanent Canadian Army was formally established in 1883, its militia regiment, which sustained the casualties, had been continuously in service since 1860 as an active component of the Canadian military primary reserves; it is on these grounds that the argument that they are Canada's military "first fallen" is based.
6. *Statement of Militia Pensions and Gratuities Awarded*, Receiver General's Department, Ottawa, February 1, 1867; *List of Pensions, Gratuities and Amounts*

for Medical Services, Department of Militia and Defence, June 21, 1868; *Compensation of Injuries, Wounds, etc., Received on Active Service Fenian Raids 1866–1868,* Fenian Raid Service Records, Adjutant General's Office, United Canada, Pensions and Land Grants, RG9 IC5; Vols. 30–32, LAC [hereinafter "FRSR"].

7. Hereward Senior points out that the celebrants forgot about the Battle of Castle Bar in 1798 in Ireland, when two thousand Irish rebels and French allies routed six thousand British troops. See *The Last Invasion of Canada: The Fenian Raids, 1866–1870,* Toronto: Dundurn Press, 1991, p. 59.
8. James Kirby (ed), *Lower Canada Law Journal,* Vol. 2, Montreal: John Lovell, 1867, pp. 6–7.
9. Captain John A. Macdonald, *Troublous Times in Canada: The History of the Fenian Raids of 1866 and 1870,* Toronto: W.S. Johnston & Co., 1910, p. 41 [hereinafter "Captain Macdonald"].
10. Toronto *Globe,* March 28, 1923. Another version of the song had a chorus that went, "Shout, shout, shout, ye loyal Britons" instead of "Tramp, tramp, tramp, our boys are marching," contrasting an unabashed imperial version with the national Canadian one.
11. C.P. Stacey, "Fenianism and the Rise of National Feeling in Canada at the Time of Confederation," *Canadian Historical Review,* Vol. 12, No. 3 (1931), pp. 238–261, p. 255.
12. *St. Catharines Constitutional,* June 21, 1866. The remaining three were as follows: "5. They have been the means of bringing out an amount of good faith and efficient effort on the part of the United States authorities to prevent the invasion of a friendly country, which will raise that nation in the opinion not only of these colonies but of the civilized world; 6. They have placed the Irish in Canada in a very cruel position—forcing them either to rebel against the government under which they enjoy liberty, equality, peace and prosperity, or to fight against their own kin; 7. They have rendered themselves a nuisance to the United States as well as to Britain and Canada and have cast discredit on all aspirations after an Irish nationality."
13. http://ve.torontopubliclibrary.ca/collected_works/performing_mapleleaf.html [accessed August 1, 2010].
14. *Globe,* June 3, 1897.
15. Paul Maroney, "'Lest We Forget': War and Meaning in English Canada, 1885–1914," *Journal of Canadian Studies,* Vol. 32, No. 4 (Winter 1997/1998); *Globe,* May 30, 1896.
16. http://www.vac-acc.gc.ca/general/sub.cfm?source=teach_resources/remdayfact ; www.calendar-updates.com/info/holidays/canada/remembrance.aspx [retrieved October 10, 2009].
17. http://www.vac-acc.gc.ca/remembers/sub.cfm?source=teach_resources/remdayfact [retrieved January 7, 2010].
18. http://www.veterans.gc.ca/remembers/sub.cfm?source=collections/books/listing [retrieved July 11, 2010].

19. Exceptional in their original research and attempt to challenge the conventional history are David Owen, *The Year of the Fenians: A Self-Guided Tour of Discovery and an Illustrated History of the Fenian Invasion of the Niagara Peninsula and the Battle of Ridgeway in 1866,* Buffalo, NY: Western New York Heritage Institute, 1990, and Brian A. Reid, "'Prepare for Cavalry!' The Battle of Ridgeway" in Donald E. Graves (ed), *Fighting for Canada: Seven Battles, 1758–1945,* Toronto: Robin Brass Studio, 2000. Interestingly, both Owen and Reid are former soldiers and locals who are personally familiar with the terrain.
20. Paul Maroney, "'Lest We Forget': War and Meaning in English Canada, 1885–1914," *Journal of Canadian Studies*, Vol. 32, No. 4 (Winter 1997/1998).
21. Captain Macdonald, p. 185.

PART 1

1. Captain Macdonald, p. 16.
2. Canadian Border Songs of the Fenian Invasion, 1870, pp. 3–4.

ONE: THE FENIAN CAUSE

1. William D'Arcy, *The Fenian Movement in the United States: 1858–1886,* Washington, DC: Catholic University of America Press, 1947, pp. 229–230; M.W. Burns, "To the Officers and Soldiers of the Irish Republican Army in Buffalo," June 14, 1866, in Captain Macdonald, p. 93.
2. W.S. Neidhardt, *Fenianism in North America,* University Park and London: Pennsylvania State University Press, 1975, p. 7; Alexander Somerville, *Narrative of the Fenian Invasion of Canada,* Hamilton, ON: Joseph Lyght, 1866, p. iii.
3. The repeal of the Irish Church Act 1869, which had required Catholics to pay tithes to the Protestant Church, is considered the final act of Catholic Emancipation in the United Kingdom.
4. See: R.F. Foster, *Modern Ireland 1600–1972,* London: Penguin Books, 1989; Robert Kee, *Ireland: A History,* London: Abacus, 1991; Brian Jenkins, *Era of Emancipation: British Government of Ireland 1812–1830*, Montreal-Kingston: McGill-Queen's University Press, 1988; David R.C. Hudson, *The Ireland We Made,* Akron, OH: University of Akron Press, 2003; Mary Frances Cusack, *History of Ireland from AD 400 to 1800* (1888), London: Senate Books Edition, 1995; Thomas Pakenham, *The Year of Liberty: The Great Irish Rebellion of 1798,* London: Weidenfeld & Nicholson, 1997; Sean Cronin, *Irish Nationalism: A History of Its Roots and Ideology,* Dublin: Academy Press, 1980; James S. Donnelly, *The Great Irish Potato Famine,* London: Sutton Publishing, 2001; D.J. Hickey & J.E. Doherty, *A New Dictionary of Irish History: From 1800*, Dublin: Gill & MacMillan, 2003; Tom Garvin, "Defenders, Ribbonmen and Others: Underground Political Networks in Pre-famine Ireland," *Past and Present,* No. 96 (Aug. 1982), p. 136; Oliver Rafferty, *The Church, the State and the Fenian Threat, 1861–75*, New York: St Martin's Press, 1999; Mike Cronin and Daryl Adair, *The Wearing of the Green: A History of St. Patrick's Day,* London: Routledge,

2002; Kenneth Moss, "St. Patrick's Day Celebrations and the Formation of Irish-American Identity, 1845–1875," *Journal of Social History*, Vol. 29, No. 1. (Autumn 1995), pp. 125–148; Michael Cottrell, "St. Patrick's Day Parades in Nineteenth-Century Toronto: A Study of Immigrant Adjustment and Elite Control," *Histoire social/Social History*, No. 49, 1992, pp. 57–73.

5. Thomas Pakenham, *The Year of Liberty: The Great Irish Rebellion of 1798*, London: Weidenfeld & Nicholson, 1997, p. 107; Cathal Póirtéir (ed), *The Great Irish Rebellion of 1798*, Dublin: Mercier Press; Boulder, CO: Irish American Book Co., 1998; Ciarán Priestley, *Clonsilla and the Rebellion of 1798*, Dublin: Four Courts Press, 2009; Jim Smyth (ed), *Revolution, Counter-Revolution and Union: Ireland in the 1790s*, Cambridge, U.K., and New York: Cambridge University Press, 2000.
6. Marta Ramón, *A Provisional Dictator: James Stephens and the Fenian Movement*, Dublin: University College Dublin Press, 2007, p. 60.
7. D'Arcy, p. 55 *n*.
8. See Brian P. Clarke, *Piety and Nationalism: Lay Voluntary Associations and the Creation of an Irish-Catholic Community in Toronto, 1850–1895*, Montreal-Kingston: McGill-Queen's University Press, 1993, for an extensive history of the HBS; also Charles P. Stacey, "A Fenian Interlude: The Story of Michael Murphy," *Canadian Historical Review*, Vol. 5 (1934), pp. 133–154; W.S. Neidhardt, "Michael Murphy," *Dictionary of Canadian Biography* [hereinafter "DCB"]; D'Arcy, p. 202, *n*.58, citing *Donahoe's Magazine*, December 1879, p. 539; Peter M. Toner, "The 'Green Ghost': Canada's Fenians and the Raids," *Eire-Ireland*, Vol. 16 (1981), p. 29, cites *Phoenix*, New York, March 24, 1866; Burton [P.C. Nolan] to McMicken, December 31, 1865, MG26 A, Vol. 236, pp. 103110–103113 [Reel C1662], LAC; Peter Vronsky, "The Hibernian Benevolent Society and Fenianism in Toronto," www.battleofridgeway.org
9. For examples of international money transfers and Fenian bond sales in France, see Mitchel to O'Mahony, March 10, 1866, in Joseph Denieffe, *A Personal Narrative of the Irish Revolutionary Brotherhood*, New York: Gael Publishing, 1906, p. 219; D'Arcy, pp. 82–84.
10. David A. Wilson, "State Security, Civil Liberty and the Fenians in Canada," 2008 Irish Studies Symposium, http://www.lac-bac.gc.ca/ireland/033001-1001.01.1-e.html [retrieved July 11, 2010].
11. For background to the Hibernian-Fenian nexus in Toronto, see Peter Vronsky, "The Hibernian Benevolent Society and Fenianism in Toronto," www.ridgewaybattle.org
12. Police Department of the City of Toronto, *Description of Fenian Prisoners*, June 9, 1866, Department of Justice, Numbered Central Registry Files, RG-13-A2, Vol. 15, LAC.
13. Quoted in Padraic Cummins Kennedy, *Political Policing in a Liberal Age: Britain's Response to the Fenian Movement 1858–1868*, PhD dissertation, Washington University, 1996, p. 88.
14. Christopher Andrew, *The Defense of the Realm: The Authorized History of MI-5*, London: Penguin Books, 2009, and *Secret Service: The Making of the British*

Intelligence Community, London: Penguin Books, 1989; Bernard Porter, *Plots and Paranoia: A History of Political Espionage in Britain 1790–1988,* London: Unwin Hyman, 1989, and *Origins of the Vigilant State: The London Metropolitan Police Special Branch Before the First World War,* London: Weidenfeld and Nicolson, 1987.

15. Porter, *Plots and Paranoia,* p. 83.
16. Ramón, pp. 162–165; Kennedy, pp. 120–121.
17. Edith J. Archibald, *Life and Letters of Sir Edward Mortimer Archibald,* Toronto: George N. Morang, 1924, p. 20.
18. Archibald to Burnley, December 12, 1864, NA/PRO, FO 5/1334, cited in Kennedy, p. 109.
19. See for details Peter Vronsky, "The Guy Fawkes' Night Incident in Toronto, 1864," www.ridgewaybattle.org; *Globe,* November 7, 1864; Toronto Board of Commissioners of Police, *Minutes,* November 12, 1864, CTA; Michael Cottrell, "Green and Orange in Mid-Nineteenth Century Toronto: The Guy Fawkes' Day Episode of 1864," *Canadian Journal of Irish Studies,* Vol. 19, No. 1 (1993); C.P. Stacey, "A Fenian Interlude."
20. *Globe,* November 7, 19, 1864.
21. *Globe,* November 7, 1864.
22. *Globe,* November 8, 9, 11, 22, 24, 1864.
23. *Globe,* November 19, 1864.
24. For a sample of material and literature on Irish Catholic immigrant vs. Protestant settler relations in Canada 1815–1860, see FitzGibbon to Baines, June 4, 1824, Upper Canada Sundries, RG 5, series A 1, Vol. 67; FitzGibbon to Hillier, June 10, 1824, CO 42, Vol. 373, p. 149, LAC; J.K. Johnson, "Colonel James FitzGibbon and the Suppression of Irish Riots in Upper Canada," *Ontario History,* Vol. 58, No. 3 (September 1966); Donald MacKay, *Flight from Famine: The Coming of the Irish to Canada,* Toronto: McClelland & Stewart, 1990, pp. 48–74; Howard Morton Brown, *Lanark Legacy: Nineteenth Century Glimpses of an Ontario County,* Perth, ON: General Store Publishing House, 1984, pp. 43–55; Carol Bennett, *The Robinson Settlers 1823–1825,* Renfrew, ON: Juniper Books, 1987; Mary Agnes FitzGibbon, *A Veteran of 1812: The Life of James FitzGibbon,* Toronto: William Briggs, 1894; Hereward Senior, *Orangeism: The Canadian Phase,* Toronto: McGraw Hill, 1972, p. 11; Michael S. Cross, "The Shiners War: Social Violence in the Ottawa Valley in the 1830s," *Canadian Historical Review,* Vol. 54, No. 1 (March 1973); Paul Romney, "A Struggle for Authority: Toronto Society and Politics in 1834" in Victor L. Russell (ed), *Forging a Consensus: Historical Essays on Toronto,* Toronto: University of Toronto Press, 1984; Paul Romney, "From the Types Riot to the Rebellion: Elite Ideology, Anti-legal Sentiment, Political Violence, and the Rule of Law in Upper Canada," *Ontario History,* Vol. 79, No. 2 (June 1987), pp. 115–140; Sean T. Cadigan, "Paternalism and Politics: Sir Francis Bond Head, the Orange Order, and the Election of 1836," *Canadian Historical Review,* Vol. 72, No. 3 (1991), pp. 319–347; J.F. Pringle, *Lunenburgh or the Old Eastern District,* Cornwall: 1890, pp. 159–160; Fitzgibbon to Joseph, June 24, 26, and July 6, 1836, Civil Secretary's Letter Book, RG7-G-16-C, Vol. 36, LAC; Ruth Bleasdale,

Unskilled Labourers on the Public Works of Canada, 1840–1880, PhD dissertation, University of Western Ontario, 1984; Ruth Bleasdale, "Class Conflict on the Canals of Upper Canada in the 1840s," *Labour/Le Travailleur,* 1981, reprinted in Laurel Sefton MacDowell and Ian Radforth (eds), *Canadian Working Class History,* 2nd Edition, Toronto: Canadian Scholar's Press, 2000, pp. 81–108; J. Lawrence Runnalls, *The Irish on the Welland Canal,* St. Catharines: St. Catharines Public Library, 1973; *St. Catharines Journal,* July 7, August 11, 1842; Michael J. Cottrell, "Political Leadership and Party Allegiance Among Irish Catholics in Victorian Toronto" in McGowan and Clarke (eds), *Catholics at the "Gathering Place,"* Toronto: Canadian Catholic Historical Association, 1993, p. 53; H.C. Pentland, "The Development of a Capitalistic Labour Market in Canada," *The Canadian Journal of Economics and Political Science*, Vol. 25, No. 4 (Nov. 1959), and see on Pentland, Donald Akenson, *Being Had: Historians, Evidence and the Irish in North America,* Toronto: P.D. Meany, 1985, pp. 111, 136; William S. Prince to Attorney General John A. Macdonald, October 28, 1865, Letter Books of the Chief Constable 1859–1921, RG9/Fond 38 Toronto Police Service, Series 90, City of Toronto Archives [hereinafter "LBCC"]; Donald Akenson, *The Orangeman: The Life and Times of Ogle Gowan,* Toronto: James Lorimer & Co., 1986; W.B. Kerr, "When Orange and Green United 1832–1839: The Alliance of Macdonell and Gowan," *Ontario History,* Vol. 34 (1942); Hereward Senior, *Orangeism: The Canadian Phase,* Toronto: McGraw Hill, 1972, pp. 7–10; John Matthew Barlow, *Fear and Loathing in Saint-Sylvestre: The Corrigan Murder Case, 1855–58,* Master's thesis, Simon Fraser University, 1998; J.R. Miller, "Anti-Catholic Thought in Victorian Canada," *Canadian Historical Review,* Vol. 66 (1985), pp. 474–494; Murray Nicolson, "Irish Tridentine Catholicism in Victorian Toronto: Vessel for Ethno-Religious Persistence" in Mark G. McGowan and David Marshall (eds), *Prophets, Priests and Prodigals: Readings in Canadian Religious History, 1608 to Present,* Toronto: 1992, pp. 117–134; J. Martin Galvin, "The Jubilee Riots in Toronto, 1875," CCHA *Report,* Vol. 26 (1959), pp. 93–107; Emmet Larkin, "The Devotional Revolution in Ireland, 1850–75," *The American Historical Review,* Vol. 77, No. 3 (June 1972), p. 651; Mark McGowan, *The Waning of the Green: Catholics, the Irish, and Identity in Toronto, 1887–1922,* Montreal-Kingston: McGill-Queen's University Press, 1999, p. 7.

25. Pikes, traditionally associated with Irish rebellion, are long-staffed spears with a hook designed for fighting cavalry. Well-trained "pikemen" were a formidable force in the short-range and inaccurate smoothbore musket age and, when deployed in force, could make short work of cavalry or musketeers within pike range.

26. [n.a.] "The Fenians," December 17, 1864, Macdonald Papers, MG26A, Vol. 56, pp. 22219–22240 [Reel C1507], LAC.

27. William F. Raney, "Recruiting and Crimping in Canada for the Northern Forces, 1861–1865," *The Mississippi Valley Historical Review,* Vol. 10, No. 1 (June 1923), pp. 21–33.

28. See Peter Vronsky, "Origins of the Canadian Secret Services, 1864–66," www.ridgewaybattle.org

29. Macdonald Papers, McMicken [Police] Reports ["Secret Service Reports"], MG26A, Vols. 232–237, pp. 100812–104234 [Reels C1660–1663], LAC.
30. For pioneering history on the Frontier Constabulary, see Jeff Keshen, "Cloak and Dagger: Canada West's Secret Police, 1864–1867," *Ontario History,* Vol. 79 (Dec. 1987), pp. 353–381 (p. 356); Gregory S. Kealey, Presidential Address, "The Empire Strikes Back: The Nineteenth-Century Origins of the Canadian Secret Service," *Journal of the CHA,* New Series, Vol. 10 (1999), pp. 3–19 (p. 9); Wayne A. Crockett, *The Uses and Abuses of the Secret Service Fund: The Political Dimension of Police Work in Canada, 1864–1877,* Master's thesis, Queen's University, Kingston, ON, 1982; and C.P. Stacey, "The Shadow of the Civil War" in *Cloak and Dagger in the Sixties,* pp. 3–4 [typescript], CBC Broadcast Script, February 1954, C.P. Stacey Papers, Box 47, University of Toronto Archives; Andrew Parnaby and Gregory S. Kealey, "The Origins of Political Policing in Canada: Class, Law and the Burden of Empire, *Osgoode Hall Law Journal,* Vol. 41, Nos. 2 & 3 (2003), pp. 211–239.
31. Susannah Ural Bruce, "'Remember Your Country and Keep Up Its Credit': Irish Volunteers and the Union Army, 1861-–1865," *Journal of Military History,* Vol. 69, No. 2 (2005), pp. 331-–359; Kevin W. Stanton, *Green Tint on Gold Bars: Irish Officers in the United States Army, 1865–1898,* PhD dissertation, University of Colorado, 2001, pp. 78–94.
32. Leon Ó Broin, *Fenian Fever: An Anglo-American Dilemma,* New York: New York University Press, 1971, pp. 2–3.
33. C.P. Stacey, *Canada and the British Army,* pp. 104–116.
34. Sweeny to Roberts [circa November 1865], *Thomas William Sweeny Papers,* MssCol 2934, New York City Public Library.
35. Captain Macdonald, p. 16.

TWO: THE MAKING OF THE CANADIAN ARMY, 1855–1866

1. Stacey, *Canada and the British Army,* p. 55.
2. Ernest J. Chambers, *The Canadian Militia: Origins and Development of the Force,* Montreal: L.M. Fresco, 1907.
3. Stephen J. Harris, *Canadian Brass: The Making of a Professional Army, 1860–1939,* Toronto: University of Toronto Press, 1988, pp. 11–21.
4. Chambers, *The Canadian Militia,* pp. 64–65.
5. Brereton Greenhous, Kingsley Brown Sr., and Kingsley Brown Jr., *Semper Paratus: The History of the Royal Hamilton Light Infantry,* Hamilton, ON: RHLI Historical Association, 1977, pp. 10, 26; Allen Andrews, *Brave Soldiers, Proud Regiments: Canada's Military Heritage,* Vancouver: Ronsdale Press, 1997, p. 215.
6. Helen G. Macdonald, *Canadian Public Opinion on the American Civil War,* New York: Columbia University Press, 1926, pp. 94–98.
7. Stacey, *Canada and the British Army,* p. 122.
8. John King, *McCaul: Croft: Forneri: Personalities of Early University Days,* Toronto: Macmillan Co. Ltd., 1894, p. 108. Thanks to Erin Fitzgerald for bringing this source to my attention.

9. *Globe,* March 28, 1864, and June 27, 1866.
10. King, p. 142.
11. Chambers, pp. 149–156.
12. [s.n.] *The Fenian Raid at Fort Erie,* Toronto: W.C. Chewett & Co., 1866, p. 52 [hereinafter "Chewett"]; Chambers, p. 54.
13. Greenhous, p. 8.
14. Greenhous, p. 31.
15. Greenhous, pp. 12–35.
16. *Defences of Canada*, p. 13.
17. John Thornley Docker, *Dunnville Heroes: The* W.T. Robb *and the Dunnville Naval Brigade in the 1866 Fenian Invasion,* Dunnville, ON: Dunnville District Heritage Association, 2003, pp. 2–3.
18. *Proceedings of the Court of Inquiry upon the Circumstances of the Engagement at Fort Erie on the 2nd of June 1866,* Adjutant General's Correspondence; Correspondence relating to complaints, courts martial and inquiries, RG9-I-C-8, Vol. 7, LAC [hereinafter "*Dennis Inquiry*"], pp. 54, 60.
19. *Dennis Inquiry,* p. 343; Docker, p. 14.
20. McCallum to Macdonald, April 6, 1865, Adjutant General Letters Received 1865, RG9 IC1, Vol. 220, File 932, LAC.
21. Stephen Beatty, *Reminiscences of the Fenian Raid 1866,* manuscript, John Colin Armour Campbell fonds, R9262-0-2-E, Notes on Military Affairs, MG29-E74, Vol. 1, Folder 4, LAC, p. 6 [hereinafter "Beatty [*ms*]"].
22. George T. Denison fonds, Reference Code: F 1009, Archives of Ontario.
23. Having served in the regiment from 1971 to 1973 as a teenage militia trooper, I can attest to the power of the Denison name's permeating the regimental lore and traditions into which every recruit was sheep-dipped. The Governor General's Horse Guard (GGHG) was based until recently in the Denison Armouries on Dufferin Street in Downsview, now torn down and replaced by a Costco. The GGHG has moved to a new Denison Armoury near Sheppard and Allan Road. The GGHG fought in South Africa, in the First and Second World Wars, and in Korea. Since 1965 it has been designated as a light-armoured reconnaissance regiment, and when I served in it, it was still commanded by a member of the Denison family. Once again today an armoured regiment, it operates with Cougar armoured cars and armoured personnel carriers (APCs) and maintains a squadron of ceremonial horse guards who ride on privately owned steeds, escorting the Governor General and the British Royal family and other dignitaries on their visits to Toronto or to the Queen's Plate race.
24. David Gagan, "George Taylor Denison, [II]," in Ramsay Cook (ed), *Dictionary of Canadian Biography* [Online], University of Toronto, http://www.utoronto.ca/dcb-dbc [hereinafter "DCB"].
25. Norman Knowles, "George Taylor Denison, [III]," DCB; Frederick C. Denison, *Historical Record of the Governor-General's Body Guard,* Toronto: 1876, p. 20.
26. Frederick C. Denison, p. 23; http://www.army.forces.gc.ca/gghg/history.html [retrieved Feb. 28, 2011].

27. *Globe,* March 30, 1861.
28. George T. Denison, *Soldiering in Canada,* Toronto: George L. Morang & Co., 1901, p. 52.
29. Adam Mayers, *Dixie & The Dominion: Canada, the Confederacy and the War for the Union,* Toronto: Dundurn Group, 2003, p. 181.
30. This is very likely the earliest record of the use of microdot photography in espionage, and as acetate-film media did not exist at the time, the process probably involved photosensitizing the metal of the buttons themselves or lining them with daguerreotype copper/silver, a photo medium with a capacity for very high resolution. According to the U.S. Consul in Toronto, "Messengers wear metal buttons, which upon the inside dispatches are most minutely photographed, not perceptible to the naked eye, but are easily read by the aid of a powerful lens ..." See Thurston to Seward, January 8, 1865, *Despatches from U.S. Consuls in Toronto, Canada 1864–1906,* United States Consular Records for Toronto; Records of the Foreign Service Posts of the Department of State, 1788–1964, RG84; (National Archives Microfilm Publication T491, Roll 1) National Archives at College Park, College Park, MD.
31. Denison, *Soldiering in Canada*, pp. 61–62.
32. See *Despatches from U.S. Consuls in Toronto, Canada 1864–1906*, T491, Roll 1, op cit.
33. Mayers, p. 133.
34. Mayers, p. 181.
35. Carl Berger, *A Sense of Power: Studies in the Ideas of Canadian Imperialism,* Toronto: University of Toronto Press, 1970, pp. 15–16.
36. Denison, *Soldiering in Canada,* p. 69.
37. George T. Denison, *Fenian Raid on Fort Erie; with an Account of the Battle of Ridgeway, June, 1866,* Toronto: Rollo & Adam, 1866.

THREE: THE THREAT OF INVASION, 1865–1866

1. D'Arcy, pp. 102–107; Senior, *Last Invasion of Canada,* pp. 40–41; Neidhardt, *Fenianism in North America,* pp. 28–33.
2. Keshen, citing Macdonald to McMicken, September 22, 1865, MG26A, Vol. 511.
3. *Cincinnati Daily Gazette,* September 23, 1865, attachment to Grant to McElderry, September 23, 1865, Macdonald Papers, MG26A, Vol. 232, p. 102831 [Reel C1662].
4. Lieutenant J.L.Granatstein, Canadian Armed Forces, Historical Section, Canadian Military Headquarters, *Report No. 2 Canadian American Defence Relations 1867–1914,* Ottawa: August 1965, p. 5, http://www.cmp-cpm.forces.gc.ca/dhh-dhp/his/rep-rap/cfhqrd-drqgfc-eng.asp?txtType=4&RfId=293 [retrieved April 2, 2011].
5. Reid, pp. 138–140; Morgan, p. 129; D'Arcy, pp. 84–85; Senior, *Last Invasion,* pp. 49–51; Rober L. Dallison, *Turning Back the Fenians: New Brunswick's Last Colonial Campaign,* Fredericton, NB: Goose Lane Editions–New Brunswick

Military Heritage Project, 2006, p. 76; Neidhardt, *The American Government and the Fenian Brotherhood*, p. 38.

6. Augustus F. Lindley, *Ti-ping Tien-kwoh: The History of the Ti-ping Revolution, Including a Narrative of the Author's Personal Adventures,* London: Day & Son Limited, 1866; Anthony Preston and John Major, *Send a Gunboat: A Study of the Gunboat and Its Role in British Policy, 1854–1904,* London: Longmans, 1967. Jonathan D. Spence, *The Search for Modern China,* New York: W.W. Norton & Co., 1990, pp. 200–201; Juliet Brendon, *Sir Robert Hart: The Romance of a Great Career,* 2nd Edition, London: 1910 [retrieved from Project Gutenberg, June 9, 2010].
7. Johannes von Gumpach, *The Burlingame Mission,* Shanghai, London, and New York: 1872, pp. 192–201; David L. Anderson, *Imperialism and Idealism: American Diplomats in China, 1861–1898,* Bloomington, IN: Indiana University Press, 1985, pp. 30–31; Frank J. Merli, *The* Alabama, *British Neutrality and the American Civil War*, Bloomington, IN: Indiana University Press, 2004; The Association to Commemorate the Chinese Serving in the American Civil War, *The Connection Between the American Civil War (1861–1865) and the Chinese Taiping Civil War (1850–1864),* http://sites.google.com/site/accsacw/Home/connection [retrieved June 10, 2010].
8. *Papers Relating to the Foreign Relations of the United States, Executive Documents Printed by the Order of the House of Representatives During the Second Session of the Thirty-Ninth Congress, 1866–'67,* Vol. 13 (1866), Part I, Washington: Government Printing Office, 1867, pp. 43–44 [hereinafter *Papers Relating to Foreign Relations*].
9. Bruce to Clarendon, March 16, 1866, Clarendon Papers cited in Barnes, p. 374.
10. Bruce to Clarendon, January 9, 1866, Clarendon Papers cited in Foner, p. 385.
11. Clarendon to Bruce, January 6, 1866, Clarendon Papers c.143, cited in Ó Broin, p. 57, in Peter Vronsky, "The Secret Anglo-American Fenian Containment Policy 1865–1866," www.ridgewaybattle.org
12. Seward to Speed, April 2, 1866, Letters Received by the Secretary of War from the President, Executive Departments, and War Department Bureaus 1862–1870 (National Archives Microfilm Publication M494, Roll 88); Records of the Office of the Secretary of War, 1791–1947, Record Group 107; National Archives Building, Washington, DC. See also Ruggles to Carlton, commander of Fort Ontario, Oswego, NY, April 2, 1866; Lawrence to Carlton, April 7, 1866; Ruggles to Carlton, April 21, 1866: WDR, NARA, and active measures taken by U.S. authorities against Fenian armed threats: Brevet Brigadier General Simon F. Barstow, adjutant for Major General George G. Meade to Brevet Colonel Ely S. Parker, March 13, 1866; March 16, 23, 26, 1866, Barstow (for Meade) to H.Q., reports on U.S. Army actions against Fenian activities in New York State, Records of the Headquarters of the Army 1828–1903, Letters Received, RG 108; Parker to Meade, April 5, 1866, Letters Received, Department of the East, Records of the U.S. Army Continental Commands, 1817–1940, RG 393; Stanton to Meade, April 16, 1866, Letters Received from Bureaus, Records of the Office of the Secretary of War, RG107; Meade to H.Q., April 19, 20; May 16, 28, 30, 1866; H.Q. to Meade, May 30, 1866, Telegrams Received, RG 108; Letters Sent, Military

Division of the Atlantic, RG 393, National Archives Building, Washington, DC, NARA.

13. Seward to Speed, April 2, 1866, Letters Received by the Secretary of War from the President, Executive Departments, and War Department Bureaus 1862–1870 (National Archives Microfilm Publication M494, Roll 88); Records of the Office of the Secretary of War, 1791–1947, Record Group 107; National Archives Building, Washington, DC.; McLeod to Simpson, February 28, March 12, 19, 26; June 2, 6, 1866, in MG26A, Vol. 57, LAC.
14. Jenkins, *The Fenians and Anglo-American Relations,* pp. 65–69.
15. Ulysses S. Grant to George G. Meade, March 12, 1866, Letters Received, War Department, Division of the Atlantic, Department of the East, RG 393: Records of the U.S. Army Continental Commands, 1817–1940, National Archives Building, Washington, DC, NARA; William Seward to Joshua Speed, U.S. Attorney General, April 2, 1866, Letters Received by the Secretary of War from the President, Executive Departments, and War Department Bureaus 1862–1870 (National Archives Microfilm Publication M494, Roll 88); Records of the Office of the Secretary of War, 1791–1947, Record Group 107, National Archives Building, Washington, DC.
16. Meade to Grant, March 31, 1866, Letters Received, RG 108, NARA.
17. Bruce to Clarendon, June 4, 1866, Clarendon Papers, cited in Barnes, p. 381.
18. See for example, Assistant Adjutant General Ruggles to Carlton, commander of Fort Ontario, Oswego, NY, March 15, 1866, WDR; Brevet Brigadier General Simon F. Barstow, adjutant for Major General George G. Meade, to Brevet Colonel Ely S. Parker, March 13, 1866, Letters Received, RG 393, NARA.
19. Sweeny to Roberts [circa November 1865], *Thomas William Sweeny Papers,* MssCol 2934: New York City Public Library [hereinafter "Sweeny Papers"].
20. Receipt, New York, "For the purpose of organizing a secret service corps in Canada," November 16, 1865, Sweeny Papers.
21. Owen, p. 68; see also testimony of Dennis Sullivan; Edward Hodder; George McMurrich, in *Queen v. John McMahon,* DFUSCT, Roll 1; *Globe,* June 6.
22. Somerville, p. 21; Tupper to McMicken, June 11, 1866, MG26 A, Vol. 237, p. 104076 [Reel C1663], LAC.
23. Owen, p. 68.
24. William Leonard to Sweeny, April 4, 1866, Sweeny Papers.
25. Mansfield to Christian, April 9, 1866, Sweeny Papers.
26. Richard Slattery to Sweeny, May 9, 1866, Sweeny Papers.
27. F.B. McNamee to Christian, March 26, 1866, Sweeny Papers; for more on Montreal Fenians, see David Wilson, "The Fenians in Montreal, 1862–68: Invasion, Intrigue, and Assassination," *Eire-Ireland: A Journal of Irish Studies*, Vol. 38, Nos. 3–4 (Fall–Winter 2003), p. 109.
28. Burton [P.C. Nolan] to McMicken, March 8, 1866, MG26A, Vol. 237, pp. 103303–103304 [Reel C1663], LAC; *Irish Canadian,* February 14, 1866.
29. McMicken to Macdonald, March 5, 1866, MG26A, Vol. 237 [Reel C1663], pp. 103296–103299.

30. Sweeny, *Official Report,* September 1866, in Denieffe, p. 255; Sweeny to Roberts [circa November 1865] and Tevis to Sweeny, March 6, 1866, Sweeny Papers; Morgan, pp. 122–123; Owen, p. 61; Neidhardt, *Fenianism in North America,* pp. 33–34; Senior, *Last Invasion of Canada,* p. 64.
31. Sweeny to Halsted, April 18, 1866, Sweeny Papers.
32. Richard Compton-Hall, *The Submarine Pioneers: The Beginnings of Underwater Warfare*, Penzance, Cornwall: Periscope Pub., 2003.
33. Kerby Miller, *Emigrants and Exiles: Ireland and the Irish Exodus to North America,* New York: Oxford University Press, 1985, p. 336.
34. D'Arcy, pp. 138–139; Neidhardt, p. 47.
35. For a recent account of the Campobello invasion, see Robert L. Dallison, *Turning Back the Fenians: New Brunswick's Last Colonial Campaign*, Fredericton, NB: Goose Lane Editions–New Brunswick Military Heritage Project, 2006.
36. Beatty [*ms*], LAC, p. 7.
37. For example, see Neidhardt, *Fenianism in North America,* pp. 56–57; Senior, *The Last Invasion of Canada,* pp. 60–61; D'Arcy, pp. 157–158.
38. Joseph W. Caddell, "Deception 101: Primer on Deception," *Conference on Strategic Deception in Modern Democracies: Ethical, Legal, and Policy Challenges,* U.S. Army War College, October 31, 2003, at the William C. Friday Conference Centre, Chapel Hill, NC.
39. Mark Twain, "The Noble Redman," *The Galaxy,* September 1870.
40. MacDougall to McMicken, October 30, 1865, MG26A, Vol. 236 [Reel C1662], pp. 102928–102931, LAC.
41. McMicken to Macdonald, November 3, 1865, MG26A, Vol. 236 [Reel C1662], pp. 102949–102951, LAC.
42. McMicken to Macdonald, July 11, 1866, MG26A, *Fenian Papers* III, pp. 700–704, LAC, quoted in C.P. Stacey, "The Fenian Troubles and Canadian Military Development," p. 28, in *Report of the Annual Meeting of the Canadian Historical Association*, 1935.
43. Captain Macdonald, p. 25.
44. Morgan, p. 124.
45. Quoted in Robert Kee, *The Bold Fenian Men,* Vol. 2, London: Penguin, 1972, p. 11.
46. Courtney to Grace, May 23, 1866, Sweeny Papers.
47. Benedict Maryniak, *The Fenian Raid and Battle of Ridgeway June 1–3, 1866,* http://www.acsu.buffalo.edu/~dbertuca/g/FenianRaid.html [retrieved October 2008] [hereinafter Maryniak].
48. Grant to Meade, May 30, 1866, Telegrams Collected, Records of the Office of the Secretary of War, RG 107, National Archives Building, Washington, DC, NARA.
49. Chewett, p. 30.
50. Bradley Alan Rodgers, *Guardian of the Great Lakes: The U.S. Paddle Frigate*

Michigan *and Iron Archetype on the Inland Seas,* PhD dissertation, Union Institute, Cincinnati, OH, 1994, p. 308.

51. Grant to Meade, May 30, 1866, Telegrams Collected.
52. Sweeny, *Official Report,* Denieffe, pp. 259–260.
53. Gerald R. Noonan, "General John O'Neill," *Clogher Record*, Vol. 6, No. 2 (Clogher Historical Society: 1967), pp. 277–319.
54. C.P. Stacey, *John O'Neill: The Story of the Fenian Paladin* [unpublished manuscript], n.d., C.P. Stacey Papers, University of Toronto Archives. Stacey cites *War of the Rebellion, Official Records*, Series I, Vol. 23, Part i, pp. 367–369, Report of Colonel Felise W. Graham (O'Neill killed two with his sabre).
55. John Savage, *Fenian Heroes and Martyrs*, Boston: Patrick Donahoe, Franklin Street, 1868, p. 385.
56. C.P. Stacey, *John O'Neill,* citing *War of the Rebellion*, *Official Records,* Vol. 31, Part i, p. 429.
57. C.P. Stacey, *John O'Neill*, citing *Official Records*, Series III, Vol. 4, pp. 766–767.
58. Reid, p. 143; Scian Dubh [James McCarroll], *Ridgeway: An Historical Romance of the Fenian Invasion of Canada,* Buffalo, NY: McCarroll & Co., 1868, pp. 75–88; J.F. Dunn, "Recollections of the Battle of Ridgeway," *Welland County Historical Society Papers and Records,* Vol. 2, Welland, Canada: 1926, pp. 50–52.
59. Gerald R. Noonan, p. 279.
60. C.P. Stacey, *John O'Neill,* p. 18.
61. Sweeny, *Official Report,* Denieffe pp. 259–260.
62. Chewett, p. 29; Jenkins, *Fenians and Anglo American Relations,* p. 143.
63. Leonard to Sweeny, February 16, 1866, Sweeny Papers.
64. Leonard to Sweeny, April 19, 1866, Sweeny Papers.
65. A.L. Morrison to T.W. Sweeny, May 13, 1866; A.L. Morrison to C.C. Tevis, May 21, 1866, Sweeny Papers.
66. Commander Andrew Bryson to Gideon Wells, June 2, 1866, Roll 85, Item 209, in Letters Received by Secretary of the Navy from Commanders, 1804–1886, Naval Records Collection of the Office of Naval Records and Library, 1691–1945, RG45; (National Archives Microfilm Publication M147, Roll 85) National Archives Building, Washington, DC, NARA [hereinafter "Commanders' Letters"].
67. James P. Kelley, *Report to Commander Bryson* [enclosure], in Bryson to Wells, June 2, 1866, Commanders' Letters.
68. Bryson to Wells, June 1, 1866, and Bryson to Wells, June 2, 1866, Commanders' Letters.
69. Logbook entry, Friday, June 1, 1866.
70. James Wood, *Militia Myths: Ideas of the Canadian Citizen Soldier 1896–1921,* Vancouver-Toronto: University of British Columbia Press, 2010, p. 11.

PART 2

1. *Globe,* March 28, 1923; Hamilton *Spectator*, December 20, 1927: Sherk, p. 64; Edith Fowke, "Canadian Variation of a Civil War Song," *Midwest Folklore,* Vol. 13, No. 2 (Summer 1963), Indiana University Press, pp. 101–104.

FOUR: THE FENIAN INVASION OF FORT ERIE, MORNING, JUNE 1, 1866

1. "Buffalo City Map 1," *Erie County 1866 Atlas*, Stone and Stewart, 1866, www.historicmapworks.com/Map/U.S./38348/Buffalo+City+1 [retrieved July 11, 2010].
2. Somerville, pp. 15–16.
3. "Map Illustrating the Fenian Raid" in [s.n.] *The Fenian Raid at Fort Erie,* Toronto: W.C. Chewett & Co., 1866. p. 97.
4. D'Arcy, pp. 229–230.
5. Charles Clarke to McMicken, May 31, 1866, MG26 A, Vol. 237, p. 103840 [Reel C1663], LAC; Joseph Newbigging, testimony, *Queen v. John McMahon*; Thomas L. Newbigging, testimony, *Queen v. Robert B. Lynch,* DFUSCT, Roll 1.
6. Thomas L. Newbigging, testimony, *Queen v. Robert B. Lynch,* DFUSCT, Roll 1.
7. Chewett, p. 29.
8. W.R. Holloway, *Indianapolis: A Historical and Statistical Sketch of the Railroad City,* Indianapolis: Indianapolis Journal Print, 1870, p. 280.
9. *Proceedings of a Court of Inquiry Held in Hamilton on Tuesday the 3rd day of July A.D. 1866 by Order of His Excellency the Commander-in-Chief on the Application of Lieutenant Colonel Booker to Examine and Report on the Circumstances Connected with the Late Engagement at Lime Ridge, dated Ottawa, June 24, 1866.* Adjutant General's Correspondence; Correspondence relating to complaints, courts martial and inquiries, RG9-I-C-8, Vol. 6 LAC [Page referenced to reprint in Captain Macdonald and hereinafter as "*Booker Inquiry*"], p. 216.
10. Eugene Courtney to John Grace, May 22, 1866; *Sweeny Official Report,* September 1866, Sweeny Papers; for Louisiana Tigers and Confederate uniforms, see the *Irish Canadian,* June 6, 1866, p. 3.
11. Reid, Appendix C, p. 378; O'Neill, *Official Report,* p. 38; Captain Macdonald, p. 26; E.A. Cruikshank, "The Fenian Raid of 1866," *Welland County Historical Society Papers and Records,* Vol. 2, Welland, Canada: 1926, pp. 20, 28; Scian Dubh [James McCarroll], pp. 164–165; Benedict Maryniak, *The Fenian Raid and Battle of Ridgeway June 1–3, 1866,* http://www.acsu.buffalo.edu/~dbertuca/g/FenianRaid.html [retrieved October 2008].
12. Reid, Appendix C, p. 378; O'Neill, *Official Report,* p. 38; Captain Macdonald, p. 26; E.A. Cruikshank, pp. 20, 28; Scian Dubh [James McCarroll], pp. 164–165; Benedict Maryniak, *The Fenian Raid and Battle of Ridgeway June 13, 1866,* http://www.acsu.buffalo.edu/~dbertuca/g/FenianRaid.html [retrieved October 2008].
13. Paddy Griffith, *Battle Tactics of the Civil War,* New Haven and London: Yale University Press, 2001, pp. 92–93. (Griffith reports that the theoretical size of a Civil War regiment was a thousand men, but the actual battlefield size averaged

between three and four hundred, and its lightness was a tactical advantage making for "a very handy and maneuverable fighting unit.")

14. Beatty [*ms*], LAC, pp. 21–22; McCallum, *Report,* [Frame 862], MRFR.
15. George Wells, "A Romance of the Raid," *Welland County Historical Society Papers and Records,* Vol. 2, Welland, Canada: 1926, pp. 80–81.
16. McLaughlin to McMicken, May 31, 1866, MG26 A, Vol. 237, pp. 103838–103845 [Reel C1663], LAC.
17. Captain John A. Macdonald, *Troublous Times in Canada,* Toronto: [s.n.] 1910, p. 28.
18. Joseph Newbigging, testimony, Judge's Notes, *The Queen v. William Havin,* DFUSCT, Roll 1.
19. Somerville, p. 38.
20. *Dennis Inquiry,* pp. 221–222.
21. George Wells, "The Fenian Raid in Willoughby," *Welland County Historical Society Papers and Records,* Vol. 2, Welland, Canada: 1926, p. 57; see also Freeman N. Blake, U.S. Consul Fort Erie, to William Seward, Secretary of State, June 20, 1866, and printed enclosure of Detective Armstrong to Colonel Lowry, June 7, 1866, in Despatches from U.S. Consuls in Fort Erie Canada 1865–1906, Records of the Foreign Service Posts of the Department of State, 1788–1964, RG84 (National Archives Microfilm Publication T465, Roll 1), National Archives at College Park, College Park, MD [hereinafter "DFUSCF"].
22. John O'Neill, *Official Report of the Battle of Ridgeway, Canada West, Fought on June 2, 1866* (June 27, 1866), New York: John A. Foster, 1870, pp. 37–38 [hereinafter O'Neill, *Official Report*]; Somerville, p. 16; Greenhous, p. 60.
23. Somerville, p. 16.
24. E.A. Cruikshank, "The Fenian Raid of 1866," *Welland County Historical Society Papers and Records,* Vol. 2, Welland, Canada: 1926, p. 24.
25. W.C. Chewett, *The Fenian Raid at Fort Erie,* Toronto: [s.n.], 1866, p. 30.
26. Somerville, p. 29.
27. Blake to Seward, Secretary of State, June 20, 1866, DFUSCF, Roll 1; Maryniak.
28. David Owen, *The Year of the Fenians,* Buffalo, NY: Western New York Heritage Institute, 1990, p. 68; see also testimony of Dennis Sullivan, Edward Hodder, George McMurrich, in *Queen v. John McMahon,* DFUSCT, Roll 1.
29. Somerville, p. 21; Tupper to McMicken, June 11, 1866, MG26 A, Vol. 237, p. 104076 [Reel C1663], LAC.
30. Owen, p. 68.
31. Somerville, p. 51, on availability of maps; see Thomas L. Newbigging, cross-examination, *The Queen v. Robert B. Lynch,* DFUSCT, Roll 1, for O'Neill's possession of road maps.
32. Cruikshank, p. 27.
33. Somerville, p.15; Cruikshank, p. 21; map of Fort Erie in *Dennis Inquiry*.
34. Cruikshank, pp. 23–24.
35. George T. Denison, *Soldiering in Canada,* p. 127.

36. Robin W. Winks, *Canada and the United States: The Civil War Years,* Montreal: McGill-Queen's University Press, 1998, pp. 178–205; Claire Hoy, *Canadians in the Civil War,* Toronto: McArthur & Co., pp. 130–131.
37. R.A. McKelvie, "Sam Johnston, Eighty-One Year Old Hero of the Fenian Raid, Now Living in Hut at Rock Creek B.C.," *Vancouver Province,* circa 1925, quoted by Louis Blake Duff in "Sam Johnston, Smuggler, Soldier and Bearer of News," *Welland County Historical Society Papers and Records,* Vol. 2, Welland, Canada: 1926, p. 87.
38. Cruikshank, p. 21; Sam Johnston in letter to Louis Blake Duff, circa 1925, quoted by Duff, p. 87.
39. Sam Johnston, *Sam Johnston's Own Narrative,* in Duff, p. 83.
40. *Earthwatch 3.0*, Larry Nagy, Elanware Inc., Ohio, 1993; Somerville, p. 16, states sunrise was at 4:25 that day.
41. Cruikshank, p. 21.
42. Cruikshank, p. 26.
43. *Dennis Statement,* October 27, 1866, p. 2 [in *Dennis Inquiry,* appended at p. 345], *Proceedings of the Court of Inquiry upon the Circumstances of the Engagement at Fort Erie on the 2nd of June 1866,* Adjutant General's Correspondence; Correspondence relating to complaints, courts martial and inquiries, RG9-I-C-8, Vol. 7, LAC.
44. Cruikshank, p. 24.
45. Robert Larmour, "With Booker's Column" [Part 1] *The Canadian Magazine,* Vol. 10, No. 2 (Dec. 1897), p. 122.
46. Larmour [Part 1], p. 122.
47. Captain Macdonald, p. 29; Larmour [Part 1], p. 123.
48. Captain Macdonald, p. 29.
49. Larmour [Part 1], p. 123.
50. Owen, p. 17.
51. Larmour [Part 1], p. 123.
52. Larmour [Part 1], p. 123.
53. Somerville, p. 14; Cruikshank, p. 21.
54. Cruikshank, p. 28.
55. *Buffalo Medical and Surgical Journal,* Vol. 5 (Buffalo 1866), p. 370.
56. http://andrewdsmith.wordpress.com/2010/11/29/macdonald-papers-online [retrieved April 2, 2010].
57. Somerville, p. 17.
58. *Buffalo Commercial Advertiser,* June 1, 1866.
59. Somerville, p. 18.
60. *Buffalo Commercial Advertiser,* June 1, 1866.
61. Somerville, p. 29.
62. Somerville, pp. 29, 73.

63. Somerville, p. 19; Blake to Seward, Secretary of State, June 20, 1866, DFUSCF, Roll 1; Tupper to McMicken, June 11, 1866, MG26 A, Vol. 237, pp. 104072–104074 [Reel C1663], LAC; George T. Denison, *The Fenian Raid at Fort Erie and an Account of the Battle of Ridgeway* [original manuscript], George Taylor Denison III fonds, MG29-E29, Vol. 43, File 1, LAC, p. 10 [hereinafter Denison, *The Fenian Raid*].
64. Captain Macdonald, p. 29.
65. Joseph Stevens, Testimony, Judge Wilson's Notes, *The Queen v. Robert B. Lynch,* October 24, 1866, DFUSCT, Roll 1.
66. Somerville, p. 20.
67. Alexander Milligan, testimony, Judge's Notes [Wilson], *The Queen v. John McMahon,* DFUSCT.
68. Hamilton *Evening Times* [5 P.M. edition], June 1, 1866.
69. M.G. Sherk, "My Recollections of the Fenian Raid," *County Historical Society Papers and Records,* Vol. 2, Welland, Canada: 1926, p. 60.
70. Duff, p. 91.
71. Sam Johnston claimed that he espied on the road between the town and the landing site a column of Fenians eight men to a rank. "I counted the columns and there were one hundred and thirty-six. At that rate there were one thousand and eighty-eight men." R.A. McKelvie, "Sam Johnston, Eighty-One Year Old Hero of the Fenian Raid, Now Living in Hut at Rock Creek B.C.," *Vancouver Province,* circa 1925, quoted by Louis Blake Duff in "Sam Johnston, Smuggler, Soldier and Bearer of News," *Welland County Historical Society Papers and Records,* Vol. 2, Welland, Canada: 1926, p. 87; Sam Johnston in letter to Louis Blake Duff, circa 1925, quoted by Duff, p. 87; Sam Johnston, *Sam Johnston's Own Narrative,* in Duff, p. 83.
72. Johnston, *Narrative,* p. 83.
73. McKelvie in *Vancouver Province* in Duff, p. 88.
74. Duff, p. 91.
75. O'Neill, *Official Report,* p. 38.
76. Captain Macdonald, p. 29; Maryniak; Microsoft, *Streets & Trips 2006,* Copyright © 1988–2005 Microsoft Corp.
77. Thomas L. Newbigging, testimony, Judge's Notes, *The Queen v. Robert B. Lynch,* October 24, 1866, DFUSCT, Roll 1.
78. Somerville, p. 32.
79. *Irish Canadian,* June 6, 1866, p. 3.
80. Dennis to McMicken, telegram, June 1, 1866, MG26 A, Vol. 237, p. 103871 [Reel C1663] LAC.
81. Charles Clarke to McMicken, telegram, June 2, 1866, MG26 A, Vol. 237 [Reel C1663], p. 103878, LAC.
82. *Dennis Inquiry*, p. 256.

FIVE: THE MILITARY RESPONSE, AFTERNOON, JUNE 1, 1866

1. Ernest J. Chambers, *The Queen's Own Rifles of Canada,* Toronto: E.L. Ruddy, 1901, p. 59.
2. Andrews, p. 167.
3. Fred H. McCallum, "Experience of a Queen's Own Rifleman at Ridgeway," *Third Annual Report of the Waterloo Historic Society,* Berlin [Kitchener]: Waterloo Historic Society, 1915, p. 24.
4. Captain J. Edwards to Colonel Gillmor, October 16, 1866, FRSR, Vol. 30, p. 45, LAC.
5. James Powell, *History of the Canadian Dollar,* Ottawa: Bank of Canada, 2005, Appendix A, p. 88.
6. Chewett, p. 91.
7. http://www.open.ac.uk/ou5/Arts/chemists/person.cfm?SearchID=4917 [retrieved December 23, 2008].
8. William H. Ellis, "The Adventures of a Prisoner of War," *The Canadian Magazine,* Vol. 13, No. 3 (July 1899), p. 199.
9. John King, *McCaul: Croft: Forneri: Personalities of Early University Days,* Toronto: Macmillan Co. Ltd., 1894, p. 145.
10. Margaret Mackenzie to Henry Croft, November 8, 1866, FRSR, Vol. 30, p. 90.
11. Harrison C. Mewburn, Compensation Application, October 26, 1866, FRSR, Vol. 30, p. 86.
12. Chewett, p. 92.
13. Mary Hannah Tempest, *Petition for Indemnity for the Loss of Her Son, William Tempest, Who Was Killed at the Battle of Ridgeway,* April 25, 1872, RG9-II-A-1, Vol. 41, File No. 6532.
14. Dr. Tempest to Lieutenant Colonel Gillmor, October 15, 1866, FRSR, Vol. 30, pp. 75–79.
15. A regimental surgeon, Dr. James Thorburn would be appointed May 26, 1866. See *List of Medical Officers of Volunteer Militia,* September 26, 1866; Adjutant General's Office, Letters Sent 1847–1868, RG9-I-C-1, Vol. 290, LAC [The list of regimental surgeons notes: "Many of the above may be dead or have left the country for aught I know to the contrary as commanding officers do not think it necessary to report such things."]
16. Dr. Tempest to Gillmor, p. 77.
17. McCallum, p. 25.
18. Irwin Silber, *Songs of the Civil War,* New York: Columbia University Press, 1960, p. 14.
19. Committee representing the Quebec Provincial Council of the Boy Scouts Association, *Songs for Canadian Boys,* Toronto: Macmillan, 1952, pp. 250–251.
20. Fowke, pp. 103–104.
21. Dr. Tempest to Gillmor, p. 76-A.
22. Andrews, p. 167.

23. Ellis, p. 199.
24. David Junor, "Taken Prisoner by the Fenians," *The Canadian Magazine,* May 1911, p. 86.
25. Chambers, p. 61.
26. Somerville, p. 44; *Globe,* June 19, 1866.
27. *Memorandum to Lt. Col Durie*, June 25, 1866; clothing and arms records relating to militia units in Ontario and Quebec, RG9-I-C-8, Vol. 18, LAC; Andrew McIntosh, manuscript, *Personal Recollections of the Fenian Raid, June 2, 1866, by One Who Was There,* MG29-E108, Vol. 1, LAC, p. 3; McCallum, p. 25.
28. *Booker Inquiry,* pp. 218, 223.
29. Somerville, p. 45.
30. Andrews, p. 166.
31. Somerville, p. 46.
32. Denison, *Soldiering in Canada,* p. 99; Peacocke to Napier, June 7, 1866, Frames 827–830, MRFR.
33. Thomas L. Newbigging, Cross-examination, *The Queen v. Robert B. Lynch,* DFUSCT, Roll 1.
34. Somerville, p. 48.
35. Somerville, p. 48.
36. Colin Frederick Read, "John Stoughton Dennis," DCB.
37. Denison, *Soldiering in Canada,* p. 33.
38. Regimental division records, *Map Military District 5,* RG9, I-C-8, Vol. 10.
39. Denison, *Soldiering in Canada,* p. 89.
40. Denison, ibid.
41. Andrews, p. 167.
42. Denison, *Soldiering in Canada,* p. 90.
43. Captain Macdonald, p. 38.
44. Captain Macdonald, p. 67.
45. Reid, p. 380.
46. Beatty [*ms*], LAC, p. 6.
47. John H. Thompson, *Jubilee History of Thorold Township and Town from the Time of the Red Man to the Present*, Thorold: Thorold and Beaverdams Historical Society, 1891, pp. 87–89; Beatty [*ms*], LAC, pp. 6–7.
48. Beatty [*ms*], LAC, p. 7.
49. *Dennis Inquiry,* p. 182.
50. Hew Strachan, *From Waterloo to Balaclava: Tactics, Technology, and the British Army 1815–1854,* Cambridge: Cambridge University Press, 1985, p. 85.
51. Beatty [*ms*], LAC, p. 7.
52. Beatty [*ms*], LAC, pp. 8–9.
53. Beatty [*ms*], LAC, pp. 17–18.
54. Beatty [*ms*], p. 18.

55. Larmour [Part 1], p. 124.
56. Larmour [Part 1], p. 124.
57. Thompson, p. 89.
58. Dennis to McMicken, telegram, June 1, 1866, MG26 A, Vol. 237, p. 103871 [Reel C1663], LAC.
59. Somerville, p. 50.
60. *Proceedings of a Board of Medical Officers to Inquire into the Nature of a Disability of Private George A. Mackenzie*, FRSR, Vol. 30, pp. 218–229.
61. *Booker Inquiry,* p. 226.
62. George A. Mackenzie, "What I Saw of the Fenian Raid," Hamilton *Spectator,* November 27, 1926. Fenian Raids Scrapbook, Hamilton Public Library.
63. *Booker Inquiry,* p. 199.
64. Mackenzie.
65. Somerville, p. 50.
66. Richard E. Ruggle, "Alfred Booker [Senior]," DCB.
67. Greenhous, p. 8.
68. George Mainer, "Alfred Booker," DCB.
69. Reid, p. 167.
70. Quoted in Greenhous, p. 33.
71. Mackenzie.
72. Somerville, p. 94.
73. Mackenzie.
74. Reid, p. 380; Beatty, *Fenian Raid 1866*, p. 18.
75. Mackenzie.
76. "Sheds New Light on Famous Battle with Fenian Raiders," Hamilton *Spectator,* June 2, 1936.
77. Booker's Statement, *Booker Inquiry,* p. 200.
78. Beatty, *The Fenian Raid 1866,* p. 17.
79. Beatty [*ms*], LAC, p. 19.
80. Beatty, *The Fenian Raid 1866,* p. 18.
81. Beatty [*ms*], LAC, p. 19.
82. Marguerite Van Die, *An Evangelical Mind: Nathanael Burwash and the Methodist Tradition in Canada, 1839–1918,* Montreal-Kingston: McGill-Queen's University Press, 1989, pp. 54–59.
83. *Biographical Notes* [*ms*], Nathanael Burwash Collection, Box 28, File 628, chapter vii, United Church Archives formerly at Victoria College (UCAVC) [hereinafter "Burwash Collection"].
84. Burwash Collection, Box 28, File 630, chapter x, p. 11, UCAVC.
85. John M'Clintock and Jame Strong, *Cyclopedia of Bibiblical, Theological, and Ecclesiastical Literature,* Supplement, Vol. II—CO–Z with Addenda—A–Z, New York: Harper & Brothers, 1887, p. 587.

86. David Inglis, *Righteousness Exalteth a Nation: A Thanksgiving Sermon,* Hamilton, C.W.: Printed at the "Spectator" Steam Press, Prince's Square, 1866, p. 2.

87. Duff Crerar, *Padres in No Man's Land: Canadian Chaplains and the Great War,* Montreal-Kingston: McGill-Queen's University Press, 1995, p. 4.

88. Burwash Collection, Box 28, File 630, chapter x, p. 11, UCAVC.

89. Field Marshal Viscount Wolseley, *A Soldier's Life,* Vol. 2, Toronto: The Book Supply Company Ltd, 1904, p. 157; Graves, p. 378; Somerville, p. 49.

90. Denison, *Soldiering in Canada,* p. 109.

91. Wolseley, p. 160.

92. Somerville, pp. 72–73.

93. Denison, *Soldiering in Canada,* pp. 90–91.

94. Peacocke, *Report*, June 4, 1866, in MRFR.

95. Denison, *Soldiering in Canada,* p. 88.

96. Peacocke, *Report,* p. 1.

97. Peacocke, *Report,* p. 1.

98. Peacocke, *Report*, June 4, 1866, in MRFR.

99. O'Neill, *Official Report,* p. 38.

100. Peacocke, *Report*, June 4, 1866, in MRFR.

101. *Booker Inquiry,* p. 200; Akers, *Report,* June 7, 1866, in MRFR.

102. See the excellent analysis of this issue in Reid, pp. 159–160.

103. Peacocke, *Report*, June 4, 1866, in MRFR.

104. Somerville, pp. 72–73.

105. Dennis, *Report,* June 4, 1866, in MRFR; Peacocke to Napier, June 6, 1866 [Frame 822], MRFR.

106. Larmour [Part 1], pp. 125–126.

107. *Dennis Inquiry,* pp. 256–257. A dispatch from Graham is inserted into the pages of the inquiry and is marked as June 1, 10 P.M.—probably written by Graham in the Fort Erie railway yard shortly before he was picked up by Larmour in the handcar. This accounts for the frequent citation of 10 P.M. as the time Graham and Dennis met, but the meeting actually must have occurred after midnight. It is also possible that the telegraph link between the Fort Erie railway yard and Port Colborne had been repaired and that the message was telegraphed to Dennis at 10 P.M.

108. Larmour [Part 1], p. 126.

109. Peacocke, *Report*, June 4, 1866, in MRFR.

110. Somerville, p. 94.

111. *Dennis Inquiry,* Letter from Graham to "Commandant at Port Colborne," inserted at p. 257.

112. *Dennis Inquiry,* William A. Rooth testimony, p. 256.

113. O'Neill, *Official Report,* p. 38.

114. Denison, *Fenian Raid* [*ms*] p. 20; Reid, p. 153.

115. O'Neill, *Official Report,* p. 39.

116. George Whale, testimony, Judge Wilson's Notes in *Queen v. John Quin*, DFUSCT.
117. Denison, *The Fenian Raid,* p. 60.
118. Denison, *The Fenian Raid* p. 62.
119. Somerville, p. 34.
120. Somerville, pp. 34–35.
121. Johnston, *Narrative*, p. 84.

SIX: MARCHING ORDERS, NIGHT, JUNE 1–2, 1866

1. *Booker Inquiry,* p. 200.
2. Somerville, p. 67; Denison, *Fenian Raid,* p. 25.
3. Peacocke to Napier, June 7, 1866, Frame 829, MRFR.
4. McCallum, p. 26.
5. Charles Clarke, telegram, June 2, 1866, p. 103878; Charles Clarke to McMicken, report, June 5, 1866, MG26 A, Vol. 237 [Reel C1663], p. 103940, LAC.
6. Larmour [Part 2], p. 228, on splicing into telegraph lines.
7. The worst-case scenario, if it is to be believed, was a crucial telegram from Peacocke received in Port Colborne at 5:20 A.M. but not delivered to Booker until 9:00 A.M. (see further below).
8. Peacocke, *Report*, June 4, 1866, Frame 812, MRFR. Chewett, p. 79, and Somerville, p. 63, also report 2 A.M.

   At Canada Archives, there is a conveniently printed version of officers' official reports, albeit with typographical errors (MG29 E74, File No. 2, Colonel Dennis, *Adjutant-General's Office: Official Reports,* June 21, 1866), which unfortunately Brian Reid used in his study (see Reid, p. 409 *n.* 55 [Reid also errs in citing E73 as the source—E74 is correct]). Peacocke is sometimes reported to have received the telegram at "10 P.M."—a typographical error in MG29 E74, as Booker had not arrived in Port Colborne until 11 P.M., and original copies from the Peacocke *Report* indicate "2 A.M."
9. Peacocke to Napier, June 7, 1866, Frame 829, MRFR.
10. Griffith, p. 124.
11. U.S. General George McClellan was an example of a "big-war science" general—a top-of-the-class graduate of West Point, a military engineer and surveyor, the inventor of the McClellan saddle, which is still used today by the mounted military and police, and a railway company president, prior to his appointment by Lincoln in 1861 as commander of the Army of the Potomac and general in chief of the U.S. Army.
12. Dennis, *Report,* June 4, 1866, in MRFR.
13. *Dennis Inquiry,* p. 343; Docker, p. 14.
14. McCallum to Macdonald, April 6, 1865, Adjutant General Letters Received 1865, RG9 IC1, Vol. 220, File 932, LAC (see Chapter 2).
15. Charles Clarke to McMicken, report, June 5, 1866, MG26 A, Vol. 237 [Reel C1663], p. 103940, LAC.
16. Larmour [Part 1], p. 126.

17. *Dennis Inquiry,* p. 216.
18. Booker, *Narrative* [undated], Courts Martial, Courts of Inquiry, 1856–1866, RG9 IC8, Vol. 6, pp. 4–5, LAC. There is a one-hour discrepancy in the intended entry time into Fort Erie between Akers (8 A.M.) and Booker (7 A.M.).
19. Griffith, p. 124.
20. Akers, *Report,* June 7, 1866, in MRFR.
21. *Dennis Inquiry,* p. 219.
22. Somerville, p. 68.
23. Denison, *Fenian Raid,* pp. 26–28; quoted extensively in Somerville, pp. 68–70.
24. Booker, *Narrative,* p. 6.
25. Peacocke to Napier, June 7, 1866, Frame 829, MRFR.
26. Beatty, *Fenian Raid 1866,* p. 21.
27. *Beatty* [*ms*], p. 21.
28. Booker, *Narrative,* p. 5.
29. Booker, *Narrative,* p. 6.
30. Akers, *Official Report,* Frame 838, MRFR. Akers writes "Dennis" instead of "Booker" because when the orders were issued to Akers, Booker had not yet relieved Dennis of his command.
31. Peacocke to Napier, June 7, 1866, Frames 827–830, MRFR.
32. *Dennis Inquiry,* pp. 216–217.
33. Denison, *Fenian Raid,* p. 28.
34. Peacocke to Napier, June 7, 1866, Frame 829, MRFR.
35. Peacocke to Napier, June 7, 1866, Frames 827–830, MRFR.
36. Peacocke, *Official Report,* Frame 812, MRFR.
37. Charles Clarke to McMicken, report, June 5, 1866, MG26 A, Vol. 237 [Reel C1663], p. 103940, LAC.
38. Somerville, p. 77.
39. Denison, *Fenian Raid,* p. 31.
40. *Globe,* November 9, 1870.
41. Booker, *Narrative,* p. 3.
42. Booker, *Narrative,* p. 6.
43. Somerville, p. 76.
44. Chambers, p. 61.
45. Somerville, p. 76.
46. Somerville, p. 77; *Hamilton Herald,* June 29, 1927.
47. Somerville, p. 77.
48. Map: "Road Lt. Col. Booker Should Have Taken," George Taylor Denison III fonds, MG29-E29, Vol. 43, File 1, LAC.
49. Denison, *Fenian Raid,* p. 24; see map in MG29-E29, Vol. 43, File No. 1, LAC.
50. Brian Reid, letter to editor, *The Reservist,* Vol. 16, No. 1 (Fall 1989).
51. See maps in Chewett, for example.

52. Peacocke to Napier, June 7, 1866, Frames 827–830, MRFR.
53. McCallum, p. 26.
54. Greenhous, p. 56.
55. See George A. Mackenzie; "Young Adventurer in '66 Tells Story of Raid," *Hamilton Herald,* June 27, 1927; "Shed New Light on Famous Battle with Fenian Raiders, Hamilton *Spectator,* June 2, 1936.
56. Ellis, p. 199.
57. Dr. Tempest to Gillmor, p. 76-A.
58. *Booker Inquiry*, pp. 218, 223.
59. Burwash Collection, Box 28, File 630, chapter x, p. 11, UCAVC.
60. Larmour [Part 1], p. 228; Johnston, *Narrative,* p. 84; Charles Clarke to McMicken, report, June 5, 1866, MG26 A, Volume 237 [Reel C1663], p. 103940, LAC.
61. *Illustrated Historical Album of the 2nd Battalion Queen's Own Rifles,* Toronto: Toronto News Company, 1894, p. 15.
62. Reid, p. 380.
63. Captain Macdonald, p. 58; "The Good Samaritan of Ridgeway," Hamilton *Spectator,* November 6, 1965; *Globe,* June 15, 1866.
64. *Booker Inquiry,* p. 202.
65. Johnston, *Narrative,* p. 84; see also, "Original Account Tells of Fenian Invasion," *Fort Erie Times Review,* November 12, 1980, p. 13.
66. Johnston, *Narrative,* p. 84.
67. Johnston, *Narrative,* p. 87.
68. Johnston, *Narrative,* p. 84.
69. Somerville, p. 80; McCallum, p. 27.
70. Booker, *Narrative,* p. 8.
71. Hamilton *Spectator,* June 2, 1936.
72. Greenhous, p. 58.
73. "Original Account Tells of Fenian Invasion," *Fort Erie Times Review,* November 12, 1980, p. 13.
74. *Booker Inquiry,* p. 202 [Booker, *Narrative,* p. 7]; *Hamilton Herald,* June 29, 1927; John A. Cooper, "The Fenian Raid 1866," *The Canadian Magazine,* Vol. 10, No. 1 (Nov. 1897), p. 50; Larmour [Part 2], p. 228; Greenhous, p. 57; Cruikshank, p. 33 [Reid argues that Booker carried ammunition with him on the wagon into the battle but bases this claim on a single remark in the testimony by Rev. Inglis—that he rode to the battle in an "ammunition waggon" (*Booker Inquiry,* p. 239)].
75. *Booker Inquiry,* pp. 218, 223, 229.
76. *Booker Inquiry,* p. 239.
77. Captain Macdonald, p. 64; *List of Medical Officers of Volunteer Militia,* September 26, 1866, Adjutant General's Office, Letters Sent 1847–1868, RG9 I-C-1, Vol. 290, LAC.
78. *Booker Inquiry,* p. 205.

79. *Booker Inquiry,* p. 221.
80. *Hamilton Herald,* June 29, 1927.
81. *Hamilton Herald,* June 29, 1927.
82. Hamilton *Spectator,* June 2, 1936.
83. N. Brewster, "Recollections of the Fenian Raid," *Welland County Historical Society Papers and Records,* Vol. 2, Welland, Canada: 1926.
84. Hamilton *Evening Times,* June 7, 1866.
85. *Booker Inquiry,* pp. 202–203; Somerville, p. 79.
86. *Booker Inquiry,* p. 224.
87. Somerville, p. 79; George A. Mackenzie, Hamilton *Spectator,* November 27, 1926.
88. *Booker Inquiry,* p. 242.
89. E.G.B. Reynolds, *Early Enfield Arms: The Muzzle Loaders,* Windsor, Berkshire: Profile Publications Ltd., 1972, p. 29; "Old English Rifles," *The Engineer,* August 20, 1886, London, http://www.researchpress.co.uk/firearms/history/oldenglish02.htm [retrieved June 22, 2009].
90. See Secretary of War, *Drill and Rifle Instruction for the Corps of Rifle Volunteers,* London: 1859, pp. 21–28; William Joseph Hardee, *Rifle and Light Infantry Tactics,* Vol. 2, Lesson 2, paragraphs 152–168, Philadelphia: J.B. Lippincott & Co., 1861; Berkley Lewis, *Small Arms and Ammunition in the U.S. Service,* Washington, DC: Smithsonian Institute, 1956 [1968 edition], p. 85.
91. Carl L. Davis, *Arming the Union: Small Arms in the Union Army,* Port Washington, NY: Kennikat Press, 1973, p. 135.
92. Griffith, pp. 84–86.
93. *Booker Inquiry,* p. 242.
94. Clothing and arms records relating to militia units in Ontario and Quebec, Stores and Ammunition, RG9-I-C-8, Vol. 18.
95. Thompson, pp. 87–89; Beatty [*ms*], LAC, pp. 6–7.
96. *Memorandum to Lt. Col Durie,* June 25, 1866; clothing and arms records relating to militia units in Ontario and Quebec, RG9-I-C-8, Vol. 18, LAC; McIntosh, p. 3; McCallum, p. 25.
97. Alexander Rose, *American Rifle: A Biography,* New York: Delacorte Press, 2008, pp. 129–131, 147–150.
98. Rose, p. 147.
99. Rose, p. 140.
100. *Memorandum to Lt. Col Durie,* June 25, 1866; clothing and arms records relating to militia units in Ontario and Quebec, RG9-I-C-8, Vol. 18, LAC.
101. *Memorandum to Lt. Col Durie,* June 25, 1866; McIntosh, p. 3; McCallum, p. 25.
102. William W. Greener, *The Gun and Its Development, 9th Edition,* Guilford, CT: Lyons Press, 2002, p. 633.
103. W.J. Hardee, *Rifle and Light Infantry Tactics for the Exercising and Manoeuvring of Troops,* Vol. 1, Lesson 4, Principle of the Double Quick Step, paragraph 117, 1855.

104. Somerville, p. 121.
105. *Booker Inquiry,* pp. 205, 221, 225.
106. Larmour [Part 2], p. 228.
107. Most sources for some reason claim "about two miles" and a one-hour march.
108. *Booker Inquiry,* p. 203.
109. Somerville, p. 95.
110. Hamilton *Spectator,* April 10, 1929.
111. Ellis, p. 200.
112. McIntosh, p. 3.
113. Somerville, p. 77.
114. Somerville, p. 72; Denison, *Fenian Raid,* p. 30.
115. Somerville quoting Armstrong, p. 93.
116. *Booker Inquiry,* p. 204.
117. Peacocke, *Report,* Frame 813; later he would claim "about 10" (see below).
118. *Booker Inquiry,* p. 204.
119. Peacocke to McMicken, June 19, 1866, MG26 A, Vol. 237, pp. 104166–104169 [Reel C1663], LAC.
120. Somerville, p. 94.
121. Somerville, p. 93; Denison, *Fenian Raid,* p. 43; Captain Macdonald, p. 48.

SEVEN: LIMESTONE RIDGE, MORNING, JUNE 2, 1866

1. *Booker Inquiry,* p. 235.
2. Somerville, p. 81.
3. Personal reconnaissance by the author; *Sketch of Field Limestone Ridge* enclosed in Durie to MacDougall, June 29, 1866, Frontier Service Reports 1865–1867, RG9 IC8, Vol. 8, LAC; see also maps in Denison, *Fenian Raid* (adopted later by both Queasly and Senior); map in Chewett, p. 96; in Somerville, p. 2; Captain Macdonald, pp. 49, 51; and maps in Reid, pp. 162, 169, 173, 174.
4. McLeod to Macdonald, June 6, 1866, MG26A, Vol. 57, p. 23126 [Reel C1508], LAC.
5. Reid, p. 162.
6. Griffith, pp. 145–150.
7. *Booker Inquiry,* p. 203.
8. *Booker Inquiry,* p. 219.
9. *Somerville,* p. 83.
10. Reid, p. 169.
11. A.G. Gilbert quoted in Chewett, p. 43.
12. Somerville, p. 83.
13. Gilbert quoted in Chewett, p. 43.
14. McIntosh, p. 3.
15. Hamilton *Spectator*, June 2, 1936.

16. Quoted in Greenhous, p. 60.
17. The Fenians carried an assortment of weapons but most commonly were armed with the 1863 Springfield .58-calibre percussion rifled musket—both weapon and ammunition were similar to what the Canadian troops were carrying, http://www.nlm.nih.gov/visibleproofs/galleries/technologies/patterns_image_4.html [retrieved June 22, 2009].
18. Greener, pp. 629–633.
19. http://www.nlm.nih.gov/visibleproofs/galleries/technologies/patterns_image_2.html [retrieved June 22, 2009].
20. https://www.grhsonline.org/File/CivilWarMedicineJuly2008.pdf [retrieved June 22, 2009].
21. Hague Declaration Concerning Expanding Bullets of July 29, 1899.
22. Ken Burns, "A Very Bloody Affair," *The Civil War,* Episode 2, Florentine Films–PBS, 1990.
23. McCallum, p. 27.
24. McIntosh, p. 3.
25. Chewett, p. 51; Dunn, p. 53.
26. *Booker Inquiry,* p. 220.
27. J.T.R. Stinson, "The Battle of Ridgeway, or Lime Ridge," *Journal of Education for Upper Canada*, Vol. 19, No. 6 (June 1866), p. 89.
28. Chewett, p. 47.
29. Captain Macdonald, p. 36.
30. George A. Mackenzie, Hamilton *Spectator,* Nov. 27, 1926.
31. Chewett, p. 51; McCallum, p. 28.
32. Inglis quoted in Chewett, p. 51.
33. McCallum, p. 28; Chewett, p. 51.
34. Burwash Collection, Box 28, File 630, chapter x, p. 15, UCAVC.
35. Burwash Collection, Box 28, File 630, chapter x, p. 15, UCAVC.
36. *Booker Inquiry,* p. 240.
37. While the regular permanent Canadian Army was not established until 1883, Canada's modern military in the form of its militia regiments, and for the purpose of "battle honours," dates back to the Militia Act of 1855.
38. *Booker Inquiry* pp. 223, 231.
39. Denison, *Fenian Raid,* p. iv.
40. Somerville, p. 85.
41. Chewett, p. 44; *Booker Inquiry,* pp. 203, 231.
42. *Booker Inquiry,* p. 215.
43. Somerville, p. 83.
44. *Nashville Press,* July 9, 1866, quoted in Somerville, p. 83.
45. O'Neill to Somerville, July 31, 1866, quoted in Somerville, p. 84.
46. Greenhous, p. 62.

47. Often referred to in histories as the "Albert Athoe farm and house," after the property's later owner.
48. *Booker Inquiry,* pp. 238, 227.
49. Griffith, p. 84.
50. *Booker Inquiry*, p. 226.
51. Mackenzie, Hamilton *Spectator,* November 27, 1926; *Hamilton Herald,* June 29, 1927.
52. Mackenzie, Hamilton *Spectator,* November 27, 1926.
53. McIntosh, p. 3.
54. Percy Routh, Compensation Application, November 2, 1866, FRSR, Vol. 30, pp. 175–176, LAC.
55. Burwash Collection, Box 28, File 630, chapter x, p. 12, UCAVC.
56. Percy Routh, Compensation Application, November 2, 1866, FRSR, p. 177, LAC.
57. Mackenzie, Hamilton *Spectator,* November 27, 1926.
58. Captain Macdonald, p. 57.
59. Percy Routh, Compensation Application, pp. 184–188.
60. Percy Routh, Compensation Application, pp. 184–188.
61. Hamilton *Evening Times,* June 2, 1866; *Globe,* June 4, 1866.
62. Percy Routh, Compensation Application, p. 174.
63. Mackenzie, Hamilton *Spectator,* November 27, 1926.
64. O'Neill, *Official Report,* p. 39.
65. Somerville, p. 85; *Booker Inquiry*, p. 226.
66. Somerville, p. 86.
67. *Booker Inquiry,* p. 228; Somerville, p. 86.
68. At the time of this writing in 2011, the house still stands on the corner of Bertie and Ridgeway roads, its north brick wall bearing golf ball–size craters (spang) from Minié ball hits.
69. O'Neill, *Official Report,* p. 39.
70. *Booker Inquiry,* pp. 203, 204, 210, 211, 236, 238; Arthur James Moody Tenny, Diary, June 2, 1866, Ridgeway Battle Museum, faxed copy, July 27, 1999, FEHM.
71. *Booker Inquiry,* p. 233.
72. Somerville, p. 86; Denison, *Fenian Raid,* p. 43.
73. *Booker Inquiry,* p. 208.
74. Ellis, p. 200.
75. *Booker Inquiry,* pp. 216, 235.
76. *Booker Inquiry,* pp. 216, 236.
77. Ellis, p. 201.
78. King, p. 141.
79. *The University College Literary & Scientific Society's Annual 1869,* Toronto: Henry Rowsell, 1869, p. 44.
80. *Trinity University Review,* 1902, p. 126.

81. *Trinity University Review,* 1902, p. 126; Junor, p. 87; King, p. 145, *n.* 1.
82. King, p. 144; J.O. Miller and F.B. Hodgins (eds), *The Year Book of the University of Toronto*, Toronto: Roswell & Hutchison, 1887, p. 92.
83. *Globe,* June 6, 1866.
84. Chambers, p. 150; King, p. 144; Junor, p. 87.
85. Ellis, pp. 200–201.
86. Ellis, pp. 200–201.
87. Ellis, pp. 200–201.
88. Somerville, p. 86.
89. Somerville, p. 86.
90. *Booker Inquiry,* p. 228.
91. *Booker Inquiry,* p. 233.
92. *Booker Inquiry,* pp. 220–221.
93. Somerville, p. 92.
94. *Booker Inquiry,* p. 223.
95. Booker, *Narrative,* pp. 11–12 [*Booker Inquiry,* p. 205].
96. A search for Somerville's notebooks proved futile and revealed previous equally futile searches by others, the last of which was by Yale University's Joseph Hamburger in 1962.
97. Somerville, p. 93.
98. *Booker Inquiry,* pp. 243–244.
99. J.T.R. Stinson, "The Battle of Ridgeway, or Lime Ridge," *Journal of Education for Upper Canada*, Vol. 19, No. 6 (June 1866), p. 89.
100. Christopher Alderson [Janet Alderson], Compensation Application, October 18, 1866, FRSR, Vol. 31, pp. 68–72, LAC.
101. *Booker Inquiry,* pp. 221–222.
102. William Smith [Rhoda Smith], Compensation Application, October 18, 1866, FRSR, Vol. 31, pp. 58–61, LAC.
103. *Booker Inquiry,* pp. 243–244.
104. *Booker Inquiry,* pp. 243–244.
105. *Booker Inquiry,* p. 228.
106. *Booker Inquiry,* pp. 220–221.
107. *Booker Inquiry,* p. 238.
108. *Booker Inquiry,* p. 211.
109. Booker, *Official Report,* Frame 848.
110. Gillmor to Napier, June 6, 1866, United Canada Subject Files, Frontier Service Reports, RG9 IC8, Vol. 9, pp. 2–3, LAC.
111. Arthur James Moody Tenny, Diary, June 2, 1866, Jacqueline Thoms to Ridgeway Battle Museum, fax, July 27, 1999, FEHM.
112. *Booker Inquiry,* p. 236.
113. Somerville, p. 91.

114. *Booker Inquiry,* p. 228.
115. *Booker Inquiry,* p. 212; Booker, *Report,* June 2, 1866, Frame 848, MRFR, LAC.
116. For comparison, the Russian AK-47 fires a 7.62 mm (.30-calibre) steel jacket round at 2,300 feet/second while the current standard U.S. rifle M4A1 fires a 5.56 mm (.233-calibre) round at 2,900 feet/second.
117. http://nmhm.washingtondc.museum/collections/archives/agalleries/civilwar/NCP3787.jpg [retrieved July 7, 2009].
118. James Stuart, Compensation Application, November 7, 1866, FRSR, Vol. 31, pp. 683–693, LAC.
119. John George Powell, Compensation Application, November 7, 1866, FRSR, Vol. 31, pp. 721–739, LAC.
120. Ibid., p. 738.
121. *Booker Inquiry,* p. 229.
122. Dunn, p. 54.
123. Captain Macdonald, p. 57.
124. Bertie Historical Society, *Battle of Ridgeway: Stories and Legends of the Fenian Raid,* June 1976, p. 1, mimeographed pamphlet in the collection of the Fort Erie Historical Museum, Ridgeway, Ontario.
125. *Globe,* June 15, 1866.
126. Mackenzie, Hamilton *Spectator,* November 27, 1926.
127. George Mackenzie, Compensation Application, November 7, 1866, FRSR, Vol. 30, p. 229, LAC.
128. George Mackenzie, Compensation Application, November 7, 1866, FRSR, Vol. 30, pp. 219–229, LAC.
129. Chewett, p. 76.
130. Francis Lackey, Compensation Application, November 23, 1866, FRSR, Vol. 30, pp. 50–56, LAC.
131. Chewett, p. 76.
132. Ellis, p. 201.
133. Ellis, p. 201.
134. Ibid., pp. 519–520.
135. Denison, *Fenian Raid,* pp. 69–70, quoted in Somerville, pp. 114–115; "Facts connected with the death of John Harriman Mewburn," June 16, 1866, Department of Justice, RG13, Vol. 15, File 656, LAC.
136. "The Good Samaritan of Ridgeway," Hamilton *Spectator,* November 6, 1965, p. 70; Chewett reports that Mewburn died of "exhaustion," or heatstroke, Chewett, p. 54.
137. Ellis, p. 201.
138. Ellis, p. 201.
139. Reid, p. 178.
140. *Booker Inquiry,* p. 236.
141. *Booker Inquiry,* p. 208.

142. *Booker Inquiry,* p. 217.
143. Forbes McHardy, Compensation Application, October 17, 1866, FRSR, Vol. 31, pp. 329–339, LAC.
144. Captain Macdonald, pp. 52–53.
145. O'Neill, *Official Report,* p. 39.
146. Griffith, p. 141.
147. Polybius, *Histories* II 29:6, Cambridge, MA: Harvard University Press, 1922; Julius Caesar, *War Commentaries of Caesar,* trans. Rex Warner, New York: New American Library, 1960, pp. 104–105, 137–38, 153–164; Gerhard Herm, *The Celts: The People Who Came Out of Darkness,* New York: St. Martin's Press, 1977, pp. 14–26; Barry Cunliffe, *The Celtic World,* London: The Bodley Head, 1979, p. 58; Grady McWhiney and Perry D. Jamieson, *Attack and Die: Civil War Tactics and the Southern Heritage,* Tuscaloosa, AL: University of Alabama Press, 1982, pp. 174–178.
148. Scian Dubh [James McCarroll], p. 206.
149. Dunn, p. 52.
150. Greenhous, p. 64.
151. *Booker Inquiry,* p. 210.
152. *Booker Inquiry,* p. 241.
153. Captain Macdonald, p. 55; FRSR, Vol. 30, pp. 272–282, LAC.
154. *Globe,* February 19, 1900.
155. *Booker Inquiry,* p. 214.
156. *Booker Inquiry,* p. 222.
157. Booker, *Narrative,* p. 13.
158. *Booker Inquiry,* pp. 213, 219.
159. Captain Macdonald, p. 56.
160. *Statement of Militia Pensions and Gratuities Awarded,* Receiver General's Department, Ottawa, February 1, 1967, FRSR, Vol. 32, LAC.
161. Brewster, pp. 75–76.
162. *Booker Inquiry,* p. 218.
163. Reel C-4300, Frame 352, MRFR, LAC.
164. Larmour to Brydges, June 2, 1866, telegram, Frame 360, MRFR, LAC.
165. C.P. Stacey, "A Fenian Interlude," p. 148; Larmour to Brydges, June 2, 1866, telegram, Frame 360, MRFR, LAC.
166. Reel C-4300, Frame 364, MRFR, LAC.
167. Reel C-4300, Frame 374, MRFR, LAC.
168. *Globe,* June 15, 1866.
169. Captain Macdonald, quoting Toronto *Leader* report, pp. 59–61.
170. Bertie Historical Society, p. 6.
171. Brewster, p. 76.
172. Brewster, p. 77.

173. Captain Macdonald, quoting Toronto *Leader* report, pp. 59–61.
174. Chewett, p. 54.
175. Mackenzie, *Hamilton Herald,* June 27, 1927.
176. Mackenzie, *Hamilton Herald,* June 27, 1927.
177. Somerville, p. 114.
178. Brewster, p. 79.
179. Denison, *The Fenian Raid,* pp. 63–64; also quoted in Somerville, p. 114.
180. Captain Macdonald, p. 54; *Globe,* June 4, 1966.
181. Petition of Mary Hannah Tempest, April 25, 1872, Deputy Minister of Militia, RG9 IIA1, Vol. 4, Docket 6532, LAC.
182. Captain Macdonald, quoting Toronto *Leader* report, pp. 59–61.
183. Captain Macdonald, pp. 52–53; *Statement of Militia Pensions and Gratuities Awarded*, Receiver General's Department, Ottawa, February 1, 1967, FRSR, Vol. 32, LAC.
184. Sherk, p. 61; Bertie Township Council Minutes, January 21, 1867, in Bertie Historical Society, p. 5.
185. Interview with Peter Simundson, Curator, Queen's Own Rifles Regimental Museum, September 17, 2009; Hamilton *Evening Times,* June 14, 1866.

EIGHT: THE STAND AT FORT ERIE, AFTERNOON, JUNE 2, 1866

1. Denison, *Soldiering in Canada,* pp. 53–55; Peacocke, *Report,* June 4, 1866.
2. Denison, *Soldiering in Canada,* p. 88.
3. Denison, *Soldiering in Canada,* p. 88.
4. Denison, *Soldiering in Canada,* p. 93.
5. Denison, *Soldiering in Canada,* p. 87.
6. Denison, *Soldiering in Canada,* p. 98.
7. Denison, *Soldiering in Canada,* p. 98.
8. Barlow Cumberland, "The Fenian Raid of 1866 and Events on the Frontier," *Royal Society of Canada Proceedings,* Vol. 4, Sec. 2 (1910), p. 91.
9. Denison, *Soldiering in Canada,* p. 99; Peacocke to Napier, June 7, 1866, Frames 827–830, MRFR.
10. Denison, *Fenian Raid,* p. 50.
11. Denison, *Fenian Raid,* p. 50.
12. Somerville, p. 75.
13. Peacocke, *Report,* June 4, 1866.
14. Peacocke, *Report,* June 4, 1866.
15. *Booker Inquiry,* p. 204; Booker, *Narrative.*
16. Peacocke, *Report,* June 4, 1866.
17. Denison, *Fenian Raid,* p. 50.
18. *Grand River Sachem,* June 20, 1866.
19. Cumberland, pp. 91–92.

20. Peacocke, *Report,* June 4, 1866.
21. Denison, *Soldiering in Canada,* p. 94.
22. Peacocke, *Report,* June 4, 1866.
23. Denison, *Soldiering in Canada,* pp. 93–94; Denison, *Fenian Raid,* p. 52; Cumberland, p. 93.
24. Denison, *Soldiering in Canada,* p. 94.
25. Denison, *Soldiering in Canada,* p. 94.
26. Denison, *Soldiering in Canada,* pp. 95–96.
27. Somerville, pp. 75–76; Chewett, pp. 61–62.
28. Denison, *Soldiering in Canada,* p. 100.
29. Denison, *Soldiering in Canada,* p. 101; see also *Dennis Inquiry,* pp. 164–168.
30. Denison, *Soldiering in Canada,* p. 101.
31. Denison, *Soldiering in Canada,* p. 101.
32. Denison, *Soldiering in Canada,* p. 102.
33. *House of Commons Debates,* November 21, 1867, Ottawa: R. Duhamel, 1967, pp. 110–116.
34. *Proceedings of the Court of Inquiry upon the Circumstances of the Engagement at Fort Erie on the 2nd of June 1866,* Adjutant General's Correspondence; Correspondence relating to complaints, courts martial and inquiries, RG9-I-C-8, Vol. 7, LAC [hereinafter "*Dennis Inquiry*"].
35. Brian A. Reid was the first historian to refer to the transcripts in his 2000 study of the Battle of Ridgeway, but he focused on Limestone Ridge and did not look into their contents in any detail or describe the battle at Fort Erie.
36. *Beatty* [*ms*], p. 21.
37. Beatty, *Fenian Raid 1866,* p. 20, lists a total of 79 men and officers by name. There are rampant variations: *Dennis Inquiry,* p. 7, Sergeant McCracken testified "54 men" in the Welland Battery; *Beatty* [*ms*], p. 20, cites 52 gunners and 18 marines; Brian Reid, p. 381, claims Naval Brigade of 43 men and 3 officers; Welland Battery cites 59 men and 3 officers; Dennis and Akers claim a total of 102 men and 8 officers; Captain Macdonald, p. 43, says 3 officers and 59 gunners and 3 officers and 43 marines, "total strength of the combatant forces 108 of all ranks"; *Dennis Inquiry,* [s.n.] Second Charge, states: "landing recklessly five officers and 68 men of the Welland Canal Field Battery and Dunnville Naval Brigade from the steamer *Robb* ..."; *Dennis Inquiry,* pp. 60–61: Naval Brigade lands 24 men"; Chewett, p. 88, cites Captain McCallum's report that 2 Naval Brigade and 13 Welland Battery remained aboard the *Robb.* There may be a discrepancy between the number of the Naval Brigade and that of the *Robb*'s crew, who might or might not have been included in the various counts.
38. *Dennis Inquiry,* p. 343; Docker, p. 14.
39. *Dennis Inquiry,* p. 182.
40. Strachan, pp. 85–86.
41. Dennis, *Report,* June 4, 1866, in MRFR; Peacocke to Napier, June 6, 1866, Frame 822, MRFR.

42. *Booker Inquiry,* p. 200.
43. Peacocke to Napier, June 5, 1866, Frame 826, MRFR.
44. *Beatty* [*ms*], p. 21; *Dennis Inquiry,* p. 46.
45. *Dennis Inquiry,* p. 5. (Several witnesses claim that the *Robb* arrived at Fort Erie at 5 A.M., but considering that the distance was over twenty miles by water, it is unlikely the *Robb* arrived so early.)
46. Dennis, *Report.*
47. Dennis, *Report.*
48. Beatty [*ms*], p. 21.
49. Beatty [*ms*], p. 21.
50. Beatty, p. 24.
51. *Dennis Inquiry,* p. 47.
52. *Dennis Inquiry,* pp. 5, 222.
53. *Dennis Inquiry,* p. 47.
54. *Dennis Inquiry,* pp. 221–222.
55. Beatty [*ms*], p. 22.
56. Macdonald testified that Dennis had a "spy glass," *Dennis Inquiry,* p. 47.
57. *Dennis Inquiry,* p. 48.
58. *Dennis Inquiry,* pp. 222–223, 338–339.
59. Dennis, *Report,* Frame 856, MRFR.
60. *Dennis Inquiry,* pp. 223–224.
61. *Dennis Inquiry,* p. 136.
62. Akers, *Report;* Dennis, *Report,* gives the time as 5:30, but that is probably too late.
63. Dennis, *Report,* Frame 857, MRFR.
64. Beatty, *The Fenian Raid 1866,* p. 25.
65. *Dennis Inquiry*, p. 339.
66. *Dennis Inquiry,* p. 143.
67. Dennis, *Report,* Frames 856–857, MRFR.
68. *Dennis Inquiry*, pp. 306–307.
69. Dennis, *Statement,* October 27, 1866, p. 1, *Dennis Inquiry* following p. 345 [hereinafter Dennis, *Statement*]; *Dennis Inquiry*, p. 306.
70. Cruikshank, p. 39.
71. *Dennis Inquiry,* p. 297.
72. *Dennis Inquiry,* p. 309.
73. *Dennis Inquiry,* p. 333.
74. *Dennis Inquiry,* pp. 224–225.
75. *Dennis Inquiry,* pp. 6, 25, 42, 65, 212.
76. *Dennis Inquiry,* p. 299.
77. *Dennis Inquiry,* p. 6.
78. *Dennis Inquiry,* pp. 6, 65, 212.

79. *Dennis Inquiry,* p. 65.
80. *Dennis Inquiry,* p. 189.
81. *Dennis Inquiry,* p. 298.
82. *Dennis Inquiry,* p. 7.
83. *Dennis Inquiry,* p. 306.
84. *Dennis Statement,* p. 2.
85. Dennis, *Report,* Frames 856–860, MRFR.
86. Dennis, *Report,* Frames 856–860, MRFR.
87. *Dennis Inquiry,* p. 109.
88. *Dennis Inquiry,* pp. 6–7, 65.
89. *Dennis Inquiry,* pp. 65, 108.
90. *Dennis Inquiry*, p. 37.
91. *Dennis Inquiry,* p. 80.
92. *Dennis Inquiry,* pp. 65, 108, 124, 134, 139, 140.
93. *Dennis Inquiry,* pp. 62, 111–112, 117, 141.
94. *Dennis Inquiry,* pp. 65, 112, 116.
95. *Dennis Inquiry,* p. 199.
96. *Dennis Inquiry,* pp. 7, 22, 65, 110, 122, 134, 183.
97. *Dennis Inquiry,* p. 112.
98. *Dennis Inquiry,* p. 87.
99. *Dennis Statement,* p. 4.
100. *Dennis Statement,* pp. 5–6.
101. *Dennis Inquiry,* p. 162.
102. *Dennis Inquiry,* pp. 172–173.
103. *Dennis Inquiry*, p. 113.
104. *Dennis Inquiry*, pp. 125, 189.
105. *Dennis Inquiry,* p. 174.
106. *Dennis Inquiry,* p. 209.
107. Beatty, *The Fenian Raid 1866*, p. 30.
108. *Dennis Inquiry,* p. 136.
109. *Dennis Inquiry,* pp. 49, 112, 312.
110. *Dennis Inquiry*, pp. 20, 50–51, 52, 80–81, 113, 170.
111. *Dennis Inquiry*, p. 250.
112. *Dennis Inquiry,* pp. 8, 22, 39, 50, 70, 80, 156.
113. *Dennis Inquiry,* p. 8.
114. *Dennis Inquiry*, pp. 15, 78, 87, 156, 188.
115. Beatty [*ms*], p. 23; Beatty, *The Fenian Raid 1866*, p. 27.
116. *Dennis Inquiry,* pp. 8, 159.
117. *Dennis Inquiry*, p. 9.

118. *Dennis Inquiry,* pp. 81, 88, 132.
119. *Dennis Inquiry,* pp. 88, 91.
120. *Dennis Inquiry,* p. 101.
121. *Dennis Inquiry,* pp. 9, 57, 97, 275, 314.
122. *Dennis Inquiry,* pp. 9, 51, 66, 106, 186.
123. *Dennis Inquiry,* p. 101.
124. *Dennis Inquiry,* pp. 20, 28, 34, 42, 66, 82, 101, 106, 114, 118, 129, 150, 164.
125. Dennis, *Report,* Frames 857–858; *Dennis Statement,* pp. 6–8.
126. *Dennis Inquiry,* pp. 68, 76, 100, 130, 186.
127. *Dennis Inquiry,* pp. 10, 23, 52, 67, 132, 145, 150, 163.
128. *Dennis Inquiry,* p. 150.
129. *Dennis Inquiry*, p. 71.
130. *Dennis Inquiry*, pp. 116, 131, 137, 142, 145–146, 164, 175; Beatty [*ms*], p. 30.
131. *Dennis Inquiry,* p. 175.
132. *Dennis Inquiry*, pp. 10, 34, 52, 142.
133. *Dennis Inquiry*, p. 174; Denison, *Fenian Raid,* p. 62.
134. Geo. H. Stowits, *History of the One Hundredth Regiment of New York State Volunteers,* Buffalo: Matthews & Warren, 1870, p. 370.
135. Albert W. Reavley, "Personal Experience in the Fenian Raid," *Welland County Historical Society Papers and Records,* Vol. 2, Welland, Canada: 1926, p. 70; Owen, p. 81.
136. *Dennis Inquiry*, pp. 105, 109, 114, 145, 189.
137. *Dennis Inquiry*, pp. 114–115, 174.
138. Fergus Scholfield, Medical Board Report, November 9, 1866, FRSR, Vol. 30, pp. 247–257, LAC.
139. *Dennis Inquiry*, pp. 88, 114, 129, 150, 169.
140. *Dennis Inquiry*, p. 153.
141. McMicken to Macdonald, June 23, 1866, MG26 A, Vol. 237, pp. 104189–104190 [Reel C1663], LAC.
142. Griffith, pp. 144–145.
143. Denison, *Fenian Raid,* p. 61.
144. *Dennis Inquiry,* p. 175.
145. *Dennis Inquiry,* p. 268.
146. Rbt. Jordan Thomas, Medical Board Report, November 8, 1866, FRSR, Vol. 30, pp. 817–831, LAC.
147. *Dennis Inquiry,* pp. 276–277.
148. *Dennis Inquiry,* p. 331.
149. *Dennis Inquiry,* pp. 315–317, 327, 330.
150. *Dennis Inquiry,* p. 90.
151. *Dennis Inquiry,* p. 144.

152. *Senator's War Tug* [*circa* 1890s], photocopy of unidentified, undated newspaper clipping originally from an Ontario Archives scrapbook, "Edwin Hilder—Ridgeway Battlefield Museum" File, FEHM.
153. Captain Macdonald, p. 75.
154. *Senator's War Tug.*
155. Captain Macdonald, p. 75.
156. *Dennis Inquiry,* p. 147.
157. Dennis, *Fenian Raid,* p. 61.
158. Captain Macdonald, pp. 72, 76.
159. Beatty, *The Fenian Raid 1866,* p. 28.
160. Beatty [*ms*], p. 30 (the six men were Gunners James H. Boyle, Isaac Dickerson, William H. Clarke, Charles Campbell, Isaac Pew, and Sergeant Major Richard Boyle).
161. Macdonald, p. 75.
162. Beatty [*ms*], p. 31.
163. Dennis, *Fenian Raid,* p. 61.
164. Beatty, *The Fenian Raid 1866,* p. 29.
165. Macdonald, p. 75.
166. Beatty, *The Fenian Raid 1866,* p. 29.
167. Beatty [*ms*], p. 31.
168. Beatty, *The Fenian Raid 1866,* p. 30.
169. Captain Macdonald, p. 73.
170. John Bradley, Medical Board Report, November 9, 1866, FRSR, Vol. 30, pp. 259–270, LAC.
171. Beatty, *The Fenian Raid 1866,* p. 28.
172. Beatty, *The Fenian Raid 1866,* p. 31.
173. Beatty [*ms*], p. 31.
174. McCallum, *Report,* Frame 862, MRFR.
175. Beatty, *The Fenian Raid 1866,* p. 32.
176. Reavley, p. 72.
177. Beatty, *The Fenian Raid 1866,* p. 32.
178. Beatty [*ms*], p. 31.
179. *Dennis Inquiry,* p. 317.
180. *Dennis Inquiry,* p. 321.
181. *Dennis Inquiry,* p. 331.
182. *Dennis Inquiry,* p. 329.
183. Denison, *Soldiering in Canada,* p. 101.
184. H.W. Hemans to Lord Monck, telegram, June 3, 1866, in [s.n.] *Correspondence Relating to the Fenian Invasion and Rebellion of the Southern States,* Ottawa: 1869, p. 142; also Colonel Lowry, *Report*, June 4, 1866, Miscellaneous Records

Relating to the Fenian Raids, British Military and Naval Records "C" Series, RG8-1, Vol. 1672, LAC Microfilm Reel C-4300, Frame 282, MRFR, LAC.

185. Beatty [*ms*], p. 32.
186. Beatty [*ms*], pp. 31–32.

PART 3

1. Major Charles Coote Grant quoted in G.C. Duggan, "The Fenians in Canada: A British Officer's Impression," *The Irish Sword* (Winter 1967); T.J. Barrow, V.A. French, & J. Seabrook (eds), *The Story of the Bedfordshire and Hertfordshire Regiment,* Vol. 2, History Committee of the Royal Anglian Regiment, circa 1988. Courtesy of Steve Fuller, www.bedfordregiment.org.uk.

NINE: BOOKER'S RUN, JUNE–JULY 1866

1. Booker, *Narrative,* p. 14.
2. *Booker Inquiry,* p. 210.
3. Booker, *Official Report,* Frame 848.
4. Gillmor to Napier, June 6, 1866, p. 2.
5. Gray to Napier, June 19, 1866, United Canada Subject Files, Frontier Service Reports, RG9 IC8, Vol. 9, p. 5, LAC.
6. Gray to Napier, June 19, 1866, p. 6.
7. Akers, *Official Report,* pp. 843–844.
8. Booker, *Narrative,* p. 15.
9. Somerville, p. 102.
10. *The Canadian Independent,* Vol. 13, No. 1 (July 1866), p. 61.
11. Gray to Napier, June 19, 1866, p. 11.
12. Booker, *Narrative,* p. 15.
13. "Gross Insult to the 13th Battalion," letter to the editor, Hamilton *Evening Times,* June 6, 1866; "Another Letter from Rev. Mr. Inglis," letter to the editor, Hamilton *Spectator,* June 6, 1866, pp. 2–3.
14. Booker, *Narrative,* p. 15.
15. Stinson, p. 90.
16. Sherk, p. 61; Bertie Township Council Minutes, January 21, 1867, in Bertie Historical Society, p. 5.
17. "A Hint to Owners of Fenian Trophies," Hamilton *Evening Times,* June 5, 1866.
18. "A Queer Idea About Parole," Hamilton *Evening Times,* June 5, 1866.
19. "A Friendly Way of 'Managing Matters,'" Hamilton *Evening Times,* June 4, 1866.
20. Percy Routh, Compensation Application, p. 186.
21. Percy Routh, Compensation Application, p. 188.
22. *Globe,* June 16, 1866.

23. Adam H. Wright, "The Stirring Commencement Period of 1866—Dr Adam Wright tells of Ridgeway and the University Company," *University of Toronto Monthly,* Vol. 21, No. 9, (June 1921), pp. 395–396.
24. *Globe,* June 4, 1866.
25. Chewett, p. 71.
26. Chewett, p. 71.
27. Chewett, p. 71.
28. King, pp. 146–147.
29. *Trinity University Review,* 1902, p. 126; Junor, p. 87 (academic duties); King, p. 144; J.O. Miller and F.B. Hodgins (eds), p. 92; *Globe,* June 6, 1866 (ordered to remain behind for service in Toronto).
30. A.J. Christie, June 6, 1866, collection of Queen's Own Rifles Regimental Museum.
31. *Graves of Fenian Raid KIA,* collection of Queen's Own Rifles Regimental Museum.
32. *Funeral Procession of the Toronto Volunteers Who Fell in Action Saturday, June 2nd,* collection of Queen's Own Rifles Regimental Museum; *Globe,* June 6, 1866, p. 2.
33. Interview with Peter Simundson, Curator, Queen's Own Rifles Regimental Museum, September 17, 2009; *Hamilton Evening Times,* June 14, 1866.
34. *Hamilton Evening Times,* June 14, 1866.
35. Somerville, p. 111.
36. Hamilton *Spectator,* June 6, 1866.
37. Somerville, p. vii.
38. Hamilton *Spectator,* June 6, 1866.
39. Elizabeth Waterston, "Alexander Somerville: Whistler at the Plough," *International Review of Scottish Studies,* Vol. 12 (1982), p. 100.
40. *The New York Times,* June 20, 1885.
41. *Globe,* June 18, 1885.
42. Alexander Somerville, *The Autobiography of a Working Man,* Manchester: Ainsworth, 1848.
43. W.M. Sandison, "Alexander Somerville," *The Border Magazine,* Vol. 18, No. 207 (March 1913), pp. 49–55.
44. Waterston, p. 101.
45. *The Spirit of Toryism Exemplified in the Brutal Conduct Exhibited Towards Alexander Sommerville* [*sic*] *of the Scots Greys,* Glasgow: Muir, Gowans & Co., 1832.
46. *Hansard,* HC Debates, August 8, 1832, Vol. 14, cc1241–1242, http://hansard.millbanksystems.com/commons/1832/aug/08/case-of-alexander-somerville [retrieved September 14, 2009].
47. Hew Strachan, *The Reform of the British Army, 1830–54,* Manchester: Manchester University Press, 1984, pp. 80–82; Sandison, p. 50.
48. Waterston, p. 102; Sandison, p. 54.

49. Edward M. Brett, *The British Auxiliary Legion in the First Carlist War,* Dublin: Four Courts Press, 2005.
50. Alexander Somerville, *History of the British Legion and the War in Spain,* London: James Pattie, 1839.
51. Waterston, p. 103.
52. Waterston, p. 103.
53. Clipping File (CF)–Biography: Alexander Somerville, *Hamilton Public Library.*
54. Somerville, p. iv.
55. Waterston, pp. 102–103.
56. Waterston, pp. 103–105.
57. Alexander Somerville, "Travels in Canada West," *The Southern Cross,* March 22, 1861, p. 6.
58. Somerville to Buchanan, January 1, 1864, Buchanan Papers, Frame 04404-04408, courtesy of Elaine Brown.
59. Somerville photographs 1871 and 1884 in Sandison, p. 51 [n. pag.].
60. Hamilton *Evening Times,* Hamilton, June 4, 1866.
61. McMicken to Macdonald, June 16, 1866, MG26 A, Vol. 237, p. 104146 [Reel C1663], LAC.
62. Hamilton *Spectator,* June 6, 1866.
63. Somerville, p. vi.
64. Somerville, *Memorandum,* April 14, 1868, Deputy Minister of Militia, RG9 IIA1, File 501, p. 3, LAC.
65. Somerville, p. iv.
66. Hamilton *Evening Times,* June 5, 1866.
67. Somerville, pp. 118–119.
68. See, for example, Hamilton *Evening Times,* "Conduct of Colonel Booker Before the Enemy," June 6, 1866; "Field Equipments: Booker," Hamilton *Evening Times,* June 13, 1866; *St. Catharines Constitutional,* "Booker's Defense," June 14, 1866; *Daily Telegraph,* June 26, 1866.
69. Hamilton *Evening Times,* June 7, 1866.
70. Reprinted in the *Globe,* June 18, 1866.
71. Hamilton *Evening Times,* June 16, 1866.
72. Hamilton *Evening Times,* "Supplies for the Thirteenth," June 8, 1866.
73. McMicken to Macdonald, June 16, 1866, MG26 A, Vol. 237, p. 104146 [Reel C1663], LAC.
74. McMicken to Macdonald, June 23, 1866, MG26 A, Vol. 237, pp. 104189–104190 [Reel C1663], LAC.
75. McMicken to Macdonald, June 23, 1866.
76. MacDougall to Denison, Ottawa, June 26, 1866, United Canada Subject Files, Courts Martial, Courts of Inquiry 1856–1866, RG9-IC8, Vol. 6, LAC.
77. Hamilton *Evening Times,* Hamilton, July 28, 1866.

78. Hamilton *Evening Times,* July 3, 1866; Denison to unknown, Toronto, June 2, 1866, United Canada Subject Files, Courts Martial, Courts of Inquiry 1856–1866, RG9-IC8, Vol. 6, LAC.
79. Lowry to MacDougall, June 18, 1866, United Canada Subject Files, Frontier Service Reports, RG9 IC8, Vol. 9, LAC.
80. *Booker Inquiry,* p. 197.
81. Hamilton *Evening Times,* July 6, 1866.
82. Somerville, *Memorandum,* p. 6.
83. Somerville, *Memorandum,* pp. 1–8.
84. Hamilton *Evening Times,* July 27, 1866.
85. *Booker Inquiry,* pp. 241–246.
86. Somerville, p. 97.
87. Hamilton *Evening Times,* July 27, 1866.
88. Hamilton *Spectator,* August 9, 1866.
89. Denison, *Fenian Raid,* p. 43.
90. Denison, *Fenian Raid,* p. 45.
91. Somerville, *Memorandum,* p. 2.
92. Somerville, pp. 118–128.
93. Somerville, *Memorandum,* pp. 1–2.
94. Hamilton *Evening Times,* August 1, 1866.
95. *Globe,* August 14, 1866.
96. Hamilton *Evening Times,* August 2, 1866.
97. Somerville, *Memorandum,* p. 5.
98. Somerville, p. 93.
99. *Grand River Sachem,* September 5, 1866.
100. George A. Mackenzie, Hamilton *Spectator,* November 27, 1926.
101. Somerville, *Memorandum,* p. 1.
102. Somerville, *Memorandum,* pp. 5–6.
103. Somerville, *Memorandum,* p. 7.
104. Somerville, *Memorandum,* p. 1.
105. Somerville, *Memorandum,* p. 8.
106. Somerville, *Memorandum,* p. 1.
107. *Globe,* July 4, 1870.
108. *Globe,* November 9, 1870.
109. Denison, *Fenian Raid,* p. 31.
110. *Globe,* November 9, 1870.
111. *The Volunteer Review and Military and Naval Gazette,* Vol. 5, No. 40 (Oct. 2, 1871), pp. 6–7.
112. T.P. Slattery, "Patrick James Whelan," DCB.
113. Sandison, p. 52.

114. Sandison, pp. 52–53.
115. Somerville to Macdonald, March 9/Feb. 24, 1868, Deputy Minister Dockets, RG9 IIA1, Docket 299, LAC.
116. *Toronto City Directory,* 1875–1885.
117. Waterston, pp. 110–111.
118. Sandison, pp. 54–55.
119. Joseph Hamburger to Mrs. Harvey Ackley, January 30, 1963, courtesy of Elaine Brown at bhsg_gen@yahoo.ca

TEN: THE DENNIS INQUIRY, AUGUST–DECEMBER 1866

1. Senior, *The Last Invasion,* p. 101.
2. Lists of Fenian names and destinations can be found in War Department Reports 1863–1872, Division of the Atlantic, Department of the East, RG 393: Records of the U.S. Army Continental Commands, 1817–1940, Inventory Identifier 1428, National Archives Building, Washington, DC (NARA).
3. Senior, *The Last Invasion,* p. 97.
4. Chewett, pp. 36–37.
5. Frank J. Keen, "Anchor, Jeep and Wings," Hamilton *Spectator,* January 4, 1957.
6. Simcoe Kerr, June 8, 1866, Adjutant-General's Office Letters Received, RG9 IC1, Vol. 272, File 910, LAC.
7. Simcoe Kerr, June 8, 1866.
8. Somerville, p. 40.
9. Senior, *The Last Invasion,* p. 111.
10. Captain Macdonald, p. 110.
11. Senior, *The Last Invasion,* pp. 123–126.
12. Senior, *The Last Invasion,* p. 126.
13. *Globe,* June 15, 1866.
14. Lowry to MacDougall, June 18, 1866, United Canada Subject Files, Frontier Service Reports, RG9 IC8, Vol. 9, LAC.
15. McCallum errs in his time of the battle, which occurred closer to between 4 and 6 P.M.
16. McCallum, *Official Report.*
17. McCallum to McDougall, June 28, 1866: Adjutant General's Correspondence; Correspondence relating to complaints, courts martial and inquiries, RG9-I-C-8, Vol. 7, LAC.
18. *The New York Times,* July 4, 1866.
19. Dennis to Durie, July 17, 1866, Adjutant General's Correspondence; Correspondence relating to complaints, courts martial and inquiries, RG9-I-C-8, Vol. 7, LAC.
20. [Michel] to MacDougall, August 16, 1866, Adjutant General's Correspondence; Correspondence relating to complaints, courts martial and inquiries, RG9-I-C-8, Vol. 7, LAC.

21. *Globe,* August 11, 1866.
22. *Globe,* August 11, 1866.
23. *Globe,* August 11, 1866.
24. *Globe,* August 11, 1866.
25. Dennis to Durie, August 15, 1866, Adjutant General's Correspondence; Correspondence relating to complaints, courts martial and inquiries, RG9-I-C-8, Vol. 7, LAC.
26. Dennis to Durie, August 15, 1866.
27. Dennis to Durie, August 15, 1866.
28. King to MacDougall, August 22, 1866, Adjutant General's Correspondence; Correspondence relating to complaints, courts martial and inquiries, RG9-I-C-8, Vol. 7, LAC.
29. King to MacDougall, August 22, 1866.
30. Denison, *Soldiering in Canada,* p. 89.
31. Denison, *Soldiering in Canada,* p. 108.
32. Denison, *Soldiering in Canada,* pp. 108–109; Denison, *The Fenian Raid,* pp. 49–56.
33. Denison, *Soldiering in Canada,* p. 109.
34. *Dennis Inquiry,* p. 2.
35. "Charges," *Dennis Inquiry,* following p. 3.
36. *Irish Canadian,* November 9, 1866.
37. *Dennis Inquiry,* pp. 164–168.
38. *Dennis Inquiry,* pp. 286–288.
39. *Dennis Inquiry,* pp. 342–356.
40. *Dennis Inquiry,* pp. 355–356.
41. *Globe,* December 17, 1866.
42. *House of Commons Debates,* November 21, 1867, Ottawa: R. Duhamel, 1967, pp. 110–116.
43. *The New York Times,* December 28, 1869.
44. Colin Read, "The Red River Rebellion and J.S. Dennis, 'Lieutenant and Conservator of the Peace,'" *Manitoba History,* No. 3 (1982), http://www.mhs.mb.ca/docs/mb_history/03/dennis_js.shtml [retrieved Sept. 25, 2009].
45. *An account of P.G. Laurie's Experiences During the Rebellion by Mrs. J. H. Storer*, n.d., p. 12, MG3 B16-2, Patrick Gammie Laurie Papers, Public Archives of Manitoba. Quoted in Read.
46. Read, "John Stoughton Dennis," DCB.
47. Berger, p. 22.
48. Berger, p. 18.
49. Gagan, pp. 56–57.
50. Knowles, DCB.
51. Robson Black, "A Dollar and Costs," *Canada Monthly,* Vol. 14, No. 4 (August

1913); George T. Denison, *Recollections of a Police Magistrate,* Toronto: Musson Co., 1920, pp. v, 7–8.

52. Henry M. Wodson, *The Whirlpool: Scenes from Toronto Police Court,* Toronto: 1917, pp. 28–29. (The arithmetic of Denison's claim casts some doubt on his assertions. Assuming Denison sat for fifty 5-day weeks a year = 250 days [11,000 court days over 44 years] x 2 hours per day = 22,000 hours = 1.32 million minutes/650,000 cases = 2 minutes average per case.)
53. Denison, *Recollections of a Police Magistrate,* p. 9.
54. Denison, *Recollections of a Police Magistrate,* p. 12.
55. Gene Howard Homel, "Denison's Court: Criminal Justice and the Police Court in Toronto, 1877–1921," *Ontario History,* LXXIII, No. 3 (September 1981), p. 174.
56. Quoted in Berger, p. 18.
57. *Dearborn Independent,* December 27, 1919, clipping in George Taylor Denison III fonds, MG29-E29, Scrapbook, 1909–1925, LAC.
58. *Canadian Courier,* November 7, 1912, clipping in George Taylor Denison III fonds, MG29-E29, Scrapbook, 1909–1925, LAC.
59. Denison, *Soldiering in Canada,* p. 117.
60. R. Blake Brown, "'Stars and Shamrocks Will Be Sown': The Fenian State Trials, 1866–67" in Barry Wright and Susan S. Binnie (eds), *Canadian State Trials, Volume III: Political Trials and Security Measures, 1840–1914*, Toronto: University of Toronto Press and the Osgoode Society, 2009, pp. 35–84.
61. George R. Gregg and E.P. Roden, *Trials of the Fenian Prisoners at Toronto,* Toronto: Leader Steam-Press, 1867. For the most recent account of the trials, see R. Blake Brown, pp. 35–84; and David Wilson in *Canadian State Trials, Volume III.*
62. Bruce to Monck, June 11, 1866, FO, 5/1338, cited in Jenkins, *Anglo-American Relations,* p. 162.
63. Bruce to F.O., A Files 157, cited in Ó Broin, p. 69.
64. Neidhardt, pp. 107–108.
65. David A. Wilson, "State Security, Civil Liberty and the Fenians in Canada," 2008 Irish Studies Symposium, http://www.lac-bac.gc.ca/ireland/033001-1001.01.1-e.html [retrieved July 11, 2010].
66. D'Arcy, p. 407.
67. D'Arcy, p. 408.
68. *The New York Times,* May 6; May 19, 1900.
69. Brigittine M. French, "'We're All Irish': Transforming Irish Identity in a Midwestern Community," *New Hibernia Review/Iris Éireannach Nua,* Vol. 11, No. 1 (Spring/Earrach 2007), pp. 9–24; John Kay and Mary Findlay, *Nebraska Historic Buildings Survey: Reconnaissance Survey Final Report of Holt County, Nebraska,* Nebraska State Historical Society—State Historic Preservation Office, June 1, 1988, p. 11, http://www.cityofoneill.com/history.htm [retrieved July 11, 2010].
70. http://en.wikipedia.org/wiki/O'Neill,_Nebraska [retrieved March 31, 2011].

71. C.P. Stacey, "John O'Neill," DCB.
72. *Unveiling of Monument to General John O'Neill,* http://www.geocities.com/CapitolHill/Lobby/8151/oneill.html [accessed April 9, 2008].
73. *Statement of Militia Pensions and Gratuities Awarded*, Receiver General's Department, Ottawa, February 1, 1967, FRSR, Vol. 32, LAC.
74. *Statement of Militia Pensions and Gratuities Awarded*, Receiver General's Department, Ottawa, February 1, 1967, FRSR, Vol. 32, LAC; for dollar value, see: James Powell, *History of the Canadian Dollar,* Ottawa: Bank of Canada, 2005, Appendix A, p. 88.
75. *List of Pensions, Gratuities and Amounts for Medical Services*, Department of Militia and Defence, June 21, 1868, FRSR, Vol. 32, LAC.

ELEVEN: RIDGEWAY FORGOTTEN, 1867–1890

1. David Inglis, *Righteousness Exalteth a Nation: A Thanksgiving Sermon,* Hamilton, C.W.: Printed at the "Spectator" Steam Press, Prince's Square, 1866, p. 2.
2. Inglis, pp. 3–14.
3. Burwash Collection, Box 28, File 630, chapter x, p. 15, UCAVC.
4. R. Blake Brown, "'Stars and Shamrocks Will Be Sown': The Fenian State Trials, 1866–67" in Barry Wright and Susan S. Binnie (eds), *Canadian State Trials, Volume III: Political Trials and Security Measures, 1840–1914,* Toronto: University of Toronto Press and the Osgoode Society, 2009, pp. 35–84.
5. Paul Romney, *Mr. Attorney: The Attorney-General for Ontario in Court, Cabinet and Legislature, 1791–1899,* Toronto: The Osgoode Society, 1986, pp. 228–229.
6. *Globe,* June 15, 1866.
7. See case files in Justice Department, RG13, Vol. 15, LAC, and Sherk, p. 63; *Irish Canadian,* June 6, 13, 1866; Hamilton *Evening Times,* June 6, 11, 1866; *St. Catharines Constitutional,* June 14, 1866.
8. Sherk, p. 63.
9. *Irish Canadian,* June 6, 1866.
10. *Irish Canadian,* June 13, 1866.
11. Hamilton *Evening Times,* June 11, 1866.
12. Hamilton *Evening Times,* June 6, 1866.
13. *St. Catharines Constitutional,* June 14, 1866.
14. Macdonald to McNabb, June 14, 1866, MG29A, Vol. 56, Roll C1507, Frame 23192, LAC.
15. Walter Laquer, *A History of Terrorism,* New York: Little Brown, 1997 [Transaction Publishers, 2001], p. 63.
16. Brian Jenkins, *The Fenian Problem: Insurgency and Terrorism in a Liberal State,* Montreal-Kingston: McGill-Queen's University Press, 2008, p. 3, citing Steven Marcus, *Engels, Manchester and the Working Class,* New York: Norton, 1974, p. 90.
17. Macdonald, circular, June 21, 1866, Department of Justice, Numbered Central Registry Files, RG13, Vol. 15, No. 667, LAC.

18. Macdonald to R. Macdonald, September 29, 1866, MG26A, Vol. 513, pp. 188–189, LAC.
19. McGowan, *The Waning of the Green.*
20. Police Department of the City of Toronto, *Description of Fenian Prisoners,* June 9, 1866, Department of Justice, Numbered Central Registry Files, RG-13-A2, Vol. 15, LAC.
21. Ernest Chambers in his history of the QOR omits Muir's name from the wounded. See p. 63.
22. *Booker Inquiry,* p. 214; Paul Green, "Alexander Muir," DCB.
23. Alexander Muir, Compensation Application, October 22, 1866, FRSR, Vol. 31, pp. 534–536, LAC.
24. www.maplecottage.ca [no longer active as of 2002]. See http://web.archive.org/web/20010305012323/www.maplecottage.ca/orangeism.html [retrieved July 11, 2010].
25. Ministry of Tourism, Culture and Recreation, Conservation Review Board, *Re: City of Toronto–Intention to Designate 62 Laing Street (Maple Cottage),* December 16, 1991, http://www.crb.gov.on.ca/stellent/idcplg/webdav/Contribution%20Folders/crb/english/toronto_laing62.pdf [retrieved July 11, 2010].
26. John Ross Robertson, *Landmarks of Toronto*, Series 6, Toronto: J. Ross Robertson, 1914, pp. 496–586.
27. "The Maple Leaf Forever," http://www.thecanadianencyclopedia.com/index.cfm?PgNm=TCE&Params=U1ARTU0002201 [retrieved July 11, 2010].
28. Robin Elliot, "(De)Constructing Nationalist Music History," *Institute for Canadian Music Newsletter,* Vol. 1, No. 1 (January 2003), pp. 10–12.
29. Paul Green, "Alexander Muir," DCB.
30. Chambers, p. 83.
31. Garry Toffoli, "CBC's Attack on Canadian Heritage," http://www.monarchist.ca/mc/cbc.htm [retrieved July 11, 2010].
32. http://en.wikipedia.org/wiki/The_Maple_Leaf_Forever [retrieved October 5, 2009].
33. *Regulations Respecting the Volunteer Militia,* Ottawa, 1866, p. 24.
34. Harris, pp. 11–21.
35. J.T. Breeze, *A Poem on the Grand Trunk Railway: Its Achievements, Institutions, Scenery, Military and Principal Characters,* Montreal: 1867, pp. 21–22.
36. See above.
37. Edith Fulton Fowke, liner notes, Alan Mills, *Canada's Story in Song,* New York: Folkways Records, 1960, p. 6.
38. *Globe,* June 18, 1866; *Booker Inquiry,* pp. 239–241.
39. James Elliott, "Irish Victory on Canadian Soil," Hamilton *Spectator,* February 2, 2001, and Brian A. Reid, "'Prepare for Cavalry!' The Battle of Ridgeway" in Donald E. Graves (ed), *Fighting for Canada: Seven Battles, 1758–1945,* Toronto: Robin Brass Studio, 2000, Appendix I, p. 395, citing Directorate of History and Heritage (DHH) 325.009 (D123) Battle Honours, Canadian Militia, LAC.

40. Lewis Perry Curtis Jr., *Apes and Angels: The Irishman in Victorian Caricature,* Washington, DC: Smithsonian Institution Press, 1971; see also Donald Power, "The Paddy Image: The Stereotype of the Irishman in Cartoon and Illustration" in Robert O'Driscoll and Lorna Reynolds (eds), *The Untold Story: The Irish in Canada,* Vol. 1, Toronto: Celtic Arts of Canada, 1988, pp. 37–58; Michael de Nie, *The Eternal Paddy: Irish Identity and the British Press, 1798–1882*, PhD dissertation, University of Wisconsin, Madison, 2001; Kathleen M. Noonan, "'The Cruell Pressure of an Enraged, Barbarous People': Irish and English Identity in Seventeenth-Century Policy and Propaganda," *The Historical Journal*, Vol. 41, No. 1 (1998), pp. 151–177; for its non-practice in Canada, see G. Bruce Retallack, "Paddy, the Priest and the Habitant: Inflecting the Irish Cartoon Stereotype in Canada," *The Canadian Journal of Irish Studies*, Vol. 28, No. 2, and Vol. 29, No. 1 (Fall 2002–Spring 2003), pp. 124–147; for an example in Canada, see Doscen Gauust, B.F.H.D. [pseudonym], *The History of the Fenian Invasion of Canada,* Hamilton, ON: W.M. Brown & Co., 1866.
41. Lewis P. Curtis Jr., *Apes and Angels: The Irishman in Victorian Caricature,* Washington, DC: Smithsonian Institute, 1971.
42. See for example Desmond Morton, *A Military History of Canada,* 4th Edition, Toronto: McClelland & Stewart, 1999, p. 89; and J.L. Granatstein and David J. Bercuson, *War and Peacekeeping,* Toronto: Key Porter Books, 1991, p. 10.
43. Jack Morgan, *Through American and Irish Wars: The Life and Times of General Thomas W. Sweeny, 1820–1892,* Dublin–Portland, OR: Irish Academic Press, 2006, p. 145.
44. *Globe,* April 5, 1892.
45. *Globe,* August 5, 1890.
46. On the "militia myth" see C.P. Stacey, "The War of 1812 in Canadian History" in Morris Zaslow (ed), *The Defended Border: Upper Canada and the War of 1812; A Collection of Writings*, Toronto: Macmillan, 1964; Desmond Morton, *Ministers and Generals: Politics and the Canadian Militia, 1868–1904,* Toronto: University of Toronto Press, 1970; Stephen J. Harris, *Canadian Brass: The Making of a Professional Army 1860–1939,* Toronto: University of Toronto Press, 1988; W.E. O'Brien, "The Growth of a Military Spirit in Canada," *Selected Papers from the Transactions of the Canadian Military Institute,* Vol. 3 (1891–1892), cited in Wood, p. 20.
47. *Globe,* July 2, 1870.
48. Baskerville, *Cariboo Sentinel,* June 16, 1869, quoted in Edith Fowke, "Canadian Variation of a Civil War Song," *Midwest Folklore,* Vol. 13, No. 2 (Summer 1963), Indiana University Press, p. 103.
49. Christopher Armstrong, *The Politics of Federalism: Ontario's Relations with the Federal Government, 1867–1942,* Toronto: University of Toronto Press, 1981; Paul Romney, "The Nature and Scope of Provincial Autonomy: Oliver Mowat, the Quebec Resolutions and the Construction of the British North America Act," *Canadian Journal of Political Science / Revue canadienne de science politique*, Vol. 25, No. 1 (March 1992), pp. 3–28, and also by Romney, *Getting It Wrong: How Canadians Forgot Their Past and Imperilled Confederation,* Toronto: University

of Toronto Press, 1999, and *Mr. Attorney: The Attorney-General for Ontario in Court, Cabinet and Legislature, 1791–1899,* Toronto: The Osgoode Society, 1986; S.F. Wise, "The Ontario Political Culture: A Study of Complexities" in Graham White (ed), *The Government and Politics of Ontario,* 4th edition, Toronto: Nelson, 1990; Robert Vipond, "1787 and 1867: The Federal Principle and Canadian Confederation Reconsidered," *Canadian Journal of Political Science,* Vol. 22, No. 1 (1989), pp. 3–25, and also by Vipond, *Federalism and the Problem of Sovereignty: Constitutional Politics and the Rise of the Provincial Rights Movement in Canada,* PhD dissertation, Harvard University, Cambridge, MA, 1983, and *Liberty and Community: Canadian Federalism and the Failure of the Constitution,* Albany, NY: State University of New York Press, 1991.

50. http://www.winnipeg.ca/police/history/story13.stm and http://www.winnipeg realtors.ca/Editorials.aspx?id=152 [retrieved September 23, 2009]; J.C. Morrison, "Oliver Mowat and the Development of Provincial Rights in Ontario: A Study in Dominion-Provincial Relations, 1867–1896" in *Three History Theses,* Toronto: Ontario Department of Public Records and Archives, 1961.
51. *Globe,* January 27, 1882.
52. *Globe,* November 30, 1872.
53. Robert Vipond, "1787 and 1867: The Federal Principle and Canadian Confederation Reconsidered," *Canadian Journal of Political Science,* Vol. 22, No. 1 (1989), pp. 3–25.
54. *Globe,* March 10, 1885.
55. *Globe,* March 10, 1885.
56. *Globe,* April 5, 1892.
57. Robin W. Winks, *Recent Trends and New Literature in Canadian History,* Washington, DC: American Historical Association, 1959, p. 3.
58. Clifford G. Holland, "William Dawson LeSueur," DCB.
59. Mackenzie-King Diaries, April 28, 1908; December 27, 1911, http://www.collectionscanada.gc.ca/king/index-e.html [retrieved July 11, 2010].
60. Morang & Co. v. LeSueur (October 3, 1911), 45 S.C.R. 95.
61. *Globe,* November 12, 13, 15, 18, 1912; Donald A. Wright, *The Professionalization of History in English Canada,* Toronto: University of Toronto Press, 2005, pp. 21–24; A.B. McKillop (ed), *A Critical Spirit: The Thought of William Dawson LeSueur,* Toronto: McClelland & Stewart, 1977, pp. 273–275; Daniel Francis, "King vs. Revisionist," *Books in Canada,* March 1979, pp. 4–7; Daniel Francis, *National Dreams: Myth, Memory, and Canadian History,* Toronto: Arsenal Pulp Press, 2002, pp. 114–119.
62. William Dawson LeSueur, *William Lyon Mackenzie: A Reinterpretation* (edited by A.B. McKillop), Toronto: Carleton Library-Macmillan, 1979.
63. Clarence M. Warner, "Canadian History as a Subject of Research," The President's Address, June 7, 1916, *Ontario Historical Society Papers and Records,* Vol. 15 (1917), p. 8.
64. Edith Fowke, p. 101.

TWELVE: MEMORY AND REMEMBRANCE, 1890–2010

1. Peter Vronsky, “Canada’s First Casualties,” *Toronto Star,* November 11, 2009.
2. Cathy Pelletier, “Decoration Day in Dunnville,” *The Chronicle,* June 8, 2010, http://www.dunnvillechronicle.com/ArticleDisplay.aspx?e=2614364 [accessed July 6, 2010].
3. *Globe,* October 26, 1866.
4. Docker, p. 52.
5. Thompson, p. 96.
6. “The Fort Erie Medal,” *The Canadian Antiquarian and Numismatic Journal,* Vol. 3, No. 2 (October 1874), pp. 89–90.
7. Hamilton *Spectator,* June 3, 1876.
8. Romney, *Getting It Wrong,* pp. 183–184.
9. See for example “In Favor of Home Rule: The Ontario Parliament Discusses the Question,” *The New York Times,* April 24, 1887.
10. *Globe,* May 31, 1890.
11. *Globe,* June 3, 1890.
12. *Globe,* June 3, 1890.
13. Hamilton *Spectator*, June 3, 1891.
14. *Globe,* June 3, 1891.
15. Paul Maroney, “‘Lest We Forget’: War and Meaning in English Canada, 1885–1914,” *Journal of Canadian Studies*, Vol. 32, No. 4 (Winter 1997/1998); *Globe,* May 30, 1896.
16. *Globe,* May 30, 1896.
17. Maroney, “‘Lest We Forget.’”
18. http://www.vac-acc.gc.ca/remembers/sub.cfm?source=teach_resources/remdayfact [retrieved January 2, 2010].
19. Cathy Pelletier, “Decoration Day in Dunnville,” *The Chronicle,* June 8, 2010, http://www.dunnvillechronicle.com/ArticleDisplay.aspx?e=2614364 [accessed July 6, 2010].
20. Katie Dawson, “Honouring Veterans During Decoration Day Ceremony,” *Cambridge Reporter,* May 19, 2010, http://www.cambridgereporter.com/news/article/210556 [accessed July 6, 2010].
21. *Globe,* June 3, 1891.
22. *Globe,* June 3, 1891.
23. *Globe,* March 11, 1896; April 12, 1897; May 24, 1897; Captain Macdonald, p. 185; Committee of Citizens Chosen to Represent the City of Toronto, “To the Queen’s Most Excellent Majesty,” circa 1897 [CIHM No. 46333].
24. *Globe,* June 2, 1896.
25. http://www.vac-acc.gc.ca/remembers/sub.cfm?source=collections/cmdp/mainmenu/group03/cgsm [retrieved Oct. 10, 2009].
26. Captain Macdonald, pp. 186–188.
27. RG 1-99 Fenian land grant records, Archives of Ontario.

28. *Globe,* February 19, 1900.
29. *Globe,* December 25, 1894.
30. Errol Boyd, "The Medals Arrive ... 34 Years Late," Hamilton *Spectator,* January 18, 1964.
31. *Globe,* July 4, 1896, and January 7, 1899; *The Canadian Magazine,* November, December 1897, January 1898, July 1899.
32. Captain Macdonald, p. 5.
33. Patent No. 21726, filing year 1885, "Portable Shield for Skirmishers," Robert Larmour, Patent Branch Records, (RG 103) R9271-2-7-E, LAC.
34. McKelvie in *Vancouver Province,* cited in Duff, p. 88.
35. Wells, p. 58.
36. Hamilton *Spectator,* April 10, 1929.
37. Women's Project of New Jersey, *Past and Promise: Lives of New Jersey Women,* Syracuse, NY: Syracuse University Press, 1997, p. 159.
38. Unidentified newspaper clipping, FEHM.
39. Barlow Cumberland, "The Fenian Raid of 1866 and Events on the Frontier," *Royal Society of Canada Proceedings,* Vol. 4, Sec. 2 (1910), p. 86.
40. Thompson, p. 59.
41. Thompson, p. 82.
42. Cathy Parks, Soldiers' Tower Committee, University of Toronto, to author, March 31, 2011.
43. Courtesy of Charles Levy, email, November 12, 2009, citing Daniel Wilson Journals, UTA-B1965-0014/004(01), p. 67, University of Toronto Archives.
44. *Estimates for the Fiscal Year Ending 30th June 1891,* Ottawa: 1890, p. 38.
45. Correspondence December 20, 1866, Adjutant-General's Office, RG9 IC1, Vol. 239, File 3289, LAC.
46. Docker, p. 56.
47. Docker, p. 57; C.H.J. Snider, "Schooner Days," *Toronto Telegram,* September 5, 1942; October 23, 1948.
48. *Globe,* June 2, 1930.
49. Hamilton *Spectator,* November 9, 1936.
50. http://www.vac-acc.gc.ca/general/sub.cfm?source=teach_resources/remdayfact and www.calendar-updates.com/info/holidays/canada/remembrance.aspx [retrieved October 10, 2009]. Wood argues that the militia lobbied in the 1890s to move Thanksgiving Day to October for the Canadian holiday in the hopes of enjoying better weather and larger audiences for its church parade. See Wood, p. 30.
51. http://www.vac-acc.gc.ca/remembers/sub.cfm?source=teach_resources/remdayfact [retrieved January 7, 2010].
52. http://www.veterans.gc.ca/eng/sub.cfm?source=collections/books [retrieved July 11, 2010].
53. Frank Jones, "How Canada Was Invaded at Fort Erie by the Fenians," *The Globe and Mail,* November 10, 1956, p. 25.

BIBLIOGRAPHY

PRIMARY SOURCES

ARCHIVES

Archives of the Roman Catholic Archdiocese of Toronto (ARCAT)
Archbishop Lynch Papers

Catholic University of America, Washington, DC
Fenian Collection: www.aladin/wrlc.org/gsdl/collect/fenian.shtml

City of Toronto Archives (CTA)
Letter Books of the Chief Constable 1859–1921; Toronto Board of Commissioners of Police, *Minutes*, 1864–1865: RG9/Fond 38 Toronto Police Service, Series 90

Toronto City Council *Minutes*

Fort Erie Historical Museum, Ridgeway (FEHM)
Fenian Raid and Battle of Ridgeway papers

Hamilton Public Library
Clipping File (CF)—Biography: Alexander Somerville

Library and Archives of Canada (LAC)
Adjutant General's Office, Letters Received, RG9 IC1, Vol. 220

Adjutant General's Office, Letters Sent 1847–1868, RG9 IC1, Vol. 290

Stephen Beatty, *Reminiscences of the Fenian Raid 1866,* manuscript, John Colin Armour Campbell fonds (R9262-0-2-E), Notes on Military Affairs, MG29-E74, Vol. 1, Folder 4

Civil Secretary's Letter Books, RG7-G-16-C, Vol. 36

George T. Denison, *The Fenian Raid at Fort Erie and an Account of the Battle of Ridgeway* [original manuscript], George Taylor Denison III fonds, MG29-E29, Vol. 43, File 1

Department of Justice, Numbered Central Registry Files, RG-13-A2, Vol. 13–16, 20

Department of Militia, Deputy Minister Dockets, RG9 IIA1

Fenian Papers, John A. Macdonald Papers, MG26 A, Vol. 56 [Microfilm Reels C1507–1508]

Fenian Raid Service Records, Adjutant General's Office, United Canada, Pensions and Land Grants, RG9 IC5; *Compensation of Injuries, Wounds, etc., Received on Active Service Fenian Raids 1866–1868*, Vol. 30–32 [FRSR]

Andrew McIntosh, manuscript, *Personal Recollections of the Fenian Raid, June 2, 1866, by one who was there,* MG29-E108, Vol. 1

Gilbert McMicken Secret Service Reports, John A. Macdonald Papers, MG26 A, Vol. 233–237 [Microfilm Reels C1660–1663]

Miscellaneous Records Relating to the Fenian Raids, British Military and Naval Records "C" Series, RG8-1, Vol. 1672 [Microfilm Reel C-4300]

Proceedings of a Court of Inquiry held in Hamilton on Tuesday the 3rd day of July A.D. 1866 by order of His Excellency the Commander-in-chief on the application of Lieutenant Colonel Booker to examine and report on the circumstances connected with the late engagement at Lime Ridge, dated Ottawa, June 24, 1866. Adjutant General's Correspondence; Correspondence relating to complaints, courts martial and inquiries, RG9-I-C-8, Vol. 6 [Booker Inquiry]

Proceedings of the Court of Inquiry upon the Circumstances of the Engagement at Fort Erie on the 2nd of June 1866, Adjutant General's Correspondence; Correspondence relating to complaints, courts martial and inquiries, RG9-I-C-8, Vol. 7 [Dennis Inquiry]

Report of the Commissioners Appointed to Consider the Defences of Canada, February 6, 1862, RG9-IIA1, Vol. 482

United Canada Subject Files, Clothing and arms records relating to militia units in Ontario and Quebec, RG9-IC8, Vol. 18

United Canada Subject Files, Frontier Service Reports 1865–1867, RG9 IC8, Vol. 8

United Canada Subject Files, Adjutant General's Correspondence; Correspondence relating to complaints, courts martial and inquiries, RG9-I-C-8, Vol. 6–7

Upper Canada Sundries, RG 5, Series A 1, Vol. 67

Missouri Historical Society

AO481 Fenian Papers 1869–1992

New York City Public Library

William Sweeny Papers, MssCol 2934 [Microfilm: NY Public Library Photographic Service, 1978]

Queen's Own Rifles Regimental Museum

Battle of Ridgeway papers

Royal Hamilton Light Infantry Wentworth Regiment Museum

Thirteenth Battalion *Order Books,* 1866

United Church of Canada Archives at Victoria College

Nathanael Burwash Collection

University of Rochester Library

The Papers of William Henry Seward, Microfilm Set in Department of Rare Books and Special Collections

U.S. National Archives and Records Administration (NARA)

Despatches from U.S. Consuls in Fort Erie 1865–1906, Records of the Foreign Service

Posts of the Department of State, 1788–1964, RG 84 (National Archives Microfilm Publication T465, Roll 1), National Archives at College Park, College Park, MD

Despatches from U.S. Consuls in Toronto, Canada, 1864–1906, Records of the Foreign Service Posts of the Department of State, 1788–1964, RG 84 (National Archives Microfilm Publication T491, Roll 1: Jan. 11, 1864–Dec. 31, 1866; Roll 2: Jan. 3, 1867–Jan. 2, 1868), National Archives at College Park, College Park, MD

Letters Received by the Secretary of War from the President, Executive Departments, and War Department Bureaus 1862–1870 (National Archives Microfilm Publication M494, Roll 88); Records of the Office of the Secretary of War, 1791–1947, RG 107, National Archives Building, Washington, DC

Letters Sent; Letters Received, Records of the Headquarters of the Army 1828–1903, RG 108; National Archives Building, Washington, DC

Provost Marshal, 30th Congressional District, New York, Letters, Records of State and District Offices, Record Group 110.4; Letters Received May 1863–December 1865 [2283]; Register of Received [2284]; Letters Received 1863–1865 [2285], Records of the Provost Marshal General's Bureau, RG 110; National Archives Building, Washington, DC

Reports 1863–1872, War Department, Records of the U.S. Army Continental Commands, 1817–1940, Division of the Atlantic, Department of the East, RG 393: Inventory Identifier 1428, National Archives Building, Washington, DC

Telegrams Collected, Records of the Office of the Secretary of War, RG 107, National Archives Building, Washington, DC

USS Michigan *Logbook No. 16*, Logbooks of U.S. Navy Ships, 1801–1940, Records of the Bureau of Naval Personnel, 1798–2003, RG 24, National Archives Building, Washington, DC

REPORTS AND GOVERNMENT PUBLICATIONS

Correspondence Respecting the Recent Fenian Aggression Upon Canada, London: 1867

Correspondence Relating to the Fenian Invasion and Rebellion of the Southern States, Ottawa: 1869

Executive Documents for the Second Session of the Fortieth Congress of the United States, 1867–'68, Washington, DC: 1868

Papers Relating to the Foreign Relations of the United States, Executive Documents Printed by the Order of the House of Representatives During the Second Session of the Thirty-Ninth Congress, 1866–'67, Vol. 13 (1866), Part I, Washington, DC: Government Printing Office, 1867

United Province of Canada, *Legislative Assembly Journals*, 1841, Appendix S, *Report of the Commissioners appointed to investigate certain proceedings at Toronto, connected with the Election for that City*, and Appendix OO

CONTEMPORARY BOOKS ON THE BATTLE OF RIDGEWAY PRE-1911

[s.n.] (*The Fenian Raid into Canada*) *The Fenian Raid at Fort Erie,* Toronto: W.C. Chewett & Co., 1866

Denison, George T. *Fenian Raid on Fort Erie; with an Account of the Battle of Ridgeway, June, 1866,* Toronto: Rollo & Adam, 1866

Gauust, Doscen, B.F.H.D. [pseudonym]. *The History of the Fenian Invasion of Canada,* Hamilton: W.M. Brown & Co., 1866

Gregg, George R. & E.P. Roden. *Trials of the Fenian Prisoners at Toronto,* Toronto: Leader Steam-Press, 1867

Macdonald, Captain John A. *Troublous Times in Canada: The History of the Fenian Raids of 1866 and 1870,* Toronto: W.S. Johnston & Co., 1910

Scian Dubh [James McCarroll]. *Ridgeway: An Historical Romance of the Fenian Invasion of Canada,* Buffalo, NY: McCarroll & Co., 1868

Somerville, Alexander. *Narrative of the Fenian Invasion of Canada,* Hamilton, ON: Joseph Lyght, 1866

CONTEMPORARY ARTICLES ON THE BATTLE OF RIDGEWAY PRE-1911

Beatty, Stephen. *Fenian Raid 1866 with Lt. Colonel J. Stoughton Dennis at Fort Erie June 2, 1866,* St. Catharines, ON: *The Star Journal*, 1910

Cumberland, Barlow. "The Fenian Raid of 1866 and Events on the Frontier," *Royal Society of Canada Proceedings,* Vol. 4, Sec. 2 (1910)

Cooper, John A. "The Fenian Raid 1866," *The Canadian Magazine,* Vol. 10, No. 1 (Nov. 1897)

Ellis, William H. "The Adventures of a Prisoner of War," *The Canadian Magazine,* Vol. 13, No. 3 (July 1899)

Larmour, Robert. "With Booker's Column" [Part 1], *The Canadian Magazine,* Vol. 10, No. 2 (Dec. 1897); [Part 2], *The Canadian Magazine,* Vol. 10, No. 3 (Jan. 1898)

Stinson, J.T.R. "The Battle of Ridgeway, or Lime Ridge," *Journal of Education for Upper Canada*, Vol. 19, No. 6 (June 1866)

CONTEMPORARY BOOKS AND OTHER MATERIAL PRE-1911

[s.n.], *Canadian Border Songs of the Fenian Invasion,* 1870

[s.n.], "The Fort Erie Medal," *The Canadian Antiquarian and Numismatic Journal,* Vol. 3, No. 2. (Oct. 1874)

[s.n.], *A Life of James Stephens: Chief Organizer of the Irish Republic,* New York: Carleton, 1866

[s.n.], *The Hand-Book of Toronto,* Toronto: Lovell & Gibson, 1858

[s.n.], *History of the Country of Middlesex Canada*, Toronto: W.A. & C.L. Goodspeed, 1889

[s.n.], *History of Welland County,* Welland Tribune Printing House, 1887

[s.n.], *Illustrated Historical Album of the 2nd Battalion Queen's Own Rifles,* Toronto: Toronto News Company, 1894

[s.n.], "Old English Rifles," *The Engineer,* August 20, 1886, London

[s.n.], *The Spirit of Toryism Exemplified in the Brutal Conduct Exhibited Towards Alexander Sommerville* [*sic*] *of the Scots Greys,* Glasgow: Muir, Gowans & Co., 1832

Breeze, J.T. *A Poem on the Grand Trunk Railway: Its Achievements, Institutions, Scenery, Military and Principal Characters,* Montreal: 1867

Buffalo City Map 1, *Erie County 1866 Atlas,* [n.p.]: Stone and Stewart, 1866

Clark, C.S. *Of Toronto the Good,* Montreal: Toronto Publishing Company, 1898

Denieffe, Joseph. *A Personal Narrative of the Irish Revolutionary Brotherhood,* New York: Gael Publishing, 1906

Davitt, Michael. *The Fall of Feudalism in Ireland,* London & New York: 1904

Denison, Frederick C. *Historical Record of the Governor-General's Body Guard,* Toronto: 1876

Denison, George T. *Soldiering in Canada,* Toronto: George L. Morang & Co., 1901

Denison, "A Visit to General Robert E. Lee," *Canadian Monthly,* March 1872

Gray, John Hamilton. *Confederation; or, the Political and Parliamentary History of Canada from the Conference at Quebec, in October, 1864 to the Admission of British Columbia, in July, 1871,* Toronto: Copp, Clark & Co., 1872

Hansard, HC Debates, August 8, 1832, Vol. 14, cc 1241–1242 http://hansard.millbanksystems.com/commons/1832/aug/08/case-of-alexander-somerville [retrieved September 14, 2009]

Hardee, W.J. *Rifle and Light Infantry Tactics for the Exercising and Manoeuvring of Troops,* Vol. 1, 1855.

Hardee, William Joseph. *Rifle and Light Infantry Tactics*, Vol. 2, Philadelphia: J.B. Lippincott & Co., 1861

Inglis, David. *Righteousness Exalteth a Nation: A Thanksgiving Sermon,* Hamilton, C.W.: Printed at the "Spectator" Steam Press, Prince's Square, 1866.

King, John. *McCaul: Croft: Forneri: Personalities of Early University Days,* Toronto: Macmillan Co. Ltd., 1894

Kirby, James (ed), *Lower Canada Law Journal*, Vol. 2., Montreal: John Lovell, 1867

O'Neill, John. *Address of General John O'Neill President F.B. to the Officers and Members of the Fenian Brotherhood on the State of Its Organization and Its Disruption,* New York, Feb. 27, 1868, New York: [s.n.] 1868

O'Neill, John. *Official Report of the Battle of Ridgeway, Canada West, Fought on June 2, 1866* (June 27, 1866), New York: John A. Foster, 1870

Rutherford, John. *The Secret History of the Fenian Conspiracy: Its Origins, Objects & Ramifications,* Vol. 1, London: C. Keegan Paul & Co., 1877

Secretary of War. *Drill and Rifle Instruction for the Corps of Rifle Volunteers*, London: 1859

Somerville, Alexander. *The Autobiography of a Working Man,* Manchester: Ainsworth, 1848

Somerville, Alexander. *History of the British Legion and the War in Spain,* London: James Pattie, 1839

Taylor, Conygham C. *The Queen's Jubilee and Toronto "Called Back" from 1887 to 1847,* Toronto: William Briggs, 1887

Thompson, John H. *Jubilee History of Thorold Township and Town from the Time of the Red Man to the Present*, Thorold: Thorold and Beaverdams Historical Society, 1891

Toronto City Directory, 1875–1885

Tracy, Basil. *The Tercentenary History of Canada*, Vol. 3, New York: P.F. Collier & Son, 1908

NEWSPAPERS

Buffalo Commercial Advertiser

Cincinnati Daily Gazette

The Evening Times (Hamilton)

Toronto *Globe*

The Globe and Mail

Hamilton Herald

Irish American

Irish Canadian (Toronto)

Toronto *Leader*

The New York Times

St. Catharines Journal

The Southern Cross (Australia)

The Spectator (Hamilton)

Toronto Telegram

The Volunteer Review and Military and Naval Gazette

SECONDARY SOURCES

BOOKS, THESES, ARTICLES, CHAPTERS, AND WEBSITES ON BATTLE OF RIDGEWAY

Andrews, Allen. *Brave Soldiers, Proud Regiments: Canada's Military Heritage*, Vancouver: Ronsdale Press, 1997

Bertie Historical Society. *Battle of Ridgeway: Stories and Legends of the Fenian Raid*, June 1976

Brewster, N. "Recollections of the Fenian Raid" in *Welland County Historical Society Papers and Records*, Vol. 2, Welland, Canada: 1926

Cruikshank, E.A. "The Fenian Raid of 1866," *Welland County Historical Society Papers and Records*, Vol. 2, Welland, Canada: 1926

Docker, John Thornley. *Dunnville Heroes: The* W.T. Robb *and the Dunnville Naval Brigade in the 1866 Fenian Invasion*, Dunnville, ON: Dunnville District Heritage Association, 2003

Duff, Louis Blake. "Sam Johnston, Smuggler, Soldier and Bearer of News," *Welland County Historical Society Papers and Records*, Vol. 2, Welland, Canada: 1926

Duggan, G.C. "The Fenians in Canada: A British Officer's Impression," *The Irish Sword* (Winter 1967)

Dunn, J.F. "Recollections of the Battle of Ridgeway," *Welland County Historical Society Papers and Records,* Vol. 2, Welland, Canada: 1926

Fryer, Mary Beacock. *Battlefields of Canada,* Toronto: Dundurn Press, 1986

Greenhous, Brereton, Kingsley Brown Sr., & Kingsley Brown Jr. *Semper Paratus: The History of the Royal Hamilton Light Infantry,* Hamilton, ON: RHLI Historical Association, 1977

Griffith, Justus A. "The Ridgeway Semi-Centennial," *Ontario Historical Society Papers and Records,* Vol. 15, 1917, pp. 18–27

Junor, David. "Taken Prisoner by the Fenians," *The Canadian Magazine,* May 1911

Mackenzie, George A. "What I Saw of the Fenian Raid," *The Spectator* (Hamilton), November 27, 1926

Mackenzie, George A. "Young Adventurer in '66 Tells Story of Raid," *Hamilton Herald,* June 27, 1927

Maryniak, Benedict. *The Fenian Raid and Battle of Ridgeway June 1–3, 1866,* http://www.acsu.buffalo.edu/~dbertuca/g/FenianRaid.html [retrieved July 11, 2010]

McCallum, Fred H. "Experience of a Queen's Own Rifleman at Ridgeway," *Third Annual Report of the Waterloo Historic Society,* Berlin [Kitchener]: Waterloo Historic Society, 1915

Ministry of Tourism, Culture and Recreation, Conservation Review Board. *Re: City of Toronto—Intention to Designate 62 Laing Street (Maple Cottage),* December 16, 1991

Neidhardt, W.S. *Fenianism in North America,* University Park and London: Pennsylvania State University Press, 1975

Owen, David. *The Year of the Fenians: A Self-Guided Tour of Discovery and an Illustrated History of the Fenian Invasion of the Niagara Peninsula and the Battle of Ridgeway in 1866,* Buffalo, NY: Western New York Heritage Institute, 1990

Quesley, F.M. "The Fenian Invasion of Canada West," *Ontario History,* Vol. 53, No. 1 (1961)

Read, Colin. "The Red River Rebellion and J. S. Dennis, 'Lieutenant and Conservator of the Peace,'" *Manitoba History,* No. 3 (1982)

Reavley, Albert W. "Personal Experience in the Fenian Raid," *Welland County Historical Society Papers and Records,* Vol. 2, Welland, Canada: 1926

Reid, Brian A. "'Prepare for Cavalry!' The Battle of Ridgeway" in Donald E. Graves (ed), *Fighting for Canada: Seven Battles, 1758–1945,* Toronto: Robin Brass Studio, 2000

Senior, Hereward. *The Last Invasion of Canada: The Fenian Raids, 1866–1870,* Toronto: Dundurn Press, 1991

Severance, Frank. "The Fenian Raid of '66" in Frank H. Severance (ed), *Publications of the Buffalo Historical Society: The Book of the Museum,* Vol. XXV, Buffalo, NY: Buffalo Historical Society, 1921

Sherk, M.G. "My Recollections of the Fenian Raid," *County Historical Society Papers and Records,* Vol. 2, Welland, Canada: 1926

Stacey, Charles P. *John O'Neill: The Story of the Fenian Paladin* [unpublished manuscript], n.d., C.P. Stacey Papers, University of Toronto Archives

Stacey, Charles P. "The Fenian Troubles and Canadian Military Development," in *Report of the Annual Meeting of the Canadian Historical Association*, 1935

Vronsky, Peter (Peter Wronski). *Combat, Memory and Remembrance in Confederation Era Canada: The Hidden History of the Battle of Ridgeway, June 2, 1866*, doctoral thesis, University of Toronto, History Department, 2011

Wells, George. "The Fenian Raid in Willoughby"; "A Romance of the Raid"; *Welland County Historical Society Papers and Records*, Vol. 2, Welland, Canada: 1926

Wright, Adam H. "The Stirring Commencement Period of 1866—Dr Adam Wright tells of Ridgeway and the University Company," *University of Toronto Monthly*, Vol. 21, No. 9 (June 1921)

UNPUBLISHED THESES

Barlow, John Matthew. *Fear and Loathing in Saint-Sylvestre: The Corrigan Murder Case, 1855–58*, MA thesis, Simon Fraser University, 1998

Bleasdale, Ruth. *Unskilled Labourers on the Public Works of Canada, 1840–1880*, PhD dissertation, London, ON: University of Western Ontario, 1984

Crockett, Wayne A. *The Uses and Abuses of the Secret Service Fund: The Political Dimension of Police Work in Canada, 1864–1877*, MA thesis, Kingston, ON: Queen's University, 1982

D'Angelo, Anthony. *The 1866 Fenian Raid on Canada West: A Study of Colonial Perceptions and Reactions Towards the Fenians in the Confederation Era*, MA thesis, Kingston, ON: Queen's University, 2009

De Nie, Michael. *The Eternal Paddy: Irish Identity and the British Press, 1798–1882*, PhD dissertation, Madison: University of Wisconsin, 2001

Kennedy, Padraic Cummins. *Political Policing in a Liberal Age: Britain's Response to the Fenian Movement 1858–1868*, PhD dissertation, Washington University, 1996

Lynch, Timothy G. *Erin's Hope: The Fenian Brotherhood of New York City, 1858–1886*, PhD dissertation, City University of New York, 2004

Neidhardt, Wilfried Steffen. *The Fenian Brotherhood and Southwestern Ontario*, MA thesis, London, ON: University of Western Ontario, 1967

O'Reilly, Rebecca. *"In a Situation of Great Distress": The Emigrant Agency, Poverty, and the Irish in Nineteenth Century Upper Canada*, MA thesis, Guelph, ON: University of Guelph, 2006

Rodgers, Bradley Alan. *Guardian of the Great Lakes: The U.S. Paddle Frigate* Michigan *and Iron Archetype on the Inland Seas*, PhD dissertation, Cincinnati, OH: Union Institute, 1994

Stanton, Kevin W. *Green Tint on Gold Bars: Irish Officers in the United States Army, 1865–1898*, PhD dissertation, University of Colorado, 2001

Vipond, Robert. *Federalism and the Problem of Sovereignty: Constitutional Politics and the Rise of the Provincial Rights Movement in Canada*, PhD dissertation, Cambridge, MA: Harvard University, 1983

GENERAL ARTICLES AND OTHER SOURCES, INCLUDING WEBSITES

Akenson, Donald. "Data: What Is Known About the Irish in North America" in O'Driscoll and Reynolds (eds), *The Untold Story: The Irish in Canada,* Vol. I, Toronto: Celtic Arts of Canada, 1988

Association to Commemorate the Chinese Serving in the American Civil War, *The Connection Between the American Civil War (1861–1865) and the Chinese Taiping Civil War (1850–1864),* http://sites.google.com/site/accsacw/Home/connection [retrieved June 10, 2010]

Baker, William M. "'God's Unfortunate People': Historiography of Irish Catholics in Nineteenth Century Canada" in O'Driscoll & Reynolds (eds), *The Untold Story: The Irish in Canada,* Vol. I, Toronto: Celtic Arts of Canada, 1988

Black, Robson. "A Dollar and Costs," *Canada Monthly,* Vol. 14, No. 4 (Aug. 1913)

Bleasdale, Ruth. "Class Conflict on the Canals of Upper Canada in the 1840s," *Labour/Le Travailleur,* 1981; reprinted in Laurel Sefton MacDowell and Ian Radforth (eds), *Canadian Working Class History,* 2nd Edition, Toronto: Canadian Scholars' Press, 2000, pp. 81–108

Brown, R. Blake. "'Stars and Shamrocks Will Be Sown': The Fenian State Trials, 1866–67," in Barry Wright & Susan S. Binnie (eds), *Canadian State Trials, Volume III: Political Trials and Security Measures, 1840–1914,* Toronto: University of Toronto Press and the Osgoode Society, 2009

Bruce, Susannah Ural. "'Remember Your Country and Keep Up Its Credit': Irish Volunteers and the Union Army, 1861–1865," *The Journal of Military History,* Vol. 69, No. 2 (2005), pp. 331–359

Buffalo Medical and Surgical Journal, Vol. 5, Buffalo: 1866

Burns, Ken. *The Civil War,* Florentine Films—PBS, 1990

Caddell, Joseph W. "Deception 101: Primer on Deception," *Conference on Strategic Deception in Modern Democracies: Ethical, Legal, and Policy Challenges,* U.S. Army War College, October 31, 2003, at the William C. Friday Conference Center, Chapel Hill, NC

Cadigan, Sean T. "Paternalism and Politics: Sir Francis Bond Head, the Orange Order, and the Election of 1836," *Canadian Historical Review,* Vol. 72, No. 3 (1991), pp. 319–347

Canadian Armed Forces, Historical Section (Lt. J.L. Granatstein), *Report No. 2 Canadian American Defence Relations 1867–1914,* August 1965

Committee Representing the Quebec Provincial Council of the Boy Scouts Association, *Songs for Canadian Boys,* Toronto: Macmillan, 1952

Cottrell, Michael. "Green and Orange in Mid-Nineteenth Century Toronto: The Guy Fawkes' Day Episode of 1864," *Canadian Journal of Irish Studies,* Vol. 19, No.1 (1993)

Cottrell, Michael J. "Political Leadership and Party Allegiance Among Irish Catholics in Victorian Toronto," in McGowan and Clarke (eds), *Catholics at the "Gathering Place,"* Toronto: Canadian Catholic Historical Association, 1993

Cottrell, Michael J. "St. Patrick's Day Parades in Nineteenth-Century Toronto: A Study of Immigrant Adjustment and Elite Control," *Histoire social/Social History,* No. 49 (1992), pp. 57–73

Cross, Michael S. "The Shiners War: Social Violence in the Ottawa Valley in the 1830s," *Canadian Historical Review,* Vol. 54, No. 1 (March 1973)

Curtis, Lewis P. *Apes and Angels: The Irishman in Victorian Caricature,* Washington, DC: Smithsonian Institute, 1971

Elliot, Robin. "(De)Constructing Nationalist Music History," *Institute for Canadian Music Newsletter,* Vol. 1, No. 1 (Jan. 2003), pp. 10–12

Foner, Eric. "Johnson and Reconstruction: The British View," *Journal of Southern History,* Vol. 41, No. 3 (Aug. 1975), pp. 381–382

Francis, Daniel. "King vs. Revisionist," *Books in Canada,* March 1979, pp. 4–7

French, Brigittine M. "'We're All Irish': Transforming Irish Identity in a Midwestern Community," *New Hibernia Review / Iris Éireannach Nua,* Vol. 11, No. 1 (Spring/Earrach 2007)

Fowke, Edith. "Canadian Variation of a Civil War Song," *Midwest Folklore,* Vol. 13, No. 2 (Summer 1963), Indiana University Press

Gagan, David. "George Taylor Denison, [II]," *Dictionary of Canadian Biography* [henceforth "DCB"]

Garvin, Tom. "Defenders, Ribbonmen and Others: Underground Political Networks in Pre-famine Ireland, *Past and Present,* No. 96 (Aug. 1982)

Green, Paul. "Alexander Muir," DCB

Hague Declaration Concerning Expanding Bullets of July 29, 1899

Holland, Clifford G. "William Dawson LeSueur," DCB

Homel, Gene Howard. "Denison's Court: Criminal Justice and the Police Court in Toronto, 1877–1921," *Ontario History,* Vol. LXXIII, No. 3 (Sept. 1981)

Houston, Cecil J. and William J. Smyth. "Irish Emigrants to Canada: Whence They Came," in O'Driscoll and Reynolds (eds), *The Untold Story: The Irish in Canada,* Vol. I, Toronto: Celtic Arts of Canada, 1988

Johnson, J.K. "Colonel James FitzGibbon and the Suppression of Irish Riots in Upper Canada," *Ontario History,* Vol. 58, No. 3 (Sept. 1966)

Jones, Frank. "Was Invaded at Fort Erie by the Fenians," *The Globe and Mail,* November 10, 1956

Kay, John and Mary Findlay. *Nebraska Historic Buildings Survey: Reconnaissance Survey Final Report of Holt County, Nebraska,* Nebraska State Historical Society–State Historic Preservation Office, June 1, 1988

Kealey, Gregory. "Orangemen and the Corporation" in Victor L. Russell (ed), *Forging a Consensus: Historical Essays on Toronto*, Toronto: University of Toronto Press, 1984

Kealey, Gregory S. "The Empire Strikes Back: The Nineteenth-Century Origins of the Canadian Secret Service," *Journal of the CHA,* New Series, Vol. 10 (1999), pp. 3–19

Kealey, Gregory. "'The Honest Workingman' and Workers' Control: The Experience of

Toronto Skilled Workers,"1860–1892, *Labour / Le Travail,* Vol. 1 (1976), pp. 32–68

Keshen, Jeff. "Cloak and Dagger: Canada West's Secret Police, 1864–1867," *Ontario History,* Vol. 79 (Dec. 1987)

Kerr, W.B. "When Orange and Green United, 1832–1839: The Alliance of Macdonell and Gowan," *Ontario History,* Vol. 34 (1942)

Knowles, Norman. "George Taylor Denison [III]," DCB

Larkin, Emmet. "The Devotional Revolution in Ireland, 1850–75," *The American Historical Review,* Vol. 77, No. 3 (June 1972)

Mainer, George. "Alfred Booker," DCB

McGowan, Mark. *Creating Historical Memory: The Case of Famine Migration of 1847,* Ottawa: Canadian Historical Association, Canada's Ethnic Group Series Booklet No. 30, 2006

McMahon, Timothy G. *The AOH in History,* Marquette University, 2005 http://www.aohmilwaukee.com/history.html [retrieved July 11, 2010]

Morrison, J.C. "Oliver Mowat and the Development of Provincial Rights in Ontario: A Study in Dominion-Provincial Relations, 1867–1896" in *Three History Theses,* Toronto: Ontario Department of Public Records and Archives, 1961

Moss, Kenneth. "St. Patrick's Day Celebrations and the Formation of Irish-American Identity, 1845–1875," *Journal of Social History*, Vol. 29, No. 1 (Autumn 1995), pp. 125–148

Neidhardt, W.S., "The Fenian Brotherhood and Western Ontario: The Final Year," *Ontario History,* Vol. 60, No. 3 (Sept. 1968), pp. 149–161

Nicolson, Murray. "William O'Grady and the Catholic Church in Toronto Prior to the Irish Famine," in McGowan and Clarke (eds), *Catholics at the "Gathering Place,"* Toronto: Canadian Catholic Historical Association, 1993

Noonan, Gerald R. "General John O'Neill," *Clogher Record*, Vol. 6, No. 2 (Clogher Historical Society, 1967), pp. 277–319

Parnaby, Andrew and Gregory S. Kealey. "The Origins of Political Policing in Canada: Class, Law and the Burden of Empire," *Osgoode Hall Law Journal,* Vol. 41, Nos. 2 & 3 (2003), pp. 211–239

Pentland, H.C. "The Development of a Capitalistic Labour Market in Canada," *The Canadian Journal of Economics and Political Science*, Vol. 25, No. 4 (Nov. 1959)

Raney, William F. "Recruiting and Crimping in Canada for the Northern Forces, 1861–1865," *The Mississippi Valley Historical Review,* Vol. 10, No. 1 (June 1923), pp. 21–33

Read, Colin Frederick. "John Stoughton Dennis," DCB

Reynolds, David. "From World War to Cold War: The Wartime Alliance and Post-war Transition, 1941–1947," *The Historical Journal,* Vol. 45, No. 1 (2002)

Romney, Paul. "A Struggle for Authority: Toronto Society and Politics in 1834," in Victor L. Russell (ed), *Forging a Consensus: Historical Essays on Toronto*, Toronto: University of Toronto Press, 1984

Romney, Paul. "From the Types Riot to the Rebellion: Elite Ideology, Anti-legal Sentiment, Political Violence, and the Rule of Law in Upper Canada," *Ontario History,* Vol. 79, No. 2 (June 1987)

Romney, Paul. "The Nature and Scope of Provincial Autonomy: Oliver Mowat, the Quebec Resolutions and the Construction of the British North America Act," *Canadian Journal of Political Science / Revue canadienne de science politique*, Vol. 25, No. 1 (March 1992), pp. 3–28

Ruggle, Richard E. "Alfred Booker [Senior]," DCB

Sandison, W.M. "Alexander Somerville," *The Border Magazine,* Vol. 18, No. 207 (March 1913)

Sheppard, George. "'God Save the Green': Fenianism and Fellowship in Victorian Ontario," *Histoire Sociale*, Vol. 20, No. 39 (1987), pp. 129–144

Slattery, T.P. "Patrick James Wheelan," DCB

Snider, C.H.J. "Schooner Days," *Toronto Telegram,* September 5, 1942; October 23, 1948

Stacey, Charles P. "A Fenian Interlude: The Story of Michael Murphy," *Canadian Historical Review*, Vol. 5 (1934), 133–154

Stacey, Charles P. "Confederation: The Atmosphere of Crisis," *Profiles of a Province,* Toronto: Ontario Historical Society, 1967

Stacey, Charles P. "Fenianism and the Rise of National Feeling in Canada at the Time of Confederation," *Canadian Historical Review,* Vol. 12, No. 3 (1931), pp. 238–261

Stacey, Charles P. "Michael Murphy," DCB

Stacey, Charles P. "John O'Neill," DCB

Toffoli, Garry. "CBC's Attack on Canadian Heritage," http://www.monarchist.ca/mc/cbc.htm [retrieved July 11, 2010]

Toner, Peter M. "The 'Green Ghost': Canada's Fenians and the Raids," *Eire-Ireland,* Vol. 16 (1981)

Twain, Mark. "The Noble Redman," *The Galaxy,* September 1870

Warner, Clarence M. "Canadian History as a Subject of Research," The President's Address, June 7, 1916, *Ontario Historical Society Papers and Records,* Vol. 15 (1917)

Waterston, Elizabeth. "Alexander Somerville: Whistler at the Plough," *International Review of Scottish Studies,* Vol. 12 (1982)

Watt, Alastair. "The Case of Alexander McLeod," *Canadian Historical Review,* Vol. 12, No. 2 (1931), pp. 145–167

Wilson, David. "The Fenians in Montreal, 1862–68: Invasion, Intrigue, and Assassination," *Eire-Ireland: A Journal of Irish Studies*, Vol. 38, Nos. 3–4 (Fall–Winter 2003)

Wilson, David. "The Irish in Canada," *Canada's Ethnic Groups,* Booklet No. 12, Ottawa: Canadian Historical Association, 1989

Wilson, David A. "State Security, Civil Liberty and the Fenians in Canada," 2008 Irish Studies Symposium, http://www.lac-bac.gc.ca/ireland/033001-1001.01.1-e.html [retrieved July 11, 2010]

Wise, S.F. "The Ontario Political Culture: A Study of Complexities" in Graham White (ed), *The Government and Politics of Ontario,* 4th edition, Toronto: Nelson, 1990

Van Die, Marguerite. *An Evangelical Mind: Nathanael Burwash and the Methodist Tradition in Canada, 1839–1918,* Montreal-Kingston: McGill-Queen's University Press, 1989

Vipond, Robert. "1787 and 1867: The Federal Principle and Canadian Confederation Reconsidered," *Canadian Journal of Political Science,* Vol. 22, No. 1 (1989), pp. 3–25

Vronsky, Peter. *Mondo Moscow: The Art and Magic of Not Being There,* feature documentary, TV Ontario–Ocean Corporation, 1991

OTHER BOOKS

Akenson, Donald. *Being Had: Historians, Evidence and the Irish in North America,* Toronto: P.D. Meany, 1985

Akenson, Donald. *The Irish in Ontario: A Study in Rural History,* Kingston and Montreal: McGill-Queen's University Press, 1984

Akenson, Donald. *The Orangeman: The Life and Times of Ogle Gowan,* Toronto: James Lorimer, 1986

Anderson, David L. *Imperialism and Idealism: American Diplomats in China, 1861–1898,* Bloomington, IN: Indiana University Press, 1985

Andrews, Allen. *Brave Soldiers, Proud Regiments: Canada's Military Heritage,* Vancouver: Ronsdale Press, 1997

Archibald, Edith J. *Life and Letters of Sir Edward Mortimer Archibald,* Toronto: George N. Morang, 1924

Armstrong, Christopher. *The Politics of Federalism: Ontario's Relations with the Federal Government, 1867–1942,* Toronto: University of Toronto Press, 1981

Arthur, Eric. *Toronto: No Mean City,* Toronto: University of Toronto Press, 1964

Barnes, James J. and Patience Barnes. *Private and Confidential: Letters for British Minister in Washington to the Foreign Secretaries in London, 1844–67,* Selinsgrove: Susquehanna University Press, 1993

Barrow, T.J., French V.A., and Seabrook, J. (eds). *The Story of the Bedfordshire and Hertfordshire Regiment,* Vol. 2, History Committee of the Royal Anglican Regiment, circa 1988

Beale, Howard K. (ed). *Diary of Gideon Welles 1861–1869*, Vol. 2, New York: Norton & Co., 1960

Benn, Carl. *Mohawks on the Nile: Natives Among the Canadian Voyageurs in Egypt, 1884–1885*, Toronto: Dundurn Press, 2009

Bennett, Carol. *The Robinson Settlers 1823–1825,* Renfrew, ON: Juniper Books, 1987

Berger, Carl. *A Sense of Power: Studies in the Ideas of Canadian Imperialism,* Toronto: University of Toronto Press, 1970

Berger, Carl. *The Writing of Canadian History: Aspects of English-Canadian Historical Writing: 1900–1970,* Toronto: Oxford University Press, 1976

Brebner, John Bartlet. *North Atlantic Triangle*, Toronto: McClelland & Stewart, 1945

Brendon, Juliet. *Sir Robert Hart: The Romance of a Great Career*, 2nd edition, [n.p.] London, 1910

Brett, Edward M. *The British Auxiliary Legion in the First Carlist War,* Dublin: Four Courts Press, 2005

Broin, Leon Ó. *Fenian Fever: An Anglo-American Dilemma,* New York: New York University Press, 1971

Brooks, Tom and Robert Trueman. *Anxious for a Little War: The Involvement of Canadians in the Civil War of the United States,* Toronto: WWEC, 1993

Brown, Arthur. *Police Governance in England and Wales,* London: Routledge, 1998

Brown, George W. *Building the Canadian Nation,* Toronto: J.M. Dent & Sons, 1942

Brown, Howard Morton. *Lanark Legacy: Nineteenth Century Glimpses of an Ontario County,* Perth, ON: General Store Publishing House, 1984

Bryce, George. *A Short History of the Canadian People*, Toronto: William Briggs, 1914

Bumsted, J.M. *The Peoples of Canada: A Post-Confederation History*, p. 12; *The Peoples of Canada: A Pre-Confederation History*, Toronto: Oxford University Press, 1992

Caesar, Julius. *War Commentaries of Caesar,* trans. Rex Warner, New York: New American Library, 1960

Careless, J.M.S. *Brown of the Globe,* Volume II, Toronto: Macmillan Company, 1963

Careless, J.M.S. *The Union of the Canadas: The Growth of Canadian Institutions, 1841–1857,* Toronto: McClelland & Stewart, 1967

Careless, J.M.S. *Toronto to 1918,* Toronto: James Lorimer & Co., 1984

Chambers, J. Ernest. *The Canadian Militia: Origins and Development of the Force,* Montreal: L.M. Fresco, 1907

Chambers, J. Ernest. *The Queen's Own Rifles of Canada,* Toronto: E.L. Ruddy, 1901

Clarke, Brian P. *Piety and Nationalism: Lay Voluntary Associations and the Creation of an Irish-Catholic Community in Toronto, 1850–1895,* Montreal-Kingston: McGill-Queen's University Press, 1993

Comerford, R.V. *The Fenians in Context: Irish Politics and Society 1848–82,* Dublin: Wolfhound Press, 1985

Cougle, Jim. *Canadian Blood, American Soil: The Story of Canada's Contribution to the American Civil War,* Fredericton, NB: 1994

Crerar, Duff. *Padres in No Man's Land: Canadian Chaplains and the Great War,* Montreal-Kingston: McGill-Queen's University Press, 1995

Creighton, Donald. *The Road to Confederation,* Toronto: MacMillan, 1964

Cronin, Mike and Daryl Adair. *The Wearing of the Green: A History of St. Patrick's Day,* London: Routledge, 2002

Cronin, Sean. *Irish Nationalism: A History of Its Roots and Ideology,* Dublin: Academy Press, 1980

Cunliffe, Barry. *The Celtic World,* London: The Bodley Head, 1979

Cusack, Mary Frances. *History of Ireland from AD 400 to 1800* (1888), London: Senate Books Edition, 1995

Dallison, Robert L. *Turning Back the Fenians: New Brunswick's Last Colonial Campaign,* Fredericton, NB: Goose Lane Editions–New Brunswick Military Heritage Project, 2006

D'Arcy, William. *The Fenian Movement in the United States: 1858–1886,* Washington, DC: Catholic University of America Press, 1947

Davis, Carl L. *Arming the Union: Small Arms in the Union Army,* Port Washington, NY: Kennikat Press, 1973

Dendy, William. *Lost Toronto,* Toronto: McClelland & Stewart, 1991

Dickinson, John A. & Brian Young. *A Short History of Quebec,* 2nd edition, Toronto: Copp Clark Pitman, 1993

Denison, George T. *Recollections of a Police Magistrate,* Toronto: Musson Co., 1920

Donnelly, James S. *The Great Irish Potato Famine,* London: Sutton Publishing, 2001

Douglas, R.A. *John Prince, 1796–1870,* Toronto: Champlain Society / University of Toronto Press, 1980

Edwards, Peter. *Delusion: The True Story of Victorian Superspy Henri Le Caron,* Toronto: Key Porter Books, 2008

Firth, Edith (ed). *The Town of York 1793–1834: A Further Collection of Documents of Early Toronto,* Toronto: The Champlain Society, 1966

FitzGibbon, Mary Agnes. *A Veteran of 1812: The Life of James FitzGibbon,* Toronto: William Briggs, 1894

Foster, R.F. *Modern Ireland 1600–1972,* London: Penguin Books, 1989

Francis, R. Douglas, Richard Jones, and Donald Smith. *Origins: Canadian History to Confederation,* 5th edition, Toronto: Thomson-Nelson, 2004

Francis, R. Douglas and Donald Smith. *Readings in Canadian History,* 6th edition, Toronto: Thomson-Nelson, 2002

Francis, Daniel. *National Dreams: Myth, Memory, and Canadian History,* Toronto: Arsenal Pulp Press, 2002

Gagan, David. *The Denison Family of Toronto, 1792–1925,* Toronto: University of Toronto Press, 1973

Greener, William W. *The Gun and Its Development,* 9th edition, Guilford, CT: Lyons Press, 2002

Greenhous, Brereton, Kingsley Brown Sr., and Kingsley Brown Jr. *Semper Paratus: The History of the Royal Hamilton Light Infantry,* Hamilton, ON: RHLI Historical Association, 1977

Greenwood, F. Murray and Barry Wright. *Canadian State Trials: Law, Politics, and Security Measures, 1608–1837,* Toronto: University of Toronto Press, 1996

Greenwood, F. Murray and Barry Wright. *Canadian State Trials II: Rebellion and Invasion in the Canadas, 1837–1839,* Toronto: University of Toronto Press, 2002

Griffith, Paddy. *Battle Tactics of the Civil War,* New Haven and London: Yale University Press, 2001

Guillet, Edwin C. *Pioneer Inns and Taverns,* Toronto: Published by author, 1954

Gumpach, Johannes von. *The Burlington Mission,* Shanghai, London, and New York: 1872

Harris, Stephen J. *Canadian Brass: The Making of a Professional Army 1860–1939,* Toronto: University of Toronto Press, 1988

Hassard, Albert R. *Famous Canadian Trials,* Toronto: Carswell Co., 1924

Herm, Gerhard. *The Celts: The People Who Came Out of Darkness,* New York: St. Martin's Press, 1977

Hickey, D.J. and J.E. Doherty. *A New Dictionary of Irish History: From 1800*, Dublin: Gill & MacMillan, 2003

Holloway, W.R. *Indianapolis: A Historical and Statistical Sketch of the Railroad City,* Indianapolis: Indianapolis Journal Print, 1870

House of Commons Debates, November 21, 1867, Ottawa: R. Duhamel, 1967

Hoy, Claire. *Canadians in the Civil War,* Toronto: McArthur & Co., 2004

Hudson, David R.C. *The Ireland We Made,* Akron, OH: University of Akron Press, 2003

Jenkins, Brian. *Era of Emancipation: British Government of Ireland 1812–1830,* Montreal-Kingston: McGill-Queen's University Press, 1988

Jenkins, Brian. *Fenians and Anglo-American Relations,* Ithaca and London: Cornell University Press, 1969.

Jenkins, Brian. *The Fenian Problem: Insurgency and Terrorism in a Liberal State,* Montreal-Kingston: McGill-Queen's University Press, 2008

Jones, James Edmund. *Pioneer Crimes and Punishments in Toronto and the Home District*, Toronto: 1924

Kee, Robert. *The Bold Fenian Men,* Vol. 2, London: Penguin, 1972

Kee, Robert. *Ireland: A History,* London: Abacus, 1991

Kinchen, Oscar A. *Confederate Operations in Canada and the North,* North Quincy, MA; Christopher Publishing House, 1970

LeSueur, William Dawson. *William Lyon Mackenzie: A Reinterpretation* (edited by A.B. McKillop), Toronto: Carleton Library–Macmillan, 1979

Lewis, Berkley. *Small Arms and Ammunition in the U.S. Service,* Washington, DC: Smithsonian Institute, 1956 [1968 edition]

Macdonald, Helen G. *Canadian Public Opinion on the American Civil War,* New York: Columbia University Press, 1926

Mackenzie King, William Lyon. *Diaries,* http://www.collectionscanada.gc.ca/king/index-e.html [retrieved July 11, 2010]

Mackinnon, Steve, Karen Teeple, and Michele Dale. *Toronto's Visual Legacy: Official City Photography from 1856 to the Present,* Toronto: James Lorimer & Co., 2009

MacLaren, Roy. *Canadians on the Nile, 1881–1898: Being the Adventures of the Voyageurs on the Khartoum Relief Expedition and Other Exploits*, Vancouver: University of British Columbia Press, 1978

Martin, Ged (ed). *The Causes of Confederation,* Fredericton, NB: Acadiensis Press, 1990

Mayers, Adam. *Dixie & The Dominion: Canada, the Confederacy and the War for the Union,* Toronto: Dundurn Group, 2003

McGowan, Mark. *The Waning of the Green: Catholics, the Irish, and Identity in Toronto, 1887–1922,* Montreal-Kingston: McGill-Queen's University Press, 1999.

McKillop, A.B. (ed). *A Critical Spirit: The Thought of William Dawson LeSueur,* Toronto: McClelland & Stewart, 1977

McWhiney, Grady and Perry D. Jamieson. *Attack and Die: Civil War Tactics and the Southern Heritage,* Tuscaloosa, AL: University of Alabama Press, 1982

Merli, Frank J. *The* Alabama, *British Neutrality and the American Civil War,* Bloomington, IN: Indiana University Press, 2004

Miller, Kerby. *Emigrants and Exiles: Ireland and the Irish Exodus to North America,* New York: Oxford University Press, 1985

Moody, T.W. *The Fenian Movement,* Cork: Mercier Press, 1968

Morgan, Jack. *Through American and Irish Wars: The Life and Times of General Thomas W. Sweeny, 1820–1892,* Dublin–Portland, OR: Irish Academic Press, 2006

Morton, Desmond. *A Military History of Canada,* 4th edition, Toronto: McClelland & Stewart, 1999

Mosier, John. *The Blitzkrieg Myth: How Hitler and the Allies Misread the Strategic Realities of World War II,* New York: Perennial, 2003

Neidhardt, W.S. *Fenianism in North America,* University Park and London: Pennsylvania State University Press, 1975

Nicholson, G.W.L. *The Gunners of Canada: The History of the Royal Regiment of Canadian Artillery,* Vol. 1, Toronto: McClelland & Stewart, 1967

Ó Broin, Leon. *Fenian Fever: An Anglo-American Dilemma,* New York: New York University Press, 1971

Oliver, Peter. *Terror to Evil-Doers: Prisons and Punishments in Nineteenth-Century Ontario,* Toronto: University of Toronto Press, 1998

Pakenham, Thomas. *The Year of Liberty: The Great Irish Rebellion of 1798,* London: Weidenfeld & Nicholson, 1997

Polybius. *Histories* II, Cambridge, MA: Harvard University Press, 1922

Porter, Bernard. *Plots and Paranoia: A History of Political Espionage in Britain 1790–1988,* London: Unwin Hyman, 1989

Powell, James. *History of the Canadian Dollar,* Ottawa: Bank of Canada, 2005

Preston, Anthony and John Major. *Send a Gunboat: A Study of the Gunboat and Its Role in British Policy, 1854–1904,* London: Longmans, 1967

Pringle, J.F. *Lunenburgh or the Old Eastern District,* Cornwall: 1890

Ramón, Marta. *A Provisional Dictator: James Stephens and the Fenian Movement,* Dublin: University College Dublin Press, 2007

Reid, Elizabeth. *The Singular Journey of O'Hea's Cross: A Unique Victoria Cross,* Yale, BC: Leamcon Press, 2005

Reynolds, E.G.B. *Early Enfield Arms: The Muzzle Loaders,* Windsor, Berkshire: Profile Publications Ltd., 1972

Robertson, John Ross. *Landmarks of Toronto*, Series 6, Toronto: J. Ross Robertson, 1914

Romney, Paul. *Getting It Wrong: How Canadians Forgot Their Past and Imperilled Confederation,* Toronto: University of Toronto Press, 1999

Romney, Paul. *Mr. Attorney: The Attorney-General for Ontario in Court, Cabinet and Legislature, 1791–1899,* Toronto: The Osgoode Society, 1986

Rose, Alexander. *American Rifle: A Biography,* New York: Delacorte Press, 2008

Ross, Charles D. *Civil War Acoustic Shadows,* Shippensburg, PA: Whitemane Books, 2001

Runnalls, J. Lawrence. *The Irish on the Welland Canal,* St. Catharines, ON: St. Catharines Public Library, 1973

Russell, Victor L. (ed). *Forging a Consensus: Historical Essays on Toronto*, Toronto: University of Toronto Press, 1984

Senior, Hereward. *The Fenians and Canada,* Toronto: Macmillan Company, 1978

Senior, Hereward. *The Last Invasion of Canada: The Fenian Raids, 1866–1870,* Toronto: Dundurn Press, 1991

Senior, Hereward. *Orangeism: The Canadian Phase,* Toronto: McGraw Hill, 1972

Silber, Irwin. *Songs of the Civil War,* New York: Columbia University Press, 1960

Skelton, O.D. *The Canadian Dominion*, New Haven: Yale University Press, 1919

Smith, Alexander William. *The Anson Guards Company C Fourteenth Regiment North Carolina Volunteers 1861–1865*, New York: Thomson Gale, 1914

Smith, Jackie G. and Hank Johnston (eds). *Globalization and Resistance: Transnational Dimensions of Social Movements,* New York: Rowman & Littlefield Publishers, 2002

Stowits, Geo. H. *History of the One Hundredth Regiment of New York State Volunteers,* Buffalo: Matthews & Warren, 1870

Spence, Jonathan D. *The Search for Modern China*, New York: W.W. Norton & Co., 1990

Stacey, Charles P. *Canada and the British Army,* Toronto: University of Toronto Press, 1963

Stacey, Charles P. (ed). *Records of the Nile Voyageurs, 1884–1885: The Canadian Voyageur Contingent in the Gordon Relief Expedition*, Toronto: The Champlain Society, 1959

Stevens, G.R. *History of the Canadian National Railways,* New York: Macmillan Company, 1973

Strachan, Hew. *From Waterloo to Balaclava: Tactics, Technology, and the British Army 1815–1854,* Cambridge: Cambridge University Press, 1985

Strachan, Hew. *The Reform of the British Army, 1830–54,* Manchester: Manchester University Press, 1984

Taylor, M. Brook. *Promoters, Patriots, and Partisans: Historiography in Nineteenth-Century English Canada,* Toronto: University of Toronto Press, 1989

Trotter, R.G. *Canadian Federation,* Toronto: J.M. Dent & Sons, 1924

Twain, Mark. "Unberlesquable Things" in Louis J. Budd (ed), *Mark Twain: Collected Tales, Sketches, Speeches and Essays, 1852–1890,* New York: 1992

Vipond, Robert. *Liberty and Community: Canadian Federalism and the Failure of the Constitution,* Albany, NY: State University of New York Press, 1991

Wallace, W. Stewart. *A First Book of Canadian History*, Toronto: MacMillan, 1928

Wallace, W. Stewart (ed). *The Encyclopaedia of Canada*, Vol. V, Toronto, University Associates of Canada, 1948

Williams, Robert Chadwell. *Horace Greeley: Champion of American Freedom*, New York: NYU Press, 2004

Wilson, David A. *Thomas D'Arcy McGee,* Vol. 1, Montreal-Kingston: McGill-Queen's University Press, 2008

Wilson, Dennis K. *Justice Under Pressure: The Saint Albans Raid and Its Aftermath,* New York: University Press of America, 1992

Winks, Robin W. *Canada and the United States: The Civil War Years,* Montreal-Kingston: McGill-Queen's University Press, 1998

Winks, Robin W. *Recent Trends and New Literature in Canadian History,* Washington, DC: American Historical Association, 1959

Wodson, Henry M. *The Whirlpool: Scenes from Toronto Police Court,* Toronto: 1917

Wolseley, Field Marshal Viscount. *A Soldier's Life,* Vol. 2, Toronto: The Book Supply Company Ltd., 1904

Women's Project of New Jersey. *Past and Promise: Lives of New Jersey Women,* Syracuse, NY: Syracuse University Press, 1997

Wright, Donald A. *The Professionalization of History in English Canada,* Toronto: University of Toronto Press, 2005

Wright, Patrick. *Tank: The Progress of a Monstrous War Machine,* New York: Penguin Books, 2003

ACKNOWLEDGMENTS

I thank the late Pierre Berton for writing *The Great Depression,* which I first read in the Kavkaz Hotel in Grozny in 1992. Before leaving for Chechnya I had "borrowed" it at random from the reading room of the Canadian embassy in Moscow, grabbing at anything to have in my camera bag to read during the seemingly endless waits for something to happen. I was thirty-six years old, and it was the first Canadian history I had read since school. Academic historians may sneer, and some say Berton smoked too much pot, but he was such a great, true storyteller that upon reading his book, so far from home in so strange a place, I found Canadian history suddenly as fascinating as any other. Berton's unashamedly biased and ferociously passionate depiction of Canada and the struggle of its peoples in the 1930s turned my head and made me ask why Chechens and Russians were the way they were and Canadians were not. I began my long journey home to find out, and *Ridgeway* in many ways is a meditation on that question.

I am most grateful to the University of Toronto's School of Graduate Studies and the History Department for giving me asylum when I finally did crash-land home in 2002, wrecked in the dot-com tech-stock bubble and 9/11, suddenly as terminally unemployed as the people I read about ten years earlier in Berton's book. The generous financial support of a U of T Graduate Fellowship and Thesis Completion Grants, along with the employment offered as a teaching historian, allowed me the opportunity to research and write the doctoral dissertation on which this book is based. I also thank Trinity College for taking me back, with no questions asked, after I had originally dropped out at the end of my second undergraduate year in the summer of 1976 to pursue what became a twenty-five-year addiction to witnessing history firsthand and recording it on film and video. Even more than politics, television, law, journalism, and the music business, it is graduate school that is the ultimate refuge of scoundrels, and I felt welcomed right at home into its fellowship.

My deepest thanks go to University of Toronto's master historian of international relations, Robert Bothwell, who committed himself to supervising my thesis and championed it against critics of its "unfashionable" storytelling nature at a time when the words *narrative history* were still being spat out like filthy expletives by some limited rearward thinkers in history departments. It was he who encouraged me to submit my dissertation as a trade book to the History of Canada series, which he co-edits with Margaret MacMillan. I owe him a world of thanks and eternal fidelity for his support, friendship, wisdom, and insight, for the beers and for his fatherly patience as my thesis advisor, for I must have been the most miscreant scholar he has ever had the misfortune to supervise.

Thanks are due to a formidable cohort of faculty from U of T who mustered behind my Ph.D. program, collectively doing everything in their power and knowledge to prevent me from making a fool of myself. Professor Bothwell took me through Canadian history, American relations, and foreign policy, while Wesley Wark at the Munk School of Global Affairs supervised my readings on espionage, and Jim Phillips at the Faculty of Law tutored me in the history of criminal and constitutional law and policing. It was like having one's learning process fine-tuned and pampered by a team of Ferrari mechanics. U of T's newest Canadianist, Steve "The Donut" Penfold, kindly coached me through my "comps," which I pray are the last exams I will ever have to write in my life. From my thesis committee, Professors Carol Chin, Mark McGowan, and Roger Sarty have my thanks for everything they did to fill the many holes in my thesis arguments, and my thanks especially to committee member Professor David Wilson, a Fenian incarnate of a historian who knows more about Canadian and Irish history than one can measure. It was David who gave me my first glimpse of that species of quasi-Talmudic complexity that they call "the history of the Irish," by teaching me that there is no such thing as *the* Irish, but an infinite multiplicity of peoples and cultures each vaguely fitting the appellation "Irish."

We often forget that Canadian history does not unfold in a vacuum tightly sealed behind our borders, but is like any other history, a component of a fluid global historical ecology—Macdonald, Marx, Garibaldi, Lincoln, Darwin, and Dostoyevsky breathed the same air and read of one another in the newspapers, and perhaps even read one another, and Canada was invaded in 1866 because the Normans invaded Ireland in 1170. History is a yin and yang of cause and effect that knows no geographical frontiers or temporal limits. My gratitude goes to some of the remarkable faculty I had at U of T during my course work, seminars, and research to fill in my inquiries into our own history with the histories of criminal justice, espionage, medicine, labour, Ireland, United States and Britain, the Third Reich and the Holocaust, Soviet Russia, and modern and medieval Europe. For the time, attention, visions, knowledge, and expertise they shared with me over these years, I thank U of T Professors Michael Bliss, John Beattie, Joseph Goering, Robert Johnson, Jacques Kornberg, Michael Marrus, Pauline Mazumdar, Edward Shorter, Arthur Silver, Giulio Silano, Denis Smyth, Thomas Socknat, and Lynne Viola. From my two-year stint at U of T in the 1970s as an undergrad, I must also thank Professors Joe Medjuck and the late Robert F. Harney; they got me started in two mad directions: film and history.

My thanks to Marilyn Laville at the Munk Centre for keeping things running smoothly and to my fellow graduate students Julie Gilmour, Geoff Hamm, Mark Laszlo-Herbert, Steven Maddox, and Cara Spittal, for their friendship and intelligence in both senses of the word.

A legion of academics and non-academics from around the world generously came to my aid in the research of this book, so many that I am sure I have forgotten to name all, and I beg those for forgiveness of my neglect.

Professor Blake R. Brown turned over to me boxes of his precious research material on the Fenian trials of 1866; Cathy Parks of the Soldiers' Tower Committee and Charles Levi and Erin Fitzgerald directed me to sources on QOR Company 9 buried in the University of Toronto Archives; Steve Fuller (www.bedfordregiment.org.uk) sent me material on the British Army in Canada; Mike Ruddy, Conner Lewis, and John Matthew Morgan shared their knowledge, enthusiasm, and sources on the Fenian Brotherhood; and military historians Brian Reid and James Wood aided me through several stages of Canadian military history.

Thanks to curators Peter Simundson, Queen's Own Rifles Historical Museum Toronto; Stan Overy, Royal Hamilton Light Infantry Museum; and Jane Davies, Fort Erie Historical Museum in Ridgeway, for the generous access granted to their museums' collections. Thanks to author-historian John T. Docker and the Dunnville District Heritage Association for sources, and a big thanks to Elaine Brown for sharing with me her material on her ancestor Alexander Somerville. I especially want to thank the staff of the Hamilton Public Library historical collections room, the Library and Archives of Canada (LAC) in Ottawa, and the National Archives and Records Administration (NARA) in Washington, D.C., and College Park, Maryland, for their care and help during my visits there; they all made it so easy and painless.

The author Dave Walker I thank for his insight into writing and telling stories, and music-history television producer Paul Eichgrun for all the working road trips, tunes, and coffees, and film director Graeme Campbell for the interest, for keeping my eye on plans ahead, and for reminding me that indeed Scorsese is the *perfectae*.

I thank Marion Dunstan, the current owner of the Angur "brick house" on Ridge Road. She graciously hosted me with coffee and cake while I tramped the battle lines haunting her property. I told her stories of what took place there on the grounds in 1866 and she in turn told me those of her survival in East Prussia and Poland during the Second World War. It is fitting that a soul like Marion's would find refuge in Ridgeway's Canada. I can imagine no more serendipitously appropriate a custodian of the heritage "brick house" than Marion.

My deep gratitude goes to the series co-editor Margaret MacMillan for her editorial support and her incisively brilliant advice on how to rework my first draft into entirely new and better directions. To have the historian and author of *Paris 1919* and *Nixon and Mao* "go over" your draft is a non-fiction writer's dream, and I was not disappointed by the experience. Thanks, Margaret, for everything.

I thank Penguin Group Canada's publishing director, the unflappable Diane Turbide, for her generous patience with the numerous postponements in the delivery of the book while I struggled through the prolonged thesis defence process. Diane graciously made sure I never felt guilty, although I was as sin, and then afterwards stoically put up with my constant whining and nagging about everything and anything.

Jonathan Webb, as senior editor on *Ridgeway*, deserves all the credit for making my manuscript readable, and Sharon Kirsch I thank for her diamond-cutter skill as copy editor. Also at Penguin, thanks to Justin Stoller and David Ross and a whole army of people I have yet to meet or whose names have slipped my mind. When people talk of the "lonely solitude of the writer's craft" they really don't know what they're talking about.

Finally, while enrolled as a graduate student at U of T, I was also beginning to practise my newly acquired craft as a historian at Ryerson University, where I have been teaching since 2005. A good part of this book was written there on the fifth floor of Jorgenson Hall in the sessional instructors' office between lectures. I could not have been thrown into a league of more extraordinary and engaging historians to work alongside and learn from. I thank all my Ryerson colleagues for making it so much fun, the inimitable Arne Kislenko for showing me the way, the Rebel historian Ron Stagg for first hiring me, Carl Benn and John Morgan for their support and counsel, and for their friendship, collegiality, and good humour, professors Art Blake, Conor Burns, Jenny Carson, and Olivier Courteaux, the late sociologist Slobodan Drakulic and his wife, Professor Patricia Albenese (coincidentally my next door neighbours), Catherine Ellis, Ross Fair, Yunxiang Gao, Des Glynn, Martin Grieg, Ingrid Hehmeyer, Jennifer Hubbard, Linda Kowal, David Mackenzie, Joey Power, Robert Teigrob, and my cellmate in the history department sessional office, Professor Mima Petrovic, who lights up that windowless room with her good humour and cheer.

I thank my late father Boris for all the toys, money, and the books and magazines (and the movies, Dad), and my mother, Svetlana, for absolutely everything else, and my cousins Lucy and John Zawadzki for all the great dinners, gifts, and art supplies, and my late cousin Leo, who taught me how to box and fight bullies when I was a kid. He saved my life.

My thanks and apologies go to my daughters, Quantel and Alisa, for having to sit through the Pogues cranked up full volume, blasting on the car stereo all the way to the cottage when I was writing about the Fenians. Q & A, you make me proud and life a joy!

My biggest thanks of all go to the beautiful woman I met on a job one night twenty-six years ago in a garden in Kingston, Jamaica; a Venetian patriot of the *serenissima*, a merchant and an artist, my wife, Anna Zinato, for putting up with all the rest of my nonsense.

Peter Vronsky
Mirvish Village
August 2011

INDEX

C

E

G

K

T

U

Y

CREDITS

Welland Railway locomotive (Library and Archives of Canada, C-002611)

Lithograph of Fenian victory (Library and Archives Canada, R9266-3316)

"The Battle of Ridgeway, C.W. June 2, 1866" (Library of Congress, Prints and Photographs Division, LC-DIG-pga-01485)

Illustration from *Leslie's Weekly,* 1866 (www.ridgewaybattle.org)

"The Queen's Own Rifles in engagement with Fenians" (www.ridgewaybattle.org)

Angur "brick house" (www.ridgewaybattle.org)

North wall of brick house (www.ridgewaybattle.org)

Toronto volunteer militia in "square" formation (www.ridgewaybattle.org)

QOR Company 10 (Queen's Own Rifles Regiment Historical Museum)

Alfred Booker, Jr. (www.ridgewaybattle.org)

Alfred Booker in uniform (Image I-2044.1 © McCord Museum, Montreal)

Major James Atchison Skinner (Library and Archives of Canada, PA-3384)

Captain Henry Holmes Croft (www.ridgewaybattle.org)

"Wesleyan Ensign" Malcolm McEachren (Queen's Own Rifles Regiment Historical Museum)

Corporal Francis Lackey (Queen's Own Rifles Regiment Historical Museum)

Lance Corporal Mark Defries (Queen's Own Rifles Regiment Historical Museum)

Private John Harriman Mewburn (Queen's Own Rifles Regiment Historical Museum)

Sergeant Hugh Matheson (Queen's Own Rifles Regiment Historical Museum)

Lieutenant Percy Gore Routh (www.ridgewaybattle.org)

Private William Fairbanks Tempest (Queen's Own Rifles Regiment Historical Museum)

Minié ball (www.ridgewaybattle.org)

Minié ball, "mushroomed" (www.ridgewaybattle.org)

Human distal femur shot with Minié ball (National Museum of Health and Medicine, Armed Forces Institute of Pathology, Washington, D.C.)

Skull showing "keyhole" gunshot trauma (National Museum of Health and Medicine, Armed Forces Institute of Pathology, Washington, D.C.)

Fenian Secretary of War Thomas W. Sweeny (www.ridgewaybattle.org)

Fenian General John O'Neill (www.ridgewaybattle.org)
"Colonel O'Neill addressing his troops" (www.ridgewaybattle.org)
"Shooting Niagara: The Invasion of Great Britain via Canada" (www.ridgewaybattle.org)
J.S. Dennis (Library and Archives of Canada, C-5833)
Captain Lachlan McCallum (Library and Archives of Canada, PA-33224)
Captain Dr. Richard Saunders King, M.D. (www.ridgewaybattle.org)
Lieutenant Walter Tyrie Robb (www.ridgewaybattle.org)
W.T. Robb (www.ridgewaybattle.org)
"Fort Erie Medal" (www.ridgewaybattle.org)
Murray Street and Niagara Boulevard, present day (www.ridgewaybattle.org)
Niagara Boulevard, looking south (www.ridgewaybattle.org)
The Lewis House (www.ridgewaybattle.org)
Alexander Somerville (www.ridgewaybattle.org)
Major George T. Denison III (www.ridgewaybattle.org)
Denison as a Lieutenant Colonel in the 1880s (www.ridgewaybattle.org)
Illustration from *Harper's Weekly,* 1866 (www.ridgewaybattle.org)
Decoration Day, mid-1920s (Niagara Falls Public Library, D416070)
Canadian Volunteers Monument at Queen's Park (www.ridgewaybattle.org)
Young rifleman at McEachren's grave (www.ridgewaybattle.org)